Contents

3

The BPP Learning Media Effective Study Package

Distance Learning from BPP Professional Education

You can access our exam-focussed interactive e-learning materials over the **Internet**, via BPP Learn Online, hosted by BPP Professional Education.

BPP Learn Online offers **comprehensive tutor support**, **revision guidance** and **exam tips**.

Visit www.bpp.com/acca/learnonline for further details.

Learning to Learn Accountancy

BPP's ground-breaking **Learning to Learn Accountancy** book is designed to be used both at the outset of your ACCA studies and throughout the process of learning accountancy. It challenges you to consider how you study and gives you helpful hints about how to approach the various types of paper which you will encounter. It can help you **focus your studies on the subject and exam**, enabling you to **acquire knowledge**, **practise and revise efficiently and effectively**.

How the BPP ACCA-approved Study Text can help you pass

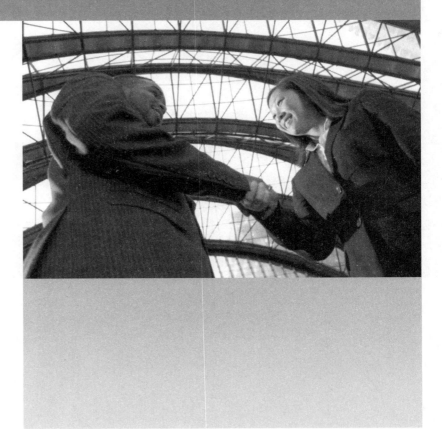

How the BPP ACCA-approved Study Text can help you pass

Tackling studying

We know that studying for a number of exams can seem daunting, particularly when you have other commitments as well.

- We therefore provide guidance on **what you need to study efficiently and effectively** – to use the limited time you have in the best way possible

- We explain the **purposes** of the **different features** in the BPP Study Text, demonstrating how they help you and improve your chances of passing

Developing exam awareness

We never forget that you're aiming to pass your exams, and our Texts are completely focused on helping you do this.

- In the section **Studying F2** we introduce the key themes of the syllabus, describe the skills you need and summarise how to succeed

- The **Introduction** to each chapter of this Study Text sets the chapter in the context of the syllabus and exam

- We provide specific tips, **Exam focus points**, on what you can expect in the exam and what to do (and not to do!) when answering questions

And our Study Text is **comprehensive**. It covers the syllabus content. No more, no less.

Using the Syllabus and Study Guide

We set out the Syllabus and Study Guide in full.

- Reading the **introduction to the Syllabus** will show you what **capabilities** (skills) you'll have to demonstrate, and how this exam links with other papers.

- The topics listed in the **Syllabus** are the **key topics** in this exam. By quickly looking through the Syllabus, you can see the breadth of the paper. Reading the Syllabus will also highlight topics to look out for when you're reading newspapers or *student accountant* magazine.

- The **Study Guide** provides the **detail**, showing you precisely what you'll be studying. Don't worry if it seems a lot when you look through it; BPP's Study Text will carefully guide you through it all.

- Remember the Study Text shows, at the start of every chapter, which areas of the Syllabus and Study Guide are covered in the chapter.

Testing what you can do

Testing yourself helps you develop the skills you need to pass the exam and also confirms that you can recall what you have learnt.

- We include **Questions** within chapters, and the **Exam Question Bank** provides lots more practice.

- Our **Quick Quizzes** test whether you have enough knowledge of the contents of each chapter.

- Question practice is particularly important if English is not your first written language. ACCA offers an **International Certificate in Financial English** promoting language skills within the international business community.

BPP
LEARNING MEDIA

Example chapter

Topic list

The Topic list gives an overview of the chapter.

Introduction

The Introduction sets the chapter in the context of the whole syllabus.

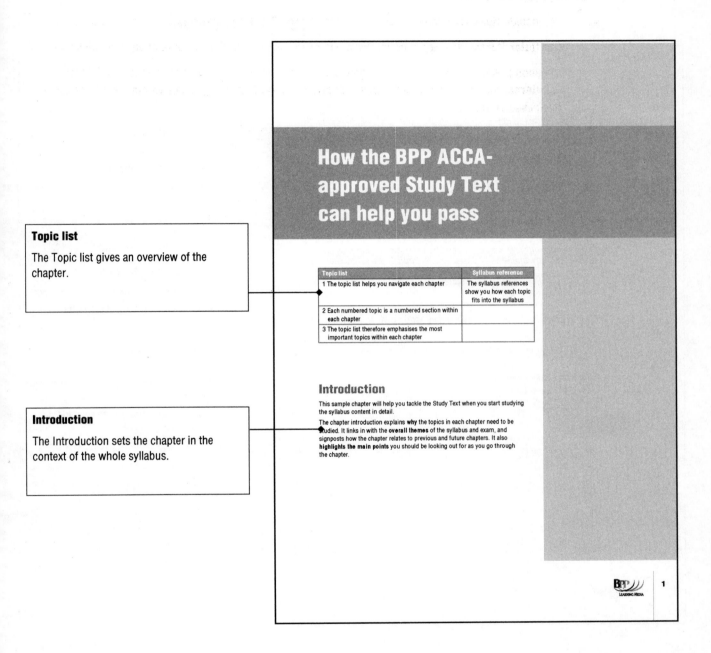

How the BPP ACCA-approved Study Text can help you pass

Topic list	Syllabus reference
1 The topic list helps you navigate each chapter	The syllabus references show you how each topic fits into the syllabus
2 Each numbered topic is a numbered section within each chapter	
3 The topic list therefore emphasises the most important topics within each chapter	

Introduction

This sample chapter will help you tackle the Study Text when you start studying the syllabus content in detail.

The chapter introduction explains **why** the topics in each chapter need to be studied. It links in with the **overall themes** of the syllabus and exam, and signposts how the chapter relates to previous and future chapters. It also **highlights the main points** you should be looking out for as you go through the chapter.

BPP LEARNING MEDIA 1

Study guide

	Intellectual level
We list the topics in ACCA's Study guide that are covered in each chapter	The intellectual level indicates the depth in which the topics will be covered

Exam guide

The Exam guide highlights ways in which the main topics covered in each chapter may be examined.

Knowledge brought forward from earlier studies

Knowledge brought forward boxes summarise information and techniques that you are **assumed to know** from your earlier studies. As the exam may test your knowledge of these areas, you should **revise** your previous study material if you are unsure about them.

1 Key topic which has a section devoted to it

FAST FORWARD Fast forwards give you a **summary** of the content of each of the main chapter sections. They are listed together in the roundup at the end of each chapter to allow you to review each chapter quickly.

1.1 Important topic within section

The headings within chapters give you a good idea of the **importance** of the topics covered. The larger the header, the more important the topic is. The headers will help you navigate through the chapter and locate the areas that have been highlighted as important in the front pages or in the chapter introduction.

Study guide

The Study guide links with ACCA's own guidance.

Exam guide

The Exam guide describes the examinability of the chapter.

Knowledge brought forward

Knowledge brought forward shows you what you need to remember from previous exams.

Fast forward

Fast forwards allow you to preview and review each section easily.

Example

Examples show you how theory is put into practice.

Key term

Key terms are the core vocabulary.

Exam focus point

Exam focus points provide specific links to the exam.

Formula to learn

You must remember these formulae in the exam.

Question

Questions provide vital practice of what you've learnt.

Case Study

Case Studies link what you've learnt with the business environment.

Example: Why examples are important

We include examples to illustrate how you should **apply key knowledge and techniques**. You therefore need to work through all examples very carefully.

Key term

Key terms are definitions of important expressions or concepts that can often earn you easy marks in the exam.

Exam focus point

Exam focus points tell you how specific topics may be examined, or if there are any **common weaknesses** in answers in these areas.

Formula to learn

This is a formula which you won't be given in the exam so you have to **learn** it. The best ways of learning it are using it in practice or writing it out a number of times until you're sure of all the terms.

Question — Practice makes perfect

Why should you attempt each question and what should you do with your answer?

Answer

You should attempt questions because they illustrate how well you **understand** what you've just read. You should check our answers against yours, and make sure you understand why they may have differed.

Case Study

Case studies show you how the topics you've covered come alive in the real world. Try to add to them with examples of your own experiences.

BPP
LEARNING MEDIA
3

Chapter Roundup

- Fast forwards give you a **summary** of the content of each of the main chapter sections. They are listed together in the roundup at the end of each chapter to allow you to review each chapter quickly.

Quick Quiz

1   What are the main purposes of the Quick Quiz?

2   What should you do if you get Quick Quiz questions wrong?

    A   Nothing as you now know where you went wrong
    B   Note the correct answer and go on to the next chapter
    C   Practise full questions on this topic when you revise
    D   Go back and look through the topic again to ensure you know it

Answers to Quick Quiz

1   The main purposes of the Quick Quiz are to check how much you've remembered of the topics covered and to practise questions in a variety of formats.

2   D   Go back and look through the topic again to ensure that you know it.

Now try the questions below from the Exam Question Bank

Number	Level	Marks	Time
Questions that give you practice of what you've learnt in each chapter	Examination	25	45 mins

Chapter Roundup

The Chapter Roundup lists all the Fast forwards.

Quick Quiz

The Quick Quiz speedily tests your knowledge.

Exam Question Bank

Each chapter cross-references to further question practice.

4   BPP
LEARNING MEDIA

Learning styles

BPP's guide to studying, *Learning to Learn Accountancy*, provides guidance on identifying how you learn and the variety of intelligences that you have. We shall summarise some of the material in *Learning to Learn Accountancy*, as it will help you understand how to you are likely to approach the Study Text:

If you like	Then you might focus on	How the Study Text helps you
Word games, crosswords, poetry	Going through the detail in the Text	Chapter introductions, Fast forwards and Key terms help you determine the detail that's most significant
Number puzzles, Sudoku, Cluedo	Understanding the Text as a logical sequence of knowledge and ideas	Chapter introductions and headers help you follow the flow of material
Drawing, cartoons, films	Seeing how the ways material is presented show what it means and how important it is	The different features and the emphasis given by headers and emboldening help you see quickly what you have to know
Attending concerts, playing a musical instrument, dancing	Identifying patterns in the Text	The sequence of features within each chapter helps you understand what material is really crucial
Sport, craftwork, hands on experience	Learning practical skills such as preparing a set of accounts	Examples and question practice help you develop the practical skills you need

If you want to learn more about developing some or all of your intelligences, *Learning to Learn Accountancy* shows you plenty of ways in which you can do so.

Studying efficiently and effectively

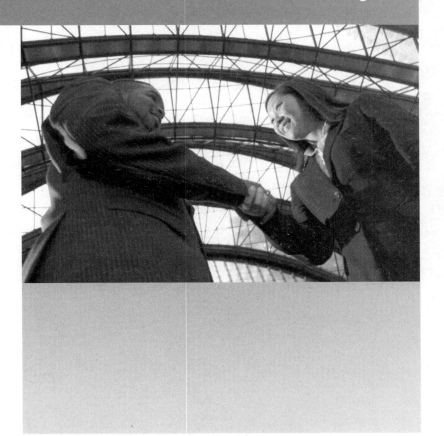

BPP
LEARNING MEDIA

What you need to study efficiently and effectively

Positive attitude

Yes there is a lot to learn. But look at the most recent ACCA pass list. See how many people have passed. They've made it; you can too. Focus on all the **benefits** that passing the exam will bring you.

Exam focus

Keep the exam firmly in your sights throughout your studies.

- Remember there's lots of **helpful guidance** about F2 in this first part of the Study Text.
- Look out for the **exam references** in the Study Text, particularly the types of question you'll be asked.

Organisation

Before you start studying you must organise yourself properly.

- We show you how to **timetable** your study so that you can ensure you have enough time to cover all of the syllabus – and revise it.

- Think carefully about the way you take **notes**. You needn't copy out too much, but if you can summarise key areas, that shows you understand them.

- Choose the notes **format** that's most helpful to you; lists, diagrams, mindmaps.

- Consider the **order** in which you tackle each chapter. If you prefer to get to grips with a theory before seeing how it's applied, you should read the explanations first. If you prefer to see how things work in practice, read the examples and questions first.

Active brain

There are various ways in which you can keep your brain active when studying and hence improve your **understanding** and **recall** of material.

- Keep asking yourself how the topic you're studying fits into the **whole picture** of this exam. If you're not sure, look back at the chapter introductions and Study Text front pages.

- Go carefully through every **example** and try every **question** in the Study Text and in the Exam Question Bank. You will be thinking deeply about the syllabus and increasing your understanding.

Review, review, review

Regularly reviewing the topics you've studied will help fix them in your memory. Your BPP Texts help you review in many ways.

- Important points are emphasised **in bold**.
- **Chapter Roundups** summarise the **Fast forward** key points in each chapter.
- **Quick Quizzes** test your grasp of the essentials.

BPP Passcards present summaries of topics in different visual formats to enhance your chances of remembering them.

Timetabling your studies

As your time is limited, it's vital that you calculate how much time you can allocate to each chapter. Following the approach below will help you do this.

Step 1   Calculate how much time you have

Work out the time you have available per week, given the following.

- The standard you have set yourself

- The time you need to set aside for work on the Practice & Revision Kit, Passcards, i-Learn and i-Pass

- The other exam(s) you are sitting

- Practical matters such as work, travel, exercise, sleep and social life

	Hours
Note your time available in box A. A	

Step 2   Allocate your time

- Take the time you have available per week for this Study Text shown in box A, multiply it by the number of weeks available and insert the result in box B.   B

- Divide the figure in box B by the number of chapters in this Study Text and insert the result in box C.   C

Remember that this is only a rough guide. Some of the chapters in this Study Text are longer and more complicated than others, and you will find some subjects easier to understand than others.

Step 3   Implement your plan

Set about studying each chapter in the time shown in box C. You'll find that once you've established a timetable, you're much more likely to study systematically.

Short of time: Skim study technique

You may find you simply do not have the time available to follow all the key study steps for each chapter, however you adapt them for your particular learning style. If this is the case, follow the **Skim study** technique below.

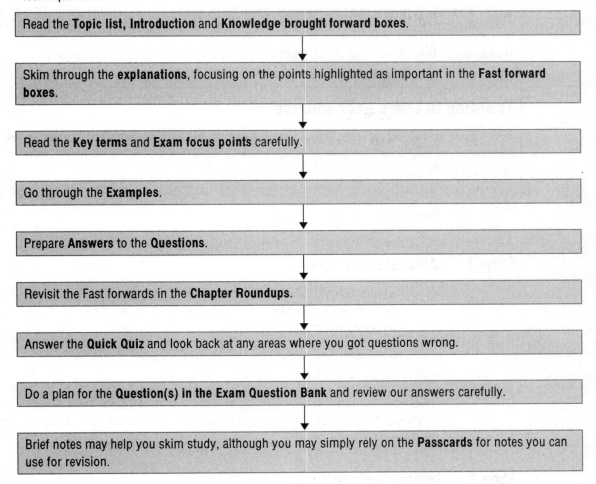

Read the **Topic list, Introduction** and **Knowledge brought forward boxes**.

Skim through the **explanations**, focusing on the points highlighted as important in the **Fast forward boxes**.

Read the **Key terms** and **Exam focus points** carefully.

Go through the **Examples**.

Prepare **Answers** to the **Questions**.

Revisit the Fast forwards in the **Chapter Roundups**.

Answer the **Quick Quiz** and look back at any areas where you got questions wrong.

Do a plan for the **Question(s) in the Exam Question Bank** and review our answers carefully.

Brief notes may help you skim study, although you may simply rely on the **Passcards** for notes you can use for revision.

Revision

When you are ready to start revising, you should still refer back to this Study Text.

- As a source of **reference** (you should find the index particularly helpful for this)

- As a way to **review** (the Fast forwards, Exam focus points, Chapter Roundups and Quick Quizzes help you here)

Remember to keep careful hold of this Study Text – you will find it invaluable in your work.

Learning to Learn Accountancy

BPP's guide to studying for accountancy exams, **Learning to Learn Accountancy**, challenges you to think about how you can study effectively and gives you lots and lots of vital tips on studying, revising and taking the exams.

Studying F2

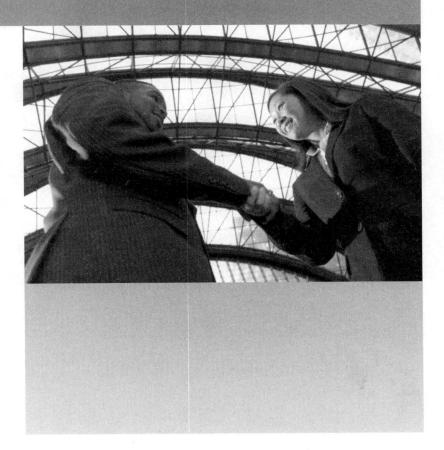

Approaching F2

1. What the paper is about

F2 is one of the three papers that form the **Knowledge** base for your ACCA studies. While Paper F1 *The Accountant in Business* gives you a broad overview of the role and function of the accountant, Papers F2 and F3 give you technical knowledge at a fundamental level concerning the two major areas of accounting – management accounting and financial reporting. Paper F2 will give you a good grounding in all the basics that you need to know in order to progress through your qualification. Thorough study for this paper will help you with papers F5 and P5 and will increase your workplace skills.

2. The skills you are expected to demonstrate

This paper is examined by computer-based exam or a written exam consisting of objective test questions, mostly multiple-choice. So you are not required, at this level, to demonstrate any written skills. However, you will have to demonstrate the following:

- Core knowledge – classification and treatment of costs, accounting for overheads, budgeting and standard costing, decision-making

- Numerical and mathematical skills – regression analysis, linear programming

- Spreadsheet skills – the paper will test your understanding of what can be done with spreadsheets. This section will be particularly useful to you in the workplace

3. How you can improve your chances of passing this paper

Bear in mind the following points:

- This exam has 50 short questions. This gives the examiner the opportunity to test pretty well everything in the syllabus, and you must expect him to do this. So you cannot leave out any area.

- The best preparation for an exam is practising lots of exam questions. When you have gone through the study text, work your way through the Practice and Revision Kit.

- In the exam read questions carefully. Beware any question that looks like one you have seen before – it's probably different in some way that you haven't spotted.

- If you really cannot answer something, move on. You can always come back to it.

Syllabus

AIM

To develop knowledge and understanding of how to prepare and process basic cost and quantitative information to support management in planning and decision-making in a variety of business contexts.

MAIN CAPABILITIES

On successful completion of this paper, candidates should be able to:

A   Explain the nature and purpose of cost and management accounting

B   Describe costs by classification, behaviour and purpose

C   Apply essential business mathematics and use computer spreadsheets

D   Explain and apply cost accounting techniques

E   Prepare and coordinate budgets and standard costing for planning, feedback and control

F   Use management accounting techniques to make and support decision-making.

RELATIONAL DIAGRAM OF MAIN CAPABILITIES

RATIONALE

The syllabus for Paper F2, *Management Accounting*, introduces candidates to costing principles and techniques, and elements of management accounting which are used to make and support decision-making.

The syllabus starts by introducing the nature and purpose of cost accounting, distinguishing it clearly from financial accounting. The next section is cost classification and behaviour. This is followed immediately by applied business mathematics and the use of computer spreadsheets, which are essential for candidates to understand the measurement and behaviour of business costs and to be able to classify them accordingly.

The next area of the syllabus represents a central part of this paper and it introduces candidates to a variety of costing techniques used in business. It is followed by the preparation and use of budgeting and standard costing as essential tools for planning and controlling business costs. The syllabus finishes with an introduction to the use of management accounting in supporting decision-making.

DETAILED SYLLABUS:

A   The nature and purpose of cost and management accounting

1.   Accounting for management

2.   Cost and management accounting versus financial accounting

B   Cost classification, behaviour and purpose

1.   Production and non-production costs

2.   Direct and indirect costs

3   Fixed and variable costs

C   Business mathematics and computer spreadsheets

1.   Dealing with uncertainty

2.   Statistics for business

3.   Use of computer spreadsheets

D   Cost accounting techniques

1.   Accounting for materials

2.   Accounting for labour

3.   Accounting for overheads

4.   Marginal and absorption costing

5.   Job and batch costing

6.   Process costing

7.   Service/operation costing

E   Budgeting and standard costing

1.   Nature and purpose of budgeting

2.   Functional budgets

3.   Flexible budgets and standard costing

4.   Basic variance analysis under absorption and marginal costing

5.   Reconciliation of budgeted profit to actual profit

F   Short-term decision-making techniques

1.   Cost-volume-profit analysis

2.   Relevant costing

3.   Limiting factors

APPROACH TO EXAMINING THE SYLLABUS

The syllabus is assessed by a two hour paper-based or computer-based examination. Questions will assess all parts of the syllabus and will include both computational and non computational elements. The examination will consist of 40 two-mark questions, and 10 one-mark questions.

5

Study Guide

A THE NATURE AND PURPOSE OF COST AND MANAGEMENT ACCOUNTING

1. Accounting for management

a) Distinguish between data and information.[1]

b) Identify and explain the attributes of good information.[1]

c) Outline the managerial processes of planning, decision making and control.[1]

d) Explain the difference between strategic, tactical and operational planning.[1]

e) Distinguish between cost, profit, investment and revenue centres.[1]

f) Describe the differing needs for information of cost, profit, investment and revenue centre managers.[1]

2. Cost and management accounting versus financial accounting

a) Describe the purpose and role of cost and management accounting within an organisation's management information system.[1]

b) Compare and contrast financial accounting with cost and management accounting.[1]

B COST CLASSIFICATION, BEHAVIOUR AND PURPOSE

1. Production and non-production costs

a) Explain and illustrate production and non-production costs.[1]

b) Describe the different elements of production cost - materials, labour and overheads.[1]

c) Describe the different elements of non-production cost – administrative, selling, distribution and finance.[1]

d) Explain the importance of the distinction between production and non-production costs when valuing output and inventories.[1]

2. Direct and indirect costs

a) Distinguish between direct and indirect costs in manufacturing and non-manufacturing organisations.[1]

b) Identify examples of direct and indirect costs in manufacturing and non-manufacturing organisations.[1]

c) Explain and illustrate the concepts of cost objects, cost units and cost centres.[1]

3. Fixed and variable costs

a) Describe and illustrate, graphically, different types of cost behaviour.[1]

b) Explain and provide examples of costs that fall into the categories of fixed, stepped fixed and variable costs.[1]

c) Use high/low analysis to separate the fixed and variable elements of total costs including situations involving stepped fixed costs and changes in the variable cost per unit.[2]

d) Explain the structure of linear functions and equations.[1]

C BUSINESS MATHEMATICS AND COMPUTER SPREADSHEETS

1. Dealing with uncertainty

a) Explain and calculate an expected value.[1]

b) Demonstrate the use of expected values in simple decision making situations.[1]

c) Explain the limitations of the expected value technique.[1]
(Decision trees and conditional profit tables are excluded).

2. Statistics for business

a) Calculate a correlation coefficient and a coefficient of determination.[1]

b) Explain the concepts in (a) and interpret the coefficients calculated in (a).[1]

c) Establish a linear function using regression analysis and interpret the results.[2]

3. Use of computer spreadsheets

a) Explain the role and features of a computer spreadsheet system.[1]

b) Demonstrate a basic understanding of the use of computer spreadsheets.[1]

c) Identify applications for computer spreadsheets in cost and management accounting.[1]

D COST ACCOUNTING TECHNIQUES

1. Accounting for materials

a) Describe the different procedures and documents necessary for the ordering, receiving and issuing of materials from inventory.[1]

b) Describe the control procedures used to monitor physical and 'book' inventory and to minimise discrepancies and losses.[1]

c) Interpret the entries and balances in the material inventory account.[1]

d) Identify and explain the costs of ordering and holding inventory.[1]

e) Calculate and interpret optimal reorder quantities.[2]

f) Calculate and interpret optimal reorder quantities when discounts apply.[1]

g) Produce calculations to minimise inventory costs when stock is gradually replenished.[1]

h) Describe and apply appropriate methods for establishing reorder levels where demand in the lead time is constant.[1]

2. Accounting for labour

a) Calculate direct and indirect costs of labour.[1]

b) Explain the methods used to relate input labour costs to work done.[1]

c) Prepare the journal and ledger entries to record labour cost inputs and outputs.[1]

d) Describe different remuneration methods: time-based systems, piecework systems and individual and group incentive schemes.[1]

e) Calculate the level, and analyse the costs and causes of labour turnover.[1]

f) Explain and calculate labour efficiency, capacity and production volume ratios.[1]

g) Interpret the entries in the labour account.[1]

3. Accounting for overheads

a) Explain the different treatment of direct and indirect expenses.[1]

b) Describe the procedures involved in determining production overhead absorption rates.[1]

c) Allocate and apportion production overheads to cost centres using an appropriate basis.[1]

d) Reapportion service cost centre costs to production cost centres (using the reciprocal method where service cost centres work for each other).[2]

e) Select, apply and discuss appropriate bases for absorption rates.[2]

f) Prepare journal and ledger entries for manufacturing overheads incurred and absorbed.[1]

g) Calculate and explain the under and over absorption of overheads.[1]

h) Apply methods of relating non-production overheads to cost units.[1]

4. Marginal and absorption costing

a) Explain the importance of, and apply, the concept of contribution.[1]

b) Demonstrate and discuss the effect of absorption and marginal costing on inventory valuation and profit determination.[2]

c) Calculate profit or loss under absorption and marginal costing.[2]

d) Reconcile the profits or losses calculated under absorption and marginal costing.[2]

e) Describe the advantages and disadvantages of absorption and marginal costing.[1]

5. Job and batch costing

a) Describe the characteristics of job and batch costing.[1]

b) Describe the situations where the use of job or batch costing would be appropriate.[1]

c) Prepare cost records and accounts in job and batch costing situations.[1]

d) Establish job costs from given information.[1]

6. Process costing

a) Describe the characteristics of process costing.[1]

b) Describe the situations where the use of process costing would be appropriate.[1]

c) Explain the concepts of normal and abnormal losses and abnormal gains.[1]

d) Calculate the cost per unit of process outputs.[1]

e) Prepare process accounts involving normal and abnormal losses and abnormal gains.[1]

f) Calculate and explain the concept of equivalent units.[1]

g) Apportion process costs between work remaining in process and transfers out of a process using the weighted average and FIFO methods.[2]

h) Prepare process accounts in situations where work remains incomplete.[2]

i) Prepare process accounts where losses and gains are identified at different stages of the process.[1]

j) Distinguish between by-products and joint products.[1]

k) Value by-products and joint products at the point of separation.[1]

l) Prepare process accounts in situations where by-products and/or joint products occur.[2] (Situations involving work in process **and** losses in the same process are excluded).

7. Service/operation costing

a) Identify situations where the use of service/operation costing is appropriate.[1]

b) Illustrate suitable unit cost measures that may be used in different service/operation situations.[1]

c) Carry out service cost analysis in simple service industry situations.[1]

E BUDGETING AND STANDARD COSTING

1. Nature and purpose of budgeting

a) Explain why organisations use budgeting.[1]

b) Explain the administrative procedures used in the budgeting process.[1]

c) Describe the stages in the budgeting process.[1]

2. Functional budgets

a) Explain the term 'principal budget factor'.[1]

b) Prepare budgets for sales, production, materials (usage and purchases), labour and overheads.[1]

3. Flexible budgets and standard costing

a) Explain and prepare fixed, flexible and flexed budgets.[1]

b) Explain the purpose and principles of standard costing.[1]

c) Establish the standard cost per unit under absorption and marginal costing.[1]

4. Basic variance analysis under absorption and marginal costing

a) Calculate the following variances: [1]
   i)   Sales price and volume
   ii) Materials total, price and usage
   iii) Labour total, rate and efficiency
   iv) Variable overhead total, expenditure and efficiency
   v)   Fixed overhead total, expenditure and, where appropriate, volume, capacity and efficiency.

b) Interpret all the variances in 4(a).[1]

c) Explain possible causes of all the variances in 4(a).[1]

d) Describe the interrelationships between the variances in 4(a).[1]

e) Calculate actual or standard figures where the variances in 4(a) are given.[1]

5. Reconciliation of budgeted profit and actual profit

a) Reconcile budgeted profit with actual profit under standard absorption costing.[1]

b) Reconcile budgeted profit or contribution with actual profit or contribution under standard marginal costing.[1]

F. SHORT-TERM DECISION-MAKING TECHNIQUES

1. Cost-volume-profit (CVP) analysis

a) Calculate and interpret a break-even point and a margin of safety.[2]

b) Demonstrate an understanding of, and use, the concepts of a target profit or revenue and a contribution to sales ratio.[2]

c) Identify the elements in traditional and contribution break-even charts and profit/volume charts.[1]

d) Apply CVP analysis to single-product situations.[2]
(Multi-product break-even charts and profit/volume charts are excluded).

2. Relevant costing

a) Explain the concept of relevant costing.[1]

b) Calculate the relevant costs for materials, labour and overheads.[2]

c) Calculate the relevant costs associated with non-current assets.[1]

d) Explain and apply the concept of opportunity cost.[1]

3. Limiting factors

a) Identify a single limiting factor.[1]

b) Determine the optimal production plan where an organisation is restricted by a single limiting factor.[2]

c) Formulate a linear programming problem involving two variables.[1]

d) Determine the optimal solution to a linear programming problem using a graphical approach.[1]

e) Use simultaneous equations, where appropriate, in the solution of a linear programming problem.[1]

The exam paper

The exam is a two-hour paper. It can be taken as a written or as a computer-based exam.

It has 50 questions – 40 two mark questions and 10 one mark questions. This gives a possible total of 90 marks.

The **pilot paper** is reproduced in full from page 31.

Pilot paper

Paper F2

Management accounting

Time allowed	2 hours

ALL questions are compulsory and MUST be attempted

Do NOT open this paper until instructed by the supervisor.

This question paper must not be removed from the examination hall.

Warning

The pilot paper cannot cover all of the syllabus nor can it include examples of every type of question that will be included in the actual exam. You may see questions in the exam that you think are more difficult than any you see in the pilot paper

---

You can see from this paper that the examiner is able to test right across the syllabus, so you must expect every topic to be examined.

If you take the paper-based exam the questions will be all 1 or 2-mark MCQs. The computer-based exam will have a variety of types of objective test questions. You will get plenty of practice doing these in the Practice and Revision Kit.

ALL 50 questions are compulsory and MUST be attempted

1   The following break-even chart has been drawn showing lines for total cost (TC), total variable cost (TVC), total fixed cost (TFC) and total sales revenue (TSR):

What is the margin of safety at the 1,700 units level of activity?

A   200 units
B   300 units
C   500 units
D   1,025 units   (2 marks)

2   The following assertions relate to financial accounting and to cost accounting:

(i)   The main users of financial accounting information are external to an organisation.

(ii)   Cost accounting is that part of financial accounting which records the cash received and payments made by an organisation.

Which of the following statements are true?

A   Assertions (i) and (ii) are both correct.
B   Only assertion (i) is correct.
C   Only assertion (ii) is correct.   (1 mark)

> This is a typical 1-mark question. Your exam will have 10 of these.

3   Regression analysis is being used to find the line of best fit (y = a + bx) from eleven pairs of data. The calculations have produced the following information:

$\Sigma x = 440$, $\Sigma y = 330$, $\Sigma x^2 = 17,986$, $\Sigma y^2 = 10,366$, $\Sigma xy = 13,467$ and $b = 0.69171$

What is the value of 'a' in the equation for the line of best fit (to 2 decimal places)?

A   0.63
B   0.69
C   2.33
D   5.33   (2 marks)

4   The purchase price of a stock item is $25 per unit. In each three month period the usage of the item is 20,000 units. The annual holding costs associated with one unit equate to 6% of its purchase price. The cost of placing an order for the item is $20.

What is the Economic Order Quantity (EOQ) for the stock item to the nearest whole unit?

A   730
B   894
C   1,461
D   1,633   **(2 marks)**

You will be given the EOQ and EBQ formulae. Make sure you can use them.

---

5   A company uses an overhead absorption rate of $3.50 per machine hour, based on 32,000 budgeted machine hours for the period. During the same period the actual total overhead expenditure amounted to $108,875 and 30,000 machine hours were recorded on actual production.

By how much was the total overhead under or over absorbed for the period?

A   Under absorbed by $3,875
B   Under absorbed by $7,000
C   Over absorbed by $3,875
D   Over absorbed by $7,000

                                                                                    (2 marks)

6   **For which of the following is a profit centre manager responsible?**

A   Costs only
B   Revenues only
C   Costs and revenues.   **(1 mark)**

7   An organisation has the following total costs at two activity levels:

Activity level (units)	16,000	22,000
Total costs ($)	135,000	170,000

Variable cost per unit is constant within this range of activity but there is a step up of $5,000 in the total fixed costs when the activity exceeds 17,500 units.

What is the total cost at an activity of 20,000 units?

A $155,000
B $158,000
C $160,000
D $163,000   **(2 marks)**

This is a typical question on the high-low method, which is very likely to be tested.

---

8   A company manufactures and sells a single product. In two consecutive months the following levels of production and sales (in units) occurred:

	Month 1	Month 2
Sales	3,800	4,400
Production	3,900	4,200

The opening inventory for Month 1 was 400 units. Profits or losses have been calculated for each month using both absorption and marginal costing principles.

Which of the following combination of profits and losses for the two months is consistent with the above data?

	Absorption costing profit/(loss)		Marginal costing profit/(loss)	
	Month 1	Month 2	Month 1	Month 2
	$	$	$	$
A	200	4,400	(400)	3,200
B	(400)	4,400	200	3,200
C	200	3,200	(400)	4,400
D	(400)	3,200	200	4,400

(2 marks)

9   **Which of the following best describes a flexible budget?**

A   A budget which shows variable production costs only.

B   A monthly budget which is changed to reflect the number of days in the month.

C   A budget which shows sales revenue and costs at different levels of activity.

D   A budget that is updated halfway through the year to incorporate the actual results for the first half of the year.   **(2 marks)**

10   Information relating to two processes (F and G) was as follows:

Process	Normal loss as %of input	Input litres	Output litres
F	8	65,000	58,900
G	5	37500	35,700

For each process, was there an abnormal loss or an abnormal gain?

	Process F	Process G
A	Abnormal gain	Abnormal gain
B	Abnormal gain	Abnormal loss
C	Abnormal loss	Abnormal gain
D	Abnormal loss	Abnormal loss

(2 marks)

11   An organisation manufactures a single product which is sold for $80 per unit. The organisation's total monthly fixed costs are $99,000 and it has a contribution to sales ratio of 45%. This month it plans to manufacture and sell 4,000 units.

What is the organisation's margin of safety this month (in units)?

A   1,250
B   1,750
C   2,250
D   2,750   **(2 marks)**

12   **Which one of the following should be classified as indirect labour?**

A   Assembly workers on a car production line
B   Bricklayers in a house building company
C   Machinists in a factory producing clothes
D   Forklift truck drivers in the stores of an engineering company.   **(2 marks)**

13 A company is evaluating a project that requires 400kg of raw material X. The company has 150kg of X in stock that were purchased six months ago for $55 per kg. The company no longer has any use for X. The inventory of X could be sold for $40 per kg. The current purchase price for X is $53 per kg.

What is the total relevant cost of raw material X for the project?

A $17,950
B $19,250
C $21,200
D $21,500 **(2 marks)**

14 **Which of the following is NOT a feasible value for the correlation coefficient?**

A +1.4
B +0.7
C 0
D −0.7 **(2 marks)**

15 The following statements relate to aspects of budget administration:

Statement (1): An important task of a budget committee is to ensure that budgets are properly coordinated.

Statement (2): A budget manual is the document produced at the end of the budget setting process.

Which of the following is true?

A Only statement (1) is correct.
B Only statement (2) is correct.
C Both statements are correct. **(1 mark)**

16 Up to a given level of activity in each period the purchase price per unit of a raw material is constant. After that point a lower price per unit applies both to further units purchased and also retrospectively to all units already purchased.

Which of the following graphs depicts the total cost of the raw materials for a period?

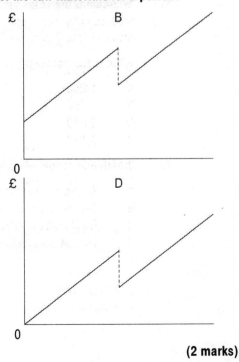

(2 marks)

17   A manufacturing organisation incurs costs relating to the following:

   (1)   Commission payable to salespersons.

   (2)   Inspecting all products.

   (3)   Packing the products at the end of the manufacturing process prior to moving them to the warehouse.

   Which of these costs are classified as production costs?

   A   (1) and (2) only
   B   (1) and (3) only
   C   (2) and (3) only
   D   (1), (2) and (3)   **(2 marks)**

18   **Which of the following is correct with regard to expected values?**

   A   Expected values provide a weighted average of anticipated outcomes.
   B   The expected value will always equal one of the possible outcomes.
   C   Expected values will show the decision maker's attitude to risk.
   D   The expected value will never equal one of the possible outcomes.   **(2 marks)**

19   There is a 60% chance that a company will make a profit of $300,000 next year and a 40% chance of making a loss of $400,000.

   What is the expected profit or loss for next year?

   A $120,000 Loss
   B $20,000 Loss
   C $20,000 Profit
   D $120,000 Profit   **(2 marks)**

20   A company's budgeted sales for last month were 10,000 units with a standard selling price of $20 per unit and a standard contribution of $8 per unit. Last month actual sales of 10,500 units at an average selling price of $19.50 per unit were achieved.

   What were the sales price and sales volume contribution variances for last month?

	Sales price variance ($)	Sales volume contribution variance ($)
A	5,250 Adverse	4,000 Favourable
B	5,250 Adverse	4,000 Adverse
C	5,000 Adverse	4,000 Favourable
D	5,000 Adverse	4,000 Adverse

                                                                                                           (2 marks)

21   A company manufactures and sells one product which requires 8 kg of raw material in its manufacture. The budgeted data relating to the next period are as follows:

	Units
Sales	19,000
Opening inventory of finished goods	4,000
Closing inventory of finished goods	3,000

	Kg
Opening inventory of raw materials	50,000
Closing inventory of raw materials	53,000

What is the budgeted raw material purchases for next period (in kg)?

A   141,000
B   147,000
C   157,000
D   163,000   **(2 marks)**

22   The following statements refer to spreadsheets:

(i)   A spreadsheet is the most suitable software for the storage of large volumes of data.

(ii)   A spreadsheet could be used to produce a flexible budget.

(iii)   Most spreadsheets contain a facility to display the data in them within them in a graphical form.

Which of these statements are correct?

A   (i) and (ii) only
B   (i) and (iii) only
C   (ii) and (iii) only
D   (i), (ii) and (iii)   **(2 marks)**

23   A company always determines its order quantity for a raw material by using the Economic Order Quantity (EOQ) model.

What would be the effects on the EOQ and the total annual holding cost of a decrease in the cost of ordering a batch of raw material?

	EOQ	*Annual holding cost*
A	Higher	Lower
B	Higher	Higher
C	Lower	Higher
D	Lower	Lower

(2 marks)

24   **Which one of the following is most likely to operate a system of service costing?**

A   A printing company
B   A hospital
C   A firm of solicitors.   **(1 mark)**

25   The following budgeted information relates to a manufacturing company for next period:

	Units		$
Production	14,000	Fixed production costs	63,000
Sales	12,000	Fixed selling costs	12,000

The normal level of activity is 14,000 units per period.

Using absorption costing the profit for next period has been calculated as $36,000.

What would the profit for next period be using marginal costing?

A $25,000
B $27,000
C $45,000
D $47,000   **(2 marks)**

26 A company manufactures a single product which it sells for $20 per unit. The product has a contribution to sales ratio of 40%. The company's weekly break- even point is sales revenue of $18,000.

What would be the profit in a week when 1,200 units are sold?

A $1,200
B $2,400
C $3,600
D $6,000 **(2 marks)**

27 The following graph relates to a linear programming problem:

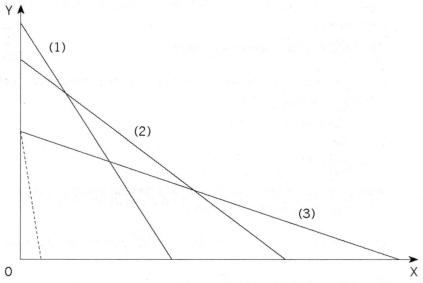

The objective is to maximise contribution and the dotted line on the graph depicts this function. There are three constraints which are all of the "less than or equal to" type which are depicted on the graph by the three solid lines labelled (1), (2) and (3).

At which of the following intersections is contribution maximised?

A Constraints (1) and (2)
B Constraints (2) and (3)
C Constraints (1) and (3)
D Constraint (1) and the x-axis **(2 marks)**

28 In an organisation manufacturing a number of different products in one large factory, the rent of that factory is an example of a direct expense when costing a product.

Is this statement true or false?

A True
B False **(1 mark)**

29 A company operates a process in which no losses are incurred. The process account for last month, when there was no opening work-in-progress, was as follows:

Process account

	$		$
Costs arising	624,000	Finished output (10,000 units)	480,000
		Closing work-in progress (4,000 units)	144,000
	624,000		624,000

The closing work-in-progress was complete to the same degree for all elements of cost.

What was the percentage degree of completion of the closing work-in-progress?

A   12%
B   30%
C   40%
D   75%   **(2 marks)**

30   A company manufactures and sells two products (X and Y) both of which utilise the same skilled labour. For the coming period, the supply of skilled labour is limited to 2,000 hours. Data relating to each product are as follows:

Product	X	Y
Selling price per unit	$20	$40
Variable cost per unit	$12	$30
Skilled labour hours per unit	2	4
Maximum demand (units) per period	800	400

In order to maximise profit in the coming period, how many units of each product should the company manufacture and sell?

A   200 units of X and 400 units of Y
B   400 units of X and 300 units of Y
C   600 units of X and 200 units of Y
D   800 units of X and 100 units of Y   **(2 marks)**

31   The following statements refer to organisations using job costing:

(i)   Work is done to customer specification.
(ii)   Work is usually completed within a relatively short period of time.
(iii)   Products manufactured tend to be all identical.

Which two of these statements are CORRECT?

A   (i) and (ii)
B   (i) and (iii)
C   (ii) and (iii)   **(1 mark)**

The following information relates to questions 32 and 33:

A company uses standard costing and the standard variable overhead cost for a product is: 6 direct labour hours @ $10 per hour

Last month when 3,900 units of the product were manufactured, the actual expenditure on variable overheads was $235,000 and 24,000 hours were actually worked.

32   **What was the variable overhead expenditure variance for last month?**

A $5,000 Adverse
B $5,000 Favourable
C $6,000 Adverse
D $6,000 Favourable   **(2 marks)**

33   **What was the variable overhead efficiency variance for last month?**

A $5,000 Adverse
B $5,000 Favourable
C $6,000 Adverse
D $6,000 Favourable   **(2 marks)**

34   When a manufacturing company operates a standard marginal costing system there are no fixed production overhead variances.

Is this statement true or false?

A   True

B   False   **(1 mark)**

35   A company operates a standard costing system. The variance analysis for last month shows a favourable materials price variance and an adverse labour efficiency variance.

The following four statements, which make comparisons with the standards, have been made:

(1)   Inferior quality materials were purchased and used.
(2)   Superior quality materials were purchased and used.
(3)   Lower graded workers were used on production.
(4)   Higher graded workers were used on production.

Which statements are consistent with the variance analysis?

A   (1) and (3)

B   (1) and (4)

C   (2) and (3)

D   (2) and (4)   **(2 marks)**

36   Which of the following best describes a principal budget factor?

A   A factor that affects all budget centres.

B   A factor that is controllable by a budget centre manager.

C   A factor which limits the activities of an organisation.

D   A factor that the management accountant builds into all budgets.   **(2 marks)**

37   Four vertical lines have been labelled G, H, J and K at different levels of activity on the following profit-volume chart:

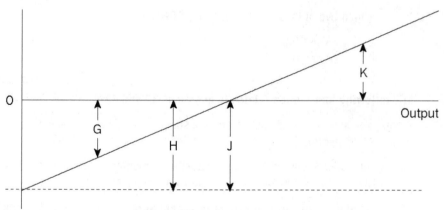

Which line represents the total contribution at that level of activity?

A   Line G

B   Line H

C   Line J

D   Line K

                                                                                              (2 marks)

38   Data is information that has been processed in such a way as to be meaningful to its recipients.

Is this statement true or false?

A   True

B   False   **(1 mark)**

39   Two products G and H are created from a joint process. G can be sold immediately after split-off. H requires further processing into product HH before it is in a saleable condition. There are no opening inventories and no work in progress of products G, H or HH. The following data are available for last period:

	$
Total joint production costs	350,000
Further processing costs of product H	66,000

Product	Production	Closing inventory
G	420,000	20,000
HH	330,000	30,000

Using the physical unit method for apportioning joint production costs, what was the cost value of the closing inventory of product HH for last period?

A $16,640
B $18,625
C $20,000
D $21,600   **(2 marks)**

40   A company purchased a machine several years ago for $50,000. Its written down value is now $10,000. The machine is no longer used on normal production work and it could be sold now for $8,000.

A project is being considered which would make use of this machine for six months. After this time the machine would be sold for $5,000.

What is the relevant cost of the machine to the project?

A $2,000
B $3,000
C $5,000
D $10,000   **(2 marks)**

41   A company operates a standard absorption costing system. The standard fixed production overhead rate is $15 per hour. The following data relate to last month: Actual hours worked 5,500 Budgeted hours 5,000 Standard hours for actual production 4,800

What was the fixed production overhead capacity variance?

A $7,500 Adverse
B $7,500 Favourable
C $10,500 Adverse
D $10,500 Favourable   **(2 marks)**

42   The following statements relate to relevant cost concepts in decision-making:

(i)   Materials can never have an opportunity cost whereas labour can.

(ii)   The annual depreciation charge is not a relevant cost.

(iii)   Fixed costs would have a relevant cost element if a decision causes a change in their total expenditure

Which statements are correct?

A   (i) and (ii) only
B   (i) and (iii) only
C   (ii) and (iii) only
D   (i), (ii) and (iii)   **(2 marks)**

43 A contract is under consideration which requires 600 labour hours to complete. There are 350 hours of spare labour capacity for which the workers are still being paid the normal rate of pay. The remaining hours for the contract can be found either by weekend overtime working paid at double the normal rate of pay or by diverting labour from other production. This other production makes a contribution, net of labour cost, of $5 per hour. The normal rate of pay is $9 per hour.

What is the total relevant cost of labour for the contract?

A $1,250
B $3,500
C $4,500
D $4,900 **(2 marks)**

44 An organisation operates a piecework system of remuneration, but also guarantees its employees 80% of a time-based rate of pay which is based on $20 per hour for an eight hour working day. Three minutes is the standard time allowed per unit of output. Piecework is paid at the rate of $18 per standard hour.

If an employee produces 200 units in eight hours on a particular day, what is the employee's gross pay for that day?

A $128
B $144
C $160
D $180 **(2 marks)**

45 A semi-variable cost is one that, in the short term, remains the same over a given range of activity but beyond that increases and then remains constant at the higher level of activity.

Is this statement true or false?

A True
B False **(1 mark)**

46 A factory consists of two production cost centres (P and Q) and two service cost centres (X and Y). The total allocated and apportioned overhead for each is as follows:

P	Q	X	Y
$95,000	$82,000	$46,000	$30,000

It has been estimated that each service cost centre does work for other cost centres in the following proportions:

	P	Q	X	Y
Percentage of service cost centre X to	50	50	–	–
Percentage of service cost centre Y to	30	60	10	

The reapportionment of service cost centre costs to other cost centres fully reflects the above proportions.

After the reapportionment of service cost centre costs has been carried out, what is the total overhead for production cost centre P?

A $124,500
B $126,100
C $127,000
D $128,500 **(2 marks)**

The following information relates to questions 47 and 48:

A company manufactures and sells two products (X and Y) which have contributions per unit of $8 and $20 respectively. The company aims to maximise profit. Two materials (G and H) are used in the manufacture of each product. Each material is in short supply – 1,000 kg of G and 1,800 kg of H are available next period. The company holds no inventories and it can sell all the units produced.

The management accountant has drawn the following graph accurately showing the constraints for materials G and H.

47 **What is the amount (in kg) of material G and material H used in each unit of product Y?**

	Material G	Material H
A	10	20
B	10	10
C	20	20
D	20	10

 (2 marks)

48 **What is the optimal mix of production (in units) for the next period?**

	Product X	Product Y
A	0	90
B	50	60
C	60	50
D	125	0

 (2 marks)

49 The following statement refers to a quality of good information: The cost of producing information should be greater than the value of the benefits of that information to management.

 Is this statement true or false?

 A True
 B False (1 mark)

50 A company which operates a process costing system had work-in-progress at the start of last month of 300 units (valued at $1,710) which were 60% complete in respect of all costs. Last month a total of 2,000 units were completed and transferred to the finished goods warehouse. The cost per equivalent unit for costs arising last month was $10. The company uses the FIFO method of cost allocation.

What was the total value of the 2,000 units transferred to the finished goods warehouse last month?

A $19,910
B $20,000
C $20,510
D $21,710 **(2 marks)**

FORMULAE SHEET

Regression analysis

$$a = \frac{\Sigma Y}{n} - \frac{b\Sigma x}{n}$$

$$b = \frac{n\Sigma xy - \Sigma x\Sigma y}{n\Sigma x^2 - (\Sigma x)^2}$$

$$r = \frac{x\Sigma xy - \Sigma x\Sigma y}{\sqrt{(n\Sigma x^2 - (\Sigma x^2)(n\Sigma y^2 - (\Sigma y)^2)}}$$

Economic order quantity

$$= \sqrt{\frac{2C_0 D}{C_h}}$$

Economic batch quantity

$$= \sqrt{\frac{2C_0 D}{C_h (1 - \frac{D}{R})}}$$

Part A
The nature and purpose of cost and management accounting

1

Information for management

Topic list	Syllabus reference
1 Information	A1 (a)
2 Planning, control and decision making	A1 (b)
3 Financial accounting and cost and management accounting	A2 (a)
4 Presentation of information to management	A1 (a)

Introduction

Welcome to **Management Accounting**– Paper F2 of the ACCA's new syllabus.

This and the following two chapters provide an introduction to **Management Accounting**. This chapter looks at **information** and introduces **cost accounting**. Chapters 2 and 3 provide basic information on how costs are classified and how they behave.

Study guide

			Intellectual level
A1	**Accounting for management**		
(a)	Distinguish between 'data' and 'information'		1
(b)	Identify and explain the attributes of good information		1
	Outline the managerial processes of planning, decision making and control		1
	Explain the difference between strategic, tactical and operational planning		1
A2	**Cost and management accounting and financial accounting**		
(a)	Describe the purpose and role of cost and management accounting within an organisation's management information system		1
	Compare and contrast financial accounting with cost and management accounting		1

Exam guide

Exam focus point

> Although this chapter is an introductory chapter it is still highly examinable. Candidates should expect questions on every study session including this one.

1 Information

1.1 Data and information

FAST FORWARD

> **Data** is the raw material for data processing. Data relate to facts, events and transactions and so forth.
>
> **Information** is data that has been processed in such a way as to be **meaningful** to the person who receives it. **Information** is anything that is communicated.

Information is sometimes referred to as **processed data**. The terms 'information' and 'data' are often used interchangeably. It is important to understand the difference between these two terms.

Researchers who conduct market research surveys might ask members of the public to complete questionnaires about a product or a service. These completed questionnaires are **data**; they are processed and analysed in order to prepare a report on the survey. This resulting report is **information** and may be used by management for decision-making purposes.

1.2 Qualities of good information

FAST FORWARD

> Good information should be **relevant**, **complete**, **accurate**, **clear**, it should **inspire confidence**, it should be **appropriately communicated**, its **volume** should be manageable, it should be **timely** and its **cost** should be less than the benefits it provides.

Let us look at those qualities in more detail.

(a) **Relevance**. Information must be relevant to the purpose for which a manager wants to use it. In practice, far too many reports fail to 'keep to the point' and contain irrelevant paragraphs which only annoy the managers reading them.

(b) **Completeness**. An information user should have all the information he needs to do his job properly. If he does not have a complete picture of the situation, he might well make bad decisions.

(c) **Accuracy**. Information should obviously be accurate because using incorrect information could have serious and damaging consequences. However, information should only be accurate enough for its purpose and there is no need to go into unnecessary detail for pointless accuracy.

(d) **Clarity**. Information must be clear to the user. If the user does not understand it properly he cannot use it properly. Lack of clarity is one of the causes of a breakdown in communication. It is therefore important to choose the most appropriate presentation medium or channel of communication.

(e) **Confidence**. Information must be trusted by the managers who are expected to use it. However not all information is certain. Some information has to be certain, especially operating information, for example, related to a production process. Strategic information, especially relating to the environment, is uncertain. However, if the assumptions underlying it are clearly stated, this might enhance the confidence with which the information is perceived.

(f) **Communication**. Within any organisation, individuals are given the authority to do certain tasks, and they must be given the information they need to do them. An office manager might be made responsible for controlling expenditures in his office, and given a budget expenditure limit for the year. As the year progresses, he might try to keep expenditure in check but unless he is told throughout the year what is his current total expenditure to date, he will find it difficult to judge whether he is keeping within budget or not.

(g) **Volume**. There are physical and mental limitations to what a person can read, absorb and understand properly before taking action. An enormous mountain of information, even if it is all relevant, cannot be handled. Reports to management must therefore be **clear** and **concise** and in many systems, control action works basically on the 'exception' principle.

(h) **Timing**. Information which is not available until after a decision is made will be useful only for comparisons and longer-term control, and may serve no purpose even then. Information prepared too frequently can be a serious disadvantage. If, for example, a decision is taken at a monthly meeting about a certain aspect of a company's operations, information to make the decision is only required once a month, and weekly reports would be a time-consuming waste of effort.

(i) **Channel of communication**. There are occasions when using one particular method of communication will be better than others. For example, job vacancies should be announced in a medium where they will be brought to the attention of the people most likely to be interested. The channel of communication might be the company's in-house journal, a national or local newspaper, a professional magazine, a job centre or school careers office. Some internal memoranda may be better sent by 'electronic mail'. Some information is best communicated informally by telephone or word-of-mouth, whereas other information ought to be formally communicated in writing or figures.

(j) **Cost**. Information should have some value, otherwise it would not be worth the cost of collecting and filing it. The benefits obtainable from the information must also exceed the costs of acquiring it, and whenever management is trying to decide whether or not to produce information for a particular purpose (for example whether to computerise an operation or to build a financial planning model) a cost/benefit study ought to be made.

Question   Value of information

The value of information lies in the action taken as a result of receiving it. What questions might you ask in order to make an assessment of the value of information?

Answer

(a)   What information is provided?
(b)   What is it used for?
(c)   Who uses it?
(d)   How often is it used?
(e)   Does the frequency with which it is used coincide with the frequency with which it is provided?
(f)   What is achieved by using it?
(g)   What other relevant information is available which could be used instead?

An assessment of the value of information can be derived in this way, and the cost of obtaining it should then be compared against this value. On the basis of this comparison, it can be decided whether certain items of information are worth having. It should be remembered that there may also be intangible benefits which may be harder to quantify.

1.3 Why is information important?

Consider the following problems and what management needs to solve these problems.

(a)   A company wishes to launch a new product. The company's pricing policy is to charge cost plus 20%. What should the price of the product be?

(b)   An organisation's widget-making machine has a fault. The organisation has to decide whether to repair the machine, buy a new machine or hire a machine. What does the organisation do if its aim is to control costs?

(c)   A firm is considering offering a discount of 2% to those customers who pay an invoice within seven days of the invoice date and a discount of 1% to those customers who pay an invoice within eight to fourteen days of the invoice date. How much will this discount offer cost the firm?

In solving these and a wide variety of other problems, **management need information**.

(a)   In problem (a) above, management would need information about the **cost of the new product**.

(b)   Faced with problem (b), management would need information on the **cost of repairing, buying and hiring the machine**.

(c)   To calculate the cost of the discount offer described in (c), information would be required about **current sales settlement patterns** and **expected changes to the pattern** if discounts were offered.

The successful management of *any* organisation depends on information: non-profit making organisations such as charities, clubs and local authorities need information for decision making and for reporting the results of their activities just as multi-nationals do. For example a tennis club needs to know the cost of undertaking its various activities so that it can determine the amount of annual subscription it should charge its members.

1.4 What type of information is needed?

Most organisations require the following types of information.

- Financial
- Non-financial
- A combination of financial and non-financial information

1.4.1 Example: Financial and non-financial information

Suppose that the management of ABC Co have decided to provide a canteen for their employees.

(a) The **financial information** required by management might include canteen staff costs, costs of subsidising meals, capital costs, costs of heat and light and so on.

(b) The **non-financial information** might include management comment on the effect on employee morale of the provision of canteen facilities, details of the number of meals served each day, meter readings for gas and electricity and attendance records for canteen employees.

ABC Co could now **combine financial and non-financial information** to calculate the **average cost** to the company of each meal served, thereby enabling them to predict total costs depending on the number of employees in the work force.

1.4.2 Non-financial information

Most people probably consider that management accounting is only concerned with financial information and that people do not matter. This is, nowadays, a long way from the truth. For example, managers of business organisations need to know whether employee morale has increased due to introducing a canteen, whether the bread from particular suppliers is fresh and the reason why the canteen staff are demanding a new dishwasher. This type of non-financial information will play its part in **planning, controlling** and **decision making** and is therefore just as important to management as financial information is.

Non-financial information must therefore be **monitored** as carefully, **recorded** as accurately and **taken into account** as fully as financial information. There is little point in a careful and accurate recording of total canteen costs if the recording of the information on the number of meals eaten in the canteen is uncontrolled and therefore produces inaccurate information.

While management accounting is mainly concerned with the provision of **financial information** to aid planning, control and decision making, the management accountant cannot ignore **non-financial influences** and should qualify the information he provides with non-financial matters as appropriate.

2 Planning, control and decision making

2.1 Planning

FAST FORWARD

Information for management is likely to be used for **planning**, **control**, and **decision making**.

An organisation should never be surprised by developments which occur gradually over an extended period of time because the organisation should have **implemented a planning process**. Planning involves the following.

- Establishing objectives
- Selecting appropriate strategies to achieve those objectives

Planning therefore forces management to think ahead systematically in both the **short term** and the **long term**.

2.2 Objectives of organisations

FAST FORWARD

An **objective** is the aim or **goal** of an organisation (or an individual). Note that in practice, the terms objective, goal and aim are often used interchangeably. A **strategy** is a possible course of action that might enable an organisation (or an individual) to achieve its objectives.

The two main types of organisation that you are likely to come across in practice are as follows.

- Profit making
- Non-profit making

The main objective of profit making organisations is to **maximise profits**. A secondary objective of profit making organisations might be to increase output of its goods/services.

The main objective of non-profit making organisations is usually to **provide goods and services**. A secondary objective of non-profit making organisations might be to minimise the costs involved in providing the goods/services.

In conclusion, the objectives of an organisation might include one or more of the following.

- Maximise profits
- Maximise shareholder value
- Minimise costs
- Maximise revenue
- Increase market share

Remember that the type of organisation concerned will have an impact on its objectives.

2.3 Strategy and organisational structure

There are two schools of thought on the link between strategy and organisational structure.

- Structure follows strategy
- Strategy follows structure

Let's consider the first idea that **structure follows strategy**. What this means is that organisations develop strategies in order that they can cope with changes in the structure of an organisation. Or do they?

The second school of thought suggests that **strategy follows structure**. This side of the argument suggests that the strategy of an organisation is determined or influenced by the structure of the organisation. The structure of the organisation therefore limits the number of strategies available.

We could explore these ideas in much more detail, but for the purposes of your **Management Accounting** studies, you really just need to be aware that there is a link between **strategy** and the **structure** of an organisation.

2.4 Long-term strategic planning

Key term

Long-term planning, also known as **corporate planning**, involves selecting appropriate strategies so as to prepare a long-term plan to attain the objectives.

The time span covered by a long-term plan depends on the **organisation**, the **industry** in which it operates and the particular **environment** involved. Typical periods are 2, 5, 7 or 10 years although longer periods are frequently encountered.

Long-term strategic planning is a **detailed, lengthy process**, essentially incorporating three stages and ending with a **corporate plan**. The diagram on the next page provides an overview of the process and shows the link between short-term and long-term planning.

2.5 Short-term tactical planning

The **long-term corporate plan** serves as the **long-term framework** for the organisation as a whole but for operational purposes it is necessary to convert the corporate plan into a series of **short-term plans**, usually covering **one year**, which relate to **sections**, **functions** or **departments**. The annual process of short-term planning should be seen as stages in the progressive fulfilment of the corporate plan as each short-term plan steers the organisation towards its long-term objectives. It is therefore vital that, to obtain the maximum advantage from short-term planning, some sort of long-term plan exists.

The planning process

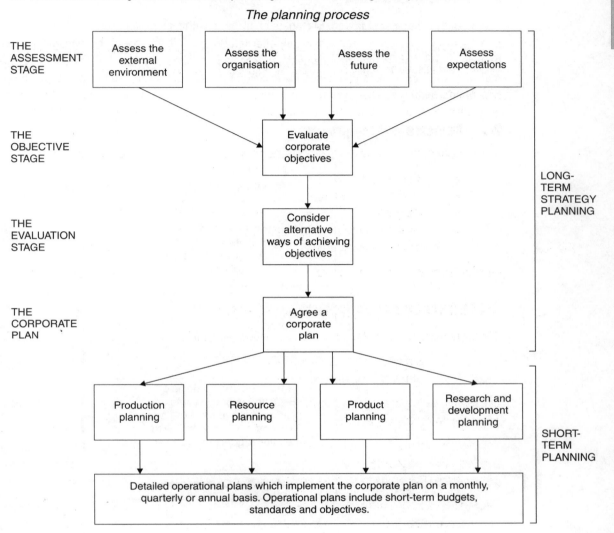

2.6 Control

There are two stages in the **control process**.

(a) The **performance of the organisation** as set out in the detailed operational plans is compared with the actual performance of the organisation on a regular and continuous basis. Any deviations from the plans can then be identified and corrective action taken.

(b) **The corporate plan** is reviewed in the light of the comparisons made and any changes in the parameters on which the plan was based (such as new competitors, government instructions and so on) to assess whether the objectives of the plan can be achieved. The plan is modified as necessary before any serious damage to the organisation's future success occurs.

> **Effective control is therefore not practical without planning, and planning without control is pointless.**

An established organisation should have a system of management reporting that produces control information in a specified format at regular intervals.

Smaller organisations may rely on informal information flows or ad hoc reports produced as required.

2.7 Decision making

Management is decision taking. Managers of all levels within an organisation take decisions. Decision making always involves a **choice between alternatives** and it is the role of the management accountant to provide information so that management can reach an informed decision. It is therefore vital that the management accountant understands the decision making process so that he can supply the appropriate type of information.

2.7.1 Decision making process

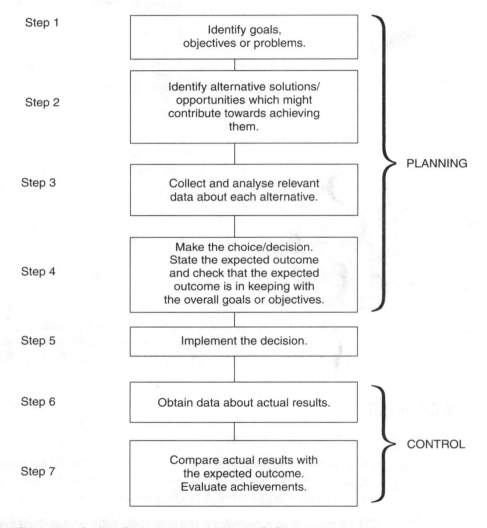

Step 1 — Identify goals, objectives or problems.

Step 2 — Identify alternative solutions/ opportunities which might contribute towards achieving them.

Step 3 — Collect and analyse relevant data about each alternative.

Step 4 — Make the choice/decision. State the expected outcome and check that the expected outcome is in keeping with the overall goals or objectives.

PLANNING

Step 5 — Implement the decision.

Step 6 — Obtain data about actual results.

Step 7 — Compare actual results with the expected outcome. Evaluate achievements.

CONTROL

2.8 Anthony's view of management activity

Anthony divides management activities into **strategic planning**, **management control** and **operational control**.

R N Anthony, a leading writer on organisational control, has suggested that the activities of **planning, control and decision making should not be separated** since all managers make planning and control decisions. He has identified three types of management activity.

(a) **Strategic planning:** 'the process of deciding on objectives of the organisation, on changes in these objectives, on the resources used to attain these objectives, and on the policies that are to govern the acquisition, use and disposition of these resources'.

(b) **Management control:** 'the process by which managers assure that resources are obtained and used effectively and efficiently in the accomplishment of the organisation's objectives'.

(c) **Operational control:** 'the process of assuring that specific tasks are carried out effectively and efficiently'.

2.8.1 Strategic planning

Strategic plans are those which **set or change the objectives**, or **strategic targets** of an organisation. They would include such matters as the selection of products and markets, the required levels of company profitability, the purchase and disposal of subsidiary companies or major fixed assets and so on.

2.8.2 Management control

Whilst strategic planning is concerned with setting objectives and strategic targets, **management control** is concerned with **decisions about the efficient and effective use of an organisation's resources** to achieve these objectives or targets.

(a) **Resources**, often referred to as the **'4 Ms'** (men, materials, machines and money).

(b) **Efficiency** in the use of resources means that optimum **output** is achieved from the **input** resources used. It relates to the combinations of men, land and capital (for example how much production work should be automated) and to the productivity of labour, or material usage.

(c) **Effectiveness** in the use of resources means that the **outputs** obtained are in line with the intended **objectives** or targets.

2.8.3 Operational control

The third, and lowest tier, in Anthony's hierarchy of decision making, consists of **operational control decisions**. As we have seen, operational control is the task of ensuring that **specific tasks** are carried out effectively and efficiently. Just as 'management control' plans are set within the guidelines of strategic plans, so too are 'operational control' plans set within the guidelines of both strategic planning and management control. Consider the following.

(a) Senior management may decide that the company should increase sales by 5% per annum for at least five years – **a strategic plan**.

(b) The sales director and senior sales managers will make plans to increase sales by 5% in the next year, with some provisional planning for future years. This involves planning direct sales resources, advertising, sales promotion and so on. Sales quotas are assigned to each sales territory – **a tactical plan** (management control).

(c) The manager of a sales territory specifies the weekly sales targets for each sales representative. This is **operational planning**: individuals are given tasks which they are expected to achieve.

Although we have used an example of selling tasks to describe operational control, it is important to remember that this level of planning occurs in all aspects of an organisation's activities, even when the activities cannot be scheduled nor properly estimated because they are non-standard activities (such as repair work, answering customer complaints).

The scheduling of unexpected or 'ad hoc' work must be done at short notice, which is a feature of much **operational planning**. In the repairs department, for example, routine preventive maintenance can be scheduled, but breakdowns occur unexpectedly and repair work must be scheduled and controlled 'on the spot' by a repairs department supervisor.

2.9 Management control systems

A **management control system** is a system which measures and corrects the performance of activities of subordinates in order to make sure that the objectives of an organisation are being met and the plans devised to attain them are being carried out.

The management function of control is the measurement and correction of the activities of subordinates in order to make sure that the goals of the organisation, or planning targets are achieved.

The basic elements of a management control system are as follows.

- **Planning:** deciding what to do and identifying the desired results
- **Recording** the plan which should incorporate standards of efficiency or targets
- **Carrying out** the plan and measuring actual results achieved
- **Comparing** actual results against the plans
- **Evaluating** the comparison, and deciding whether further action is necessary
- Where **corrective action** is necessary, this should be implemented

2.10 Types of information

Information within an organisation can be analysed into the three levels assumed in Anthony's hierarchy: **strategic**; **tactical**; and **operational**.

2.10.1 Strategic information

Strategic information is used by senior managers to plan the objectives of their organisation, and to assess whether the objectives are being met in practice. Such information includes **overall** profitability, the profitability of different segments of the business, capital equipment needs and so on.

Strategic information therefore has the following features.

- It is derived from both **internal** and **external** sources.
- It is summarised at a **high level**.
- It is relevant to the **long term**.
- It deals with the **whole organisation** (although it might go into some detail).
- It is often prepared on an **'ad hoc'** basis.
- It is both **quantitative** and **qualitative** (see below).
- It cannot provide complete certainty, given that the future cannot be predicted.

2.10.2 Tactical information

Tactical information is used by middle management to decide how the resources of the business should be employed, and to monitor how they are being and have been employed. Such information includes **productivity measurements** (output per man hour or per machine hour), **budgetary control** or **variance analysis reports**, and **cash flow forecasts** and so on.

Tactical information therefore has the following features.

- It is primarily generated internally.
- It is summarised at a lower level.
- It is relevant to the short and medium term.
- It describes or analyses activities or departments.
- It is prepared routinely and regularly.
- It is based on quantitative measures.

2.10.3 Operational information

Operational information is used by 'front-line' managers such as foremen or head clerks to ensure that specific tasks are planned and carried out properly within a factory or office and so on. In the payroll office, for example, information at this level will relate to day-rate labour and will include the hours worked each week by each employee, his rate of pay per hour, details of his deductions, and for the purpose of wages analysis, details of the time each man spent on individual jobs during the week. In this example, the information is required weekly, but more urgent operational information, such as the amount of raw materials being input to a production process, may be required daily, hourly, or in the case of automated production, second by second.

Operational information has the following features.

- It is derived almost entirely from internal sources.
- It is highly detailed, being the processing of raw data.
- It relates to the immediate term.
- It is task-specific.
- It is prepared constantly, or very frequently.
- It is largely quantitative.

3 Financial accounting and cost and management accounting

3.1 Financial accounts and management accounts

Financial accounting systems ensure that the assets and liabilities of a business are properly accounted for, and provide information about profits and so on to shareholders and to other interested parties. **Management accounting systems** provide information specifically for the use of managers within an organisation.

Management information provides a common source from which is drawn information for two groups of people.

(a) **Financial accounts** are prepared for individuals **external** to an organisation: shareholders, customers, suppliers, tax authorities, employees.

(b) **Management accounts** are prepared for **internal** managers of an organisation.

The data used to prepare financial accounts and management accounts are the same. The differences between the financial accounts and the management accounts arise because the data is analysed differently.

3.2 Financial accounts versus management accounts

Financial accounts	Management accounts
Financial accounts detail the performance of an organisation over a defined period and the state of affairs at the end of that period.	Management accounts are used to aid management record, plan and control the organisation's activities and to help the decision-making process.
Limited liability companies must, by law, prepare financial accounts.	There is no legal requirement to prepare management accounts.
The format of published financial accounts is determined by local law, by International Accounting Standards and International Financial Reporting Standards. In principle the accounts of different organisations can therefore be easily compared.	The format of management accounts is entirely at management discretion: no strict rules govern the way they are prepared or presented. Each organisation can devise its own management accounting system and format of reports.
Financial accounts concentrate on the business as a whole, aggregating revenues and costs from different operations, and are an end in themselves.	Management accounts can focus on specific areas of an organisation's activities. Information may be produced to aid a decision rather than to be an end product of a decision.
Most financial accounting information is of a monetary nature.	Management accounts incorporate non-monetary measures. Management may need to know, for example, tons of aluminium produced, monthly machine hours, or miles travelled by salesmen.
Financial accounts present an essentially historic picture of past operations.	Management accounts are both an historical record and a future planning tool.

Question   Management accounts

Which of the following statements about management accounts is/are true?

(i)   There is a legal requirement to prepare management accounts.
(ii)   The format of management accounts is largely determined by law.
(iii)   They serve as a future planning tool and are not used as a historical record.

A   (i) and (ii)
B   (ii) and (iii)
C   (iii) only
D   None of the statements are correct.

Answer

D

Statement (i) is incorrect. Limited liability companies must, by law, prepare **financial** accounts.

The format of published financial accounts is determined by law. Statement (ii) is therefore incorrect.

Management accounts do serve as a future planning tool but they are also useful as a historical record of performance. Therefore all three statements are incorrect and D is the correct answer.

3.3 Cost accounts

Cost accounting and management accounting are terms which are often used interchangeably. It is *not* correct to do so. **Cost accounting is part of management accounting. Cost accounting provides a bank of data for the management accountant to use.**

Cost accounting is concerned with the following.

- Preparing statements (eg budgets, costing)
- Cost data collection
- Applying costs to inventory, products and services

Management accounting is concerned with the following.

- Using financial data and communicating it as information to users

3.3.1 Aims of cost accounts

(a) The **cost** of goods produced or services provided.

(b) The **cost** of a department or work section.

(c) What **revenues** have been.

(d) The **profitability** of a product, a service, a department, or the organisation in total.

(e) **Selling prices** with some regard for the costs of sale.

(f) The **value of inventories of goods** (raw materials, work in progress, finished goods) that are still held in store at the end of a period, thereby aiding the preparation of a balance sheet of the company's assets and liabilities.

(g) **Future costs** of goods and services (costing is an integral part of budgeting (planning) for the future).

(h) **How actual costs compare with budgeted costs.** (If an organisation plans for its revenues and costs to be a certain amount, but they actually turn out differently, the differences can be measured and reported. Management can use these reports as a guide to whether corrective action (or 'control' action) is needed to sort out a problem revealed by these differences between budgeted and actual results. This system of control is often referred to as budgetary control.

(i) **What information management needs** in order to make sensible decisions about profits and costs.

It would be wrong to suppose that cost accounting systems are restricted to manufacturing operations, although they are probably more fully developed in this area of work. **Service industries**, **government departments** and **welfare activities** can all make use of cost accounting information. Within a manufacturing organisation, the cost accounting system should be applied not only to **manufacturing** but also to **administration**, **selling and distribution**, **research and development** and all other departments.

4 Presentation of information to management

4.1 Reports

Data and information are usually presented to management in the form of a **report**. The main features of a report are: TITLE; TO; FROM; DATE; and SUBJECT.

In small organisations it is possible, however, that information will be communicated in a less formal manner than writing a report (orally or using informal reports/memos).

Throughout this Study Text, you will come across a number of techniques which allow financial information to be collected. Once it has been collected it is usually analysed and reported back to management in the form of a **report**.

4.2 Main features of a report

- **TITLE**

  Most reports are usually given a heading to show that it is a report.

- **WHO IS THE REPORT INTENDED FOR?**

  It is vital that the intended recipients of a report are clearly identified. For example, if you are writing a report for Joe Bloggs, it should be clearly stated at the head of the report.

- **WHO IS THE REPORT FROM?**

  If the recipients of the report have any comments or queries, it is important that they know who to contact.

- **DATE**

  We have already mentioned that information should be communicated at the most appropriate **time**. It is also important to show this timeliness by giving your report a date.

- **SUBJECT**

  What is the report about? Managers are likely to receive a great number of reports that they need to review. It is useful to know what a report is about before you read it!

- **APPENDIX**

  In general, information is summarised in a report and the more detailed calculations and data are included in an appendix at the end of the report.

4.3 Report format

We recommend that you should use the following format when writing a report in an examination.

REPORT

To: Board of Directors

From: Cost Accountant   Date:

Subject: Report Format

Body of report

Signed: Cost Accountant

Exam focus
point

When producing reports in an examination, remember that they must include the following.

- **Title** – REPORT
- **To** – Who is the report to?
- **From** – Who is the report from?
- **Date** – What is the date of report?
- **Subject** – What is the subject of the report?

Chapter roundup

- **Data** is the raw material for data processing. Data relate to facts, events and transactions and so forth.

  Information is data that has been processed in such a way as to be **meaningful** to the person who receives it. **Information** is anything that is communicated.

- Good information should be **relevant, complete, accurate, clear**, it should **inspire confidence**, it should be **appropriately communicated**, its **volume** should be manageable, it should be **timely** and its **cost** should be less than the benefits it provides.

- Information for management accounting is likely to be used for **planning, control** and **decision making**.

- An **objective** is the aim or **goal** of an organisation (or an individual). Note that in practice, the terms objective, goal and aim are often used interchangeably. A **strategy** is a possible course of action that might enable an organisation (or an individual) to achieve its objectives.

- Anthony divides management activities into **strategic planning, management control** and **operational control**.

- A **management control system** is a system which measures and corrects the performance of activities of subordinates in order to make sure that the objectives of an organisation are being met and the plans devised to attain them are being carried out.

- Information within an organisation can be analysed into the three levels assumed in Anthony's hierarchy: **strategic; tactical**; and **operational**.

- **Financial accounting systems** ensure that the assets and liabilities of a business are properly accounted for, and provide information about profits and so on to shareholders and to other interested parties. **Management accounting systems** provide information specifically for the use of managers within the organisation.

- Cost accounting and management accounting are terms which are often used interchangeably. It is not correct to do so. **Cost accounting is part of management accounting. Cost accounting provides a bank of data for the management accountant to use**.

- Data and information are usually presented to management in the form of a report. The main features of a report are: TITLE; TO; FROM; DATE; and SUBJECT.

Quick quiz

1   Define the terms **data** and **information**.

2   The four main qualities of good information are:

   - ....

   - ....

   - ....

   - ....

3   In terms of management accounting, information is most likely to be used for (1) ...., (2) .... or (3) ....

4   A strategy is the aim or goal of an organisation.

   True   ☐

   False   ☐

5 | **Organisation** | **Objective** |
     | --- | --- |
     | Profit making | |
     | Non-profit making | |

6   What are the three types of management activity identified by R N Anthony?

   (1)   ....

   (2)   ....

   (3)   ....

7   A management control system is

   A   a possible course of action that might enable an organisation to achieve its objectives

   B   a collective term for the hardware and software used to drive a database system

   C   a set up that measures and corrects the performance of activities of subordinates in order to make sure that the objectives of an organisation are being met and their associated plans are being carried out

   D   a system that controls and maximises the profits of an organisation

8   List six differences between financial accounts and management accounts.

9   When preparing reports, what are the five key points to remember?

   (1)   ....

   (2)   ....

   (3)   ....

   (4)   ....

   (5)   ....

Answers to quick quiz

1   **Data** is the raw material for data processing. **Information** is data that has been processed in such a way as to be meaningful to the person who receives it. **Information** is anything that is communicated.

2   - Relevance
    - Completeness
    - Accuracy
    - Clarity

3   (1)   Planning
    (2)   Control
    (3)   Decision making

4   False. This is the definition of an **objective**. A strategy is a possible course of action that might enable an organisation to **achieve** its objectives.

5   Profit making = maximise profits
    Non-profit making = provide goods and services

6   (1)   Strategic planning
    (2)   Management control
    (3)   Operational control

7   C

8   See Paragraph 3.2

9   - Title
    - Who is the report to
    - Who is the report from
    - Date
    - Subject

Now try the question below from the Exam Question Bank

Now try the questions below from the Exam Question Bank

Number	Level	Marks	Time
Q1	MCQ	n/a	n/a

Part B
Cost classification, behaviour and purpose

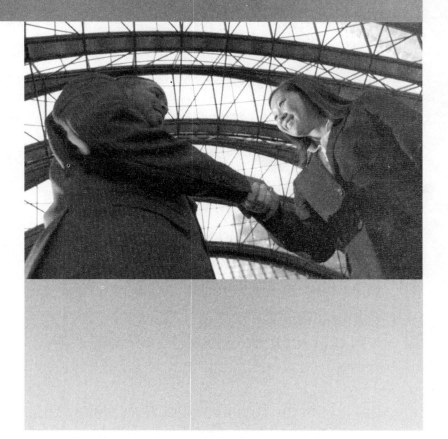

Cost classification

Topic list	Syllabus reference
1 Total product/service costs	B1 (a)
2 Direct costs and indirect costs	B2 (a)
3 Functional costs	B1 (a)
4 Fixed costs and variable costs	B1 (d)
5 Production and non-production costs	B1 (a)
6 Other cost classifications	B1 (c)
7 Cost units, cost objects and responsibility centres	A1 (a)

Introduction

The **classification of costs** as either **direct** or **indirect**, for example, is essential in the costing method used by an organisation to determine the cost of a unit of product or service.

The **fixed** and **variable cost classifications**, on the other hand, are important in **absorption** and **marginal costing**, **cost behaviour** and **cost-volume-profit analysis**. You will meet all of these topics as we progress through the Study Text.

This chapter therefore acts as a foundation stone for a number of other chapters in the text and hence an understanding of the concepts covered in it is vital before you move on.

Study guide

		Intellectual level
A1	**Accounting for Management**	
(a)	Distinguish between cost, profit, investment and revenue centres	1
(b)	Describe the differing needs for information of cost, profit, investment and revenue centre managers	1
B1	**Production and non-production costs**	
(a)	Explain and illustrate production and non-production costs	1
(b)	Describe the different elements of production cost – material, labour and overheads	1
(c)	Describe the different elements of non-production cost – administrative, selling, distribution and finance	1
(d)	Explain the importance of the distinction between production and non-production costs when valuing output and inventories	1
B2	**Direct and indirect costs**	
(a)	Distinguish between direct and indirect costs in manufacturing and non-manufacturing organisations	1
(b)	Identify examples of direct and indirect costs in manufacturing and non-manufacturing organisations	1
(c)	Explain and illustrate the concepts of cost objects, cost units and cost centres	1

Exam guide

Cost classification is one of the key areas of the syllabus and you can therefore expect to see it in the exam that you will be facing.

1 Total product/service costs

The total cost of making a product or providing a service consists of the following.

    (a)   Cost of **materials**

    (b)   Cost of the **wages** and **salaries** (labour costs)

    (c)   Cost of **other expenses**

        •   Rent and rates
        •   Electricity and gas bills
        •   Depreciation

2 Direct costs and indirect costs

2.1 Materials, labour and expenses

FAST FORWARD

A **direct cost** is a cost that can be traced in full to the product, service, or department that is being costed. An **indirect cost** (or **overhead**) is a cost that is incurred in the course of making a product, providing a service or running a department, but which cannot be traced directly and in full to the product, service or department.

Materials, labour costs and other expenses can be classified as either **direct costs** or **indirect costs**.

(a) **Direct material costs** are the costs of materials that are known to have been used in making and selling a product (or even providing a service).

(b) **Direct labour costs** are the specific costs of the workforce used to make a product or provide a service. Direct labour costs are established by measuring the time taken for a job, or the time taken in 'direct production work'.

(c) **Other direct expenses** are those expenses that have been incurred in full as a direct consequence of making a product, or providing a service, or running a department.

Examples of indirect costs include supervisors' wages, cleaning materials and buildings insurance.

2.2 Analysis of total cost

Materials	=	Direct materials	+	Indirect materials
+		+		+
Labour	=	Direct labour	+	Indirect labour
+		+		+
Expenses	=	Direct expenses	+	Indirect expenses
Total cost	=	Direct cost	+	Overhead

2.3 Direct material

Key term

Direct material is all material becoming part of the product (unless used in negligible amounts and/or having negligible cost).

Direct material costs are charged to the product as part of the **prime cost**. Examples of direct material are as follows.

(a) **Component parts**, specially purchased for a particular job, order or process.

(b) **Part-finished work** which is transferred from department 1 to department 2 becomes finished work of department 1 and a direct material cost in department 2.

(c) **Primary packing materials** like cartons and boxes.

2.4 Direct labour

Key term

Direct wages are all wages paid for labour (either as basic hours or as overtime) expended on work on the product itself.

Direct wages costs are charged to the product as part of the **prime cost**.

Examples of groups of labour receiving payment as direct wages are as follows.

(a) Workers engaged in **altering** the condition or composition of the product.

(b) Inspectors, analysts and testers **specifically required** for such production.

(c) Foremen, shop clerks and anyone else whose wages are **specifically identified.**

Two **trends** may be identified in **direct labour costs.**

- The ratio of direct labour costs to total product cost is falling as the use of machinery increases, and hence depreciation charges increase.

- Skilled labour costs and sub-contractors' costs are increasing as direct labour costs decrease.

Question

Classify the following labour costs as either direct or indirect.

(a) The basic pay of direct workers (cash paid, tax and other deductions)
(b) The basic pay of indirect workers
(c) Overtime premium
(d) Bonus payments
(e) Social insurance contributions
(f) Idle time of direct workers
(g) Work on installation of equipment

Answer

(a) The basic pay of direct workers is a direct cost to the unit, job or process.

(b) The basic pay of indirect workers is an indirect cost, unless a customer asks for an order to be carried out which involves the dedicated use of indirect workers' time, when the cost of this time would be a direct labour cost of the order.

(c) Overtime premium paid to both direct and indirect workers is an indirect cost, except in two particular circumstances.

    (i) If overtime is worked at the specific request of a customer to get his order completed, the overtime premium paid is a direct cost of the order.

    (ii) If overtime is worked regularly by a production department in the normal course of operations, the overtime premium paid to direct workers could be incorporated into the (average) direct labour hourly rate.

(d) Bonus payments are generally an indirect cost.

(e) Employer's National Insurance contributions (which are added to employees' total pay as a wages cost) are normally treated as an indirect labour cost.

(f) Idle time is an overhead cost, that is an indirect labour cost.

(g) The cost of work on capital equipment is incorporated into the capital cost of the equipment.

2.5 Direct expenses

Key term

> **Direct expenses** are any expenses which are incurred on a specific product other than direct material cost and direct wages

Direct expenses are charged to the product as part of the **prime** cost. Examples of direct expenses are as follows.

- The **hire of tools** or equipment for a particular job
- **Maintenance costs** of tools, fixtures and so on

Direct expenses are also referred to as **chargeable expenses.**

2.6 Production overhead

Production (or factory) overhead includes all indirect material costs, indirect wages and indirect expenses incurred in the factory from receipt of the order until its completion.

Production overhead includes the following.

(a) **Indirect materials** which cannot be traced in the finished product.

- Consumable stores, eg material used in negligible amounts

(b) **Indirect wages**, meaning all wages not charged directly to a product.

- Wages of non-productive personnel in the production department, eg foremen

(c) **Indirect expenses** (other than material and labour) not charged directly to production.

- Rent, rates and insurance of a factory
- Depreciation, fuel, power, maintenance of plant, machinery and buildings

2.7 Administration overhead

Administration overhead is all indirect material costs, wages and expenses incurred in the direction, control and administration of an undertaking.

Examples of administration overhead are as follows.

- **Depreciation** of office buildings and equipment.
- **Office salaries**, including salaries of directors, secretaries and accountants.
- Rent, rates, insurance, lighting, cleaning, telephone charges and so on.

2.8 Selling overhead

Selling overhead is all indirect materials costs, wages and expenses incurred in promoting sales and retaining customers.

Examples of selling overhead are as follows.

- **Printing** and **stationery**, such as catalogues and price lists.
- **Salaries** and **commission** of salesmen, representatives and sales department staff.
- **Advertising** and **sales promotion**, market research.
- Rent, rates and insurance of sales offices and showrooms, bad debts and so on.

2.9 Distribution overhead

Distribution overhead is all indirect material costs, wages and expenses incurred in making the packed product ready for despatch and delivering it to the customer.

Examples of distribution overhead are as follows.

- Cost of packing cases.
- Wages of packers, drivers and despatch clerks.
- Insurance charges, rent, rates, depreciation of warehouses and so on.

Question
Direct labour cost

A direct labour employee's wage in week 5 consists of the following.

		$
(a)	Basic pay for normal hours worked, 36 hours at $4 per hour =	144
(b)	Pay at the basic rate for overtime, 6 hours at $4 per hour =	24
(c)	Overtime shift premium, with overtime paid at time-and-a-quarter ¼ × 6 hours × $4 per hour =	6
(d)	A bonus payment under a group bonus (or 'incentive') scheme – bonus for the month =	30
	Total gross wages in week 5 for 42 hours of work	204

What is the direct labour cost for this employee in week 5?

A $144   B $168   C $198   D $204

Answer

Let's start by considering a general approach to answering multiple choice questions (MCQs). In a numerical question like this, the best way to begin is to ignore the available options and work out your own answer from the available data. If your solution corresponds to one of the four options then mark this as your chosen answer and move on. Don't waste time working out whether any of the other options might be correct. If your answer does not appear among the available options then check your workings. If it still does not correspond to any of the options then you need to take a calculated guess.

Do not make the common error of simply selecting the answer which is closest to yours. The best thing to do is to first eliminate any answers which you know or suspect are incorrect. For example you could eliminate C and D because you know that group bonus schemes are usually indirect costs. You are then left with a choice between A and B, and at least you have now improved your chances if you really are guessing.

The correct answer is B because the basic rate for overtime is a part of direct wages cost. It is only the overtime premium that is usually regarded as an overhead or indirect cost.

3 Functional costs

3.1 Classification by function

FAST FORWARD

> **Classification by function** involves classifying costs as production/manufacturing costs, administration costs or marketing/selling and distribution costs.

In a 'traditional' costing system for a manufacturing organisation, costs are classified as follows.

(a) **Production** or **manufacturing costs.** These are costs associated with the factory.

(b) **Administration costs.** These are costs associated with general office departments.

(c) **Marketing**, or **selling** and **distribution costs.** These are costs associated with sales, marketing, warehousing and transport departments.

Classification in this way is known as **classification by function**. Expenses that do not fall fully into one of these classifications might be categorised as **general overheads** or even listed as a classification on their own (for example research and development costs).

3.2 Full cost of sales

In costing a small product made by a manufacturing organisation, direct costs are usually restricted to some of the production costs. A commonly found build-up of costs is therefore as follows.

	$
Production costs	
Direct materials	A
Direct wages	B
Direct expenses	C
Prime cost	A+B+C
Production overheads	D
Full factory cost	A+B+C+D
Administration costs	E
Selling and distribution costs	F
Full cost of sales	A+B+C+D+E+F

3.3 Functional costs

(a) **Production costs** are the costs which are incurred by the sequence of operations beginning with the supply of raw materials, and ending with the completion of the product ready for warehousing as a finished goods item. Packaging costs are production costs where they relate to 'primary' packing (boxes, wrappers and so on).

(b) **Administration costs** are the costs of managing an organisation, that is, planning and controlling its operations, but only insofar as such administration costs are not related to the production, sales, distribution or research and development functions.

(c) **Selling costs**, sometimes known as marketing costs, are the costs of creating demand for products and securing firm orders from customers.

(d) **Distribution costs** are the costs of the sequence of operations with the receipt of finished goods from the production department and making them ready for despatch and ending with the reconditioning for reuse of empty containers.

(e) **Research costs** are the costs of searching for new or improved products, whereas **development costs** are the costs incurred between the decision to produce a new or improved product and the commencement of full manufacture of the product.

(f) **Financing costs** are costs incurred to finance the business such as loan interest.

Question | Cost classification

Within the costing system of a manufacturing company the following types of expense are incurred.

Reference number

1	Cost of oils used to lubricate production machinery
2	Motor vehicle licences for lorries
3	Depreciation of factory plant and equipment
4	Cost of chemicals used in the laboratory
5	Commission paid to sales representatives
6	Salary of the secretary to the finance director
7	Trade discount given to customers
8	Holiday pay of machine operatives

9	Salary of security guard in raw material warehouse
10	Fees to advertising agency
11	Rent of finished goods warehouse
12	Salary of scientist in laboratory
13	Insurance of the company's premises
14	Salary of supervisor working in the factory
15	Cost of typewriter ribbons in the general office
16	Protective clothing for machine operatives

Required

Complete the following table by placing each expense in the correct cost classification.

Cost classification	Reference number					
Production costs						
Selling and distribution costs						
Administration costs						
Research and development costs						

Each type of expense should appear only once in your answer. You may use the reference numbers in your answer.

Answer

Cost classification	Reference number					
Production costs	1	3	8	9	14	16
Selling and distribution costs	2	5	7	10	11	
Administration costs	6	13	15			
Research and development costs	4	12				

4 Fixed costs and variable costs

4.1 Introduction

FAST FORWARD

A different way of analysing and classifying costs is into **fixed costs** and **variable costs.** Many items of expenditure are part-fixed and part-variable and hence are termed **semi-fixed** or **semi-variable costs.**

Key terms

A **fixed cost** is a cost which is incurred for a particular period of time and which, within certain activity levels, is unaffected by changes in the level of activity.

A **variable cost** is a cost which tends to vary with the level of activity.

4.2 Examples of fixed and variable costs

(a)   Direct material costs are **variable costs** because they rise as more units of a product are manufactured.

(b)   Sales commission is often a fixed percentage of sales turnover, and so is a **variable cost** that varies with the level of sales.

(c) Telephone call charges are likely to increase if the volume of business expands, but there is also a fixed element of line rental, and so they are a **semi-fixed** or **semi-variable overhead cost.**

(d) The rental cost of business premises is a constant amount, at least within a stated time period, and so it is a **fixed cost.**

5 Production and non-production costs

For the preparation of financial statements, costs are often classified as **production costs** and **non-production costs**. Production costs are costs identified with goods produced for resale. Non-production costs are cost deducted as expenses during the current period.

Production costs are all the costs involved in the manufacture of goods. In the case of manufactured goods, these costs consist of direct material, direct labour and manufacturing overhead.

Non-production costs are taken directly to the profit and loss account as expenses in the period in which they are incurred; such costs consist of selling and administrative expenses.

5.1 Production and non-production costs

The distinction between production and non-production costs is the basis of valuing inventory.

5.2 Example

A business has the following costs for a period:

	$
Materials	600
Labour	1,000
Production overheads	500
Administration overheads	700
	2,800

During the period 100 units are produced. If all of these costs were allocated to production units, each unit would be valued at $28.

This would be incorrect. Only **production** costs are allocated to units of inventory. Administrative overheads are **non-production** costs.

So each unit of inventory should be valued at $21((600 + 1,000 + 500)/100)

This affects both gross profit and the valuation of closing inventory. If during the period 80 units are sold at $40 each, the gross profit will be:

	$
Sales (80 × 40)	3,200
Cost of sales (80 × 21)	(1,680)
Gross profit	1,520

The value of closing (unsold) inventory will be $420 (20 × 21).

6 Other cost classifications

Avoidable costs are specific costs of an activity or business which would be avoided if the activity or business did not exist.

Unavoidable costs are costs which would be incurred whether or not an activity or sector existed.

A **controllable cost** is a cost which can be influenced by management decisions and actions.

An **uncontrollable cost** is any cost that cannot be affected by management within a given time span.

Discretionary costs are costs which are likely to arise from decisions made during the budgeting process. They are likely to be fixed amounts of money over fixed periods of time.

Examples of discretionary costs are as follows.

- Advertising
- Research and Development
- Training

7 Cost units, cost objects and responsibility centres

7.1 Cost centres

FAST FORWARD

Cost centres are collecting places for costs before they are further analysed. Costs are further analysed into cost units once they have been traced to cost centres.

Costs consist of the costs of the following.

- Direct materials
- Direct labour
- Direct expenses
- Production overheads
- Administration overheads
- General overheads

When costs are incurred, they are generally allocated to a **cost centre**. Cost centres may include the following.

- A department
- A machine, or group of machines
- A project (eg the installation of a new computer system)
- Overhead costs eg rent, rates, electricity (which may then be allocated to departments or projects)

Cost centres are an essential 'building block' of a costing system. They are the starting point for the following.

(a) The classification of actual costs incurred.
(b) The preparation of budgets of planned costs.
(c) The comparison of actual costs and budgeted costs (management control).

7.2 Cost units

FAST FORWARD

A **cost unit** is a unit of product or service to which costs can be related. The cost unit is the basic control unit for costing purposes.

Once costs have been traced to cost centres, they can be further analysed in order to establish a **cost per cost unit**. Alternatively, some items of cost may be charged directly to a cost unit, for example direct materials and direct labour costs.

Examples of cost units include the following.

- Patient episode (in a hospital)
- Barrel (in the brewing industry)
- Room (in a hotel)

Question
Cost units

Suggest suitable cost units which could be used to aid control within the following organisations.

(a)   A hotel with 50 double rooms and 10 single rooms
(b)   A hospital
(c)   A road haulage business

Answer

(a)   • Guest/night
       • Bed occupied/night
       • Meal supplied

(b)   • Patient/night
       • Operation
       • Outpatient visit

(c)   • Tonne/mile
       • Mile

7.3 Cost objects

FAST FORWARD
> A **cost object** is any activity for which a separate measurement of costs is desired.

If the users of management information wish to know the cost of something, this something is called a **cost object**. Examples include the following.

- The cost of a product
- The cost of a service
- The cost of operating a department

7.4 Profit centres

FAST FORWARD
> **Profit centres** are similar to cost centres but are accountable for **costs** *and* **revenues**.

We have seen that a cost centre is where costs are collected. Some organisations, however, work on a profit centre basis.

Profit centre managers should normally have control over how revenue is raised and how costs are incurred. Often, several cost centres will comprise one profit centre. The profit centre manager will be able to make decisions about both purchasing and selling and will be expected to do both as profitably as possible.

A profit centre manager will want information regarding both revenues and costs. He will be judged on the profit margin achieved by his division. In practice, it may be that there are fixed costs which he cannot control, so he should be judged on contribution, which is revenue less variable costs. In this case he will want information about which products yield the highest contribution.

7.5 Revenue centres

Revenue centres are similar to cost centres and profit centres but are accountable for **revenues only**. Revenue centre managers should normally have control over how revenues are raised

A revenue centre manager is not accountable for costs. He will be aiming purely to maximise sales revenue. He will want information on markets and new products and he will look closely at pricing and the sales performance of competitors – in addition to monitoring revenue figures.

7.6 Investment centres

An **investment centre** is a profit centre with additional responsibilities for capital investment and possibly for financing, and whose performance is measured by its return on investment.

An investment centre manager will take the same decisions as a profit centre manager but he also has additional responsibility for investment. So he will be judged additionally on his handling of cash surpluses and he will seek to make only those investments which yield a higher percentage than the company's notional cost of capital. So the investment centre manager will want the same information as the profit centre manager and in addition he will require quite detailed appraisals of possible investments and information regarding the results of investments already undertaken. He will have to make decisions regarding the purchase or lease of non-current assets and the investment of cash surpluses. Most of these decisions involve large sums of money.

7.7 Responsibility centres

A **responsibility centre** is a department or organisational function whose performance is the direct responsibility of a specific manager.

Cost centres, revenue centres, profit centres and investment centres are also known as **responsibility centres**.

Question

Investment centre

Which of the following is a characteristic of an investment centre?

A   Managers have control over marketing.

B   Management have a sales team.

C   Management have a sales team and are given a credit control function.

D   Managers can purchase capital assets.

Answer

D

Exam focus point

This chapter has introduced a number of new terms and definitions. The topics covered in this chapter are key areas of the syllabus and are likely to be tested in the **Management Accounting** examination.

Chapter roundup

- A **direct cost** is a cost that can be traced in full to the product, service or department being costed. An **indirect cost** (or overhead) is a cost that is incurred in the course of making a product, providing a service or running a department, but which cannot be traced directly and in full to the product, service or department.

- **Classification by function** involves classifying costs as production/manufacturing costs, administration costs or marketing/selling and distribution costs.

- A different way of analysing and classifying costs is into **fixed costs** and **variable costs**. Many items of expenditure are part-fixed and part-variable and hence are termed **semi-fixed** or **semi-variable** costs.

- For the preparation of financial statements, costs are often classified as **production costs** and **non-production costs**. Production costs are costs identified with goods produced or purchased for resale. Non-production costs are costs deducted as expenses during the current period.

- **Cost centres** are collecting places for costs before they are further analysed. Costs are further analysed into cost units once they have been traced to cost centres.

- A **cost unit** is a unit of product or service to which costs can be related. The cost unit is the basic control unit for costing purposes.

- A **cost object** is any activity for which a separate measurement of costs is desired.

- **Profit centres** are similar to cost centres but are accountable for both **costs** *and* **revenues**.

- **Revenue centres** are similar to cost centres and profit centres but are accountable for **revenues only**.

- An **investment centre** is a profit centre with additional responsibilities for capital investment and possibly financing, and whose performance is measured by its return on investment.

- A **responsibility centre** is a department or organisational function whose performance is the direct responsibility of a specific manager.

Quick quiz

1 Give two examples of direct expenses.

2 Give an example of an administration overhead, a selling overhead and a distribution overhead.

3 What are functional costs?

4 What is the distinction between fixed and variable costs?

5 What are production costs and non-production costs?

6 What is a cost centre?

7 What is a cost unit?

8 What is a profit centre?

9 What is an investment centre?

Answers to quick quiz

1   • The hire of tools or equipment for a particular job
    • Maintenance costs of tools, fixtures and so on

2   • **Administration overhead** = Depreciation of office buildings and equipment
    • **Selling overhead** = Printing and stationery (catalogues, price lists)
    • **Distribution overhead** = Wages of packers, drivers and despatch clerks

3   Functional costs are classified as follows.

    • **Production** or **manufacturing costs**
    • **Administration costs**
    • **Marketing** or **selling and distribution costs**

4   A **fixed cost** is a cost which is incurred for a particular period of time and which, within certain activity levels, is unaffected by changes in the level of activity.

    A **variable cost** is a cost which tends to vary with the level of activity.

5   **Production costs** are costs identified with a finished product. Such costs are initially identified as part of the value of inventory. They become expenses only when the inventory is sold.

    Non-production costs are costs that are deducted as expenses during the current period without ever being included in the value of inventory held.

6   A **cost centre** acts as a collecting place for certain costs before they are analysed further.

7   A **cost unit** is a unit of product or service to which costs can be related. The cost unit is the basic control unit for costing purposes.

8   A **profit centre** is similar to a cost centre but is accountable for **costs** and **revenues**.

9   An **investment centre** is a profit centre with additional responsibilities for capital investment and possibly financing.

Now try the questions below from the Exam Question Bank

Number	Level	Marks	Time
Q2	MCQ/OTQ	n/a	n/a

3

Cost behaviour

Topic list	Syllabus reference
1 Introduction to cost behaviour	B3 (b)
2 Cost behaviour patterns	B3 (a)
3 Determining the fixed and variable elements of semi-variable costs	B3 (c)

Introduction

So far in this text we have introduced you to the subject of management information and explained in general terms what it is and what it does. In Chapter 2 we considered the principal methods of classifying costs. In particular, we introduced the concept of the division of costs into those that vary directly with changes in activity levels (**variable costs**) and those that do not (**fixed costs**). This chapter examines further this two-way split of **cost behaviour** and explains one method of splitting semi-variable costs into these two elements, the **high-low** method.

Study guide

		Intellectual level
B3	**Fixed and variable cost**	
(a)	Describe and illustrate graphically different types of cost behaviour	1
(b)	Explain and provide examples of costs that fall into categories of fixed, stepped fixed and variable costs	1
(c)	Use high-low analysis to separate the fixed and variable elements of total costs including situations involving stepped fixed costs and changes in the variable cost per unit	2

Exam guide

Cost behaviour is a key area of the **Management Accounting** syllabus and you need to understand fixed and variable elements and the use of high-low analysis.

1 Introduction to cost behaviour

1.1 Cost behaviour and decision making

FAST FORWARD

> **Cost behaviour** is the way in which costs are affected by changes in the volume of output.

Management decisions will often be based on how costs and revenues vary at different activity levels. Examples of such decisions are as follows.

- What should the **planned activity level** be for the next period?
- Should the **selling price** be reduced in order to sell more units?
- Should a particular component be **manufactured internally** or **bought in**?
- Should a **contract** be undertaken?

1.2 Cost behaviour and cost control

If the accountant does not know the level of costs which should have been incurred as a result of an organisation's activities, how can he or she hope to control costs?

1.3 Cost behaviour and budgeting

Knowledge of cost behaviour is obviously essential for the tasks of **budgeting**, **decision making** and **control accounting**.

Exam focus point

Remember that the behavioural analysis of costs is important for planning, control and decision-making.

1.4 Cost behaviour and levels of activity

There are many factors which may influence costs. The major influence is **volume of output**, or the **level of activity**. The level of activity may refer to one of the following.

- Number of units produced
- Value of items sold
- Number of items sold

- Number of invoices issued
- Number of units of electricity consumed

1.5 Cost behaviour principles

The basic principle of cost behaviour is that **as the level of activity rises, costs will usually rise**. It will cost more to produce 2,000 units of output than it will cost to produce 1,000 units.

This principle is common sense. The problem for the accountant, however, is to determine, for each item of cost, the way in which costs rise and by how much as the level of activity increases. For our purposes here, the level of activity for measuring cost will generally be taken to be the **volume of production**.

1.6 Example: cost behaviour and activity level

Hans Bratch has a fleet of company cars for sales representatives. Running costs have been estimated as follows.

(a) Cars cost $12,000 when new, and have a guaranteed trade-in value of $6,000 at the end of two years. Depreciation is charged on a straight-line basis.

(b) Petrol and oil cost 15 cents per mile.

(c) Tyres cost $300 per set to replace; replacement occurs after 30,000 miles.

(d) Routine maintenance costs $200 per car (on average) in the first year and $450 in the second year.

(e) Repairs average $400 per car over two years and are thought to vary with mileage. The average car travels 25,000 miles per annum.

(f) Tax, insurance, membership of motoring organisations and so on cost $400 per annum per car.

Required

Calculate the average cost per annum of cars which travel 15,000 miles per annum and 30,000 miles per annum.

Solution

Costs may be analysed into fixed, variable and stepped cost items, a stepped cost being a cost which is fixed in nature but only within certain levels of activity.

(a) **Fixed costs**

	$ per annum
Depreciation $(12,000 − 6,000) ÷ 2	3,000
Routine maintenance $(200 + 450) ÷ 2	325
Tax, insurance etc	400
	3,725

(b) **Variable costs**

	Cents per mile
Petrol and oil	15.0
Repairs ($400 ÷ 50,000 miles)	0.8
	15.8

(c) Step costs are tyre replacement costs, which are $300 at the end of every 30,000 miles.

    (i) If the car travels less than or exactly 30,000 miles in two years, the tyres will not be changed. Average cost of tyres per annum = $0.

(ii)   If a car travels more than 30,000 miles and up to (and including) 60,000 miles in two years, there will be one change of tyres in the period. Average cost of tyres per annum = $150 ($300 ÷ 2).

(iii)   If a car exceeds 60,000 miles in two years (up to 90,000 miles) there will be two tyre changes. Average cost of tyres per annum = $300 ($600 ÷ 2).

The estimated costs per annum of cars travelling 15,000 miles per annum and 30,000 miles per annum would therefore be as follows.

	15,000 miles per annum $	30,000 miles per annum $
Fixed costs	3,725	3,725
Variable costs (15.8c per mile)	2,370	4,740
Tyres	–	150
Cost per annum	6,095	8,615

2 Cost behaviour patterns

2.1 Fixed costs

FAST FORWARD

> A **fixed cost** is a cost which tends to be unaffected by increases or decreases in the volume of output.

Fixed costs are a **period charge**, in that they relate to a span of time; as the time span increases, so too will the fixed costs (which are sometimes referred to as period costs for this reason). It is important to understand that **fixed costs always have a variable element**, since an increase or decrease in production may also bring about an increase or decrease in fixed costs.

A sketch graph of fixed cost would look like this.

Examples of a fixed cost would be as follows.

- The salary of the managing director (per month or per annum)
- The rent of a single factory building (per month or per annum)
- Straight line depreciation of a single machine (per month or per annum)

2.2 Step costs

FAST FORWARD

> A **step cost** is a cost which is fixed in nature but only within certain levels of activity.

Consider the depreciation of a machine which may be fixed if production remains below 1,000 units per month. If production exceeds 1,000 units, a second machine may be required, and the cost of depreciation (on two machines) would go up a step. A sketch graph of a step cost could look like this.

Graph of step cost

Other examples of step costs are as follows.

    (a)   Rent is a step cost in situations where accommodation requirements increase as output levels get higher.

    (b)   Basic pay of employees is nowadays usually fixed, but as output rises, more employees (direct workers, supervisors, managers and so on) are required.

    (c)   Royalties.

2.3 Variable costs

A **variable cost** is a cost which tends to vary directly with the volume of output. The variable cost per unit is the same amount for each unit produced.

Graph of variable cost (1)

A constant variable cost per unit implies that the price per unit of say, material purchased is constant, and that the rate of material usage is also constant.

    (a)   The most important variable cost is the **cost of raw materials** (where there is no discount for bulk purchasing since bulk purchase discounts reduce the cost of purchases).

    (b)   **Direct labour costs** are, for very important reasons, classed as a variable cost even though basic wages are usually fixed.

    (c)   **Sales commission** is variable in relation to the volume or value of sales.

    (d)   **Bonus payments** for productivity to employees might be variable once a certain level of output is achieved, as the following diagram illustrates.

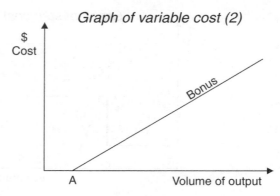

Graph of variable cost (2)

Up to output A, no bonus is earned.

2.4 Non-linear or curvilinear variable costs

> If the relationship between total variable cost and volume of output can be shown as a curved line on a graph, the relationship is said to be **curvilinear**.

Two typical relationships are as follows.

(a)

(b)

Each extra unit of output in graph (a) causes a **less than proportionate** increase in cost whereas in graph (b), each extra unit of output causes **a more than proportionate** increase in cost.

The cost of a piecework scheme for individual workers with differential rates could behave in a **curvilinear** fashion if the rates increase by small amounts at progressively higher output levels.

2.5 Semi-variable costs (or semi-fixed costs or mixed costs)

> A **semi-variable/semi-fixed/mixed cost** is a cost which contains both fixed and variable components and so is partly affected by changes in the level of activity.

Examples of these costs include the following.

(a) **Electricity and gas bills**

- Fixed cost = standing charge
- Variable cost = charge per unit of electricity used

(b) **Salesman's salary**

- Fixed cost = basic salary
- Variable cost = commission on sales made

(c)   **Costs of running a car**

- Fixed cost = road tax, insurance
- Variable costs = petrol, oil, repairs (which vary with miles travelled)

2.6 Other cost behaviour patterns

Other cost behaviour patterns may be appropriate to certain cost items. Examples of two other cost behaviour patterns are shown below.

(a)   *Cost behaviour pattern (1)*   (b)   *Cost behaviour pattern (2)*

- Graph (a) represents an item of cost which is variable with output up to a certain maximum level of cost.

- Graph (b) represents a cost which is variable with output, subject to a minimum (fixed) charge.

2.7 Cost behaviour and total and unit costs

The following table relates to different levels of production of the zed. The variable cost of producing a zed is $5. Fixed costs are $5,000.

	1 zed $	10 zeds $	50 zeds $
Total variable cost	5	50	250
Variable cost per unit	5	5	5
Total fixed cost	5,000	5,000	5,000
Fixed cost per unit	5,000	500	100
Total cost (fixed and variable)	5,005	5,050	5,250
Total cost per unit	5,005	505	105

What happens when activity levels rise can be summarised as follows.

- The variable cost per unit remains constant
- The fixed cost per unit falls
- The total cost per unit falls

This may be illustrated graphically as follows.

Question	Fixed, variable, mixed costs

Are the following likely to be fixed, variable or mixed costs?

(a)   Telephone bill
(b)   Annual salary of the chief accountant
(c)   The management accountant's annual membership fee to CIMA (paid by the company)
(d)   Cost of materials used to pack 20 units of product X into a box
(e)   Wages of warehousemen

Answer

(a)   Mixed
(b)   Fixed
(c)   Fixed
(d)   Variable
(e)   Variable

Exam focus point

> An exam question may give you a graph and require you to extract information from it.

2.8 Assumptions about cost behaviour

Assumptions about cost behaviour include the following.

(a)   Within the normal or **relevant range** of output, costs are often assumed to be either **fixed**, **variable** or **semi-variable** (mixed).

(b)   Departmental costs within an organisation are assumed to be **mixed costs**, with a **fixed** and a **variable** element.

(c)   Departmental costs are assumed to rise in a straight line as the volume of activity increases. In other words, these costs are said to be **linear**.

The **high-low method** of determining fixed and variable elements of mixed costs relies on the assumption that mixed costs are linear. We shall now go on to look at this method of cost determination.

3 Determining the fixed and variable elements of semi-variable costs

3.1 Analysing costs

FAST FORWARD

> The fixed and variable elements of semi-variable costs can be determined by the **high-low method**.

It is generally assumed that costs are one of the following.

- Variable
- Fixed
- Semi-variable

Cost accountants tend to separate semi-variable costs into their variable and fixed elements. They therefore generally tend to treat costs as either **fixed** or **variable**.

There are several methods for identifying the fixed and variable elements of semi-variable costs. Each method is only an estimate, and each will produce different results. One of the principal methods is the **high-low method.**

3.2 High-low method

Follow the steps below to estimate the fixed and variable elements of semi-variable costs.

Step 1   Review records of costs in previous periods.

- Select the period with the **highest** activity level.
- Select the period with the **lowest** activity level.

Step 2   Determine the following.

- Total cost at high activity level
- Total costs at low activity level
- Total units at high activity level
- Total units at low activity level

Step 3   Calculate the following.

$$\frac{\text{Total cost at high activity level} - \text{total cost at low activity level}}{\text{Total units at high activity level} - \text{total units at low activity level}} = \text{variable cost per unit (v)}$$

Step 4   The fixed costs can be determined as follows. (Total cost at high activity level) –(total units at high activity level × variable cost per unit)

The following graph demonstrates the high-low method.

Demonstration of high-low method

3.3 Example: The high-low method

DG Co has recorded the following total costs during the last five years.

Year	Output volume Units	Total cost $
20X0	65,000	145,000
20X1	80,000	162,000
20X2	90,000	170,000
20X3	60,000	140,000
20X4	75,000	160,000

Required

Calculate the total cost that should be expected in 20X5 if output is 85,000 units.

Solution

Step 1
- Period with highest activity = 20X2
- Period with lowest activity = 20X3

Step 2
- Total cost at high activity level = 170,000
- Total cost at low activity level = 140,000
- Total units at high activity level = 90,000
- Total units at low activity level = 60,000

Step 3   Variable cost per unit

$$= \frac{\text{total cost at high activity level} - \text{total cost at low activity level}}{\text{total units at high activity level} - \text{total units at low activity level}}$$

$$= \frac{170,000 - 140,000}{90,000 - 60,000} = \frac{30,000}{30,000} = \$1 \text{ per unit}$$

Step 4   Fixed costs = (total cost at high activity level) − (total units at high activity level × variable cost per unit)

= 170,000 − (90,000 × 1) = 170,000 − 90,000 = $80,000

Therefore the costs in 20X5 for output of 85,000 units are as follows.

		$
Variable costs =	85,000 × $1 =	85,000
Fixed costs =		80,000
		165,000

3.4 Example: The high-low method with stepped fixed costs

The following data relate to the overhead expenditure of contract cleaners (for industrial cleaning) at two activity levels.

Square metres cleaned	12,750	15,100
Overheads	$73,950	$83,585

When more than 20,000 square metres are industrially cleaned, it is necessary to have another supervisor and so the fixed costs rise to $43,350.

Required

Calculate the estimated overhead expenditure if 22,000 square metres are to be industrially cleaned.

Solution

	Units		$
High output	15,100	Total cost	83,585
Low output	12,750	Total cost	73,950
	2,350		9,635

$$\text{Variable cost} = \frac{\$9,635}{2,350}$$

= $4.10 per square metre

Estimated overhead expenditure if 22,000 square metres are to be industrially cleaned:

	$
Fixed costs	43,350
Variable costs (22,000 × $4.10)	90,200
	133,550

3.5 Example: The high-low method with a change in the variable cost per unit

Same data as the previous question.

Additionally, a round of wage negotiations have just taken place which will cost an additional $1 per square metre.

Solution

Estimated overheads to clean 22,000 square metres.

Variable cost = $\frac{\$9,635}{2,350}$ =	$4.10	per square metre
Additional variable cost	£1.00	per square metre
Total variable cost	$5.10	per square metre

Cost for 22,000 square metres:

	$
Fixed	43,350
Variable costs (22,000 × $5.10)	112,200
	155,550

Question
High-low method

The Valuation Department of a large firm of surveyors wishes to develop a method of predicting its total costs in a period. The following past costs have been recorded at two activity levels.

	Number of valuations (V)	Total cost (TC)
Period 1	420	82,200
Period 2	515	90,275

The total cost model for a period could be represented as follows.

A   TC = $46,500 + 85V
B   TC = $42,000 + 95V
C   TC = $46,500 – 85V
D   TC = $51,500 – 95V

Answer

Although we only have two activity levels in this question we can still apply the high-low method.

	Valuations V	Total cost $
Period 2	515	90,275
Period 1	420	82,200
Change due to variable cost	95	8,075

∴ Variable cost per valuation = $8,075/95 = $85.

Period 2: fixed cost = $90,275 – (515 × $85)
= $46,500

Using good MCQ technique, you should have managed to eliminate C and D as incorrect options straightaway. The variable cost must be added to the fixed cost, rather than subtracted from it. Once you had calculated the variable cost as $85 per valuation (as shown above), you should have been able to select option A without going on to calculate the fixed cost (we have shown this calculation above for completeness).

Chapter roundup

- **Cost behaviour** is the way in which costs are affected by changes in the volume of output.

- The basic principle of cost behaviour is that **as the level of activity rises, costs will usually rise**. It will cost more to produce 2,000 units of output than it will to produce 1,000 units.

- Costs which are not affected by the level of activity are **fixed** costs or **period** costs.

- A **fixed cost** is a cost which tends to be unaffected by increases or decreases in the volume of output.

- A **step cost** is a cost which is fixed in nature but only within certain levels of activity.

- A **variable cost** is a cost which tends to vary directly with the volume of output. The variable cost per unit is the same amount for each unit produced.

- If the relationship between total variable cost and volume of output can be shown as a curved line on a graph, the relationship is said to be **curvilinear**.

- A **semi-variable/semi-fixed/mixed cost** is a cost which contains both fixed and variable components and so is partly affected by changes in the level of activity.

- The fixed and variable elements of semi-variable costs can be determined by the **high-low method**.

Quick quiz

1 Cost behaviour is ....

2 The basic principle of cost behaviour is that as the level of activity rises, costs will usually rise/fall.

3 Fill in the gaps for each of the graph titles below.

(a)

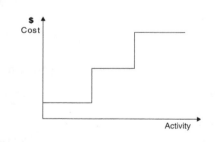

Graph of a ....…....cost

Example:

(b)

Graph of a ....…....cost

Example:

BPP
LEARNING MEDIA

(c)

Graph of a ....cost

Example:

(d)

Graph of a ....cost

Example:

4   Costs are assumed to be either fixed, variable or semi-variable within the normal or relevant range of output.

True

False

5   The costs of operating the canteen at 'Eat a lot Company' for the past three months is as follows.

Month	Cost	Employees
	$	
1	72,500	1,250
2	75,000	1,300
3	68,750	1,175

Variable cost (per employee per month) =

Fixed cost per month =

Answers to quick quiz

1   The variability of input costs with activity undertaken.

2   Rise

3   (a)   Step cost. Example: rent, supervisors' salaries
        (b)   Variable cost. Example: raw materials, direct labour
        (c)   Semi-variable cost. Example: electricity and telephone
        (d)   Fixed. Example: rent, depreciation (straight-line)

4   True

5   Variable cost = $50 per employee per month
       Fixed costs = $10,000 per month

	Activity	Cost
		$
High	1,300	75,000
Low	1,175	68,750
	125	6,250

Variable cost per employee = $6,250/125 = $50

For 1,175 employees, total cost = $68,750

Total cost   = variable cost + fixed cost
$68,750   = (1,175 × $50) + fixed cost

∴ Fixed cost   = $68,750 − $58,750
             = $10,000

Now try the questions below from the Exam Question Bank

Number	Level	Marks	Time
Q3	MCQ/OTQ	n/a	n/a

Part C
Business mathematics and computer spreadsheets

Correlation and regression; expected values

Topic list	Syllabus reference
1 Correlation	C2 (a)
2 The correlation coefficient and the coefficient of determination	C2 (a)
3 Lines of best fit	C2 (c)
4 Least squares method of linear regression analysis	C2 (c)
5 The reliability of regression analysis forecasts	C2 (b)
6 Expected values	C1 (a)
7 Expectation and decision-making	C1 (b) (c)

Introduction

In chapter 3, we looked at how costs behave and how total costs can be split into fixed and variable costs using the **high-low method**. In this chapter, we shall be looking at another method which is used to split total costs. This method is used to determine whether there is a linear relationship between two variables. If a **linear function** is considered to be appropriate, **regression analysis** is used to establish the equation (this equation can then be used to make forecasts or predictions).

Study guide

		Intellectual level
B3	**Fixed and variable costs**	
(a)	Explain the structure of linear functions and equations	1
C1	**Dealing with uncertainty**	
(a)	Explain and calculate an expected value	1
(b)	Demonstrate the use of expected values in simple decision making situations	1
(c)	Explain the limitations of the expected value technique	1
C2	**Statistics for business**	
(a)	Calculate a correlation coefficient and a coefficient of determination	1
(b)	Explain and interpret coefficients calculated	1
(c)	Establish a linear function using regression analysis and interpret the results	2

Exam guide

This is a very important topic and it is vital that you are able to establish linear equations using regression analysis.

1 Correlation

1.1 Introduction

Two variables are said to be correlated if a change in the value of one variable is accompanied by a change in the value of another variable. This is what is meant by **correlation**.

Examples of variables which might be correlated are as follows.

- A person's height and weight
- The distance of a journey and the time it takes to make it

1.2 Scattergraphs

One way of showing the correlation between two related variables is on a **scattergraph** or **scatter diagram**, plotting a number of pairs of data on the graph. For example, a scattergraph showing monthly selling costs against the volume of sales for a 12-month period might be as follows.

BPP
LEARNING MEDIA

This scattergraph suggests that there is some correlation between selling costs and sales volume, so that as sales volume rises, selling costs tend to rise as well.

1.3 Degrees of correlation

Two variables might be **perfectly correlated**, **partly correlated** or **uncorrelated**. Correlation can be **positive** or **negative**.

The differing degrees of correlation can be illustrated by scatter diagrams.

1.3.1 Perfect correlation

All the pairs of values lie on a straight line. An exact **linear relationship** exists between the two variables.

1.3.2 Partial correlation

In (a), although there is no exact relationship, low values of X tend to be associated with low values of Y, and high values of X with high values of Y.

In (b) again, there is no exact relationship, but low values of X tend to be associated with high values of Y and vice versa.

1.3.3 No correlation

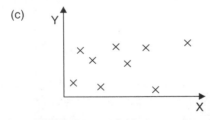

The values of these two variables are not correlated with each other.

1.3.4 Positive and negative correlation

Correlation, whether perfect or partial, can be **positive** or **negative**.

Positive correlation means that low values of one variable are associated with low values of the other, and high values of one variable are associated with high values of the other.

Negative correlation means that low values of one variable are associated with high values of the other, and high values of one variable with low values of the other.

2 The correlation coefficient and the coefficient of determination

2.1 The correlation coefficient

FAST FORWARD

The degree of correlation between two variables is measured by the **Pearsonian** (product moment) **correlation coefficient, r**. The nearer r is to +1 or −1, the stronger the relationship.

When we have measured the **degree of correlation** between two variables we can decide, using actual results in the form of pairs of data, whether two variables are perfectly or partially correlated, and if they are partially correlated, whether there is a **high** or **low degree of partial correlation.**

Exam formula

Correlation coefficient, $r = \dfrac{n\sum XY - \sum X \sum Y}{\sqrt{[n\sum X^2 - (\sum X)^2][n\sum Y^2 - (\sum Y)^2]}}$

where X and Y represent pairs of data for two variables X and Y

n = the number of pairs of data used in the analysis

Exam focus point

The formula for the correlation coefficient is given in the exam.

The correlation coefficient, r must always fall between −1 and +1. If you get a value outside this range you have made a mistake.

- $r = $ **+1** means that the variables are perfectly positively correlated
- $r = $ **−1** means that the variables are perfectly negatively correlated
- $r = $ **0** means that the variables are uncorrelated

2.2 Example: the correlation coefficient

The cost of output at a factory is thought to depend on the number of units produced. Data have been collected for the number of units produced each month in the last six months, and the associated costs, as follows.

Month	Output '000s of units X	Cost $'000 Y
1	2	9
2	3	11
3	1	7
4	4	13
5	3	11
6	5	15

Required

Assess whether there is there any correlation between output and cost.

Solution

$$r = \frac{n\sum XY - \sum X \sum Y}{\sqrt{[n\sum X^2 - (\sum X)^2][n\sum Y^2 - (\sum Y)^2]}}$$

We need to find the values for the following.

(a) $\sum XY$ Multiply each value of X by its corresponding Y value, so that there are six values for XY. Add up the six values to get the total.

(b) $\sum X$ Add up the six values of X to get a total. $(\sum X)^2$ will be the square of this total.

(c) $\sum Y$ Add up the six values of Y to get a total. $(\sum Y)^2$ will be the square of this total.

(d) $\sum X^2$ Find the square of each value of X, so that there are six values for X^2. Add up these values to get a total.

(e) $\sum Y^2$ Find the square of each value of Y, so that there are six values for Y^2. Add up these values to get a total.

Workings

X	Y	XY	X^2	Y^2
2	9	18	4	81
3	11	33	9	121
1	7	7	1	49
4	13	52	16	169
3	11	33	9	121
5	15	75	25	225
$\sum X = $ 18	$\sum Y = $ 66	$\sum XY = $ 218	$\sum X^2 = $ 64	$\sum Y^2 = $ 766

$(\sum X)^2 = 18^2 = 324$ $(\sum Y)^2 = 66^2 = 4,356$

n   =   6

$$r = \frac{(6 \times 218) - (18 \times 66)}{\sqrt{(6 \times 64 - 324) \times (6 \times 766 - 4,356)}}$$

$$= \frac{1,308 - 1,188}{\sqrt{(384 - 324) \times (4,596 - 4,356)}}$$

$$= \frac{120}{\sqrt{60 \times 240}} = \frac{120}{\sqrt{14,400}} = \frac{120}{120} = 1$$

There is **perfect positive correlation** between the volume of output at the factory and costs which means that there is a perfect linear relationship between output and costs.

2.3 Correlation in a time series

Correlation exists in a time series if there is a relationship between the period of time and the recorded value for that period of time. The correlation coefficient is calculated with time as the X variable although it is convenient to use simplified values for X instead of year numbers.

For example, instead of having a series of years 20X1 to 20X5, we could have values for X from 0 (20X1) to 4 (20X5).

Note that whatever starting value you use for X (be it 0, 1, 2 ... 721, ... 953), the value of r will always be the same.

Correlation

Sales of product A between 20X7 and 20Y1 were as follows.

Year	Units sold ('000s)
20X7	20
20X8	18
20X9	15
20Y0	14
20Y1	11

Required

Determine whether there is a trend in sales. In other words, decide whether there is any correlation between the year and the number of units sold.

Answer

Workings

Let 20X7 to 20Y1 be years 0 to 4.

X	Y	XY	X^2	Y^2
0	20	0	0	400
1	18	18	1	324
2	15	30	4	225
3	14	42	9	196
4	11	44	16	121
$\sum X = 10$	$\sum Y = 78$	$\sum XY = 134$	$\sum X^2 = 30$	$\sum Y^2 = 1{,}266$

$(\sum X)^2 = 100$ $(\sum Y)^2 = 6{,}084$

$n = 5$

$$r = \frac{(5 \times 134) - (10 \times 78)}{\sqrt{(5 \times 30 - 100) \times (5 \times 1{,}266 - 6{,}084)}}$$

$$= \frac{670 - 780}{\sqrt{(150 - 100) \times (6{,}330 - 6{,}084)}} = \frac{-110}{\sqrt{50 \times 246}}$$

$$= \frac{-110}{\sqrt{12{,}300}} = \frac{-110}{110.90537} = -0.992$$

There is **partial negative correlation** between the year of sale and units sold. The value of r is close to −1, therefore a **high degree of correlation exists**, although it is not quite perfect correlation. This means that there is a **clear downward trend** in sales.

2.4 The coefficient of determination, r^2

FAST FORWARD

The **coefficient of determination**, r^2 (alternatively R^2) measures the proportion of the total variation in the value of one variable that can be explained by variations in the value of the other variable.

Unless the correlation coefficient r is exactly or very nearly +1, −1 or 0, its meaning or significance is a little unclear. For example, if the correlation coefficient for two variables is +0.8, this would tell us that the variables are positively correlated, but the correlation is not perfect. It would not really tell us much else. A more meaningful analysis is available from **the square of the correlation coefficient, r**, which is called the **coefficient of determination**, r^2

In the question above entitled 'Correlation' shows that r = –0.992, therefore r^2 = 0.984. This means that over 98% of variations in sales can be explained by the passage of time, leaving 0.016 (less than 2%) of variations to be explained by other factors.

Similarly, if the correlation coefficient between a company's output volume and maintenance costs was 0.9, r^2 would be 0.81, meaning that 81% of variations in maintenance costs could be explained by variations in output volume, leaving only 19% of variations to be explained by other factors (such as the age of the equipment).

Note, however, that if r^2 = 0.81, we would say that 81% of **the variations in y can be explained by variations in x**. We do not necessarily conclude that 81% of variations in y are *caused* by the variations in x. We must beware of reading too much significance into our statistical analysis.

2.5 Correlation and causation

If two variables are well correlated, either positively or negatively, this may be due to **pure chance** or there may be a **reason** for it. The larger the number of pairs of data collected, the less likely it is that the correlation is due to chance, though that possibility should never be ignored entirely.

If there is a reason, it may not be causal. For example, monthly net income is well correlated with monthly credit to a person's bank account, for the logical (rather than causal) reason that for most people the one equals the other.

Even if there is a causal explanation for a correlation, it does not follow that variations in the value of one variable cause variations in the value of the other. For example, sales of ice cream and of sunglasses are well correlated, not because of a direct causal link but because the weather influences both variables.

3 Lines of best fit

3.1 Linear relationships

Correlation enables us to determine the strength of any relationship between two variables but it does not offer us any method of forecasting values for one variable, Y, given values of another variable, X.

If we assume that there is a **linear relationship** between the two variables, however, and we determine the **equation of a straight line (Y = a + bX)** which is a good fit for the available data plotted on a scattergraph, we can use the equation for forecasting: we can substitute values for X into the equation and derive values for Y. If you need reminding about linear equations and graphs, refer to your Basic Maths appendix.

3.2 Estimating the equation of the line of best fit

There are a number of techniques for estimating the equation of a line of best fit. We will be looking at **simple linear regression analysis**. This provides a technique for estimating values for a and b in the equation

$$Y = a + bX$$

where X and Y are the related variables and
       a and b are estimated using pairs of data for X and Y.

4 Least squares method of linear regression analysis

4.1 Introduction

Linear regression analysis (the **least squares method**) is one technique for estimating a line of best fit. Once an equation for a line of best fit has been determined, forecasts can be made.

Exam formulae

The **least squares method of linear regression analysis** involves using the following formulae for a and b in Y = a + bX.

$$b = \frac{n\sum XY - \sum X \sum Y}{n\sum X^2 - (\sum X)^2}$$

$$a = \frac{\sum Y}{n} - b\frac{\sum X}{n}$$

where n is the number of pairs of data

Exam focus point

The formulae will be given in the exam.

The line of best fit that is derived represents the **regression of Y upon X**.

A different line of best fit could be obtained by interchanging X and Y in the formulae. This would then represent the regression of X upon Y (X = a + bY) and it would have a slightly different slope. For examination purposes, always use the regression of Y upon X, where X is the independent variable, and Y is the dependent variable whose value we wish to forecast for given values of X. In a time series, X will represent time.

4.2 Example: the least squares method

(a)   Given that there is a fairly high degree of correlation between the output and the costs detailed in the example in Paragraph 4.1 (so that a linear relationship can be assumed), calculate an equation to determine the expected level of costs, for any given volume of output, using the least squares method.

(b)   Prepare a budget for total costs if output is 22,000 units.

(c)   Confirm that the degree of correlation between output and costs is high by calculating the correlation coefficient.

Solution

(a)   *Workings*

X	Y	XY	X^2	Y^2
20	82	1,640	400	6,724
16	70	1,120	256	4,900
24	90	2,160	576	8,100
22	85	1,870	484	7,225
18	73	1,314	324	5,329
$\sum X = 100$	$\sum Y = 400$	$\sum XY = 8,104$	$\sum X^2 = 2,040$	$\sum Y^2 = 32,278$

n   =   5 (There are five pairs of data for x and y values)

$$b = \frac{n\sum XY - \sum X \sum Y}{n\sum X^2 - (\sum X)^2} = \frac{(5 \times 8{,}104) - (100 \times 400)}{(5 \times 2{,}040) - 100^2}$$

$$= \frac{40{,}520 - 40{,}000}{10{,}200 - 10{,}000} = \frac{520}{200} = 2.6$$

$$a = \frac{\sum Y}{n} - b\frac{\sum X}{n} = \frac{400}{5} - 2.6 \times \left(\frac{100}{5}\right) = 28$$

Y   =   28 + 2.6X

where   Y = total cost, in thousands of pounds
X = output, in thousands of units.

Note that the fixed costs are $28,000 (when X = 0 costs are $28,000) and the variable cost per unit is $2.60.

(b)   If the output is 22,000 units, we would expect costs to be

28 + 2.6 × 22 = 85.2 = $85,200.

(c) $$r = \frac{520}{\sqrt{200 \times \left(5 \times 32{,}278 - 400^2\right)}} = \frac{520}{\sqrt{200 \times 1{,}390}} = \frac{520}{527.3} = +0.99$$

4.3 Regression lines and time series

The same technique can be applied to calculate a **regression line** (a **trend line**) for a time series. This is particularly useful for purposes of forecasting. As with correlation, years can be numbered from 0 upwards.

Question   **Trend line**

Using the data in the question entitled 'Correlation', calculate the trend line of sales and forecast sales in 20Y2 and 20Y3.

Answer

Using workings from the question entitled 'Correlation':

$$b = \frac{(5 \times 134) - (10 \times 78)}{(5 \times 30) - (10)^2} = \frac{670 - 780}{150 - 100} = -2.2$$

$$a = \frac{\sum Y}{n} - b\frac{\sum X}{n} = \frac{78}{5} - \frac{(-2.2 \times 10)}{5} = 20$$

∴ Y = 20 – 2.2X where X = 0 in 20X7, X = 1 in 20X8 and so on.

Using the trend line, predicted sales in 20Y2 (year 5) would be:

20 – (2.2 × 5) = 9 ie 9,000 units

and predicated sales in 20Y3 (year 6) would be:

20 – (2.2 × 6) = 6.8 ie 6,800 units.

Question

Regression analysis was used to find the equation Y = 300 – 4.7X, where X is time (in quarters) and Y is sales level in thousands of units. Given that X = 0 represents 20X0 quarter 1 what are the forecast sales levels for 20X5 quarter 4?

Answer

X = 0 corresponds to 20X0 quarter 1

Therefore X = 23 corresponds to 20X5 quarter 4

Forecast sales   = 300 – (4.7 × 23)
                   = 191.9 = 191,900 units

Question

Over a 36 month period sales have been found to have an underlying regression line of Y = 14.224 + 7.898X where Y is the number of items sold and X represents the month.

What are the forecast number of items to be sold in month 37?

Answer

Y   = 14.224 + 7.898X
      = 14.224 + (7.898 × 37)
      = 306.45 = 306 units

5 The reliability of regression analysis forecasts

FAST FORWARD   As with all forecasting techniques, the results from regression analysis will not be wholly reliable. There are a number of factors which affect the reliability of forecasts made using regression analysis.

(a)   **It assumes a linear relationship exists between the two variables** (since linear regression analysis produces an equation in the linear format) whereas a non-linear relationship might exist.

(b)   It **assumes that the value of one variable, Y, can be predicted or estimated from the value of one other variable, X**. In reality the value of Y might depend on several other variables, not just X.

(c)   When it is used for forecasting, **it assumes that what has happened in the past will provide a reliable guide to the future**.

(d)   When calculating a line of best fit, there will be a range of values for X. In the example in Paragraph 4.2, the line Y = 28 + 2.6X was predicted from data with output values ranging from X = 16 to X = 24. Depending on the degree of correlation between X and Y, we might safely use the estimated line of best fit to predict values for Y in the future, provided that the value of X remains within the range 16 to 24. We would be on less safe ground if we used the formula to predict a value for Y when X = 10, or 30, or any other value outside the range

16 to 24, because we would have to **assume that the trend line applies outside the range of X values used to establish the line in the first place**.

    (i)   **Interpolation** means using a line of best fit to predict a value within the two extreme points of the observed range.

    (ii)   **Extrapolation** means using a line of best fit to predict a value outside the two extreme points.

When linear regression analysis is used for forecasting a time series (when the X values represent time) it **assumes that the trend line can be extrapolated into the future**. This might not necessarily be a good assumption to make.

(e)   As with any forecasting process, **the amount of data available is very important**. Even if correlation is high, if we have fewer than about ten pairs of values, we must regard any forecast as being somewhat unreliable. (It is likely to provide more reliable forecasts than the scattergraph method, however, since it uses all of the available data.)

(f)   **The reliability of a forecast will depend on the reliability of the data collected to determine the regression analysis equation**. If the data is not collected accurately or if data used is false, forecasts are unlikely to be acceptable.

A check on the reliability of the estimated line Y= 28 + 2.6X can be made, however, by calculating the coefficient of correlation. From the answer to the example in Paragraph 4.2, we know that r = 0.99. This is a high positive correlation, and r^2 = 0.9801, indicating that 98.01% of the variation in cost can be explained by the variation in volume. This would suggest that a **fairly large degree of reliance** can probably be placed on estimates .

If there is a **perfect linear relationship** between X and Y (r = $\pm$1) then we can predict Y from any given value of X with **great confidence**.

If correlation is high (for example r = 0.9) the actual values will all lie quite close to the regression line and so predictions should not be far out. If correlation is below about 0.7, predictions will only give a very rough guide as to the likely value of Y.

6 Expected values

An **expected value** (or **EV**) is a weighted average value, based on probabilities. The expected value for a single event can offer a helpful guide for management decisions.

6.1 How to calculate expected values

If the probability of an outcome of an event is p, then the expected number of times that this outcome will occur in n events (the expected value) is equal to n × p.

For example, suppose that the probability that a transistor is defective is 0.02. How many defectives would we expect to find in a batch of 4,000 transistors?

EV = 4,000 × 0.02
     = 80 defectives

6.2 Example: Expected values

The daily sales of Product T may be as follows.

Units	Probability
1,000	0.2
2,000	0.3
3,000	0.4
4,000	0.1
	1.0

Required

Calculate the expected daily sales.

Solution

The EV of daily sales may be calculated by multiplying each possible outcome (volume of daily sales) by the probability that this outcome will occur.

	Probability	Expected value
Units		Units
1,000	0.2	200
2,000	0.3	600
3,000	0.4	1,200
4,000	0.1	400
		EV of daily sales 2,400

In the long run the expected value should be approximately the actual average, if the event occurs many times over. In the example above, we do not expect sales on any one day to equal 2,400 units, but in the long run, over a large number of days, average sales should equal 2,400 units a day.

6.3 Expected values and single events

The point made in the preceding paragraph is an important one. An **expected value** can be calculated when the **event will only occur once or twice**, but it will not be a true long-run average of what will actually happen, because there is no long run.

6.4 Example: Expected values and single events

Suppose, for example, that a businessman is trying to decide whether to invest in a project. He estimates that there are three possible outcomes.

Outcome	Profit/(loss)	Probability
	$	
Success	10,000	0.2
Moderate success	2,000	0.7
Failure	(4,000)	0.1

The expected value of profit may be calculated as follows.

Profit/(loss)	Probability	Expected value
$		$
10,000	0.2	2,000
2,000	0.7	1,400
(4,000)	0.1	(400)
		Expected value of profit 3,000

In this example, the project is a one-off event, and as far as we are aware, it will not be repeated. The actual profit or loss will be $10,000, $2,000 or $(4,000), and the average value of $3,000 will not actually happen. There is no long-run average of a single event.

Nevertheless, the expected value can be used to help the manager decide whether or not to invest in the project.

Question
Expected values

A company manufactures and sells product D. The selling price of the product is $6 per unit, and estimates of demand and variable costs of sales are as follows.

Probability	Demand Units	Probability	Variable cost per unit $
0.3	5,000	0.1	3.00
0.6	6,000	0.3	3.50
0.1	8,000	0.5	4.00
		0.1	4.50

The unit variable costs do not depend on the volume of sales.

Fixed costs will be $10,000.

Required

Calculate the expected profit.

Answer

The EV of demand is as follows.

Demand Units	Probability	Expected value Units
5,000	0.3	1,500
6,000	0.6	3,600
8,000	0.1	800
		EV of demand 5,900

The EV of the variable cost per unit is as follows.

Variable costs $	Probability	Expected value $
3.00	0.1	0.30
3.50	0.3	1.05
4.00	0.5	2.00
4.50	0.1	0.45
		EV of unit variable costs 3.80

		$
Sales	5,900 units × $6.00	35,400
Less: variable costs	5,900 units × $3.80	22,420
Contribution		12,980
Less: fixed costs		10,000
Expected profit		2,980

6.5 The expected value equation

The expected value is summarised in equation form as follows.

$E(x) = \sum xP(x)$

This is read as 'the expected value of a particular outcome "x" is equal to the sum of the products of each value of x and the corresponding probability of that value of x occurring'.

7 Expectation and decision making

7.1 Decision making

FAST FORWARD

Probability and expectation should be seen as an aid to decision making.

The concepts of probability and expected value are vital in **business decision making**. The expected values for single events can offer a helpful guide for management decisions.

- A project with a positive EV should be accepted
- A project with a negative EV should be rejected

Another decision rule involving expected values that you are likely to come across is the choice of an option or alternative which has the **highest EV of profit** (or the **lowest EV of cost**).

Choosing the option with the highest EV of profit is a decision rule that has both merits and drawbacks, as the following simple example will show.

7.2 Example: The expected value criterion

Suppose that there are two mutually exclusive projects with the following possible profits.

Project A		Project B	
Probability	Profit	Probability	Profit/(loss)
	$		$
0.8	5,000	0.1	(2,000)
0.2	6,000	0.2	5,000
		0.6	7,000
		0.1	8,000

Required

Determine which project should be chosen.

Solution

The EV of profit for each project is as follows.

				$
(a)	Project A $(0.8 \times 5,000) + (0.2 \times 6,000)$		=	5,200
(b)	Project B $(0.1 \times (2,000)) + (0.2 \times 5,000) + (0.6 \times 7,000) + (0.1 \times 8,000)$		=	5,800

Project B has a higher EV of profit. This means that on the balance of probabilities, it could offer a better return than A, and so is arguably a better choice.

On the other hand, the minimum return from project A would be $5,000 whereas with B there is a 0.1 chance of a loss of $2,000. So project A might be a safer choice.

Expected values

A company is deciding whether to invest in a project. There are three possible outcomes of the investment:

Outcome	Profit/(Loss) $'000
Optimistic	19.2
Most likely	12.5
Pessimistic	(6.7)

There is a 30% chance of the optimistic outcome, and a 60% chance of the most likely outcome arising. The expected value of profit from the project is

A $7,500
B $12,590
C $13,930
D $25,000

Answer

B   Since the probabilities must total 100%, the probability of the pessimistic outcome = 100% − 60% − 30% = 10%.

Outcome	Profit/(Loss) $	Probability	Expected value $
Optimistic	19,200	0.3	5,760
Most likely	12,500	0.6	7,500
Pessimistic	(6,700)	0.1	(670)
		1.0	12,590

If you selected option A, you calculated the expected value of the most likely outcome instead of the entire project.

If you selected option C, you forgot to treat the 6,700 as a loss, ie as a negative value.

If you selected option D, you forgot to take into account the probabilities of the various outcomes arising.

7.3 Payoff tables

Decisions have to be taken about a wide variety of matters (capital investment, controls on production, project scheduling and so on) and under a wide variety of conditions from **virtual certainty** to **complete uncertainty**.

There are, however, certain common factors in many business decisions.

   (a)   When a decision has to be made, there will be a range of possible **actions**.

   (b)   Each action will have certain **consequences**, or **payoffs** (for example, profits, costs, time).

   (c)   The payoff from any given action will depend on the **circumstances** (for example, high demand or low demand), which may or may not be known when the decision is taken. Frequently each circumstance will be assigned a probability of occurrence. The circumstances are *not* dependent on the action taken.

For a decision with these elements, a **payoff table** can be prepared.

A payoff table is simply a table with **rows for circumstances** and **columns for actions** (or vice versa), and the payoffs in the cells of the table.

For example, a decision on the level of advertising expenditure to be undertaken given different states of the economy, would have payoffs in $'000 of profit after advertising expenditure as follows.

		Actions: expenditure		
		High	Medium	Low
Circumstances:	Boom	+50	+30	+15
the state of the	Stable	+20	+25	+5
economy	Recession	0	−10	−35

Question

Pay off tables

In a restaurant there is a 30% chance of five apple pies being ordered a day and a 70% chance of ten being ordered. Each apple pie sells for $2. It costs $1 to make an apple pie. Using a payoff table, decide how many apple pies the restaurant should prepare each day, bearing in mind that unsold apple pies must be thrown away at the end of each day.

Answer

		Prepared	
		Five	Ten
Demand	Five (P = 0.3)	5	0
	Ten (P = 0.7)	5	10

Prepare five, profit = ($5 × 0.3) + ($5 × 0.7) = $5
Prepare ten, profit = ($0 × 0.3) + ($10 × 0.7) = $7

Ten pies should be prepared.

7.4 Limitations of expected values

Evaluating decisions by using expected values have a number of limitations.

(a) The **probabilities** used when calculating expected values are likely to be estimates. They may therefore be **unreliable** or **inaccurate**.

(b) Expected values are **long-term averages** and may not be suitable for use in situations involving **one-off decisions**. They may therefore be useful as a **guide** to decision making.

(c) Expected values do not consider the **attitudes to risk of** the people involved in the decision-making process. They do not, therefore, take into account all of the factors involved in the decision.

(d) The time value of money may not be taken into account: $100 now is worth more than $100 in ten years' time.

Chapter roundup

- Two variables are said to be correlated if a change in the value of one variable is accompanied by a change in the value of another variable. This is what is meant by **correlation**.

- Two variables might be **perfectly correlated**, **partly correlated** or **uncorrelated**. Correlation can be **positive** or **negative**.

- The **degree of correlation** between two variables is measured by the **Pearsonian** (product moment) **correlation coefficient, r**. The nearer r is to +1 or −1, the stronger the relationship.

- The **coefficient of determination, r^2** (alternatively **R^2**) measures the proportion of the total variation in the value of one variable that can be explained by variations in the value of the other variable.

- **Linear regression analysis** (the **least squares method**) is one technique for estimating a line of best fit. Once an equation for a line of best fit has been determined, forecasts can be made.

- As with all forecasting techniques, the results from regression analysis will not be wholly reliable. There are a number of factors which affect the reliability of forecasts made using regression analysis.

- An **expected value** (or EV) is a weighted average value, based on probabilities. The expected value for a single event can offer a helpful guide for management decisions.

- **Probability** and **expectation** should be seen as an aid to decision making.

- A **payoff table** is simply a table with rows for circumstances and columns for actions (or vice versa) and the payoffs in the cells of the table.

Quick quiz

1   ……………….. means that low values of one variable are associated with low values of the other, and high values of one variable are associated with high values of the other.

2   ……………….. means that low values of one variable are associated with high values of the other, and high values of one variable with low values of the other.

3   • Perfect positive correlation,   r = ………………..
     • Perfect negative correlation,   r = ………………..
     • No correlation,   r = ………………..

     The correlation coefficient, r, must always fall within the range ……………….. to ……………….. .

4   If the correlation coefficient of a set of data is 0.9, what is the coefficient of determination and how is it interpreted?

5   (a)   The equation of a straight line is given as $Y = a + bX$. Give two methods used for estimating the above equation.

     (b)   If $Y = a + bX$, it is best to use the regression of Y upon X where X is the dependent variable and Y is the independent variable.

            True

            False

6   List five factors affecting the reliability of regression analysis forecasts.

7   What is an expected value?.

Answers to quick quiz

1   Positive correlation

2   Negative correlation

3   • r = +1
     • r = −1
     • r = 0

     The correlation coefficient, r, must always fall within the range −1 to +1.

4   Correlation coefficient = r = 0.9

     Coefficient of determination = $r^2 = 0.9^2 = 0.81$ or 81%

     This tells us that over 80% of the variations in the dependent variable (Y) can be explained by variations in the independent variable, X.

5   (a)   • Scattergraph method (line of best fit)
            • Simple linear regression analysis

     (b)   False. When using the regression of Y upon X, X is the independent variable and Y is the dependent variable (the value of Y will depend upon the value of X).

6   (a)   It assumes a linear relationship exists between the two variables.

       (b)   It assumes that the value of one variable, Y, can be predicted or estimated from the value of another variable, X.

       (c)   It assumes that what happened in the past will provide a reliable guide to the future.

       (d)   It assumes that the trend line can be extrapolated into the future.

       (e)   The amount of data available.

7   A weighted average value based on probabilities.

Now try the questions below from the Exam Question Bank

Number	Level	Marks	Time
Q4	MCQ	n/a	n/a

Spreadsheets

Topic list	Syllabus reference
1 Features and functions of spreadsheets	C3 (a)
2 Examples of spreadsheet formula	C3 (a)
3 Basic skills	C3 (b)
4 Spreadsheet construction	C3 (b)
5 Formulae with conditions	C3 (b)
6 Charts and graphs	C3 (b)
7 Spreadsheet format and appearance	C3 (b)
8 Other issues	C3 (b)
9 Three dimensional (multi-sheet) spreadsheets	C3 (b)
10 Macros	C3 (a)
11 Advantage and disadvantages of spreadsheet software	C3 (c)
12 Uses of spreadsheet software	C3 (c)

Introduction

Spreadsheet skills are essential for people working in a management accounting environment as much of the information produces is analysed or presented using spreadsheet software.

This chapter will look at features and functions of commonly used spreadsheet software, its advantages and its disadvantages and how it is used in the day-to-day work of an accountant.

Study guide

		Intellectual level
C3	**Use of spreadsheet models**	
(a)	Explain the role and features of a spreadsheet system	1
(b)	Demonstrate a basic understanding of the use of spreadsheets	1
(c)	Identify applications for spreadsheets in cost and management accounting	1

Exam guide

This topic will account for no more than about 4 marks in the examination and if you are familiar with spreadsheets you may want to skip a lot of this chapter. We have covered this topic in some depth as an aid to those students who do not normally use spreadsheets.

1 Features and functions of spreadsheets

> **FAST FORWARD**
>
> Use of spreadsheets is an essential part of the day-to-day work of an accountant.

1.1 What is a spreadsheet?

> **FAST FORWARD**
>
> A spreadsheet is an electronic piece of paper divided into **rows** and **columns**. The intersection of a row and a column is known as a **cell**.

A spreadsheet is divided into **rows** (horizontal) and **columns** (vertical). The rows are numbered 1, 2, 3 . . . etc and the columns lettered A, B C . . . etc. Each individual area representing the intersection of a row and a column is called a 'cell'. A cell address consists of its row and column reference. For example, in the spreadsheet below the word '*Jan*' is in cell B2. The cell that the cursor is currently in or over is known as the 'active cell'.

The main examples of spreadsheet packages are Lotus 1 2 3 and Microsoft Excel. We will be referring to **Microsoft Excel**, as this is the most widely-used spreadsheet. A simple Microsoft Excel spreadsheet, containing budgeted sales figures for three geographical areas for the first quarter of the year, is shown below.

	A	B	C	D	E	F
1	**BUDGETED SALES FIGURES**					
2		Jan	Feb	Mar	Total	
3		$'000	$'000	$'000	$'000	
4	North	2,431	3,001	2,189	7,621	
5	South	6,532	5,826	6,124	18,482	
6	West	895	432	596	1,923	
7	Total	9,858	9,259	8,909	28,026	
8						

1.2 Why use spreadsheets?

Spreadsheets provide a tool for calculating, analysing and manipulating numerical data. Spreadsheets make the calculation and manipulation of data easier and quicker. For example, the spreadsheet above has been set up to calculate the totals **automatically.** If you changed your estimate of sales in February for the North region to $3,296, when you input this figure in cell C4 the totals (in E4 and C7) would change accordingly.

1.2.1 Uses of spreadsheets

Spreadsheets can be used for a wide range of tasks. Some common applications of spreadsheets are:

- Management accounts
- Cash flow analysis and forecasting
- Reconciliations
- Revenue analysis and comparison
- Cost analysis and comparison
- Budgets and forecasts

1.2.2 Cell contents

The contents of any cell can be one of the following.

(a) **Text**. A text cell usually contains **words**. Numbers that do not represent numeric values for calculation purposes (eg a Part Number) may be entered in a way that tells Excel to treat the cell contents as text. To do this, enter an apostrophe before the number eg '451.

(b) **Values**. A value is a **number** that can be used in a calculation.

(c) **Formulae**. A formula **refers to other cells** in the spreadsheet, and performs some sort of computation with them. For example, if cell C1 contains the formula =A1-B1, cell C1 will display the result of the calculation subtracting the contents of cell B1 from the contents of cell A1. In Excel, a formula always begins with an equals sign: = . There are a wide range of formulae and functions available.

1.2.3 Formula bar

The following illustration shows the formula bar. (If the formula bar is not visible, choose **View**, **Formula bar** from Excel's main menu.)

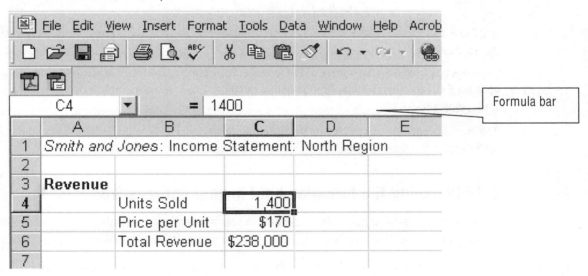

The formula bar allows you to see and edit the contents of the active cell. The bar also shows the cell address of the active cell (C3 in the example above).

Exam focus point

Questions on spreadsheets are likely to focus on the main features of spreadsheets and their issues.

2 Examples of spreadsheet formulae

FAST FORWARD

Formulas in Microsoft Excel follow a specific syntax.

All Excel formulae start with the equals sign =, followed by the elements to be calculated (the operands) and the calculation operators. Each operand can be a value that does not change (a constant value), a cell or range reference, a label, a name, or a worksheet function.

Formulae can be used to perform a variety of calculations. Here are some examples.

(a)   =C4*5. This formula **multiplies** the value in C4 by 5. The result will appear in the cell holding the formula.

(b)   =C4*B10. This **multiplies** the value in C4 by the value in B10.

(c)   =C4/E5. This **divides** the value in C4 by the value in E5. (* means multiply and / means divide by.)

(d)   =C4*B10-D1. This **multiplies** the value in C4 by that in B10 and then subtracts the value in D1 from the result. Note that generally Excel will perform multiplication and division before addition or subtraction. If in any doubt, use brackets (parentheses): =(C4*B10)–D1.

(e)   =C4*117.5%. This **adds** 17.5% to the value in C4. It could be used to calculate a price including 17.5% sales tax.

(f)   =(C4+C5+C6)/3. Note that the **brackets** mean Excel would perform the addition first. Without the brackets, Excel would first divide the value in C6 by 3 and then add the result to the total of the values in C4 and C5.

(g)   = 2^2 gives you 2 **to the power** of 2, in other words 2^2. Likewise = 2^3 gives you 2 cubed and so on.

(h)   = 4^ (1/2) gives you the **square root** of 4. Likewise 27^(1/3) gives you the cube root of 27 and so on.

Without brackets, Excel calculates a formula from left to right. You can control how calculation is performed by changing the syntax of the formula. For example, the formula =5+2*3 gives a result of 11 because Excel calculates multiplication before addition. Excel would multiply 2 by 3 (resulting in 6) and would then add 5.

You may use parentheses to change the order of operations. For example =(5+2)*3 would result in Excel firstly adding the 5 and 2 together, then multiplying that result by 3 to give 21.

2.1 Displaying the formulae held in your spreadsheet

It is sometimes useful to see all formulae held in your spreadsheet to enable you to see how the spreadsheet works. There are two ways of making Excel **display the formulae** held in a spreadsheet.

(a)   You can 'toggle' between the two types of display by pressing **Ctrl +** ` (the latter is the key above the Tab key). Press Ctrl + ` again to get the previous display back.

(b)   You can also click on Tools, then on Options, then on View and tick the box next to 'Formulas'.

In the following paragraphs we provide examples of how spreadsheets and formulae may be used in an accounting context.

2.1.1 Example: formulae

	A	B	C	D	E	F
1	BUDGETED SALES FIGURES					
2		Jan	Feb	Mar	Total	
3		$'000	$'000	$'000	$'000	
4	North	2,431	3,001	2,189	7,621	
5	South	6,532	5,826	6,124	18,482	
6	West	895	432	596	1,923	
7	Total	9,858	9,259	8,909	28,026	
8						

(a) In the spreadsheet shown above, which of the cells have had a number typed in, and which cells display the result of calculations (ie which cells contain a formula)?

(b) What formula would you put in each of the following cells?

   (i) Cell B7
   (ii) Cell E6
   (iii) Cell E7

(c) If the February sales figure for the South changed from $5,826 to $5,731, what other figures would change as a result? Give cell references.

Solution

(a) Cells into which you would need to enter a value are: B4, B5, B6, C4, C5, C6, D4, D5 and D6. Cells which would perform calculations are B7, C7, D7, E4, E5, E6 and E7.

(b) (i) =B4+B5+B6 *or better* =SUM(B4:B6)

   (ii) =B6+C6+D6 *or better* =SUM(B6:D6)

   (iii) =E4+E5+E6 *or better* =SUM(E4:E6) Alternatively, the three monthly totals could be added across the spreadsheet: = SUM (B7: D7)

(c) The figures which would change, besides the amount in cell C5, would be those in cells C7, E5 and E7. (The contents of E7 would change if any of the sales figures changed.)

Question   **Sum formulae**

The following spreadsheet shows sales of two products, the Ego and the Id, for the period July to September.

	A	B	C	D	E
1	**Sigmund Co**				
2	*Sales analysis - Q3 20X7*				
3		M7	M8	M9	Total
4		$	$	$	$
5	Ego	3,000	4,000	2,000	9,000
6	Id	2,000	1,500	4,000	7,500
7	Total	5,000	5,500	6,000	16,500
8					

Devise a suitable formula for each of the following cells.

(a) Cell B7
(b) Cell E6
(c) Cell E7

Answer

(a) =SUM(B5:B6)

(b) =SUM(B6:D6)

(c) =SUM (E5:E6) *or* =SUM(B7:D7)

or (best of all) =IF(SUM(E5:E6) =SUM(B7:D7),SUM(B7:D7),"ERROR") Don't worry if you don't understand this formula when first attempting this question – we cover IF statements later in this Chapter.

Question

Formulae

The following spreadsheet shows sales, exclusive of sales tax, in row 6.

	A	B	C	D	E	F	G	H
1	**Taxable supplies Co**							
2	*Sales analysis - Branch C*							
3	*Six months ended 30 June 200X*							
4		Jan	Feb	Mar	Apr	May	Jun	Total
5		$	$	$	$	$	$	$
6	Net sales	2,491.54	5,876.75	3,485.01	5,927.7	6,744.52	3,021.28	27,546.80
7	Sales tax							
8	Total							
9								

Your manager has asked you to insert formulae to calculate sales tax at 17½% in row 7 and also to produce totals.

(a) Devise a suitable formula for cell B7 and cell E8.

(b) How could the spreadsheet be better designed?

Answer

(a) For cell B7 =B6*0.175 For cell E8 =SUM(E6:E7)

(b) By using a separate 'variables' holding the sales tax rate and possibly the Sales figures. The formulae could then refer to these cells as shown below.

	A	B	C	D	E	F	G	H
1	**Taxable Supplies Co**							
2	*Sales analysis - Branch C*							
3	*Six months ended 30 June 200X*							
4		Jan	Feb	Mar	Apr	May	Jun	Total
5		$	$	$	$	$	$	$
6	Net sales	=B12	=C12	=D12	=E12	=F12	=G12	=SUM(B6:G6)
7	Sales tax	=B6*$B$13	=C6*$B$13	=D6*$B$13	=E6*$B$13	=F6*$B$13	=G6*$B$13	=SUM(B7:G7)
8	Total	=SUM(B6:B7)	=SUM(C6:C7)	=SUM(D6:D7)	=SUM(E6:E7)	=SUM(F6:F7)	=SUM(G6:G7)	=SUM(H6:H7)
9								
10								
11	*Variables*							
12	Sales	2491.54	5876.75	3485.01	5927.7	6744.52	3021.28	
13	Sales tax rate	0.175						

3 Basic skills

Essential basic skills include how to **move around** within a spreadsheet, how to **enter** and **edit** data, how to **fill** cells, how to **insert** and **delete** columns and rows and how to improve the basic **layout** and **appearance** of a spreadsheet.

In this section we explain some **basic spreadsheeting skills**. We give instructions for Microsoft Excel, the most widely used package. Our examples should be valid with all versions of Excel released since 1997.

You should read this section while sitting at a computer and trying out the skills we describe **'hands-on'**.

3.1 Moving about

The F5 key is useful for moving around within large spreadsheets. If you press the function key **F5,** a **Go To** dialogue box will allow you to specify the cell address you would like to move to. Try this out.

Also experiment by holding down Ctrl and pressing each of the direction arrow keys in turn to see where you end up. Try using the **Page Up** and **Page Down** keys and also try **Home** and **End** and Ctrl + these keys. Try **Tab** and **Shift + Tab**, too. These are all useful shortcuts for moving quickly from one place to another in a large spreadsheet.

3.2 Editing cell contents

Suppose cell A2 currently contains the value 456. If you wish to **change the entry** in cell A2 from 456 to 123456 there are four options – as shown below.

(a) Activate cell A2, **type** 123456 and press **Enter**.

To undo this and try the next option press **Ctrl + Z**: this will always undo what you have just done.

(b) **Double-click** in cell A2. The cell will keep its thick outline but you will now be able to see a vertical line flashing in the cell. You can move this line by using the direction arrow keys or the Home and the End keys. Move it to before the 4 and type 123. Then press Enter.

When you have tried this press Ctrl + Z to undo it.

(c) **Click once** before the number 456 in the formula bar. Again you will get the vertical line and you can type in 123 before the 4. Then press Enter. Undo this before moving onto (d).

(d) Press the **function key F2**. The vertical line cursor will be flashing in cell A2 at the *end* of the figures entered there (after the 6). Press Home to get to a position before the 4 and then type in 123 and press Enter, as before.

3.3 Deleting cell contents

You may delete the contents of a cell simply by making the cell the active cell and then pressing **Delete**. The contents of the cell will disappear. You may also highlight a range of cells to delete and then delete the contents of all cells within the range.

For example, enter any value in cell A1 and any value in cell A2. Move the cursor to cell A2. Now hold down the **Shift** key (the one above the Ctrl key) and keeping it held down press the ↑ arrow. Cell A2 will stay white but cell A1 will go black. What you have done here is **selected** the range A1 and A2. Now press the Delete key. The contents of cells A1 and A2 will be deleted.

3.4 Filling a range of cells

Start with a blank spreadsheet. Type the number 1 in cell A1 and the number 2 in cell A2. Now select cells A1: A2, this time by positioning the mouse pointer over cell A1, holding down the left mouse button and moving the pointer down to cell A2. When cell A2 is highlighted release the mouse button.

Now position the mouse pointer at the **bottom right hand corner** of cell A2. When you have the mouse pointer in the right place it will turn into a **black cross**.

Then, hold down the left mouse button again and move the pointer down to cell A10. You will see an outline surrounding the cells you are trying to 'fill'.

Release the mouse button when you have the pointer over cell A10. You will find that the software **automatically** fills in the numbers 3 to 10 below 1 and 2.

Try the following variations of this technique.

(a) Delete what you have just done and type in **Jan** in cell A1. See what happens if you select cell A1 and fill down to cell A12: you get the months **Feb, Mar, Apr** and so on.

(b) Type the number 2 in cell A1. Select A1 and fill down to cell A10. What happens? The cells should fill up with 2's.

(c) Type the number 2 in cell A1 and 4 in cell A2. Then select A1: A2 and fill down to cell A10. What happens? You should get 2, 4, 6, 8, and so on.

(d) Try **filling across** as well as down.

(e) If you click on the bottom right hand corner of the cell using the **right mouse button**, drag down to a lower cell and then release the button you should see a menu providing a variety of options for filling the cells.

3.5 The SUM button Σ

We will explain how to use the SUM button by way of a simple example. Start with a blank spreadsheet, then enter the following figures in cells A1:B5.

	A	B
1	400	582
2	250	478
3	359	264
4	476	16
5	97	125

Make cell B6 the active cell and click once on the SUM button (the button with a Σ symbol on the Excel toolbar - the Σ symbol is the mathematical sign for 'the sum of'). A formula will appear in the cell saying =SUM(B1:B5). Above cell B6 you will see a flashing dotted line encircling cells B1:B5. Accept the suggested formula by hitting the Enter key.

The formula =SUM(B1:B5) will be entered, and the number 1465 will appear in cell B6.

Next, make cell A6 the active cell and **double-click** on the SUM button. The number 1582 should appear in cell A6.

3.6 Multiplication

Continuing on with our example, next select cell C1. Type in an = sign then click on cell A1. Now type in an **asterisk** * (which serves as a **multiplication sign**) and click on cell B1. Watch how the formula in cell C1 changes as you do this. (Alternatively you can enter the cell references by moving the direction arrow keys.) Finally press Enter. Cell C1 will show the result (232,800) of multiplying the figure in Cell A1 by the one in cell B1.

Your next task is to select cell C1 and **fill in** cells C2 to C5 automatically using the **dragging technique** described above. If you then click on each cell in column C and look above at the line showing what the cell contains you will find that the software has automatically filled in the correct cell references for you: A2*B2 in cell C2, A3*B3 in cell C3 and so on.

(**Note**: The forward slash / is used to represent division in spreadsheet formulae.)

3.7 Inserting columns and rows

Suppose we also want to add each row, for example cells A1 and B1. The logical place to do this would be cell C1, but column C already contains data. We have three options that would enable us to place this total in column C.

(a)   Highlight cells C1 to C5 and position the mouse pointer on one of the **edges**. (It will change to an arrow shape.) Hold down the **left** mouse button and drag cells C1 to C5 into column D. There is now space in column C for our next set of sums. Any **formulae** that need to be changed as a result of moving cells using this method should be changed **automatically** – but always check them.

(b)   The second option is to highlight cells C1 to C5 as before, position the mouse pointer anywhere **within** column C and click on the **right** mouse button. A menu will appear offering you an option **Insert…** . If you click on this you will be asked where you want to shift the cells that are being moved. In this case you want to move them to the right so choose this option and click on OK.

(c)   The third option is to **insert a whole new column**. You do this by clicking on the letter at the top of the column (here C) to highlight the whole of it then proceeding as in (b). The new column will always be inserted to the **left** of the one you highlight.

You can now display the sum of each of the rows in column C.

You can also insert a new row in a similar way (or stretch rows).

(a)   To **insert** one row, perhaps for headings, click on the row number to highlight it, click with the right mouse button and choose insert. One row will be inserted **above** the one you highlighted. Try putting some headings above the figures in columns A to C.

(b)   To insert **several** rows click on the row number immediately **below** the point where you want the new rows to appear and, holding down the left mouse button highlight the number of rows you wish to insert. Click on the highlighted area with the right mouse button and choose Insert (or if you prefer, choose **Insert**, **Rows** from the main menu).

3.8 Changing column width

You may occasionally find that a cell is not wide enough to display its contents. When this occurs, the cell displays a series of hashes ######. There are two options available to solve this problem.

(a)   One is to **decide for yourself** how wide you want the columns to be. Position the mouse pointer at the head of column A directly over the little line dividing the letter A from the letter B. The mouse **pointer** will change to a sort of **cross**. Hold down the left mouse button and, by moving your mouse, stretch Column A to the right, to about the middle of column D, until the words you typed fit. You can do the same for column B. Then make your columns too narrow again so you can try option (b).

(b)   Often it is easier to **let the software decide for you**. Position the mouse pointer over the little dividing line as before and get the cross symbol. Then double-click with the left mouse button. The column automatically adjusts to an appropriate width to fit the widest cell in that column.

You can either adjust the width of each column individually or you can do them all in one go. To do the latter click on the button in the top left hand corner to **select the whole sheet** and then **double-click** on just one of the dividing lines: all the columns will adjust to the '**best fit**' width.

3.9 Keyboard shortcuts and toolbar buttons

Here are a few tips to improve the **appearance** of your spreadsheets and speed up your work. To do any of the following to a cell or range of cells, first **select** the cell or cells and then:

(a) Press Ctrl + B to make the cell contents **bold.**

(b) Press Ctrl + I to make the cell contents *italic.*

(c) Press **Ctrl + C** to **copy** the contents of the cells.

(d) Move the cursor and press **Ctrl + V** to **paste** the cell you just copied into the new active cell or cells.

There are also **buttons** in the Excel toolbar (shown below) that may be used to carry out these and other functions. The best way to learn about these features is to use them - enter some numbers and text into a spreadsheet and experiment with keyboard shortcuts and toolbar buttons.

4 Spreadsheet construction

FAST FORWARD

A wide range of **formulae** and functions are available within Excel.

Spreadsheet models that will be used mainly as a calculation tool for various scenarios should ideally be constructed in **three sections**, as follows.

1 An inputs section containing the variables (eg the amount of a loan and the interest rate).

2 A calculations section containing formulae (eg the loan term and interest rate).

Example: spreadsheet construction

In practice, in many situations it is often **more convenient** to combine the results and calculations areas as follows.

	A	B	C	D	E	F	G
1	*Results*						
2		$					
3	Interest due:	200.00					
4							
5							
6							
7	*Variables*						
8	Loan	$2,000.00					
9	Interest rate	10.00%					
10							
11							
12							

Cell B3 contains the formula =B8*B9

The variables are typed in as numbers (just as they are shown here)

If we took out another loan of $4,789 at an interest rate of 7.25% we would simply need to **overwrite the figures in the variable section** of the spreadsheet with the new figures to calculate the interest.

Question

Answer questions (a) and (b) below, which relate to the following spreadsheet.

	A	B	C	D
1	**Boilermakers Ltd**			
2	*Department B*			
3				
4	*Production data*	Machine A	Machine B	Machine C
5	Shift 1	245.84	237.49	231.79
6	Shift 2	241.14	237.62	261.31
7	Shift 3	244.77	201.64	242.71
8	Shift 4	240.96	238.18	234.50
9				
10	*Usage data*	Machine A	Machine B	Machine C
11	Maintenance	35	71	6
12	Operational	8.47	7.98	9.31
13	Idle	1.42	2.40	0.87
14	Recovery	0	15	4
15			24.875	

(a) Cell B9 needs to contain an average of all the preceding numbers in column B. Suggest a formula which would achieve this.

(b) Cell C16 contains the formula

=C12+C13/C14-C15

What would the result be, displayed in cell C16?

Answer

This question tests whether you can evaluate formulae in the correct order. In part (a) you must remember to put brackets around the numbers required to be added, otherwise the formula will automatically divide cell B8 by 4 first and add the result to the other numbers. Similarly, in part (b), the formula performs the multiplication before the addition and subtraction.

(a)   =SUM(B5:B8)/4   An alternative is = AVERAGE(B5:B8).

(b)   59.325

4.1 Example: Constructing a cash flow projection

Suppose you wanted to set up a simple six-month cash flow projection, in such a way that you could use it to estimate how the **projected cash balance** figures will **change** in total when any **individual item** in the projection is **altered**. You have the following information.

(a)   Sales were $45,000 per month in 20X5, falling to $42,000 in January 20X6. Thereafter they are expected to increase by 3% per month (ie February will be 3% higher than January, and so on).

(b)   Debts are collected as follows.

   (i)   60% in month following sale.
   (ii)   30% in second month after sale.
   (iii) 7% in third month after sale.
   (iv)   3% remains uncollected.

(c)   Purchases are equal to cost of sales, set at 65% of sales.

(d)   Overheads were $6,000 per month in 20X5, rising by 5% in 20X6.

(e)   Opening cash is an overdraft of $7,500.

(f)   Dividends: $10,000 final dividend on 20X5 profits payable in May.

(g)   Capital purchases: plant costing $18,000 will be ordered in January. 20% is payable with order, 70% on delivery in February and the final 10% in May.

4.1.1 Headings and layout

The first step is to put in the various **headings** required for the cash flow projection. At this stage, your spreadsheet might look as follows.

	A	B	C	D	E	F	G
1	**EXCELLENT PLC**						
2	*Cash flow projection - six months ending 30 June 20X6*						
3		*Jan*	*Feb*	*Mar*	*Apr*	*May*	*Jun*
4		$	$	$	$	$	$
5	Sales						
6	*Cash receipts*						
7	1 month in arrears						
8	2 months in arrears						
9	3 months in arrears						
10	Total operating receipts						
11							
12	Cash payments						
13	Purchases						
14	Overheads						
15	Total operating payments						
16							
17	Dividends						
18	Capital purchases						
19	Total other payments						
20							
21	Net cash flow						
22	Cash balance b/f						
23	Cash balance c/f						
24							

Note the following points.

(a) We have **increased the width** of column A to allow longer pieces of text to be inserted. Had we not done so, only the first part of each caption would have been displayed (and printed).

(b) We have developed a **simple style for headings**. Headings are essential, so that users can identify what a spreadsheet does. We have **emboldened** the company name and *italicised* other headings.

(c) When **text** is entered into a cell it is usually **left-aligned** (as for example in column A). We have **centred** the headings above each column by highlighting the cells and using the relevant buttons at the top of the screen.

(d) **Numbers** should be **right-aligned** in cells.

(e) We have left **spaces** in certain rows (after blocks of related items) to make the spreadsheet **easier to use and read**.

4.1.2 Inserting formulae

The next step is to enter the **formulae** required. For example, in cell B10 you want total operating receipts, =SUM(B7:B9).

Look for a moment at cell C7. We are told that sales in January were $42,000 and that 60% of customers settle their accounts one month in arrears. We could insert the formula =B5*0.6 in the cell and fill in the other cells along the row so that it is replicated in each month. However, consider the effect of a change in payment patterns to a situation where, say, 55% of customer debts are settled after one month. This would necessitate a **change to each and every cell** in which the 0.6 ratio appears.

An alternative approach, which makes **future changes much simpler** to execute, is to put the relevant ratio (here, 60% or 0.6) in a cell **outside** the main table and cross-refer each cell in the main table to that cell. This means that, if the percentage changes, the change need only be reflected in **one cell**, following which all cells which are dependent on that cell will **automatically use the new percentage**. We will therefore input such values in separate parts of the spreadsheet, as follows. Look at the other assumptions which we have inserted into this part of the spreadsheet.

	A	B	C	D	E	F
25						
26	*This table contains the key variables for the 20X6 cash flow projections*					
27						
28	Sales growth factor per month		1.03			
29	Purchases as % of sales		-0.65			
30						
31	Debts paid within 1 month		0.6			
32	Debts paid within 2 months		0.3			
33	Debts paid within 3 months		0.07			
34	Irrecoverable debts		0.03			
35						
36	Increase in overheads		1.05			
37						
38	Dividends (May)		-10000			
39						
40	Capital purchases		-18000			
41	January		0.2			
42	February		0.7			
43	May		0.1			
44						
45						
46	*This table contains relevant opening balance data as at Jan 20X6*					
47						
48	Monthly sales 20X5		45000			
49	January 20X6 sales		42000			
50	Monthly overheads 20X5		-6000			
51	Opening cash		-7500			
52						

Now we can go back to cell C7 and input =B5*C31 and then fill this in across the '1 month in arrears' row. (Note that, as we have no December sales figure, we will have to deal with cell B7 separately.) If we assume for the moment that we are copying to cells D7 through to G7 and follow this procedure, the contents of cell D7 would be shown as =C5*D31, and so on, as shown below.

	A	B	C	D	E	F	G
3		*Jan*	*Feb*	*Mar*	*Apr*	*May*	*Jun*
4		$	$	$	$	$	$
5	Sales						
6	*Cash receipts*						
7	1 month in arrears		=B5*C31	=C5*D31	=D5*E31	=E5*F31	=F5*G31
8	2 months in arrears						
9	3 months in arrears						
10	Total operating receipts						
11							

You may have noticed a problem. While the formula in cell C7 is fine - it multiplies January sales by 0.6 (the 1 month ratio stored in cell C31) - the remaining formulae are useless, as they **refer to empty cells** in row 31. This is what the spreadsheet would look like (assuming, for now, constant sales of $42,000 per month).

BPP
LEARNING MEDIA

	A	B	C	D	E	F	G
3		Jan	Feb	Mar	Apr	May	Jun
4		$	$	$	$	$	$
5	Sales	42000	42000	42000	42000	42000	42000
6	Cash receipts						
7	1 month in arrears		25200	0	0	0	0
8	2 months in arrears						
9	3 months in arrears						
10	Total operating receipts						
11							

This problem highlights the important distinction between **relative** cell references and **absolute** cell references. Usually, cell references are **relative**. A formula of =SUM(B7:B9) in cell B10 is relative. It does not really mean 'add up the numbers in cells B7 to B9'; it actually means '**add up the numbers in the three cells above this one**'. If this formula was copied to cell C10 (as we will do later), it would become =SUM(C7:C9).

This is what is causing the problem encountered above. The spreadsheet thinks we are asking it to 'multiply the number two up and one to the left by the number twenty-four cells down', and that is indeed the effect of the instruction we have given. But we are actually intending to ask it to 'multiply the number two up and one to the left by the number in cell C31'. This means that we need to create an **absolute** (unchanging) **reference** to cell C31.

Absolute cell references use **dollar signs** ($). A dollar sign before the column letter makes the column reference absolute, and one before the row number makes the row number absolute. You do not need to type the dollar signs - add them as follows.

(a) Make cell C7 the active cell and press F2 to edit it.

(b) Note where the cursor is flashing: it should be after the 1. If it is not move it with the direction arrow keys so that it is positioned somewhere next to or within the cell reference C31.

(c) Press F4.

The **function key F4** adds dollar signs to the cell reference: it becomes $C$31. Press F4 again: the reference becomes C$31. Press it again: the reference becomes $C31. Press it once more, and the simple relative reference is restored: C31.

(a) A dollar sign **before a letter** means that the **column** reference stays the same when you copy the formula to another cell.

(b) A dollar sign **before a number** means that the **row** reference stays the same when you copy the formula to another cell.

In our example we have now altered the reference in cell C7 and filled in across to cell G7, overwriting what was there previously. This is the result.

(a) Formulae

	A	B	C	D	E	F	G
3		Jan	Feb	Mar	Apr	May	Jun
4		$	$	$	$	$	$
5	Sales	42000	42000	42000	42000	42000	42000
6	Cash receipts						
7	1 month in arrears		=B5*$C$31	=C5*$C$31	=D5*$C$31	=E5*$C$31	=F5*$C$31
8	2 months in arrears						
9	3 months in arrears						
10	Total operating receipts						
11							

(b)   Numbers

	A	B	C	D	E	F	G
1		Jan	Feb	Mar	Apr	May	Jun
2		$	$	$	$	$	$
3	Sales	42000	42000	42000	42000	42000	42000
4	*Cash receipts*						
5	1 month in arrears		25200	25200	25200	25200	25200
6	2 months in arrears						
7	3 months in arrears						
8	Total operating receipts						
9							

Other formulae required for this projection are as follows.

(a)   **Cell B5** refers directly to the information we are given - **sales of $42,000** in January. We have input this variable in cell C49. The other formulae in row 5 (sales) reflect the predicted sales growth of 3% per month, as entered in cell C28.

(b)   Similar formulae to the one already described for row 7 are required in rows 8 and 9.

(c)   **Row 10** (total operating receipts) will display simple **subtotals**, in the form =SUM(B7:B9).

(d)   **Row 13 (purchases)** requires a formula based on the data in row 5 **(sales)** and the value in cell C29 **(purchases** as a % of sales). This model assumes no changes in stock levels from month to month, and that stocks are sufficiently high to enable this. The formula is B5 * $C$29. Note that C29 is negative.

(e)   **Row 15** (total operating payments), like row 10, requires **formulae** to create **subtotals**.

(f)   **Rows 17 and 18** refer to the **dividends and capital purchase data** input in cells C38 and C40 to 43.

(g)   **Row 21** (net cash flow) requires a **total** in the form =B10 + B15 + B21.

(h)   **Row 22** (balance b/f) requires the contents of the **previous month's closing cash** figure.

(i)   **Row 23** (balance b/f) requires the **total** of the **opening cash** figure and the **net cash flow** for the month.

The following image shows the formulae that should now be present in the spreadsheet.

	A	B	C	D	E	F	G
1	EXCELLENT CO						
2	Cash flow projection - six month						
3		Jan	Feb	Mar	Apr	May	Jun
4		$	$	$	$	$	$
5	Sales	=C49	=B5*$C$28	=C5*$C$28	=D5*$C$28	=E5*$C$28	=F5*$C$28
6	Cash receipts						
7	1 month in arrears	=$C$48*$C$31	=B5*$C$31	=C5*$C$31	=D5*$C$31	=E5*$C$31	=F5*$C$31
8	2 months in arrears	=$C$48*$C$32	=$C$48*$C$32	=B5*$C$32	=C5*$C$32	=D5*$C$32	=E5*$C$32
9	3 months in arrears	=$C$48*$C$33	=$C$48*$C$33	=$C$48*$C$33	=B5*$C$33	=C5*$C$33	=D5*$C$33
10	Total operating receipts	=SUM(B7:B9)	=SUM(C7:C9)	=SUM(D7:D9)	=SUM(E7:E9)	=SUM(F7:F9)	=SUM(G7:G9)
11							
12	Cash payments						
13	Purchases	=B5*$C$29	=C5*$C$29	=D5*$C$29	=E5*$C$29	=F5*$C$29	=G5*$C$29
14	Overheads	=$C$50*$C$36	=$C$50*$C$36	=$C$50*$C$36	=$C$50*$C$36	=$C$50*$C$36	=$C$50*$C$36
15	Total operating payments	=SUM(B13:B14)	=SUM(C13:C14)	=SUM(D13:D14)	=SUM(E13:E14)	=SUM(F13:F14)	=SUM(G13:G14)
16							
17	Dividends	0	0	0	0	=C38	0
18	Capital purchases	=C40*C41	=C40*C42	0	0	=C40*C43	0
19	Total other payments	=SUM(B17:B18)	=SUM(C17:C18)	=SUM(D17:D18)	=SUM(E17:E18)	=SUM(F17:F18)	=SUM(G17:G18)
20							
21	Net cash flow	=B10+B15+B19	=C10+C15+C19	=D10+D15+D19	=E10+E15+E19	=F10+F15+F19	=G10+G15+G19
22	Cash balance b/f	=C51	=B23	=C23	=D23	=E23	=F23
23	Cash balance c/f	=SUM(B21:B22)	=SUM(C21:C22)	=SUM(D21:D22)	=SUM(E21:E22)	=SUM(F21:F22)	=SUM(G21:G22)
24							

Be careful to ensure you use the correct sign (negative or positive) when manipulating numbers. For example, if total operating payments in row 15 are shown as **positive**, you would need to **subtract** them from total operating receipts in the formulae in row 23. However if you have chosen to make them **negative**, to represent outflows, then you will need to **add** them to total operating receipts.

Here is the spreadsheet in its normal 'numbers' form.

	A	B	C	D	E	F	G
1	**EXCELLENT CO**						
2	*Cash flow projection - six months ending 30 June 20X6*						
3		*Jan*	*Feb*	*Mar*	*Apr*	*May*	*Jun*
4		$	$	$	$	$	$
5	Sales	42,000	43,260	44,558	45,895	47,271	48,690
6	*Cash receipts*						
7	1 month in arrears	27,000	25,200	25,956	26,735	27,537	28,363
8	2 months in arrears	13,500	13,500	12,600	12,978	13,367	13,768
9	3 months in arrears	3,150	3,150	3,150	2,940	3,028	3,119
10	Total operating receipts	43,650	41,850	41,706	42,653	43,932	45,250
11							
12	*Cash payments*						
13	Purchases	-27,300	-28,119	-28,963	-29,831	-30,726	-31,648
14	Overheads	-6,000	-6,300	-6,300	-6,300	-6,300	-6,300
15	Total operating payments	-33,300	-34,419	-35,263	-36,131	-37,026	-37,948
16							
17	Dividends	0	0	0	0	-10,000	0
18	Capital purchases	-3,600	-12,600	0	0	-1,800	0
19	Total other payments	-3,600	-12,600	0	0	-11,800	0
20							
21	Net cash flow	6,450	-5,169	6,443	6,521	-4,894	7,302
22	Cash balance b/f	-7,500	-1,050	-6,219	224	6,746	1,852
23	Cash balance c/f	-1,050	-6,219	224	6,746	1,852	9,154
24							

4.1.3 Tidy the spreadsheet up

Our spreadsheet needs a little **tidying up**. We will do the following.

(a) Add in **commas** to denote thousands of dollars.

(b) Put **zeros** in the cells with no entry in them.

(c) Change **negative numbers** from being displayed with a **minus sign** to being displayed in **brackets**.

	A	B	C	D	E	F	G	
1	**EXCELLENT CO**							
2	*Cash flow projection - six months ending 30 June 20X6*							
3		*Jan*	*Feb*	*Mar*	*Apr*	*May*	*Jun*	
4		$	$	$	$	$	£	
5	Sales	42,000	43,260	44,558	45,895	47,271	48,690	
6	*Cash receipts*							
7	1 month in arrears	27,000	25,200	25,956	26,735	27,537	28,363	
8	2 months in arrears	13,500	13,500	12,600	12,978	13,367	13,768	
9	3 months in arrears	3,150	3,150	3,150	2,940	3,028	3,119	
10	Total operating receipts	43,650	41,850	41,706	42,653	43,932	45,250	
11								
12	*Cash payments*							
13	Purchases	(27,300)	(28,119)	(28,963)	(29,831)	(30,726)	(31,648)	
14	Overheads	(6,300)	(6,300)	(6,300)	(6,300)	(6,300)	(6,300)	
15	Total operating payments	(33,600)	(34,419)	(35,263)	(36,131)	(37,026)	(37,948)	
16								
17	Dividends	0	0	0	0	(10,000)	0	
18	Capital purchases	(3,600)	(12,600)	0	0	(1,800)	0	
19	Total other payments	(3,600)	(12,600)	0	0	(11,800)	0	
20								
21	Net cash flow	6,450	(5,169)	6,443	6,521	(4,894)	7,302	
22	Cash balance b/f	(7,500)	(1,050)	(6,219)	224	6,746	1,852	
23	Cash balance c/f	(1,050)	(6,219)	224	6,746	1,852	9,154	
24								

4.1.4 Changes in assumptions (what if? analysis)

We referred to earlier to the need to design a spreadsheet so that **changes in assumptions** do **not** require **major changes** to the spreadsheet. This is why we set up two separate areas of the spreadsheet, one for 20X6 assumptions and one for opening balances. Consider each of the following.

(a) Negotiations with suppliers and gains in productivity have resulted in cost of sales being reduced to 62% of sales.

(b) The effects of a recession have changed the cash collection profile so that receipts in any month are 50% of prior month sales, 35% of the previous month and 10% of the month before that, with bad debt experience rising to 5%.

(c) An insurance claim made in 20X5 and successfully settled in December has resulted in the opening cash balance being an overdraft of $3,500.

(d) Sales growth will only be 2% per month.

All of these changes can be made quickly and easily. The two tables are revised as follows.

	A	B	C	D	E	F
25						
26	This table contains the key variables for the 20X6 cash flow projections					
27						
28	Sales growth factor per month		1.02			
29	Purchases as % of sales		-0.62			
30						
31	Debts paid within 1 month		0.5			
32	Debts paid within 2 months		0.35			
33	Debts paid within 3 months		0.1			
34	Irrecoverable debts		0.05			
35						
36	Increase in overheads		1.05			
37						
38	Dividends (May)		-10000			
39						
40	Capital purchases		-18000			
41	January		0.2			
42	February		0.7			
43	May		0.1			
44						
45						
46	This table contains relevant opening balance data as at Jan 20X6					
47						
48	Monthly sales 19X5		45000			
49	January 1996 sales		42000			
50	Monthly overheads 19X5		-6000			
51	Opening cash		-3500			
52						

The resulting (recalculated) spreadsheet would look like this.

	A	B	C	D	E	F	G
1	EXCELLENT PLC						
2	Cash flow projection - six months ending 30 June 20X6						
3		Jan	Feb	Mar	Apr	May	Jun
4		$	$	$	$	$	$
5	Sales	42,000	42,840	43,697	44,571	45,462	46,371
6	Cash receipts						
7	1 month in arrears	22,500	21,000	21,420	21,848	22,285	22,731
8	2 months in arrears	15,750	15,750	14,700	14,994	15,294	15,600
9	3 months in arrears	4,500	4,500	4,500	4,200	4,284	4,370
10	Total operating receipts	42,750	41,250	40,620	41,042	41,863	42,701
11							
12	Cash payments						
13	Purchases	-26,040	-26,561	-27,092	-27,634	-28,187	-28,750
14	Overheads	-6,300	-6,300	-6,300	-6,300	-6,300	-6,300
15	Total operating payments	-32,340	-32,861	-33,392	-33,934	-34,487	-35,050
16							
17	Dividends	0	0	0	0	-10,000	0
18	Capital purchases	-3,600	-12,600	0	0	-1,800	0
19	Total other payments	-3,600	-12,600	0	0	-11,800	0
20							
21	Net cash flow	6,810	-4,211	7,228	7,109	-4,423	7,650
22	Cash balance b/f	-3,500	3,310	-901	6,327	13,436	9,012
23	Cash balance c/f	3,310	-901	6,327	13,436	9,012	16,663
24							

Question

The following four insurance salesmen each earn a basic salary of $14,000 pa. They also earn a commission of 2% of sales. The following spreadsheet has been created to process their commission and total earnings. Give an appropriate formula for each of the following cells.

(a) Cell D4

(b) Cell E6

(c) Cell D9

(d) Cell E9

	A	B	C	D	E	
1	Sales team salaries and commissions - 200X					
2	Name	Sales	Salary	Commission	Total earnings	
3		$	$	$	$	
4	Northington	284,000	14,000	5,680	19,680	
5	Souther	193,000	14,000	3,860	17,860	
6	Weston	12,000	14,000	240	14,240	
7	Easterman	152,000	14,000	3,040	17,040	
8						
9	Total	641,000	56,000	12,820	68,820	
10						
11						
12	Variables					
13	Basic Salary	14,000				
14	Commission rate	0.02				
15						

Answer

Possible formulae are as follows.

(a) =B4*$B$14

(b) =C6+D6

(c) =SUM(D4:D7)

(d) There are a number of possibilities here, depending on whether you set the cell as the total of the earnings of each salesman (cells E4 to E7) or as the total of the different elements of remuneration (cells C9 and D9). Even better, would be a formula that checked that both calculations gave the same answer. A suitable formula for this purpose would be:

=IF(SUM(E4:E7)=SUM(C9:D9),SUM(E4:E7),"ERROR")

We will explain this formula in more detail in the next section.

5 Formulae with conditions

If statements are used in conditional formulae.

Suppose the company employing the salesmen in the above question awards a bonus to those salesmen who exceed their target by more than $1,000. The spreadsheet could work out who is entitled to the bonus.

To do this we would enter the appropriate formula in cells F4 to F7. For salesperson Easterman, we would enter the following in cell F7:

=IF(D4>1000,"BONUS"," ")

We will now explain this formula.

IF statements follow the following structure (or syntax).

=IF(logical_test,value_if_true,value_if_false)

The logical_test is any value or expression that can be evaluated to Yes or No. For example, D4>1000 is a logical expression; if the value in cell D4 is over 1000, the expression evaluates to Yes. Otherwise, the expression evaluates to No.

Value_if_true is the value that is returned if the answer to the logical_test is Yes. For example, if the answer to D4>1000 is Yes, and the value_if_true is the text string "BONUS", then the cell containing the IF function will display the text "BONUS".

Value_if_false   is the value that is returned if the answer to the logical_test is No. For example, if the value_if_false is two sets of quote marks "" this means display a blank cell if the answer to the logical test is No. So in our example, if D4 is not over 1000, then the cell containing the IF function will display a blank cell.

Note the following symbols which can be used in formulae with conditions:

<	less than (like L (for 'less') on its side)
<=	less than or equal to
=	equal to
>=	greater than or equal to
>	greater than
<>	not equal to

Care is required to ensure **brackets** and **commas** are entered in the right places. If, when you try out this kind of formula, you get an error message, it may well be a simple mistake, such as leaving a comma out.

5.1 Examples of formulae with conditions

A company offers a discount of 5% to customers who order more than $1,000 worth of goods. A spreadsheet showing what customers will pay might look like this.

	A	B	C	D
1	**Discount Traders Co**			
2	*Sales analysis - April 200X*			
3	Customer	Sales	5% discount	Sales (net)
4		$	$	$
5	Arthur	956.00	0.00	956.00
6	Dent	1423.00	71.15	1351.85
7	Ford	2894.00	144.70	2749.30
8	Prefect	842.00	0.00	842.00
9				

The formula in cell C5 is: =IF(B5>1,000,(0.05*B5),0). This means, if the value in B5 is greater than $1,000 multiply it by 0.05, otherwise the discount will be zero. Cell D5 will calculate the amount net of discount, using the formula: =B5-C5. The same conditional formula with the cell references changed will be found in cells C6, C7 and C8. **Strictly**, the variables $1,000 and 5% should be entered in a **different part** of the spreadsheet.

Here is another example. Suppose the pass mark for an examination is 50%. You have a spreadsheet containing candidate's scores in column B. If a score is held in cell B10, an appropriate formula for cell C10 would be:

=IF(B10<50,"FAILED","PASSED").

6 Charts and graphs

Excel includes the facility to produce a range of charts and graphs. The **chart wizard** provides a tool to simplify the process of chart construction.

Using Microsoft Excel, It is possible to display data held in a range of spreadsheet cells in a variety of charts or graphs. We will use the Discount Traders Co spreadsheet shown below to generate a chart.

	A	B	C	D
1	**Discount Traders Co**			
2	*Sales analysis - April 200X*			
3	Customer	Sales	5% discount	Sales (net)
4		$	$	$
5	Arthur	956.00	0.00	956.00
6	Dent	1423.00	71.15	1351.85
7	Ford	2894.00	144.70	2749.30
8	Prefect	842.00	0.00	842.00
9				

The data in the spreadsheet could be used to generate a chart, such as those shown below. We explain how later in this section.

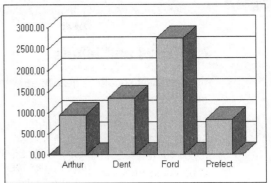

The Chart Wizard, which we explain in a moment, may also be used to generate a line graph. A line graph would normally be used to track a trend over time. For example, the chart below graphs the Total Revenue figures shown in Row 7 of the following spreadsheet.

	A	B	C	D	E	F	G	H	I
1									
2	**Revenue 2003-2006**								
3									
4	**Net revenue:**	2003	2004	2005	2006				
5	Products	24,001	27,552	34,823	39,205				
6	Services	5,306	5,720	6,104	6,820				
7	Total Revenue	29,307	33,272	40,927	46,025				
8									
9									

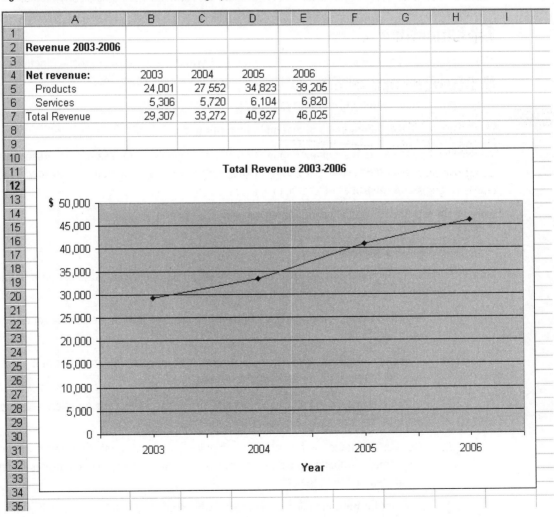

7 Spreadsheet format and appearance

Good presentation can help people understand the contents of a spreadsheet.

7.1 Titles and labels

A spreadsheet should be headed up with a title which **clearly defines its purpose**. Examples of titles are follows.

(a) Income statement for the year ended 30 June 200X.

(b) (i) Area A: Sales forecast for the three months to 31 March 200X.
     (ii) Area B: Sales forecast for the three months to 31 March 200X.
     (iii) Combined sales forecast for the three months to 31 March 200X.

(c) Salesmen: Analysis of earnings and commission for the six months ended 30 June 200X.

Row and **column** headings (or labels) should clearly identify the contents of the row/column. Any assumptions made that have influenced the spreadsheet contents should be clearly stated.

7.2 Formatting

There are a wide range of options available under the **Format** menu. Some of these functions may also be accessed through toolbar **buttons**. Formatting options include the ability to:

(a) Add **shading** or **borders** to cells.

(b) Use **different sizes of text** and different **fonts**.

(c) Choose from a range of options for presenting values, for example to present a number as a **percentage** (eg 0.05 as 5%), or with commas every third digit, or to a specified number of **decimal places** etc.

Experiment with the various formatting options yourself.

7.2.1 Formatting numbers

Most spreadsheet programs contain facilities for presenting numbers in a particular way. In Excel you simply click on **Format** and then **Cells ...**to reach these options.

(a) **Fixed format** displays the number in the cell rounded off to the number of decimal places you select.

(b) **Currency format** displays the number with a '$' in front, with commas and not more than two decimal places, eg $10,540.23.

(c) **Comma format** is the same as currency format except that the numbers are displayed without the '$'.

(d) **General format** is the format assumed unless another format is specified. In general format the number is displayed with no commas and with as many decimal places as entered or calculated that fit in the cell.

(e) **Percent format** multiplies the number in the display by 100 and follows it with a percentage sign. For example the number 0.548 in a cell would be displayed as 54.8%.

(f) **Hidden format** is a facility by which values can be entered into cells and used in calculations but are not actually displayed on the spreadsheet. The format is useful for hiding sensitive information.

7.3 Gridlines

One of the options available under the **Tools**, **Options** menu, on the **View** tab, is an option to remove the gridlines from your spreadsheet.

Compare the following two versions of the same spreadsheet. Note how the formatting applied to the second version has improved the spreadsheet presentation.

	A	B	C	D	E
1	Sales team salaries and commissions - 200X				
2	Name	Sales	Salary	Commis	Total earnings
3		$	$	$	$
4	Northington	284,000	14,000	5,680	19,680
5	Souther	193,000	14,000	3,860	17,860
6	Weston	12,000	14,000	240	14,240
7	Easterman	152,000	14,000	3,040	17,040
8					
9	Total	641,000	56,000	12,820	68,820
10					

	A	B	C	D	E
1	Sales team salaries and commissions - 200X				
2	Name	Sales	Salary	Commission	Total earnings
3		$	$	$	$
4	Northington	284,000	14,000	5,680	19,680
5	Souther	193,000	14,000	3,860	17,860
6	Weston	12,000	14,000	240	14,240
7	Easterman	152,000	14,000	3,040	17,040
8					
9	Total	641,000	56,000	12,820	68,820
10					

8 Other issues: printing; controls; using spreadsheets with word processing software

Backing up is a key security measure. **Cell protection** and **passwords** can also be used to prevent unauthorised access.

8.1 Printing spreadsheets

The print options for your spreadsheet may be accessed by selecting **File** and then **Page Setup**. The various Tabs contain a range of options. You specify the area of the spreadsheet to be printed in the Print area box on the Sheet tab. Other options include the ability to repeat headings on all pages and the option to print gridlines if required (normally they wouldn't be!)

Experiment with these options including the options available under Header/Footer.

8.2 Controls

There are facilities available in spreadsheet packages which can be used as controls – to prevent unauthorised or accidental amendment or deletion of all or part of a spreadsheet.

(a)   **Saving** and **back-up**. When working on a spreadsheet, save your file regularly, as often as every ten minutes. This will prevent too much work being lost in the advent of a system crash. Spreadsheet files should be included in standard back-up procedures.

(b)   **Cell protection**. This prevents the user from inadvertently changing or erasing cells that should not be changed. Look up how to protect cells using Excel's Help facility. (Select Help from the main menu within Excel, then select Contents and Index, click on the Find tab and enter the words 'cell protection'.)

(c)   **Passwords.** You can set a password for any spreadsheet that you create. In Excel, simply click on **Tools,** then on **Protection,** then on **Protect Sheet** or **Protect Workbook**, as appropriate.

8.3 Using spreadsheets with word processing software

There may be a situation where you wish to incorporate the contents of all or part of a spreadsheet into a **word processed report**. There are a number of options available to achieve this.

(a)   The simplest, but least professional option, is to **print out** the spreadsheet and interleave the page or pages at the appropriate point in your word processed document.

(b)   A neater option if you are just including a small table is to select and **copy** the relevant cells from the spreadsheet to the computer's clipboard by selecting the cells and choosing Edit, Copy. Then switch to the word processing document, and **paste** them in at the appropriate point.

(c)   Office packages, such as Microsoft Office allow you to easily use spreadsheets and word processing files together.

For example, a new, blank spreadsheet can be 'embedded' in a document by selecting Insert, Object then, from within the Create New tab, selecting Microsoft Excel worksheet.

The spreadsheet is then available to be worked upon, allowing the easy manipulation of numbers using all the facilities of the spreadsheet package. Clicking outside the spreadsheet will result in the spreadsheet being inserted in the document.

The contents of an existing spreadsheet may be inserted into a Word document by choosing Insert, Object and then activating the Create from File tab. Then click the Browse button and locate the spreadsheet file. Highlight the file, then click Insert, and then OK. You may then need to move and resize the object, by dragging its borders, to fit your document.

9 Three dimensional (multi-sheet) spreadsheets

FAST FORWARD Spreadsheet packages permit the user to work with **multiple sheets** that refer to each other.

9.1 Background

In early spreadsheet packages, a spreadsheet file consisted of a single worksheet. Excel provides the option of multi-sheet spreadsheets, consisting of a series of related sheets. Excel files which contain more than one worksheet are often called **workbooks**.

For example, suppose you were producing a profit forecast for two regions, and a combined forecast for the total of the regions. This situation would be suited to using separate worksheets for each region and another for the total. This approach is sometimes referred to as working in **three dimensions**, as you are able to flip between different sheets stacked in front or behind each other. Cells in one sheet may **refer** to cells in another sheet. So, in our example, the formulae in the cells in the total sheet would refer to the cells in the other sheets.

Excel has a series of 'tabs', one for each worksheet at the foot of the spreadsheet.

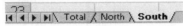

9.2 How many sheets?

Excel can be set up so that it always opens a fresh file with a certain number of worksheets ready and waiting for you. Click on **Tools ... Options** ... and then the **General** tab and set the number *Sheets in new workbook* option to the number you would like each new spreadsheet file to contain (sheets may be added or deleted later).

If you subsequently want to insert more sheets you just **right click** on the index tab after which you want the new sheet to be inserted and choose **Insert** ... and then **Worksheet**. By default sheets are called **Sheet 1, Sheet 2** etc. However, these may be changed. To **rename** a sheet in **Excel, right click** on its index tab and choose the rename option.

9.3 Pasting from one sheet to another

When building a spreadsheet that will contain a number of worksheets with identical structure, users often set up one sheet, then copy that sheet and amend the sheet contents. [To copy a worksheet in Excel, from within the worksheet you wish to copy, select Edit, Move or Copy sheet, and tick the Create a copy box.] A 'Total' sheet would use the same structure, but would contain formulae totalling the individual sheets.

9.4 Linking sheets with formulae

Formulae on one sheet may refer to data held on another sheet. The links within such a formula may be established using the following steps.

Step 1 In the cell that you want to refer to a cell from another sheet, type =.

Step 2 Click on the index tab for the sheet containing the cell you want to refer to and select the cell in question.

Step 3 Press Enter or Return.

9.5 Uses for multi-sheet spreadsheets

There are a wide range of situations suited to the multi-sheet approach. A variety of possible uses follow.

(a) A model could use one sheet for variables, a second for calculations, and a third for outputs.

(b) To enable quick and easy **consolidation** of similar sets of data, for example the financial results of two subsidiaries or the budgets of two departments.

(c) To provide **different views** of the same data. For instance you could have one sheet of data sorted in product code order and another sorted in product name order.

10 Macros

> **FAST FORWARD**
>
> A **macro** is an automated process that may be written by recording key-strokes and mouse clicks.

A macro is a sort of mini-program that automates keystrokes or actions. Macros are often used within spreadsheets. Macros may be written using a type of code – like a programming language. However, most spreadsheet users produce macros by asking the spreadsheet to record their actions – this automatically generates the macro 'code' required.

Macros can get **very complex** indeed – in fact you **can** build whole applications using them. (Doing so is a very good introduction to programming proper.)

We are **not** going to be demonstrating anything very elaborate, here. We are just going to show you how macros can be used to **eliminate a few key-strokes and mouse clicks** for tasks that you have to **perform frequently** enough to warrant writing a macro in the first place.

We are going to explain the basic principles of macros by reference to Microsoft **Excel.**

10.1 A simple macro

Suppose you decided that **every spreadsheet you created** should have your **first name and surname** in the bottom right corner of the footer in **Arial 8pt font**. You could write a macro and do all of this just by pressing two keys.

To write this macro you would proceed as follows. Follow this example through **hands-on** if possible.

Step 1 **Excel:** Open a fresh file. Click on the **Tools** menu and then on the option **Macro**

Step 2 This gives a sub-menu including the option **Record New Macro**. Select this.

Step 3 A dialogue box like the following will appear.

Step 4   Give the macro a name such as InsertName and press **Tab**. Excel will not allow spaces within macro names.

Step 5   Choose a shortcut key. This must be a **letter**, and it should be one that you don't frequently use for other purposes such as Ctrl + C or Ctrl + B. We will choose **Ctrl + m**

(Note that we use lower case **m**; if we had used **M** we would subsequently have to type Ctrl +**Shift** +m to start the macro).

Step 6   Accept the option to store the macro in **This Workbook** and **click on OK**

Step 7   Everything you do is now being **recorded**.

Step 8   From the menu select **View, Header and Footer.**

Step 9   Click on **Custom Footer** and click into the **Right section**.

Step 10   Type your name and highlight the text by clicking and dragging the cursor over it.

Step 11   Click on the **A** button to activate the font menu, and select Arial 8pt.

Step 12   Close the menus by clicking on **OK**. (Three **OK** boxes require clicking.)

Step 13   Click on the stop recording button.

Always start a macro by **returning the cursor to cell A1** (by pressing Ctrl + Home), even if it is already there. You may well not want to make your first entry in cell A1, but if you select your first real cell (B4 say) **before** you start recording, the macro will always begin at the currently active cell, whether it is B4 or Z256.

Always finish a macro by **selecting the cell** where the **next entry** is required.

That's all there is to it. Test your macro now by **selecting a fresh sheet** and then pressing Ctrl + m together. Then type 'Test' in cell A1 (as Excel will not Print Preview a blank sheet), and select **File, Print Preview.** You will see your name has been inserted into the footer.

Save your file with a suitable name and **close down** your spreadsheet package completely. Then open it up again and open a completely **new file**. Press Ctrl + m. Regrettably, nothing will happen. This does not mean that your macro is lost forever, just that it is not currently in the computer's memory (because you closed down the package).

However, if you **open up the file you just saved**, your macro will work again, because it is actually **stored** in that file. If you want your macro to be **available to you whenever** you want it you have the following choices.

(a)   Keep this file, with no contents other than your 'name' macro (and any others you may write) and always use it as the basis for any new spreadsheets you create, which will subsequently be saved with new file names.

(b)   You can add the macro to your **Personal Macro Workbook.** You do this at the point when you are naming your workbook and choosing a shortcut key, by changing the option in the **Store macro in:** box from This Workbook to Personal Macro Workbook. The macro will then be loaded into memory whenever you start up Excel and be available in any spreadsheet you create.

If you forget to assign a keyboard shortcut to a macro (or do not want to do so), you can still run your macros by clicking on Tools …Macro … Macros. This gives you a list of all the macros currently available. Select the one you want then click on Run.

Do not accept the default names offered by Excel of Macro1, Macro2 etc. You will soon forget what these macros do, unless you give them a meaningful name.

11 Advantages and disadvantages of spreadsheet software

11.1 Advantages of spreadsheets

- Excel is easy to learn and to use
- Spreadsheets make the calculation and manipulation of data easier and quicker
- They enable the analysis, reporting and sharing of financial information
- They enable 'what-if' analysis to be performed very quickly

11.2 Disadvantages of spreadsheets

- A spreadsheet is only as good as its original design, garbage in = garbage out!
- Formulae are hidden from sight so the underlying logic of a set of calculations may not be obvious
- A spreadsheet presentation may make reports appear infallible
- Research shows that a high proportion of large models contain critical errors
- A database may be more suitable to use with large volumes of data

Question	Spreadsheet advantages

An advantage of a spreadsheet program is that it

A   Can answer 'what if?' questions
B   Checks for incorrect entries
C   Automatically writes formulae
D   Can answer 'when is?' questions

Answer

The correct answer is A.

12 Uses of spreadsheet software

FAST FORWARD

Spreadsheets can be used in a variety of accounting contexts. You should practise using spreadsheets, **hands-on experience** is the key to spreadsheet proficiency.

Management accountants will use spreadsheet software in activities such as budgeting, forecasting, reporting performance and variance analysis.

12.1 Budgeting

Spreadsheet packages for budgeting have a number of advantages.

(a) Spreadsheet packages have a facility to perform **'what if' calculations** at great speed. For example, the consequences throughout the organisation of sales growth per month of nil, $1/2$%, 1%, $1^1/2$% and so on can be calculated very quickly.

(b) Preparing budgets may be complex; budgets may need to go through several drafts. If one or two figures are changed, the **computer will automatically make all the computational changes to the other figures**.

(c) A spreadsheet model will **ensure that the preparation of the individual budgets is co-ordinated**. Data and information from the production budget, for example, will be automatically fed through to the material usage budget (as material usage will depend on production levels).

These advantages of spreadsheets make them ideal for taking over the **manipulation of numbers**, leaving staff to get involved in the real planning process.

Chapter Roundup

- Use of spreadsheets is an essential part of the day-to-day work of the Management Accountant.

- A spreadsheet is an electronic piece of paper divided into **rows** and **columns**. The intersection of a row and a column is known as a **cell**.

- Formulas in Microsoft Excel follow a specific syntax.

- Essential basic skills include how to **move around** within a spreadsheet, how to **enter** and **edit** data, how to **fill** cells, how to **insert** and **delete** columns and rows and how to improve the basic **layout** and **appearance** of a spreadsheet.

- A wide range of **formulae** and functions are available within Excel.

- **If statements** are used in conditional formulae.

- Excel includes the facility to produce a range of charts and graphs. The **chart wizard** provides a tool to simplify the process of chart construction.

- Good presentation can help people understand the contents of a spreadsheet.

- **Backing up** is a key security measure. **Cell protection** and **passwords** can also be used to prevent unauthorised access.

- Spreadsheet packages permit the user to work with **multiple sheets** that refer to each other.

- A **macro** is an automated process that may be written by recording key-strokes and mouse clicks.

- Spreadsheets can be used in a variety of accounting contexts. You should practise using spreadsheets, **hands-on experience** is the key to spreadsheet proficiency.

Quick quiz

1   List three types of cell contents.

2   What do the F5 and F2 keys do in Excel?

3   What technique can you use to insert a logical series of data such as 1, 2 .... 10, or Jan, Feb, March etc?

4   How do you display formulae instead of the results of formulae in a spreadsheet?

5   Which function key may be used to change cell references within a selected formula from absolute to relative – and vice-versa?

6   List five possible changes that may improve the appearance of a spreadsheet.

7   List three possible uses for a multi-sheet (3D) spreadsheet.

8   You are about to key an exam mark into cell B4 of a spreadsheet. Write an IF statement, to be placed in cell C4, that will display PASS in C4 if the student mark is 50 or above - and or will display FAIL if the mark is below 50 (all student marks are whole numbers).

9   Give two ways of starting Excel's function wizard.

Answers to quick quiz

1   Text, values or formulae.

2   F5 opens a GoTo dialogue box which is useful for navigating around large spreadsheets. F2 puts the active cell into edit mode.

3   You can use the technique of 'filling' - selecting the first few items of a series and dragging the lower right corner of the selection in the appropriate direction.

4   Select Tools, Options, ensure the View tab is active then tick the Formulas box within the window options area.

5   The F4 key.

6   Removing gridlines, adding shading, adding borders, using different fonts and font sizes, presenting numbers as percentages or currency or to a certain number of decimal places.

7   The construction of a spreadsheet model with separate Input, Calculation and Output sheets. They can help consolidate data from different sources. They can offer different views of the same data.

8   =IF(A4>49,"PASS","FAIL ")

9   You could click on the *fx* symbol in the toolbar, or use the menu item Insert, Function, to start the function wizard.

Now try the questions below from the Exam Question Bank

Number	Level	Marks	Time
5	MCQ/OTQ	n/a	n/a

Part D
Cost accounting techniques

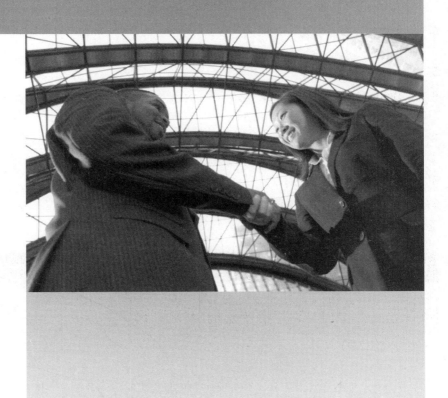

Material costs

Topic list	Syllabus reference
1 What is inventory control?	D1 (b)
2 The ordering, receipt and issue of raw materials	D1 (a)
3 The storage of raw materials	D1 (c), (d)
4 Inventory control levels	D1 (e)-(h)

Introduction

The investment in inventory is a very important one for most businesses, both in terms of monetary value and relationships with customers (no inventory, no sale, loss of customer goodwill). It is therefore vital that management establish and maintain an **effective inventory control system**.

This chapter will concentrate on a **inventory control system** for materials, but similar problems and considerations apply to all forms of inventory.

Study guide

		Intellectual level
D1	**Accounting for materials**	
(a)	Describe the different procedures and documents necessary for ordering, receiving and issuing materials from inventory	1
(b)	Describe the control procedures used to monitor physical and 'book' inventory and to minimise discrepancies and losses	1
(c)	Interpret the entries and balances in the material inventory account	1
(d)	Identify and explain the costs of ordering and holding inventory	1
(e)	Calculate and interpret optimal recorder quantities	2
(f)	Calculate and interpret optimal reorder quantities when discounts apply	2
(g)	Produce calculations to minimise inventory costs when inventory is gradually replenished	2
(h)	Describe and apply appropriate methods for establishing reorder levels where demand in the lead time is constant	2

Exam guide

Material costs is another key area of the syllabus so expect questions on this topic. Make sure you understand and can use the EOQ formula. It will be given to you in the exam.

1 What is inventory control?

1.1 Introduction

FAST FORWARD

> **Inventory control** includes the functions of inventory ordering and purchasing, receiving goods into store, storing and issuing inventory and controlling levels of inventory.

Classifications of inventories

- Raw materials
- Work in progress
- Spare parts/consumables
- Finished goods

This chapter will concentrate on an **inventory control system** for materials, but similar problems and considerations apply to all forms of inventory. Controls should cover the following functions.

- The **ordering** of inventory
- The **purchase** of inventory
- The **receipt** of goods into store
- **Storage**
- The **issue** of inventory and maintenance of inventory at the most appropriate level

1.2 Qualitative aspects of inventory control

We may wish to **control inventory** for the following reasons.

- Holding costs of inventory may be expensive.
- Production will be disrupted if we run out of raw materials.
- Unused inventory with a short shelf life may incur unnecessary expenses.

If manufactured goods are made out of low quality materials, the end product will be of low quality also. It may therefore be necessary to control the quality of inventory, in order to maintain a good reputation with consumers.

2 The ordering, receipt and issue of raw materials

2.1 Ordering and receiving materials

FAST FORWARD

Every movement of a material in a business should be documented using the following as appropriate: purchase requisition; purchase order; GRN; materials requisition note; materials transfer note and materials returned note.

Proper records must be kept of the physical procedures for ordering and receiving a consignment of materials to ensure the following.

- That enough inventory is held
- That there is no duplication of ordering
- That quality is maintained
- That there is adequate record keeping for accounts purposes

2.2 Purchase requisition

Current inventories run down to the level where a reorder is required. The stores department issues a **purchase requisition** which is sent to the purchasing department, authorising the department to order further inventory. An example of a purchase requisition is shown below.

PURCHASE REQUISITION Req. No.				
Department/job number: Suggested Supplier:		Date		
		Requested by: Latest date required:		
Quantity	Code number	Description	Estimated Cost	
			Unit	$
Authorised signature:				

2.3 Purchase order

The purchasing department draws up a **purchase order** which is sent to the supplier. (The supplier may be asked to return an acknowledgement copy as confirmation of his acceptance of the order.) Copies of the purchase order must be sent to the accounts department and the storekeeper (or receiving department).

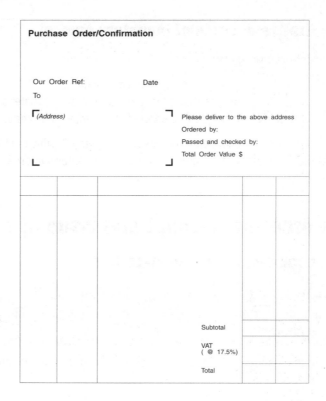

Purchase Order/Confirmation

Our Order Ref: Date

To

⌐ *(Address)*

Please deliver to the above address

Ordered by:

Passed and checked by:

Total Order Value $

		Subtotal		
		VAT (@ 17.5%)		
		Total		

2.4 Quotations

The purchasing department may have to obtain a number of quotations if either a new inventory line is required, the existing supplier's costs are too high or the existing supplier no longer stocks the goods needed. Trade discounts (reduction in the price per unit given to some customers) should be negotiated where possible.

2.5 Delivery note

The supplier delivers the consignment of materials, and the storekeeper signs a **delivery note** for the carrier. The packages must then be checked against the copy of the purchase order, to ensure that the supplier has delivered the types and quantities of materials which were ordered. (Discrepancies would be referred to the purchasing department.)

2.6 Goods received note

If the delivery is acceptable, the storekeeper prepares a **goods received note (GRN)**, an example of which is shown below.

```
┌─────────────────────────────────────────────────────────────────┐
│         GOODS RECEIVED NOTE  WAREHOUSE COPY                       │
│    DATE:                    TIME:            NO  5565             │
│    OUR ORDER NO:                        WAREHOUSE A              │
│    SUPPLIER AND SUPPLIER'S ADVICE NOTE NO:                       │
│  ─────────────────────────────────────────────────────────────  │
│    QUANTITY     CAT NO       DESCRIPTION                          │
│                                                                   │
│                                                                   │
│                                                                   │
│                                                                   │
│                                                                   │
│  ─────────────────────────────────────────────────────────────  │
│    RECEIVED IN GOOD CONDITION:                    (INITIALS)     │
└─────────────────────────────────────────────────────────────────┘
```

A copy of the **GRN** is sent to the accounts department, where it is matched with the copy of the purchase order. The supplier's invoice is checked against the purchase order and GRN, and the necessary steps are taken to pay the supplier. The invoice may contain details relating to discounts such as trade discounts, quantity discounts (order in excess of a specified amount) and settlement discounts (payment received within a specified number of days).

Question
Ordering materials

What are the possible consequences of a failure of control over ordering and receipt of materials?

Answer

(a)   Incorrect materials being delivered, disrupting operations
(b)   Incorrect prices being paid
(c)   Deliveries other than at the specified time (causing disruption)
(d)   Insufficient control over quality
(e)   Invoiced amounts differing from quantities of goods actually received or prices agreed

You may, of course, have thought of equally valid consequences.

2.7 Materials requisition note

Materials can only be issued against a **materials/stores requisition**. This document must record not only the quantity of goods issued, but also the cost centre or the job number for which the requisition is being made. The materials requisition note may also have a column, to be filled in by the cost department, for recording the cost or value of the materials issued to the cost centre or job.

Materials requisition note			
Date required _ _ _ _ _ _ _ _ .		Cost centre No/ Job No _ _ _ _ _ _ _ _ _ _ .	
Quantity	Item code	Description	$
Signature of requisitioning Manager/ Foreman _ .		Date _ _ _ _ _ _	

2.8 Materials transfers and returns

Where materials, having been issued to one job or cost centre, are later transferred to a different job or cost centre, without first being returned to stores, a **materials transfer note** should be raised. Such a note must show not only the job receiving the transfer, but also the job from which it is transferred. This enables the appropriate charges to be made to jobs or cost centres.

Material returns must also be documented on a **materials returned note**. This document is the 'reverse' of a requisition note, and must contain similar information. In fact it will often be almost identical to a requisition note. It will simply have a different title and perhaps be a distinctive colour, such as red, to highlight the fact that materials are being returned.

2.9 Computerised inventory control systems

Many inventory control systems these days are computerised. Computerised inventory control systems vary greatly, but most will have the features outlined below.

(a)   **Data must be input into the system**. For example, details of goods received may simply be written on to a GRN for later entry into the computer system. Alternatively, this information may be keyed in directly to the computer: a GRN will be printed and then signed as evidence of the transaction, so that both the warehouse and the supplier can have a hard copy record in case of dispute. Some systems may incorporate the use of devices such as bar code readers.

Other types of transaction which will need to be recorded include the following.

(i)   **Transfers** between different categories of inventory (for example from work in progress to finished goods)

(ii)   **Despatch**, resulting from a sale, of items of finished goods to customers

(iii)   **Adjustments** to inventory records if the amount of inventory revealed in a physical inventory count differs from the amount appearing on the inventory records

(b)   **An inventory master file is maintained**. This file will contain details for every category of inventory and will be updated for new inventory lines. A database file may be maintained.

Question   **Inventory master file**

What type of information do you think should be held on an inventory master file?

Answer

Here are some examples.

(a)   Inventory code number, for reference
(b)   Brief description of inventory item
(c)   Reorder level
(d)   Reorder quantity
(e)   Cost per unit
(f)   Selling price per unit (if finished goods)
(g)   Amount in inventory
(h)   Frequency of usage

The file may also hold details of inventory movements over a period, but this will depend on the type of system in operation. In a **batch system**, transactions will be grouped and input in one operation and details of the movements may be held in a separate transactions file, the master file updated in total only. In an **on-line system**, transactions may be input directly to the master file, where the record of movements is thus likely to be found. Such a system will mean that the inventory records are constantly up to date, which will help in monitoring and controlling inventory.

The system may generate orders automatically once the amount in inventory has fallen to the reorder level.

(c)   **The system will generate outputs**. These may include, depending on the type of system, any of the following.

(i)   **Hard copy** records, for example a printed GRN, of transactions entered into the system.

(ii)   Output on a **VDU** screen in response to an enquiry (for example the current level of a particular line of inventory, or details of a particular transaction).

(iii)   Various **printed reports**, devised to fit in with the needs of the organisation. These may include inventory movement reports, detailing over a period the movements on all inventory lines, listings of GRNs, despatch notes and so forth.

A computerised inventory control system is usually able to give more up to date information and more flexible reporting than a manual system but remember that both manual and computer based inventory control systems need the same types of data to function properly.

3 The storage of raw materials

3.1 Objectives of storing materials

- Speedy **issue** and **receipt** of materials
- Full **identification** of all materials at all times
- Correct **location** of all materials at all times
- **Protection** of materials from damage and deterioration
- Provision of **secure stores** to avoid pilferage, theft and fire
- **Efficient** use of storage space
- **Maintenance** of correct inventory levels
- Keeping correct and up-to-date **records** of receipts, issues and inventory levels

3.2 Recording inventory levels

One of the objectives of storekeeping is to maintain accurate records of current inventory levels. This involves the accurate recording of inventory movements (issues from and receipts into stores). The most frequently encountered system for recording inventory movements is the use of bin cards and stores ledger accounts.

3.2.1 Bin cards

A **bin card** shows the level of inventory of an item at a particular stores location. It is kept with the actual inventory and is updated by the storekeeper as inventories are received and issued. A typical bin card is shown below.

Bin card

Part code no _ _ _ _ _ _ _ _ _ _ _		Location _ _ _ _ _ _ _ _ _ _ _ _ _ _ _				
Bin number _ _ _ _ _ _ _ _ _ _ _		Stores ledger no _ _ _ _ _ _ _ _ _ _ _				
Receipts			Issues			Inventory balance
Date	Quantity	G.R.N. No.	Date	Quantity	Req. No.	

The use of bin cards is decreasing, partly due to the difficulty in keeping them updated and partly due to the merging of inventory recording and control procedures, frequently using computers.

3.2.2 Stores ledger accounts

A typical stores ledger account is shown below. Note that it shows the value of inventory.

Stores ledger account

Material _ _ _ _ _ _ _ _ _ _ _ _ _ _ _ .				Maximum Quantity _ _ _ _ _ _ _ _ _ _ _ _ _ _						
Code _ _ _ _ _ _ _ _ _ _ _ _ _ _ _ _				Minimum Quantity _ _ _ _ _ _ _ _ _ _ _ _ _ _						
Date	Receipts				Issues				Inventory		
	G.R.N No.	Quantity	Unit price $	Amount $	Stores Req. No	Quantity	Unit price $	Amount $	Quantity	Unit price $	Amount $

The above illustration shows a card for a manual system, but even when the inventory records are computerised, the same type of information is normally included in the computer file. The running balance on the stores ledger account allows inventory levels and valuation to be monitored.

3.2.3 Free inventory

Managers need to know the **free inventory balance** in order to obtain a full picture of the current inventory position of an item. Free inventory represents what is really **available for future use** and is calculated as follows.

	Materials in inventory	X
+	Materials on order from suppliers	X
−	Materials requisitioned, not yet issued	(X)
	Free inventory balance	X

Knowledge of the level of physical inventory assists inventory issuing, inventory counting and controlling maximum and minimum inventory levels: knowledge of the level of free inventory assists ordering.

Question

A wholesaler has 8,450 units outstanding for Part X100 on existing customers' orders; there are 3,925 units in inventory and the calculated free inventory is 5,525 units.

How many units does the wholesaler have on order with his supplier?

A 9,450   B 10,050   C 13,975   D 17,900

Answer

Free inventory balance	=	units in inventory + units on order – units ordered, but not yet issued
5,525	=	3,925 + units on order – 8,450
Units on order	=	10,050

The correct answer is B.

3.3 Identification of materials: inventory codes (materials codes)

Materials held in stores are **coded** and **classified**. Advantages of using code numbers to identify materials are as follows.

(a)   Ambiguity is avoided.

(b)   Time is saved. Descriptions can be lengthy and time-consuming.

(c)   Production efficiency is improved. The correct material can be accurately identified from a code number.

(d)   Computerised processing is made easier.

(e)   Numbered code systems can be designed to be flexible, and can be expanded to include more inventory items as necessary.

The digits in a code can stand for the type of inventory, supplier, department and so forth.

3.4 The inventory count (stocktake)

FAST FORWARD

The **inventory count (stocktake)** involves counting the physical inventory on hand at a certain date, and then checking this against the balance shown in the inventory records. The count can be carried out on a **continuous** or **periodic** basis.

Key terms

Periodic stocktaking is a process whereby all inventory items are physically counted and valued at a set point in time, usually at the end of an accounting period.

Continuous stocktaking is counting and valuing selected items at different times on a rotating basis. This involves a specialist team counting and checking a number of inventory items each day, so that each item is checked at least once a year. Valuable items or items with a high turnover could be checked more frequently.

3.4.1 Advantages of continuous stocktaking compared to periodic stocktaking

(a)   The annual stocktaking is unnecessary and the disruption it causes is avoided.

(b)   Regular skilled stocktakers can be employed, reducing likely errors.

(c)   More time is available, reducing errors and allowing investigation.

(d)   Deficiencies and losses are revealed sooner than they would be if stocktaking were limited to an annual check.

(e)   Production hold-ups are eliminated because the stores staff are at no time so busy as to be unable to deal with material issues to production departments.

(f)   Staff morale is improved and standards raised.

(g)   Control over inventory levels is improved, and there is less likelihood of overstocking or running out of inventory.

3.4.2 Inventory discrepancies

There will be occasions when inventory checks disclose discrepancies between the physical amount of an item in inventory and the amount shown in the inventory records. When this occurs, the cause of the discrepancy should be investigated, and appropriate action taken to ensure that it does not happen again.

3.4.3 Perpetual inventory

FAST FORWARD

Perpetual inventory refers to a inventory recording system whereby the records (bin cards and stores ledger accounts) are updated for each receipt and issue of inventory as it occurs.

This means that there is a continuous record of the balance of each item of inventory. The balance on the stores ledger account therefore represents the inventory on hand and this balance is used in the calculation of closing inventory in monthly and annual accounts. In practice, physical inventories may not agree with recorded inventories and therefore continuous stocktaking is necessary to ensure that the perpetual inventory system is functioning correctly and that minor inventory discrepancies are corrected.

3.4.4 Obsolete, deteriorating and slow-moving inventories and wastage

FAST FORWARD

Obsolete inventories are those items which have become out-of-date and are no longer required. Obsolete items are written off and disposed of.

Inventory items may be wasted because, for example, they get broken. All **wastage** should be noted on the inventory records immediately so that physical inventory equals the inventory balance on records and the cost of the wastage written off.

Slow-moving inventories are inventory items which are likely to take a long time to be used up. For example, 5,000 units are in inventory, and only 20 are being used each year. This is often caused by overstocking. Managers should investigate such inventory items and, if it is felt that the usage rate is unlikely to increase, excess inventory should be written off as for obsolete inventory, leaving perhaps four or five years' supply in inventory.

4 Inventory control levels

4.1 Inventory costs

Inventory costs include purchase costs, holding costs, ordering costs and costs of running out inventory.

The costs of purchasing inventory are usually one of the largest costs faced by an organisation and, once obtained, inventory has to be carefully controlled and checked.

4.1.1 Reasons for holding inventories

- To ensure sufficient goods are available to meet expected demand
- To provide a buffer between processes
- To meet any future shortages
- To take advantage of bulk purchasing discounts
- To absorb seasonal fluctuations and any variations in usage and demand
- To allow production processes to flow smoothly and efficiently
- As a necessary part of the production process (such as when maturing cheese)
- As a deliberate investment policy, especially in times of inflation or possible shortages

4.1.2 Holding costs

If inventories are too high, **holding costs** will be incurred unnecessarily. Such costs occur for a number of reasons.

(a) **Costs of storage and stores operations.** Larger inventories require more storage space and possibly extra staff and equipment to control and handle them.

(b) **Interest charges**. Holding inventories involves the tying up of capital (cash) on which interest must be paid.

(c) **Insurance costs**. The larger the value of inventories held, the greater insurance premiums are likely to be.

(d) **Risk of obsolescence**. The longer a inventory item is held, the greater is the risk of obsolescence.

(e) **Deterioration**. When materials in store deteriorate to the extent that they are unusable, they must be thrown away with the likelihood that disposal costs would be incurred.

4.1.3 Costs of obtaining inventory

On the other hand, if inventories are kept low, small quantities of inventory will have to be ordered more frequently, thereby increasing the following **ordering or procurement costs**.

(a) **Clerical and administrative costs** associated with purchasing, accounting for and receiving goods

(b) **Transport costs**

(c) **Production run costs**, for inventory which is manufactured internally rather than purchased from external sources

4.1.4 Stockout costs (running out of inventory)

An additional type of cost which may arise if inventory are kept too low is the type associated with running out of inventory. There are a number of causes of **stockout costs**.

- Lost contribution from lost sales
- Loss of future sales due to disgruntled customers
- Loss of customer goodwill
- Cost of production stoppages
- Labour frustration over stoppages
- Extra costs of urgent, small quantity, replenishment orders

4.1.5 Objective of inventory control

The overall objective of inventory control is, therefore, to maintain inventory levels so that the total of the following costs is minimised.

- Holding costs
- Ordering costs
- Stockout costs

4.2 Inventory control levels

FAST FORWARD

Inventory control levels can be calculated in order to maintain inventories at the optimum level. The three critical control levels are reorder level, minimum level and maximum level.

Based on an analysis of past inventory usage and delivery times, inventory control levels can be calculated and used to maintain inventory at their optimum level (in other words, a level which minimises costs). These levels will determine 'when to order' and 'how many to order'.

4.2.1 Reorder level

When inventories reach this level, an order should be placed to replenish inventories. The reorder level is determined by consideration of the following.

- The maximum rate of consumption
- The maximum lead time

The maximum lead time is the time between placing an order with a supplier, and the inventory becoming available for use

Formula to learn

Reorder level = maximum usage × maximum lead time

4.2.2 Minimum level

This is a warning level to draw management attention to the fact that inventories are approaching a dangerously low level and that stockouts are possible.

Formula to learn

Minimum level = reorder level − (average usage × average lead time)

4.2.3 Maximum level

This also acts as a warning level to signal to management that inventories are reaching a potentially wasteful level.

Formula to learn

Maximum level = reorder level + reorder quantity − (minimum usage × minimum lead time)

Question

A large retailer with multiple outlets maintains a central warehouse from which the outlets are supplied. The following information is available for Part Number SF525.

Average usage	350 per day
Minimum usage	180 per day
Maximum usage	420 per day
Lead time for replenishment	11-15 days
Re-order quantity	6,500 units
Re-order level	6,300 units

(a)　Based on the data above, what is the maximum level of inventory?

　　　A 5,250　　　　　　B 6,500　　　　　　C 10,820　　　　　　D 12,800

(b)　Based on the data above, what is the approximate number of Part Number SF525 carried as buffer inventory?

　　　A 200　　　　　　B 720　　　　　　C 1,680　　　　　　D 1,750

Answer

(a)　Maximum inventory level = reorder level + reorder quantity – (min usage × min lead time)
　　　　　　　= 6,300 + 6,500 – (180 × 11)
　　　　　　　= 10,820

The correct answer is C.

Using good MCQ technique, if you were resorting to a guess you should have eliminated option A. The maximum inventory level cannot be less than the reorder quantity.

(b)　Buffer inventory　= minimum level

Minimum level　　= reorder level – (average usage × average lead time)
　　　　　　　= 6,300 – (350 × 13) = 1,750.

The correct answer is D.

Option A could again be easily eliminated. With minimum usage of 180 per day, a buffer inventory of only 200 would not be much of a buffer!

4.2.4 Reorder quantity

This is the quantity of inventory which is to be ordered when inventory reaches the reorder level. If it is set so as to minimise the total costs associated with holding and ordering inventory, then it is known as the economic order quantity.

4.2.5 Average inventory

The formula for the average inventory level assumes that inventory levels fluctuate evenly between the minimum (or safety) inventory level and the highest possible inventory level (the amount of inventory immediately after an order is received, ie safety inventory + reorder quantity).

Formula to learn

> **Average inventory** = safety inventory + ½ reorder quantity

| Question | Average inventory |

A component has a safety inventory of 500, a re-order quantity of 3,000 and a rate of demand which varies between 200 and 700 per week. The average inventory is approximately

A 2,000   B 2,300   C 2,500   D 3,500

| Answer |

Average inventory   = safety inventory + ½ reorder quantity
                    = 500 + (0.5 × 3,000)
                    = 2,000

The correct answer is A.

4.3 Economic order quantity (EOQ)

FAST FORWARD

The **economic order quantity (EOQ)** is the order quantity which minimises inventory costs. The EOQ can be calculated using a table, graph or formula.

Economic order theory assumes that the average inventory held is equal to one half of the reorder quantity (although as we saw in the last section, if an organisation maintains some sort of buffer or safety inventory then average inventory = buffer inventory + half of the reorder quantity). We have seen that there are certain costs associated with holding inventory. These costs tend to increase with the level of inventories, and so could be reduced by ordering smaller amounts from suppliers each time.

On the other hand, as we have seen, there are costs associated with ordering from suppliers: documentation, telephone calls, payment of invoices, receiving goods into stores and so on. These costs tend to increase if small orders are placed, because a larger number of orders would then be needed for a given annual demand.

4.3.1 Example: Economic order quantity

Suppose a company purchases raw material at a cost of $16 per unit. The annual demand for the raw material is 25,000 units. The holding cost per unit is $6.40 and the cost of placing an order is $32.

We can tabulate the annual relevant costs for various order quantities as follows.

Order quantity (units)		100	200	300	400	500	600	800	1,000
Average inventory (units)	(a)	50	100	150	200	250	300	400	500
Number of orders	(b)	250	125	83	63	50	42	31	25
		$	$	$	$	$	$	$	$
Annual holding cost	(c)	320	640	960	1,280	1,600	1,920	2,560	3,200
Annual order cost	(d)	8,000	4,000	2,656	2,016	1,600	1,344	992	800
Total relevant cost		8,320	4,640	3,616	3,296	3,200	3,264	3,552	4,000

Notes

(a)   Average inventory = Order quantity ÷ 2 (ie assuming no safety inventory)
(b)   Number of orders = annual demand ÷ order quantity
(c)   Annual holding cost = Average inventory × $6.40
(d)   Annual order cost = Number of orders × $32

You will see that the economic order quantity is 500 units. At this point the total annual relevant costs are at a minimum.

4.3.2 Example: Economic order quantity graph

We can present the information tabulated in Paragraph 4.3.1 in graphical form. The vertical axis represents the relevant annual costs for the investment in inventories, and the horizontal axis can be used to represent either the various order quantities or the average inventory levels; two scales are actually shown on the horizontal axis so that both items can be incorporated. The graph shows that, as the average inventory level and order quantity increase, the holding cost increases. On the other hand, the ordering costs decline as inventory levels and order quantities increase. The total cost line represents the sum of both the holding and the ordering costs.

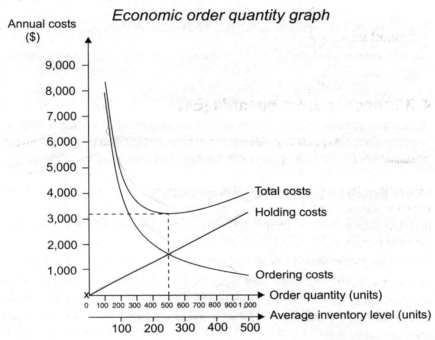

Economic order quantity graph

Note that the total cost line is at a minimum for an order quantity of 500 units and occurs at the point where the ordering cost curve and holding cost curve intersect. **The EOQ is therefore found at the point where holding costs equal ordering costs.**

4.3.3 EOQ formula

The formula for the EOQ will be provided in your examination.

$$EOQ = \sqrt{\frac{2C_0 D}{C_H}} \quad \text{(given in exam)}$$

where C_H = cost of holding one unit of inventory for one time period
C_0 = cost of ordering a consignment from a supplier
D = demand during the time period

Question   EOQ

Calculate the EOQ using the formula and the information in Paragraph 4.3.1.

Answer

$$\text{EOQ} = \sqrt{\frac{2 \times \$32 \times 25,000}{\$6.40}}$$

$$= \sqrt{250,000}$$

$$= 500 \text{ units}$$

4.4 Economic batch quantity (EBQ)

The **economic batch quantity** (EBQ) is a modification of the EOQ and is used when resupply is gradual instead of instantaneous.

$$\text{EBQ} = \sqrt{\frac{2C_0 D}{C_H(1 - D/R)}}$$

Typically, a manufacturing company might hold inventories of a finished item, which is produced in batches. Once the order for a new batch has been placed, and the production run has started, finished output might be used before the batch run has been completed.

4.4.1 Example: Economic batch quantity

If the daily demand for an item of inventory is ten units, and the storekeeper orders 100 units in a batch. The rate of production is 50 units a day.

(a) On the first day of the batch production run, the stores will run out of its previous inventories, and re-supply will begin. 50 units will be produced during the day, and ten units will be consumed. The closing inventory at the end of day 1 will be 50 – 10 = 40 units.

(b) On day 2, the final 50 units will be produced and a further ten units will be consumed. Closing inventory at the end of day 2 will be (40 + 50 – 10) = 80 units.

(c) In eight more days, inventories will fall to zero.

The minimum inventory in this example is zero, and the maximum inventory is 80 units. The maximum inventory is the quantity ordered (Q = 100) minus demand during the period of the batch production run which is Q × D/R, where

D   is the rate of demand
R   is the rate of production
Q   is the quantity ordered.

In our example, the maximum inventory is $(100 - \frac{10}{50} \times 100)$ = 100 – 20 = 80 units.

The maximum inventory level, given gradual re-supply, is thus $Q - \frac{QD}{R} = Q(1 - D/R)$.

4.4.2 Example: Economic batch quantity graph

The position in Paragraph 4.4.1 can be represented graphically as follows.

An amended EOQ (economic batch quantity, or EBQ) formula is required because average inventories are not Q/2 but Q(1 – D/R)/2.

4.4.3 EBQ Formula

The **EBQ** is $\sqrt{\dfrac{2C_oD}{C_H(1-\frac{D}{R})}}$ (given in exam)

where   R   = the production rate per time period (which must exceed the inventory usage)
         Q   = the amount produced in each batch
         D   = the usage per time period
         C_o = the set up cost per batch
         C_H = the holding cost per unit of inventory per time period

Question   Economic production run

A company is able to manufacture its own components for inventory at the rate of 4,000 units a week. Demand for the component is at the rate of 2,000 units a week. Set up costs for each production run are $50. The cost of holding one unit of inventory is $0.001 a week.

Required

Calculate the economic production run.

Answer

$Q = \sqrt{\dfrac{2 \times 50 \times 2,000}{0.001(1 - 2,000/4,000)}}$ = 20,000 units (giving an inventory cycle of 10 weeks)

4.5 Bulk discounts

The solution obtained from using the simple EOQ formula may need to be modified if bulk discounts (also called quantity discounts) are available. The following graph shows the effect that discounts granted for orders of certain sizes may have on total costs.

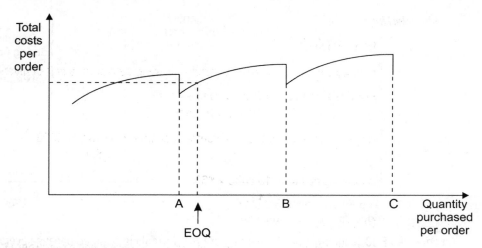

The graph above shows the following.

- Differing bulk discounts are given when the order quantity exceeds A, B and C
- The minimum total cost (ie when quantity B is ordered rather than the EOQ)

To decide mathematically whether it would be worthwhile taking a discount and ordering larger quantities, it is necessary to **minimise** the total of the following.

- Total material costs
- Ordering costs
- Inventory holding costs

The **total cost** will be **minimised** at one of the following.

- At the **pre-discount EOQ level**, so that a discount is not worthwhile
- At the **minimum order size** necessary to earn the discount

4.5.1 Example: Bulk discounts

The annual demand for an item of inventory is 45 units. The item costs $200 a unit to purchase, the holding cost for one unit for one year is 15% of the unit cost and ordering costs are $300 an order.

The supplier offers a 3% discount for orders of 60 units or more, and a discount of 5% for orders of 90 units or more.

Required

Calculate the cost-minimising order size.

Solution

(a) The EOQ ignoring discounts is $\sqrt{\dfrac{2 \times 300 \times 45}{15\% \text{ of } 200}} = 30$

	$
Purchases (no discount) 45 × $200	9,000
Holding costs (W1)	450
Ordering costs (W2)	450
Total annual costs	9,900

Workings

1 **Holding costs**

Holding costs = Average stock × holding cost for one unit of inventory per annum

Average inventory = Order quantity ÷ 2
= 30 ÷ 2 = 15 units

Holding cost for one unit of inventory per annum = 15% × $200
= $30

∴ Holding costs = 15 units × $30
= $450

2 **Ordering costs**

Ordering costs = Number of orders × ordering costs per order ($300)

Number of orders = Annual demand ÷ order quantity
= 45 ÷ 30
= 1.5 orders

∴ ordering costs = 1.5 orders × $300
= $450

scount of 3% and an order quantity of 60, units costs are as follows.

	$
s $9,000 × 97%	8,730
osts (W3)	873
costs (W4)	225
al costs	9,828

lding costs

ding costs = Average inventory × holding cost for one unit of inventory per annum

rage inventory = Order quantity ÷ 2
= 60 ÷ 2 = 30 units

ding cost for one unit of inventory per annum = 15% × 97% × $200 = $29.10

e. 97% = 100% − 3% discount

olding costs = 30 units × $29.10
= $873

ering costs

ering costs = Number of orders × ordering costs per order ($300)

ber of orders = Annual demand ÷ order quantity
= 45 ÷ 60
= 0.75 orders

rdering costs = 0.75 orders × $300
= $225

(c)   With a discount of 5% and an order quantity of 90, units costs are as follows.

	$
Purchases $9,000 × 95%	8,550.0
Holding costs (W5)	1,282.5
Ordering costs (W6)	150.0
Total annual costs	9,982.5

Workings

5   **Holding costs**

Holding costs   = Average inventory × holding cost for one unit of inventory per annum

Average inventory   = order quantity ÷ 2
                    = 90 ÷ 2
                    = 45 units

Holding cost for one unit of inventory per annum   = 15% × 95% × $200
                                                   = $28.50

Note. 95% = 100% − 5% discount

∴ Holding costs   = 45 units × $28.50
                    = $1,282.50

6   **Ordering costs**

Ordering costs   = Number of orders × ordering costs per order ($300)

Number of orders   = Annual demand ÷ order quantity
                   = 45 ÷ 90
                   = 0.5 orders

∴ ordering costs   = 0.5 orders × $300
                   = $150

The cheapest option is to order 60 units at a time.

Note that the value of C_H varied according to the size of the discount, because C_H was a percentage of the purchase cost. This means that **total holding costs are reduced because of a discount**. This could easily happen if, for example, most of C_H was the cost of insurance, based on the cost of inventory held.

Question

Discounts

A company uses an item of inventory as follows.

Purchase price:	$96 per unit
Annual demand:	4,000 units
Ordering cost:	$300
Annual holding cost:	10% of purchase price
Economic order quantity:	500 units

Required

Ascertain whether the company should order 1,000 units at a time in order to secure an 8% discount.

Answer

The total annual cost at the economic order quantity of 500 units is as follows.

	$
Purchases 4,000 × $96	384,000
Ordering costs $300 × (4,000/500)	2,400
Holding costs $96 × 10% × (500/2)	2,400
	388,800

The total annual cost at an order quantity of 1,000 units would be as follows.

	$
Purchases $384,000 × 92%	353,280
Ordering costs $300 × (4,000/1,000)	1,200
Holding costs $96 × 92% × 10% × (1,000/2)	4,416
	358,896

The company should order the item 1,000 units at a time, saving $(388,800 − 358,896) = $29,904 a year.

4.6 Other systems of stores control and reordering

4.6.1 Order cycling method

Under the order cycling method, quantities on hand of each stores item are reviewed periodically (every 1, 2 or 3 months). For low-cost items, a technique called the 90-60-30 day technique can be used, so that when inventories fall to 60 days' supply, a fresh order is placed for a 30 days' supply so as to boost inventories to 90 days' supply. For high-cost items, a more stringent stores control procedure is advisable so as to keep down the costs of inventory holding.

4.6.2 Two-bin system

The two-bin system of stores control (or visual method of control) is one whereby each stores item is kept in two storage bins. When the first bin is emptied, an order must be placed for re-supply; the second bin will contain sufficient quantities to last until the fresh delivery is received. This is a simple system which is not costly to operate but it is not based on any formal analysis of inventory usage and may result in the holding of too much or too little inventory.

4.6.3 Classification of materials

Materials items may be classified as expensive, inexpensive or in a middle-cost range. Because of the practical advantages of simplifying stores control procedures without incurring unnecessary high costs, it may be possible to segregate materials for selective stores control.

(a) Expensive and medium-cost materials are subject to careful stores control procedures to minimise cost.

(b) Inexpensive materials can be stored in large quantities because the cost savings from careful stores control do not justify the administrative effort required to implement the control.

This selective approach to stores control is sometimes called the **ABC method** whereby materials are classified A, B or C according to their expense-group A being the expensive, group B the medium-cost and group C the inexpensive materials.

4.6.4 Pareto (80/20) distribution

A similar selective approach to stores control is the **Pareto (80/20) distribution** which is based on the finding that in many stores, 80% of the value of stores is accounted for by only 20% of the stores items, and inventories of these more expensive items should be controlled more closely.

Chapter roundup

- **Inventory control** includes the functions of inventory ordering and purchasing, receiving goods into store, storing and issuing inventory and controlling the level of inventories.

- Every movement of material in a business should be documented using the following as appropriate: purchase requisition, purchase order, GRN, materials requisition note, materials transfer note and materials returned note.

- **Inventory counting** involves counting the physical inventory on hand at a certain date, and then checking this against the balance shown in the inventory records. The inventory count can be carried out on a **continuous** or **periodic** basis.

- **Perpetual inventory** refers to a inventory recording system whereby the records (bin cards and stores ledger accounts) are updated for each receipt and issue of inventory as it occurs.

- **Obsolete inventories** are those items which have become out of date and are no longer required. Obsolete items are written off and disposed of.

- **Inventory costs** include purchase costs, holding costs, ordering costs and costs of running out of inventory.

- **Inventory control levels** can be calculated in order to maintain inventories at the optimum level. The three critical control levels are reorder level, minimum level and maximum level.

- The **economic order quantity** (EOQ) is the order quantity which minimises inventory costs. The EOQ can be calculated using a table, graph or formula.

$$EOQ = \sqrt{\frac{2C_oD}{C_H}}$$

- The **economic batch quantity (EBQ)** is a modification of the EOQ and is used when resupply is gradual instead of instantaneous.

$$EBQ = \sqrt{\frac{2C_oD}{C_H(1-D/R)}}$$

Quick quiz

1   List six objectives of storekeeping.

•   ....

•   ....

•   ....

•   ....

•   ....

•   ....

2   Free inventory represents..

3   Free inventory is calculated as follows. (Delete as appropriate)

(a)	+ –	Materials in inventory	X
(b)	+ –	Materials in order	X
(c)	+ –	Materials requisitioned (not yet issued)	X
		Free inventory balance	X

4   How does periodic inventory counting differ from continuous inventory counting?

5   Match up the following.

Reorder level   Maximum usage × maximum lead time

Minimum level   Safety inventory + ½ reorder level

Maximum level   ?   Reorder level – (average usage × average lead time)

Average inventory   Reorder level + reorder quantity – (minimum usage × minimum lead time)

6    $EOQ = \sqrt{\dfrac{2C_oD}{C_H}}$

Where

(a) C_H = ...

(b) C_o = ...

(c)   D = ...

7   When is the economic batch quantity used?

Answers to quick quiz

1 • Speedy **issue** and **receipt** of materials
  • Full **identification** of all materials at all times
  • Correct **location** of all materials at all times
  • **Protection** of materials from damage and deterioration
  • Provision of **secure stores** to avoid pilferage, theft and fire
  • **Efficient** use of storage space
  • **Maintenance** of correct inventory levels
  • Keeping correct and up-to-date **records** of receipts, issues and inventory levels

2 Inventory that is readily available for future use.

3 (a) +
  (b) +
  (c) −

4 **Periodic inventory counting.** All inventory items physically counted and valued, usually annually.

  Continuous inventory counting. Counting and valuing selected items at different times of the year (at least once a year).

5

Reorder level	Maximum usage × maximum lead time
Minimum level	Safety inventory + ½ reorder level
Maximum level	Reorder level − (average usage × average lead time)
Average inventory	Reorder level + reorder quantity − (minimum usage × minimum lead time)

6 (a) Cost of holding one unit of inventory for one time period
  (b) Cost of ordering a consignment from a supplier
  (c) Demand during the time period

7 When resupply of a product is gradual instead of instantaneous.

Now try the questions below from the Exam Question Bank

Number	Level	Marks	Time
Q6	MCQ	n/a	n/a

7

Labour costs

Topic list	Syllabus reference
1 Measuring labour activity	D2 (a) (f)
2 Remuneration methods	D2 (d)
3 Recording labour costs	D2 (b)
4 Labour turnover	D2 (e)
5 Accounting for labour costs	D2 (c) (g)

Introduction

Just as management need to control inventories and operate an appropriate valuation policy in an attempt to control material costs, so too must they be aware of the most suitable **remuneration policy** for their organisation. We will be looking at a number of methods of remuneration and will consider the various types of **incentive scheme** that exist. We will also examine the procedures and documents required for the accurate **recording of labour costs**. **Labour turnover** will be studied too.

Study guide

		Intellectual level
D2	**Accounting for labour**	
(a)	Calculate, direct and indirect labour costs	1
(b)	Explain the methods used to relate input labour costs to work done	1
(c)	Prepare journal and ledger entries to record labour cost inputs and outputs	1
(d)	Describe different remuneration methods, time-based systems, piecework systems and individual and group incentive schemes	1
(e)	Calculate the level, and analyse the costs and causes of, labour turnover	1
(f)	Explain and calculate labour efficiency, capacity and production volume ratios	1
(g)	Interpret the entries in the labour account	1

Exam guide

You may get a question just on labour costs or on working out an employee's pay or you may have to deal with labour as a component of variable cost or overhead.

1 Measuring labour activity

Production and productivity are common methods of measuring labour activity.

1.1 Production and productivity

FAST FORWARD

Production is the quantity or volume of output produced. **Productivity** is a measure of the efficiency with which output has been produced. An increase in production without an increase in productivity will not reduce unit costs

1.2 Example: Production and productivity

Suppose that an employee is expected to produce three units in every hour that he works. The standard rate of productivity is three units per hour, and one unit is valued at $\frac{1}{3}$ of a standard hour of output. If, during one week, the employee makes 126 units in 40 hours of work the following comments can be made.

(a)   **Production** in the week is 126 units.

(b)   **Productivity** is a relative measure of the hours actually taken and the hours that should have been taken to make the output.

(i)	**Either**, 126 units should take	42 hours
	But did take	40 hours
	Productivity ratio = 42/40 × 100% =	105%
(ii)	**Or alternatively**, in 40 hours, he should make (× 3)	120 units
	But did make	126 units
	Productivity ratio = 126/120 × 100% =	105%

A productivity ratio greater than 100% indicates that actual efficiency is better than the expected or 'standard' level of efficiency.

Key term

> **Standard hour of production** is a concept used in standard costing, and means the number of units that can be produced by one worker working in the standard way at the standard rate for one hour.

1.3 Planning and controlling production and productivity

Management will wish to **plan** and **control** both production levels and labour productivity.

(a) **Production levels can be raised** as follows.

- Working overtime
- Hiring extra staff
- Sub-contracting some work to an outside firm
- Managing the work force so as to achieve more output.

(b) **Production levels can be reduced** as follows.

- Cancelling overtime
- Laying off staff

(c) **Productivity**, if improved, will enable a company to achieve its production targets in fewer hours of work, and therefore at a lower cost.

1.4 Productivity and its effect on cost

Improved productivity is an important means of reducing total unit costs. In order to make this point clear, a simple example will be used.

1.4.1 Example: Productivity and its effect on cost

Clooney Co has a production department in its factory consisting of a work team of just two men, Doug and George. Doug and George each work a 40 hour week and refuse to do any overtime. They are each paid $100 per week and production overheads of $400 per week are charged to their work.

(a) In week one, they produce 160 units of output between them. Productivity is measured in units of output per man hour.

Production	160 units
Productivity (80 man hours)	2 units per man hour
Total cost	$600 (labour plus overhead)
Cost per man hour	$7.50
Cost per unit	$3.75

(b) In week two, management pressure is exerted on Doug and George to increase output and they produce 200 units in normal time.

Production	200 units (up by 25%)
Productivity	2.5 units per man hour (up by 25%)
Total cost	$600
Cost per man hour	$7.50 (no change)
Cost per unit	$3.00 (a saving of 20% on the previous cost; 25% on the new cost)

(c) In week three, Doug and George agree to work a total of 20 hours of overtime for an additional $50 wages. Output is again 200 units and overhead charges are increased by $100.

Production	200 units (up 25% on week one)
Productivity (100 man hours)	2 units per hour (no change on week one)
Total cost ($600 + $50 + $100)	$750
Cost per unit	$3.75

(d)   Conclusions

(i)   An increase in production without an increase in productivity will not reduce unit costs (week one compared with week three).

(ii)   An **increase in productivity will reduce unit costs** (week one compared with week two).

1.4.2 Automation

Labour cost control is largely concerned with **productivity**. Rising wage rates have increased automation, which in turn has improved productivity and reduced costs.

Where **automation** is introduced, productivity is often, but misleadingly, measured in terms of **output per man-hour**.

1.4.3 Example: Automation

Suppose, for example, that a work-team of six men (240 hours per week) is replaced by one machine (40 hours per week) and a team of four men (160 hours per week), and as a result output is increased from 1,200 units per week to 1,600 units.

	Production	Man hours	Productivity
Before the machine	1,200 units	240	5 units per man hour
After the machine	1,600 units	160	10 units per man hour

Labour productivity has doubled because of the machine, and employees would probably expect extra pay for this success. For control purposes, however, it is likely that a new measure of productivity is required, **output per machine hour**, which may then be measured against a standard output for performance reporting.

1.5 Efficiency, capacity and production volume ratios

Other measures of labour activity include the following.

- Production volume ratio, or activity ratio
- Efficiency ratio (or productivity ratio)
- Capacity ratio

$$\text{Efficiency ratio} \times \text{Capacity ratio} = \text{Production volume ratio}$$

$$\frac{\text{Expected hours to make output}}{\text{Actual hours taken}} \times \frac{\text{Actual hours worked}}{\text{Hours budgeted}} = \frac{\text{Output measured in expected or standard hours}}{\text{Hours budgeted}}$$

These ratios are usually expressed as percentages.

1.5.1 Example: Labour activity ratios

Rush and Fluster Co budgets to make 25,000 standard units of output (in four hours each) during a budget period of 100,000 hours.

Actual output during the period was 27,000 units which took 120,000 hours to make.

Required

Calculate the efficiency, capacity and production volume ratios.

Solution

(a) Efficiency ratio $\dfrac{(27,000 \times 4) \text{ hours}}{120,000} \times 100\% = 90\%$

(b) Capacity ratio $\dfrac{120,000 \text{ hours}}{100,000 \text{ hours}} \times 100\% = 120\%$

(c) Production volume ratio $\dfrac{(27,000 \times 4) \text{ hours}}{100,000} \times 100\% = 108\%$

(d) The production volume ratio of 108% (more output than budgeted) is explained by the 120% capacity working, offset to a certain extent by the poor efficiency (90% × 120% = 108%).

Where efficiency standards are associated with remuneration schemes they generally allow 'normal time' (that is, time required by the average person to do the work under normal conditions) plus an allowance for rest periods and possible delays. There should therefore be a readily achievable standard of efficiency (otherwise any remuneration scheme will fail to motivate employees), but without being so lax that it makes no difference to the rate at which work is done.

2 Remuneration methods

FAST FORWARD

> There are three basic groups of **remuneration** method: **time work**; **piecework schemes**; **bonus/incentive schemes**.

Labour remuneration methods have an effect on the following.

- The cost of finished products and services.
- The morale and efficiency of employees.

2.1 Time work

Formula to earn

> The most common form of **time work** is a **day-rate system** in which wages are calculated by the following formula.
>
> Wages = Hours worked × rate of pay per hour

2.1.1 Overtime premiums

If an employee works for more hours than the basic daily requirement he may be entitled to an **overtime payment**. Hours of overtime are usually paid at a **premium rate**. For instance, if the basic day-rate is $4 per hour and overtime is paid at time-and-a-quarter, eight hours of overtime would be paid the following amount.

	$
Basic pay (8 × $4)	32
Overtime premium (8 × $1)	8
Total (8 × $5)	40

The **overtime premium** is the extra rate per hour which is paid, not the whole of the payment for the overtime hours.

If employees work unsocial hours, for instance overnight, they may be entitled to a **shift premium**. The extra amount paid per hour, above the basic hourly rate, is the **shift premium**.

2.1.2 Summary of day-rate systems

(a)   They are easy to understand.

(b)   They do not lead to very complex negotiations when they are being revised.

(c)   They are most appropriate when the quality of output is more important than the quantity, or where there is no basis for payment by performance.

(d)   There is no incentive for employees who are paid on a day-rate basis to improve their performance.

2.2 Piecework schemes

Formula to learn

In a **piecework scheme**, wages are calculated by the following formula.

Wages = Units produced × Rate of pay per unit

Suppose for example, an employee is paid $1 for each unit produced and works a 40 hour week. Production overhead is added at the rate of $2 per direct labour hour.

Weekly production	Pay (40 hours)	Overhead	Conversion cost	Conversion cost per unit
Units	$	$	$	$
40	40	80	120	3.00
50	50	80	130	2.60
60	60	80	140	2.33
70	70	80	150	2.14

As his output increases, his wage increases and at the same time unit costs of output are reduced.

It is normal for pieceworkers to be offered a **guaranteed minimum wage**, so that they do not suffer loss of earnings when production is low through no fault of their own.

If an employee makes several different types of product, it may not be possible to add up the units for payment purposes. Instead, a **standard time allowance** is given for each unit to arrive at a total of piecework hours for payment.

Question

Weekly pay

Penny Pincher is paid 50c for each towel she weaves, but she is guaranteed a minimum wage of $60 for a 40 hour week. In a series of four weeks, she makes 100, 120, 140 and 160 towels.

Required

Calculate her pay each week, and the conversion cost per towel if production overhead is added at the rate of $2.50 per direct labour hour.

Answer

Week	Output		Pay	Production overhead	Conversion cost	Unit conversion cost
	Units		$	$	$	$
1	100	(minimum)	60	100	160	1.60
2	120		60	100	160	1.33
3	140		70	100	170	1.21
4	160		80	100	180	1.13

There is no incentive to Penny Pincher to produce more output unless she can exceed 120 units in a week. The guaranteed minimum wage in this case is too high to provide an incentive.

2.2.1 Example: Piecework

An employee is paid $5 per piecework hour produced. In a 35 hour week he produces the following output.

	Piecework time allowed per unit
3 units of product A	2.5 hours
5 units of product B	8.0 hours

Required

Calculate the employee's pay for the week.

Solution

Piecework hours produced are as follows.

Product A	3 × 2.5 hours	7.5 hours
Product B	5 × 8 hours	40.0 hours
Total piecework hours		47.5 hours

Therefore employee's pay = 47.5 × $5 = $237.50 for the week.

2.2.2 Differential piecework scheme

Differential piecework schemes offer an incentive to employees to increase their output by paying higher rates for increased levels of production. For example:

up to 80 units per week, rate of pay per unit	=	$1.00
80 to 90 units per week, rate of pay per unit	=	$1.20
above 90 units per week, rate of pay per unit	=	$1.30

Employers should obviously be careful to make it clear whether they intend to pay the increased rate on all units produced, or on the extra output only.

2.2.3 Summary of piecework schemes

They enjoy fluctuating popularity.

occasionally used by employers as a means of increasing pay levels.

drive employees to work too hard to earn a satisfactory wage.

ensure that quality doesn't fall as production increases.

es

oduced to compensate workers paid under a time-based system for working more efficiently. Various types of incentive and bonus courage greater productivity. The characteristics of such schemes are as follows.

(a) Employees are paid more for their efficiency.

(b) The profits arising from productivity improvements are shared between employer and employee.

(c) Morale of employees is likely to improve since they are seen to receive extra reward for extra effort.

A bonus scheme must satisfy certain conditions to operate successfully.

(a) Its **objectives** should be **clearly stated** and **attainable** by the employees.

(b) The **rules** and conditions of the scheme should be **easy to understand**.

(c) It must **win** the full **acceptance** of everyone concerned.

(d) It should be seen to be **fair to employees and employers**..

(e) The bonus should ideally be **paid soon after the extra effort has been made** by the employees.

(f) **Allowances** should be made for external factors outside the employees' control which reduce their productivity (machine breakdowns, material shortages).

(g) Only those employees who make the extra effort should be rewarded.

(h) The scheme must be **properly communicated** to employees.

We shall be looking at the following types of incentive schemes in detail.

- High day rate system
- Individual bonus schemes
- Group bonus schemes
- Profit sharing schemes
- Incentive schemes involving shares
- Value added incentive schemes

Some organisations employ a variety of incentive schemes. A scheme for a production labour force may not necessarily be appropriate for white-collar workers. An organisation's incentive schemes may be regularly reviewed, and altered as circumstances dictate.

2.4 High day-rate system

Key term

> A **high day-rate system** is a system where employees are paid a high hourly wage rate in the expectation that they will work more efficiently than similar employees on a lower hourly rate in a different company.

2.4.1 Example: High day-rate system

For example if an employee would make 100 units in a 40 hour week if he were paid $2 per hour, but 120 units if he were paid $2.50 per hour, and if production overhead is added to cost at the rate of $2 per direct labour hour, costs per unit of output would be as follows.

(a) Costs per unit of output on the low day-rate scheme would be:

$$\frac{(40 \times \$4)}{100} = \$1.60 \text{ per unit}$$

(b) Costs per unit of output on the high day-rate scheme would be:

$$\frac{(40 \times \$4.50)}{120} = \$1.50 \text{ per unit}$$

(c) Note that in this example the labour cost per unit is lower in the first scheme (80c) than in the second (83.3c), but the unit conversion cost (labour plus production overhead) is higher because overhead costs per unit are higher at 80c than with the high day-rate scheme (66.7c).

(d) In this example, the high day-rate scheme would reward both employer (a lower unit cost by 10c) and employee (an extra 50c earned per hour).

2.4.2 Advantages and disadvantages of high day rate schemes

There are two **advantages** of a high day-rate scheme over other incentive schemes.

(a) It is **simple** to calculate and **easy** to understand.

(b) It **guarantees** the employee a consistently **high wage**.

The **disadvantages** of such schemes are as follows.

(a) **Employees cannot earn more than the fixed hourly rate for their extra effort**. In the previous example, if the employee makes 180 units instead of 120 units in a 40 hour week on a high day-rate pay scheme, the cost per unit would fall to $1 but his wage would be the same – 40 hours at $4.50. All the savings would go to benefit the company and none would go to the employee.

(b) **There is no guarantee that the scheme will work consistently**. The high wages may become the accepted level of pay for normal working, and supervision may be necessary to ensure that a high level of productivity is maintained. Unit costs would rise.

(c) **Employees may prefer to work at a normal rate of output**, even if this entails accepting the lower wage paid by comparable employers.

2.5 Individual bonus schemes

> An **individual bonus scheme** is a remuneration scheme whereby **individual** employees qualify for a bonus on top of their basic wage, with each person's bonus being calculated separately.

(a) The bonus is **unique** to the individual. It is not a share of a group bonus.

(b) The individual can earn a bonus by working at an **above-target** standard of efficiency.

(c) The individual earns a **bigger bonus the greater his efficiency**, although the bonus scheme might incorporate quality safeguards, to prevent individuals from sacrificing quality standards for the sake of speed and more pay.

To be successful, however, an **individual bonus scheme** must take account of the following factors.

(a) Each individual should be rewarded for the **work done by that individual**. This means that each person's output and time must be measured separately. Each person must therefore work without the assistance of anyone else.

(b) Work should be **fairly routine**, so that standard times can be set for jobs.

(c) The bonus should be **paid soon after the work is done**, to provide the individual with the incentive to try harder.

2.6 Group bonus schemes

> A **group bonus scheme** is an incentive plan which is related to the output performance of an entire group of workers, a department, or even the whole factory.

Where individual effort cannot be measured, and employees work as a team, an individual incentive scheme is impracticable but a **group bonus scheme** would be feasible.

The other **advantages** of group bonus schemes are as follows.

(a)   They are **easier to administer** because they reduce the clerical effort required to measure output and calculate individual bonuses.

(b)   They **increase co-operation** between fellow workers.

(c)   They have been found to **reduce** accidents, spoilage, waste and absenteeism.

Serious **disadvantages** would occur in the following circumstances.

(a)   The employee groups demand **low efficiency standards** as a condition of accepting the scheme.

(b)   Individual employees are browbeaten by their fellow workers for working too slowly.

2.7 Profit-sharing schemes

Key term

> A **profit sharing scheme** is a scheme in which employees receive a certain proportion of their company's year-end profits (the size of their bonus being related to their position in the company and the length of their employment to date).

The advantage of these schemes is that the company will only pay what it can afford out of actual profits and the bonus can be paid also to non-production personnel.

The disadvantages of profit sharing are as follows.

(a)   Employees must **wait until the year end** for a bonus. The company is therefore expecting a long-term commitment to greater efforts and productivity from its workers without the incentive of immediate reward.

(b)   **Factors** affecting profit may be **outside the control** of employees, in spite of their greater efforts.

(c)   **Too many employees** are involved in a single scheme for the scheme to have a great motivating effect on individuals.

2.7.1 Incentive schemes involving shares

It is becoming increasingly common for companies to use their shares, or the right to acquire them, as a form of incentive.

Key terms

> A **share option scheme** is a scheme which gives its members the right to buy shares in the company for which they work at a set date in the future and at a price usually determined when the scheme is set up.
>
> An **employee share ownership plan** is a scheme which acquires shares on behalf of a number of employees, and it must distribute these shares within a certain number of years of acquisition.

Some governments have encouraged companies to set up schemes of this nature in the hope that workers will feel they have a stake in the company which employs them. The **disadvantages** of these schemes are as follows.

(a)   The benefits are not certain, as the market value of shares at a future date cannot realistically be predicted in advance.

(b)   The benefits are not immediate, as a scheme must be in existence for a number of years before members can exercise their rights.

2.7.2 Value added incentive schemes

Value added is an alternative to profit as a business performance measure and it can be used as the basis of an incentive scheme. It is calculated as follows.

> **Value added** = sales − cost of bought-in materials and services

The advantage of value added over profit as the basis for an incentive scheme is that it excludes any bought-in costs, and is affected only by costs incurred internally, such as labour.

A basic value added figure would be agreed as the target for a business, and some of any excess value added earned would be paid out as a bonus. For example, it could be agreed that value added should be, say, treble the payroll costs and a proportion of any excess earned, say one third, would be paid as bonus.

Payroll costs for month	$40,000
Therefore, value added target (× 3)	$120,000
Value added achieved	$150,000
Therefore, excess value added	$30,000
Employee share to be paid as bonus	$10,000

2.7.3 Example: incentive schemes

Swetton Tyres Co manufactures a single product. Its work force consists of 10 employees, who work a 36-hour week exclusive of lunch and tea breaks. The standard time required to make one unit of the product is two hours, but the current efficiency (or productivity) ratio being achieved is 80%. No overtime is worked, and the work force is paid $4 per attendance hour.

Because of agreements with the work force about work procedures, there is some unavoidable idle time due to bottlenecks in production, and about four hours per week per person are lost in this way.

The company can sell all the output it manufactures, and makes a 'cash profit' of $20 per unit sold, deducting currently achievable costs of production but *before* deducting labour costs.

An incentive scheme is proposed whereby the work force would be paid $5 per hour in exchange for agreeing to new work procedures that would reduce idle time per employee per week to two hours and also raise the efficiency ratio to 90%.

Required

Evaluate the incentive scheme from the point of view of profitability.

Solution

The current situation

Hours in attendance	10 × 36	= 360 hours
Hours spent working	10 × 32	= 320 hours
Units produced, at 80% efficiency	$\frac{320}{2} \times \frac{80}{100}$	= 128 units

	$
Cash profits before deducting labour costs (128 × $20)	2,560
Less labour costs ($4 × 360 hours)	1,440
Net profit	1,120

The incentive scheme

Hours spent working	10 × 34	= 340 hours
Units produced, at 90% efficiency	$\frac{340}{2} \times \frac{90}{100}$	= 153 units

	$
Cash profits before deducting labour costs (153 × $20)	3,060
Less labour costs ($5 × 360)	1,800
Net profit	1,260

In spite of a 25% increase in labour costs, profits would rise by $140 per week. The company and the workforce would both benefit provided, of course, that management can hold the work force to their promise of work reorganisation and improved productivity.

Question

Labour cost

The following data relate to work at a certain factory.

Normal working day	8 hours
Basic rate of pay per hour	$6
Standard time allowed to produce 1 unit	2 minutes
Premium bonus	75% of time saved at basic rate

What will be the labour cost in a day when 340 units are made?

A $48	B $51	C $63	D $68

Answer

Standard time for 340 units (× 2 minutes)	680 minutes
Actual time (8 hours per day)	480 minutes
Time saved	200 minutes

	$
Bonus = 75% × 200 minutes × $6 per hour	15
Basic pay = 8 hours × $6	48
Total labour cost	63

Therefore the correct answer is C.

Using basic MCQ technique you can eliminate option A because this is simply the basic pay without consideration of any bonus. You can also eliminate option D, which is based on the standard time allowance without considering the basic pay for the eight-hour day. Hopefully your were not forced to guess, but had you been you would have had a 50% chance of selecting the correct answer (B or C) instead of a 25% chance because you were able to eliminate two of the options straightaway.

3 Recording labour costs

FAST FORWARD

Labour attendance time is recorded on, for example, an attendance record or clock card. Job time may be recorded on daily time sheets, weekly time sheets or job cards depending on the circumstances. The manual recording of times on time sheets or job cards is, however, liable to error or even deliberate deception and may be unreliable. The labour cost of pieceworkers is recorded on a piecework ticket/operation card.

BPP
LEARNING MEDIA

3.1 Organisation for controlling and measuring labour costs

Several departments and management groups are involved in the collection, recording and costing of labour. These include the following.

- Personnel
- Production planning
- Timekeeping
- Wages
- Cost accounting

3.2 Personnel department

The **personnel department** is responsible for the following:

- Engagement, transfer and discharge of employees.
- Classification and method of remuneration.

The department is headed by a **professional personnel officer** trained in personnel management, labour laws, company personnel policy and industry conditions who should have an understanding of the needs and problems of the employees.

When a person is engaged a **personnel record card** should be prepared showing full personal particulars, previous employment, medical category and wage rate. Other details to be included are social security number, address, telephone number, transfers, promotions, changes in wage rates, sickness and accidents and, when an employee leaves, the reason for leaving.

Personnel departments sometimes **maintain records of overtime and shift working**. Overtime has to be sanctioned by the works manager or personnel office who advise the time-keepers who control the time booked.

The personnel department is responsible for issuing **reports to management** on normal and overtime hours worked, absenteeism and sickness, lateness, labour turnover and disciplinary action.

3.3 Production planning department

This department is responsible for the following.

- Scheduling work
- Issuing job orders to production departments
- Chasing up jobs when they run late

3.4 Timekeeping department

The **timekeeping department** is responsible for recording the attendance time and job time of the following.

- The time spent in the factory by each worker
- The time spent by each worker on each job

Such timekeeping provides basic data for statutory records, payroll preparation, labour costs of an operation or overhead distribution (where based on wages or labour hours) and statistical analysis of labour records for determining productivity and control of labour costs.

3.5 Attendance time

The bare minimum record of employees' time is a simple **attendance record** showing days absent because of holiday, sickness or other reason. A typical record of attendance is shown as follows.

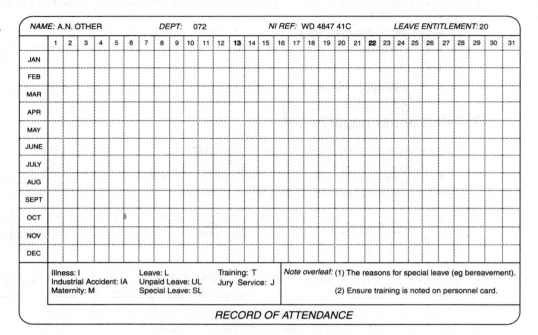

RECORD OF ATTENDANCE

It is also necessary to have a record of the following.

- Time of arrival
- Time of breaks
- Time of departure

These may be recorded as follows.

- In a signing-in book
- By using a time recording clock which stamps the time on a clock card
- By using swipe cards (which make a computer record)

An example of a clock card is shown as follows.

3.6 Job time

Continuous production. Where **routine, repetitive** work is carried out it might not be practical to record the precise details. For example if a worker stands at a conveyor belt for seven hours his work can be measured by keeping a note of the number of units that pass through his part of the process during that time.

Job costing. When the work is not of a repetitive nature the records required might be one or several of the following.

(a) **Daily time sheets**. A time sheet is filled in by the employee as a record of how their time has been spent. The total time on the time sheet should correspond with time shown on the attendance record.

(b) **Weekly time sheets**. These are similar to daily time sheets but are passed to the cost office at the end of the week. An example of a weekly timesheet is shown below.

Time Sheet No. _ _ _ _ _ _ _ _ _ _ _ _ _ _ _							
Employee Name _ _ _ _ _ _ _ _ _ Clock Code _ _ _ _ _ _ _ _ _ Dept _ _ _ _ _ _ _							
Date _ _ _ _ _ _ _ _ _ _ _ _ _ _ _ _ _ _ . Week No. _ _ _ _ _ _ _ _ _ _ _ _ _							
Job No.	Start Time	Finish Time	Qty	Checker	Hrs	Rate	Extension

(c) **Job cards**. Cards are prepared for each job or batch. When an employee works on a job he or she records on the job card the time spent on that job. Job cards are therefore likely to contain entries relating to numerous employees. On completion of the job it will contain a full record of the times and quantities involved in the job or batch. A typical job card is shown as follows.

JOB CARD			
Department _ _ _ _ _ _ _ _ _ _ _ _ _ _ _ _ _ _ _ Job no _ _ _ _ _ _ _ _ _ _ _ _ _ _ _ _ _ _ _ .			
Date _ . Operation no _ _ _ _ _ _ _ _ _ _ _ _ _ _ _ _			
Time allowance _ _ _ _ _ _ _ _ _ _ _ _ _ _ _ _ Time started _ _ _ _ _ _ _ _ _ _ _ _ _ _ _ _ _ _			
	Time finished _ _ _ _ _ _ _ _ _ _ _ _ _ _ _ _ _ _		
	Hours on the job _ _ _ _ _ _ _ _ _ _ _ _ _ _ _ _ _ .		
Description of job	Hours	Rate	Cost
Employee no _ _ _ _ _ _ _ _ _ _ _ _ _ _ _ _ _ _ Certified by _ _ _ _ _ _ _ _ _ _ _ _ _ _ _ _ _ _ _			
Signature _ _ _ _ _ _ _ _ _ _ _ _ _ _ _ _ _ _ _			

A job card will be given to the employee, showing the work to be done and the expected time it should take. The employee will record the time started and time finished for each job. Breaks for tea and lunch may be noted on the card, as standard times, by the production planning department. The hours actually taken and the cost of those hours will be calculated by the accounting department.

Piecework. The wages of pieceworkers and the labour cost of work done by them is determined from what is known as a **piecework ticket** or an **operation card**. The card records the total number of items (or 'pieces') produced and the number of rejects. Payment is only made for 'good' production.

OPERATION CARD				
Operator's Name _ _ _ _ _ _ _ _ _ _ _ _ _ _ _ _ _ _ _		Total Batch Quantity _ _ _ _ _ _ _ _ _ _ _ _ _		
Clock No _		Start Time _ _ _ _ _ _ _ _ _ _ _ _ _ _ _ _ _ _ _		
Pay week No _ _ _ _ _ _ _ _ _ . Date _ _ _ _ _ _ _ _ _		Stop Time _		
Part No _		Works Order No _ _ _ _ _ _ _ _ _ _ _ _ _ _ _ _		
Operation _		Special Instructions _ _ _ _ _ _ _ _ _ _ _ _ _		
Quantity Produced	No Rejected	Good Production	Rate	$
Inspector _		Operative _		
Foreman _		Date _		
PRODUCTION CANNOT BE CLAIMED WITHOUT A PROPERLY SIGNED CARD				

Note that the attendance record of a pieceworker is required for calculations of holidays, sick pay and so on.

Other types of work. Casual workers are paid from job cards or time sheets. Time sheets are also used where outworkers are concerned.

Office work can be measured in a similar way, provided that the work can be divided into distinct jobs. Firms of accountants and advertising agencies, for example, book their staff time to individual clients and so make use of time sheets for salaried staff.

3.7 Salaried labour

Even though salaried staff are paid a flat rate monthly, they may be required to prepare timesheets. The reasons are as follows.

(a)   Timesheets provide management with information (eg product costs).

(b)   Timesheet information may provide a basis for billing for services provided (eg service firms where clients are billed based on the number of hours work done).

(c)   Timesheets are used to record hours spent and so support claims for overtime payments by salaried staff.

An example of a timesheet (as used in the service sector) is shown as follows.

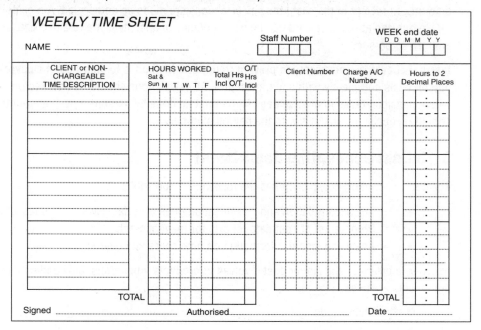

3.8 Idle time

FAST FORWARD

Idle time has a cost because employees will still be paid their basic wage or salary for these unproductive hours and so there should be a record of idle time.

Idle time occurs when employees cannot get on with their work, through no fault of their own. Examples are as follows.

- Machine breakdowns
- Shortage of work

A record of idle time may simply comprise an entry on time sheets coded to 'idle time' generally, or separate idle time cards may be prepared. A supervisor might enter the time of a stoppage, its cause, its duration and the employees made idle on an idle time record card. Each stoppage should have a reference number which can be entered on time sheets or job cards.

3.9 Wages department

Responsibilities of the payroll department include the following.

- Preparation of the payroll and payment of wages.
- Maintenance of employee records.
- Summarising wages cost for each cost centre.
- Summarising the hours worked for each cost centre.
- Summarising other payroll information eg bonus payment, pensions etc.
- Providing an internal check for the preparation and payout of wages.

Attendance cards are the basis for payroll preparation. For **time workers**, the gross wage is the product of time attended and rate of pay. To this is added any overtime premium or bonus. For **piece workers**, gross wages are normally obtained by the product of the number of good units produced and the unit rate, with any premiums, bonuses and allowances for incomplete jobs added.

After calculation of net pay, a pay slip is prepared showing all details of earnings and deductions. The wage envelope or the attendance card may be used for this purpose.

When the payroll is complete, a coin and note analysis is made and a cheque drawn to cover the total amount. On receipt of the cash, the pay envelopes are made up and sealed. A receipt is usually obtained on payout (the attendance card can be used). Wages of absentees are retained until claimed by an authorised person.

Internal checks are necessary to prevent fraud. One method is to distribute the payroll work so that no person deals completely with any transaction. All calculations should be checked on an adding machine where possible. Makeup of envelopes should not be done by persons who prepare the payroll. The cashier should reconcile his analysis with the payroll summary.

3.10 Cost accounting department

The cost accounting department has the following responsibilities.

- The accumulation and classification of all cost data (which includes labour costs).
- Preparation of cost data reports for management.
- Analysing labour information on time cards and payroll.

In order to establish the labour cost involved in products, operations, jobs and cost centres, the following documents are used.

- Clock cards
- Job cards
- Idle time cards
- Payroll

Analyses of labour costs are used for the following.

(a) Charging wages directly attributable to production to the appropriate job or operation.

(b) Charging wages which are not directly attributable to production as follows.

   (i) Idle time of production workers is charged to indirect costs as part of the overheads.

   (ii) Wages costs of supervisors, or store assistants are charged to the overhead costs of the relevant department.

(c) Producing idle time reports which show a summary of the hours lost through idle time, and the cause of the idle time. Idle time may be analysed as follows.

   - Controllable eg lack of materials.
   - Uncontrollable eg power failure.

3.11 Idle time ratio

Formula to learn

$$\text{Idle time ratio} = \frac{\text{Idle hours}}{\text{Total hours}} \times 100\%$$

The idle time ratio is useful because it shows the proportion of available hours which were lost as a result of idle time.

Exam focus point

Make sure you understand the distinction between direct and indirect labour costs and the classification of overtime premium.

4 Labour turnover

Labour turnover is the rate at which employees leave a company and this rate should be kept as low as possible. The cost of labour turnover can be divided into **preventative** and **replacement costs**.

4.1 The reasons for labour turnover

Some employees will leave their job and go to work for another company or organisation. Sometimes the reasons are unavoidable.

- Illness or accidents
- A family move away from the locality
- Marriage, pregnancy or difficulties with child care provision
- Retirement or death

Other causes of labour turnover are to some extent controllable.

- Paying a lower wage rate than is available elsewhere.
- Requiring employees to work in unsafe or highly stressful conditions.
- Requiring employees to work uncongenial hours.
- Poor relationships between management and staff.
- Lack of opportunity for career enhancement.
- Requiring employees to work in inaccessible places (eg no public transport).
- Discharging employees for misconduct, bad timekeeping or unsuitability.

4.2 Measuring labour turnover

Key term

Labour turnover is a measure of the number of employees leaving/being recruited in a period of time expressed as a percentage of the total labour force.

Formula to learn

$$\text{Labour turnover rate} = \frac{\text{Replacements}}{\text{Average number of employees in period}} \times 100\%$$

4.3 Example : Labour turnover rate

Revolving Doors Inc had a staff of 2,000 at the beginning of 20X1 and, owing to a series of redundancies caused by the recession, 1,000 at the end of the year. Voluntary redundancy was taken by 1,500 staff at the end of June, 500 more than the company had anticipated, and these excess redundancies were immediately replaced by new joiners.

The labour turnover rate is calculated as follows.

$$\text{Rate} = \frac{500}{(2,000 + 1,000) \div 2} \times 100\% = 33\%$$

4.4 The costs of labour turnover

The costs of labour turnover can be large and management should attempt to keep labour turnover as low as possible so as to minimise these costs. The **cost of labour turnover** may be divided into the following.

- Preventative costs
- Replacement costs

4.4.1 Replacement costs

These are the costs incurred as a result of hiring new employees. and they include the following.

- Cost of selection and placement
- Inefficiency of new labour; productivity will be lower
- Costs of training
- Loss of output due to delay in new labour becoming available
- Increased wastage and spoilage due to lack of expertise among new staff
- The possibility of more frequent accidents at work
- Cost of tool and machine breakages

4.4.2 Preventative costs

These are costs incurred in order to prevent employees leaving and they include the following.

- Cost of personnel administration incurred in maintaining good relationships
- Cost of medical services including check-ups, nursing staff and so on
- Cost of welfare services, including sports facilities and canteen meals
- Pension schemes providing security to employees

4.5 The prevention of high labour turnover

Labour turnover will be reduced by the following actions.

- Paying satisfactory wages
- Offering satisfactory hours and conditions of work
- Creating a good informal relationship between members of the workforce
- Offering good training schemes and a well-understood career or promotion ladder
- Improving the content of jobs to create job satisfaction
- Proper planning so as to avoid redundancies
- Investigating the cause of an apparently high labour turnover

5 Accounting for labour costs

We will use an example to briefly review the principal bookkeeping entries for wages.

5.1 Example: The wages control account

The following details were extracted from a weekly payroll for 750 employees at a factory.

Analysis of gross pay

	Direct workers $	Indirect workers $	Total $
Ordinary time	36,000	22,000	58,000
Overtime: basic wage	8,700	5,430	14,130
premium	4,350	2,715	7,065
Shift allowance	3,465	1,830	5,295
Sick pay	950	500	1,450
Idle time	3,200	–	3,200
	56,665	32,475	89,140
Net wages paid to employees	$45,605	$24,220	$69,825

Required

Prepare the wages control account for the week.

Solution

(a)   **The wages control account** acts as a sort of 'collecting place' for net wages paid and deductions made from gross pay. The gross pay is then analysed between direct and indirect wages.

(b)   The first step is to determine which wage costs are **direct** and which are **indirect**. The direct wages will be debited to the work in progress account and the indirect wages will be debited to the production overhead account.

(c)   There are in fact only two items of direct wages cost in this example, the ordinary time ($36,000) and the basic overtime wage ($8,700) paid to direct workers. All other payments (including the overtime premium) are indirect wages.

(d)   The net wages paid are debited to the control account, and the balance then represents the deductions which have been made for tax, social insurance, and so on.

WAGES CONTROL ACCOUNT

	$		$
Bank: net wages paid	69,825	Work in progress – direct labour	44,700
Deductions control accounts*		Production overhead control:	
($89,140 – $69,825)	19,315	Indirect labour	27,430
		Overtime premium	7,065
		Shift allowance	5,295
		Sick pay	1,450
		Idle time	3,200
	89,140		89,140

* In practice there would be a separate deductions control account for each type of deduction made (for example, tax and social insurance).

5.2 Direct and indirect labour costs

We had a brief look at direct and indirect labour costs in Chapter 3. Have a go at the following questions to remind yourself about the classification of labour costs.

Question	Direct and indirect costs

A direct labour employee's wage in week 5 consists of the following.

		$
(a)	Basic pay for normal hours worked, 36 hours at $4 per hour =	144
(b)	Pay at the basic rate for overtime, 6 hours at $4 per hour =	24
(c)	Overtime shift premium, with overtime paid at time-and-a-quarter ¼ × 6 hours × $4 per hour =	6
(d)	A bonus payment under a group bonus (or 'incentive') scheme – bonus for the month =	30
	Total gross wages in week 5 for 42 hours of work	204

Required

Establish which costs are direct costs and which are indirect costs.

Answer

Items (a) and (b) are direct labour costs of the items produced in the 42 hours worked in week 5.

Overtime premium, item (c), is usually regarded as an overhead expense, because it is 'unfair' to charge the items produced in overtime hours with the premium. Why should an item made in overtime be more costly just because, by chance, it was made after the employee normally clocks off for the day?

Group bonus scheme payments, item (d), are usually overhead costs, because they cannot normally be traced directly to individual products or jobs.

In this example, the direct labour employee costs were $168 in direct costs and $36 in indirect costs.

Question
Overtime

Jaffa plc employs two types of labour: skilled workers, considered to be direct workers, and semi-skilled workers considered to be indirect workers. Skilled workers are paid $10 per hour and semi-skilled $5 per hour.

The skilled workers have worked 20 hours overtime this week, 12 hours on specific orders and 8 hours on general overtime. Overtime is paid at a rate of time and a quarter.

The semi-skilled workers have worked 30 hours overtime, 20 hours for a specific order at a customer's request and the rest for general purposes. Overtime again is paid at time and a quarter.

What would be the total overtime pay considered to be a direct cost for this week?

A $275
B $355
C $375
D $437.50

Answer

		Direct cost $	Indirect cost $
Skilled workers			
Specific overtime	(12 hours × $10 × 1.25)	150	
General overtime	(8 hours × $10 × 1)	80	
	(8 hours × $10 × 0.25)		20
Semi-skilled workers			
Specific overtime	(20 hours × $5 × 1.25)	125	
General overtime	(10 hours × $5 × 1.25)		62.50
		355	82.50

The correct answer is therefore B.

If you selected option A, you forgot to include the direct cost of the general overtime of $80 for the skilled workers.

If you selected option C, you included the overtime premium for skilled workers' general overtime of $20.

If you selected option D, you calculated the total of direct cost + indirect cost instead of the direct cost.

xam focus
oint

The study guide for this paper states that candidates should be able to explain the difference between and calculate direct and indirect labour costs.

Chapter roundup

- **Production** is the quantity or volume of output produced. **Productivity** is a measure of the efficiency with which output has been produced. An increase in production without an increase in productivity will not reduce unit costs.

- There are three basic groups of **remuneration** method: **time work**; **piecework schemes**; and **bonus/incentive** schemes.

- Labour attendance time is recorded on, for example, an attendance record or clock card. Job time may be recorded on daily time sheets, weekly time sheets or job cards depending on the circumstances. The manual recording of times on time sheets or job cards, is however, liable to error or even deliberate deception and may be unreliable. The labour cost of pieceworkers is recorded on a piecework ticket/operation card.

- **Idle time** has a cost because employees will still be paid their basic wage or salary for these unproductive hours and so there should be a record of idle time.

- **Labour turnover** is the rate at which employees leave a company and this rate should be kept as low as possible. The cost of labour turnover can be divided into **preventative** and **replacement** costs.

Quick quiz

1   Distinguish between the terms production and productivity.

2   List five types of incentive scheme.

3   What are the requirements for a successful individual bonus scheme?

4   What is a value added incentive scheme?

5   When does idle time occur?

6   What are the responsibilities of a typical wages department?

7   Define the idle time ratio.

8   List six methods of reducing labour turnover.

Answers to quick quiz

1 • **Production** is the quantity or volume of output produced
  • **Productivity** is a measure of the efficiency with which output has been produced

2 • High day rate system
  • Individual bonus schemes
  • Group bonus schemes
  • Profit sharing schemes
  • Incentive schemes involving shares
  • Value added incentive schemes

3 • Each individual should be rewarded for the work done by that individual
  • Work should be fairly routine, so that standard times can be set for jobs
  • The bonus should be paid soon after the work is done

4 **Value added** is an alternative to profit as a business performance measure and it can be used as the basis of an incentive scheme

  Value added = Sales – cost of bought-in materials and services

5 **Idle time** occurs when employees cannot get on with their work, through no fault of their own, for example when machines break down or there is a shortage of work.

6 • Preparation of the payroll and payment of wages
  • Maintenance of employee records
  • Summarising wages cost for each cost centre
  • Summarising the hours worked for each cost centre
  • Summarising other payroll information, eg bonus payment, pensions etc
  • Providing an internal check for the preparation and payout of wages

7 Idle time ratio = $\dfrac{\text{Idle hours}}{\text{Total hours}} \times 100\%$

8 Any six from:

  • Paying satisfactory wages
  • Offering satisfactory hours and conditions of work
  • Creating a good informal relationship between members of the workforce
  • Offering good training schemes and a well-understood career or promotion ladder
  • Improving the content of jobs to create job satisfaction
  • Proper planning so as to avoid redundancies
  • Investigating the cause of an apparently high labour turnover

Now try the questions below from the Exam Question Bank

Number	Level	Marks	Time
Q7	MCQ	n/a	n/a

Overheads and absorption costing

Topic list	Syllabus reference
1 Overheads	D3 (a)
2 Absorption costing: an introduction	D3 (b)
3 Overhead allocation	D3 (c)
4 Overhead apportionment	D3 (d)
5 Overhead absorption	D3 (e)
6 Blanket absorption rates and departmental absorption rates	D3 (e)
7 Over and under absorption of overheads	D3 (g)
8 Ledger entries relating to overheads	D3 (f)
9 Non-manufacturing overheads	D3 (h)

Introduction

Absorption costing is a method of accounting for overheads. It is basically a method of sharing out overheads incurred amongst units produced.

This chapter begins by explaining why absorption costing might be necessary and then provides an overview of how the cost of a unit of product is built up under a system of absorption costing. A detailed analysis of this costing method is then provided, covering the three stages of absorption costing: **allocation**, **apportionment** and **absorption**.

Study guide

		Intellectual level
D3	**Accounting for overheads 1**	
(a)	Explain the different treatment of direct and indirect expenses	1
(b)	Describe the procedures involved in determining production overhead absorption rates	1
(c)	Allocate and apportion production overheads to cost centres using an appropriate basis	1
(d)	Reapportion service centre costs including the use of the reciprocal method	2
(e)	Select, apply and discuss appropriate bases for absorption rates	2
(f)	Prepare journal and ledger entries for manufacturing overheads incurred and absorbed	1
(g)	Calculate and explain under– and over-absorbed overheads	1
(h)	Apply methods of relating non-production overheads to cost units	1

Exam guide

Overhead apportionment and absorption is one of the most important topics in your Management Accounting studies and is almost certain to appear in the exam. Make sure that you study the contents of this chapter and work through the calculations very carefully.

1 Overheads

FAST FORWARD

Overhead is the cost incurred in the course of making a product, providing a service or running a department, but which cannot be traced directly and in full to the product, service or department.

Overhead is actually the total of the following.

- Indirect materials
- Indirect labour
- Indirect expenses

The total of these indirect costs is usually split into the following.

- **Production** overhead
- **Administration** overhead
- **Selling and distribution** overhead

In cost accounting there are two schools of thought as to the correct method of dealing with overheads.

- Absorption costing
- Marginal costing

2 Absorption costing: an introduction

The objective of absorption costing is to include in the total cost of a product an appropriate share of the organisation's total overhead. An appropriate share is generally taken to mean an amount which reflects the amount of time and effort that has gone into producing a unit or completing a job.

An organisation with one production department that produces identical units will divide the total overheads among the total units produced. **Absorption costing is a method for sharing overheads between different products on a fair basis.**

2.1 Is absorption costing necessary?

Suppose that a company makes and sells 100 units of a product each week. The prime cost per unit is $6 and the unit sales price is $10. Production overhead costs $200 per week and administration, selling and distribution overhead costs $150 per week. The weekly profit could be calculated as follows.

	$	$
Sales (100 units × $10)		1,000
Prime costs (100 × $6)	600	
Production overheads	200	
Administration, selling and distribution costs	150	
		950
Profit		50

In absorption costing, overhead costs will be added to each unit of product manufactured and sold.

	$ per unit
Prime cost per unit	6
Production overhead ($200 per week for 100 units)	2
Full factory cost	8

The weekly profit would be calculated as follows.

	$
Sales	1,000
Less factory cost of sales	800
Gross profit	200
Less administration, selling and distribution costs	150
Net profit	50

Sometimes, but not always, the overhead costs of administration, selling and distribution are also added to unit costs, to obtain a full cost of sales.

	$ per unit
Prime cost per unit	6.00
Factory overhead cost per unit	2.00
Administration etc costs per unit	1.50
Full cost of sales	9.50

The weekly profit would be calculated as follows.

	$
Sales	1,000
Less full cost of sales	950
Profit	50

It may already be apparent that the weekly profit is $50 no matter how the figures have been presented. So, how does absorption costing serve any useful purpose in accounting?

The **theoretical justification** for using absorption costing is that all production overheads are incurred in the production of the organisation's output and so each unit of the product receives some benefit from these costs. Each unit of output should therefore be charged with some of the overhead costs.

2.2 Practical reasons for using absorption costing

The main reasons for using absorption costing are for **inventory valuations**, **pricing decisions**, and **establishing the profitability of different products**.

(a) **Inventory valuations**. Inventory in hand must be valued for two reasons.

  (i) For the closing inventory figure in the balance sheet

  (ii) For the cost of sales figure in the income statement

  The valuation of inventory will affect profitability during a period because of the way in which the cost of sales is calculated.

  The cost of goods produced
  + the value of opening inventories
  − the value of closing inventories
  = the cost of goods sold.

  In our example, closing inventories might be valued at prime cost ($6), but in absorption costing, they would be valued at a fully absorbed factory cost, $8 per unit. (They would not be valued at $9.50, the full cost of sales, because the only costs incurred in producing goods for finished inventory are factory costs.)

(b) **Pricing decisions**. Many companies attempt to fix selling prices by calculating the full cost of production or sales of each product, and then adding a margin for profit. In our example, the company might have fixed a gross profit margin at 25% on factory cost, or 20% of the sales price, in order to establish the unit sales price of $10. 'Full cost plus pricing' can be particularly useful for companies which do jobbing or contract work, where each job or contract is different, so that a standard unit sales price cannot be fixed. Without using absorption costing, a full cost is difficult to ascertain.

(c) **Establishing the profitability of different products**. This argument in favour of absorption costing is more contentious, but is worthy of mention here. If a company sells more than one product, it will be difficult to judge how profitable each individual product is, unless overhead costs are shared on a fair basis and charged to the cost of sales of each product.

2.3 International Accounting Standard 2 (IAS 2)

Absorption costing is recommended in financial accounting by IAS 2 *Inventories*. IAS 2 deals with **financial accounting systems**. The cost accountant is (in theory) free to value inventories by whatever method seems best, but where companies integrate their financial accounting and cost accounting systems into a single system of accounting records, the valuation of closing inventories will be determined by IAS 2.

IAS 2 states that costs of all inventories should comprise those costs which have been incurred in the normal course of business in **bringing the inventories to their 'present location and condition'**. These costs incurred will include all related production overheads, even though these overheads may accrue on a time basis. In other words, in financial accounting, closing inventories should be valued at full factory cost, and it may therefore be convenient and appropriate to value inventories by the same method in the cost accounting system.

2.4 Absorption costing stages

The three stages of absorption costing are:
- Allocation
- Apportionment
- Absorption

We shall now begin our study of absorption costing by looking at the process of **overhead allocation**.

3 Overhead allocation

3.1 Introduction

Allocation is the process by which whole cost items are charged direct to a cost unit or cost centre.

Cost centres may be one of the following types.

(a)   A **production department**, to which production overheads are charged

(b)   A **production area service department**, to which production overheads are charged

(c)   An **administrative department**, to which administration overheads are charged

(d)   A **selling** or a **distribution department**, to which sales and distribution overheads are charged

(e)   An **overhead cost centre**, to which items of expense which are shared by a number of departments, such as rent and rates, heat and light and the canteen, are charged

The following costs would therefore be charged to the following cost centres via the process of allocation.

- Direct labour will be charged to a production cost centre.
- The cost of a warehouse security guard will be charged to the warehouse cost centre.
- Paper (recording computer output) will be charged to the computer department.
- Costs such as the canteen are charged direct to various overhead cost centres.

3.2 Example: Overhead allocation

Consider the following costs of a company.

Wages of the foreman of department A	$200
Wages of the foreman of department B	$150
Indirect materials consumed in department A	$50
Rent of the premises shared by departments A and B	$300

The cost accounting system might include three overhead cost centres.

Cost centre:	101	Department A
	102	Department B
	201	Rent

Overhead costs would be allocated directly to each cost centre, ie $200 + $50 to cost centre 101, $150 to cost centre 102 and $300 to cost centre 201. The rent of the factory will be subsequently shared between the two production departments, but for the purpose of day to day cost recording, the rent will first of all be charged in full to a separate cost centre.

4 Overhead apportionment

Apportionment is a procedure whereby indirect costs are spread fairly between cost centres. Service cost centre costs may be apportioned to production cost centres by using the reciprocal method.

4.1 Stage 1: Apportioning general overheads

Overhead apportionment follows on from overhead allocation. The first stage of overhead apportionment is to identify all overhead costs as production department, production service department, administration or selling and distribution overhead. The costs for heat and light, rent and rates, the canteen and so on (ie costs allocated to general overhead cost centres) must therefore be shared out between the other cost centres.

4.2 Bases of apportionment

It is considered important that overhead costs should be shared out on a **fair basis**. You will appreciate that because of the complexity of items of cost it is rarely possible to use only one method of apportioning costs to the various departments of an organisation. The bases of apportionment for the most usual cases are given below.

Overhead to which the basis applies	Basis
Rent, rates, heating and light, repairs and depreciation of buildings	Floor area occupied by each cost centre
Depreciation, insurance of equipment	Cost or book value of equipment
Personnel office, canteen, welfare, wages and cost offices, first aid	Number of employees, or labour hours worked in each cost centre
Heating, lighting (see above)	Volume of space occupied by each cost centre

4.3 Example: Overhead apportionment

Burton Court Co has incurred the following overhead costs.

	$
Depreciation of factory	1,000
Factory repairs and maintenance	600
Factory office costs (treat as production overhead)	1,500
Depreciation of equipment	800
Insurance of equipment	200
Heating	390
Lighting	100
Canteen	900
	5,490

Information relating to the production and service departments in the factory is as follows.

	Department			
	Production A	Production B	Service X	Service Y
Floor space (square metres)	1,200	1,600	800	400
Volume (cubic metres)	3,000	6,000	2,400	1,600
Number of employees	30	30	15	15
Book value of equipment	$30,000	$20,000	$10,000	$20,000

Required

Determine how the overhead costs should be apportioned between the four departments.

Solution

Item of cost	Basis of apportionment	Total cost $	A $	B $	X $	Y $
				To Department		
Factory depreciation	(floor area)	1,000	300	400	200	100
Factory repairs	(floor area)	600	180	240	120	60
Factory office costs	(number of employees)	1,500	500	500	250	250
Equipment depreciation	(book value)	800	300	200	100	200
Equipment insurance	(book value)	200	75	50	25	50
Heating	(volume)	390	90	180	72	48
Lighting	(floor area)	100	30	40	20	10
Canteen	(number of employees)	900	300	300	150	150
Total		5,490	1,775	1,910	937	868

4.4 Stage 2: Service department cost apportionment

The second stage of overhead apportionment concerns **the treatment of service cost centres**. A factory is divided into several production cost centres and also many service cost centres. Service cost centres might include the stores or the canteen

Only the production cost centres are directly involved in the manufacture of the units. In order to be able to add production overheads to unit costs, it is necessary to have all the overheads charged to (or located in) the production cost centres.

The next stage in absorption costing is therefore to apportion the costs of service cost centres to the production cost centres.

There are three methods by which the apportionment of service cost centre costs can be done.

(a) Apportion the costs of each service cost centre to production cost centres only (the **direct** method).

(b) Apportion the costs of each service cost centre not only to production cost centres, but also to other service cost centres which make use of its services. Eventually apportion all costs to the production cost centres alone by a gradual process of **repeated distribution** (the reciprocal method).

(c) Apportion the costs of each service cost centre, not only to production cost centres, but also to some (but not all) of the service cost centres that make use of its services. This is known as the **step-down** method.

The direct and step-down methods are not in your syllabus. We will be covering the **reciprocal** method.

4.5 Basis of apportionment

Whichever method is used to apportion service cost centre costs, **the basis of apportionment must be fair**. A different apportionment basis may be applied for each service cost centre. This is demonstrated in the following table.

Service cost centre	Possible basis of apportionment
Stores	Number or cost value of material requisitions
Maintenance	Hours of maintenance work done for each cost centre
Production planning	Direct labour hours worked in each production cost centre

4.6 The reciprocal (repeated distribution) method of apportionment

Apportionment is a procedure whereby indirect costs are spread fairly between cost centres. It could therefore be argued that a fair sharing of service cost centre costs is not possible **unless consideration is given to the work done by each service cost centre for other service cost centres.**

4.6.1 Example: The reciprocal method of apportionment

Suppose a company has two production departments and two service departments (stores and maintenance). The following information about activity in a recent costing period is available.

	Production departments		Stores department	Maintenance department
	1	2		
Overhead costs	$10,030	$8,970	$10,000	$8,000
Value of material requisitions	$30,000	$50,000	–	$20,000
Maintenance hours used	8,000	1,000	1,000	–

The problem is that the stores department uses the maintenance department, and the maintenance department uses the stores. This is known as **reciprocal servicing.**

(a)   If service department overheads were apportioned directly to production departments, ignoring the reciprocal servicing, the apportionment would be as follows.

Service department	Basis of apportionment	Total cost	1	2
		$	$	$
Stores	Material requisitions (W1)	10,000	3,750	6,250
Maintenance	Maintenance hours (W2)	8,000	7,111	889
		18,000	10,861	7,139
Overheads of departments 1 and 2		19,000	10,030	8,970
		37,000	20,891	16,109

Workings

1   **Apportionment of stores department overheads**

The overhead costs of the stores department are apportioned on the basis of the value of material requisitions.

Total value of material requisitions raised by production departments only = $30,000 (Production department 1) + $50,000 (Production department 2) = $80,000.

$$\therefore \text{Overheads apportioned to Production department 1} = \frac{30,000}{80,000} \times \$10,000$$

$$= \frac{3}{8} \times \$10,000$$

$$= \$3,750$$

$$\therefore \text{Overheads apportioned to Production department 2} = \frac{50,000}{80,000} \times \$10,000$$

$$= \frac{5}{8} \times \$10,000$$

$$= \$6,250$$

2   **Apportionment of maintenance department overheads**

The overhead costs of the maintenance department are apportioned on the basis of the number of maintenance hours used.

Total maintenance hours used by production departments only = 8,000 (Production department 1) + 1,000 (Production department 2) = 9,000.

$$\therefore \text{Overheads apportioned to production department 1} = \frac{8,000}{9,000} \times \$8,000$$

$$= \frac{8}{9} \times \$8,000$$

$$= \$7,111$$

$$\therefore \text{Overheads apportioned to Production department 2} = \frac{1,000}{9,000} \times \$8,000$$

$$= \frac{1}{9} \times \$8,000$$

$$= \$889$$

(b)   If, however, recognition is made of the fact that **the stores and maintenance department do work for each other,** and the basis of apportionment remains the same, we ought to apportion service department costs as follows. The percentages are based on the value of materials requisitions and the maintenance hours.

	Production departments		Stores department	Maintenance department
	1	2		
Stores (100%)	30%	50%	–	20%
Maintenance (100%)	80%	10%	10%	–

This may be done using the **reciprocal** or **repeated distribution method of apportionment** as follows.

4.6.2 Example: Reciprocal (repeated distribution) method of apportionment

	Production departments		Stores department	Maintenance department
	1	2		
	$	$	$	$
Overhead costs	10,030	8,970	10,000	8,000
Apportion stores (see note (a))	3,000	5,000	(10,000)	2,000
			0	10,000
Apportion maintenance	8,000	1,000	1,000	(10,000)
			1,000	0
Repeat: Apportion stores	300	500	(1,000)	200
Repeat: Apportion maintenance	160	20	20	(200)
Repeat: Apportion stores	6	10	(20)	4
Repeat: Apportion maintenance (b)	4	–	–	(4)
	21,500	15,500	0	0

Notes

(a)   The first apportionment could have been the costs of maintenance, rather than stores; there is no difference to the final results. The apportionments are based on the percentages calculated in paragraph 4.6.1.

(b)   When the repeated distributions bring service department costs down to small numbers (here $4), the final apportionment to production departments is an approximate rounding.

The total overhead of $37,000 has now been apportioned to the production departments. Have a look at the difference in the final overhead apportionments to each production department using the different apportionment methods. Unless the difference is substantial, the direct method which ignores the reciprocal servicing, might be preferred because it is **clerically simpler to use.**

4.7 Using algebra

The results of the reciprocal method of apportionment may also be obtained using **algebra** and **simultaneous equations**.

4.7.1 Example: Using algebra

Let us use the same data as the example in Paragraph 4.6.1.

(a)   Let S be the total stores department overhead for apportionment, after it has been apportioned overhead from Maintenance.

(b)   Let M be the total of maintenance department overhead after it has been apportioned overhead from Stores.

We can set up our equations as follows.

$$S = 0.1M* + \$10,000 \qquad (1)$$
$$M = 0.2S** + \$8,000 \qquad (2)$$

*   10% × maintenance department overhead
**   20% × stores department overhead

Multiplying (2) by 5 gives us

$$5M = S + \$40,000 \qquad (3), \text{which can be rearranged so that}$$
$$S = 5M - \$40,000 \qquad (4)$$

Subtracting (1) from (4)

$$S = 5M - \$40,000 \qquad (4)$$
$$S = 0.1M + \$10,000 \qquad (1)$$
$$0 = 4.9M - \$50,000$$
$$M = \frac{\$50,000}{4.9} = \$10,204$$

Substituting in (1)

$$S = 0.1 \times (\$10,204) + \$10,000$$
$$S = \$11,020$$

These overheads can be apportioned as follows, using the percentages in Paragraph 4.6.1. Note that the result is the same as that obtained when using the reciprocal (repeated distribution) method.

	Production dept A $	Production dept B $	Stores $	Maintenance $
Overhead costs	10,030	8,970	10,000	8,000
Apportion stores total	3,306	5,510	(11,020)	2,204
Apportion maintenance total	8,164	1,020	1,020	(10,204)
	21,500	15,500	–	–

Exam focus point

You must never ignore the existence of reciprocal services unless a question clearly instructs you to do so. Examination questions will usually indicate clearly if you are required to use a specific method of reciprocal apportionment.

Question
Reapportionment

Sandstorm is a jobbing engineering concern which has three production departments (forming, machines and assembly) and two service departments (maintenance and general).

The following analysis of overhead costs has been made for the year just ended.

	$	$
Rent and rates		8,000
Power		750
Light, heat		5,000
Repairs, maintenance:		
Forming	800	
Machines	1,800	
Assembly	300	
Maintenance	200	
General	100	
		3,200
Departmental expenses:		
Forming	1,500	
Machines	2,300	
Assembly	1,100	
Maintenance	900	
General	1,500	
		7,300
Depreciation:		
Plant		10,000
Fixtures and fittings		250
Insurance:		
Plant		2,000
Buildings		500
Indirect labour:		
Forming	3,000	
Machines	5,000	
Assembly	1,500	
Maintenance	4,000	
General	2,000	
		15,500
		52,500

Other available data are as follows.

	Floor area sq. ft	Plant value $	Fixtures & fittings $	Effective horse-power	Direct cost for year $	Labour hours worked	Machine hours worked
Forming	2,000	25,000	1,000	40	20,500	14,400	12,000
Machines	4,000	60,000	500	90	30,300	20,500	21,600
Assembly	3,000	7,500	2,000	15	24,200	20,200	2,000
Maintenance	500	7,500	1,000	5	–	–	–
General	500	–	500	–	–	–	–
	10,000	100,000	5,000	150	75,000	55,100	35,600

Service department costs are apportioned as follows.

	Maintenance %	General %
Forming	20	20
Machines	50	60
Assembly	20	10
General	10	–
Maintenance	–	10
	100	100

Required

Using the data provided prepare an analysis showing the distribution of overhead costs to departments. Reapportion service cost centre costs using the reciprocal method.

Answer

Analysis of distribution of actual overhead costs

	Basis	Forming $	Machines $	Assembly $	Machining $	General $	Total $
Directly allocated overheads:							
Repairs, maintenance		800	1,800	300	200	100	3,200
Departmental expenses		1,500	2,300	1,100	900	1,500	7,300
Indirect labour		3,000	5,000	1,500	4,000	2,000	15,500
Apportionment of other overheads:							
Rent, rates	1	1,600	3,200	2,400	400	400	8,000
Power	2	200	450	75	25	0	750
Light, heat	1	1,000	2,000	1,500	250	250	5,000
Depreciation of plant	3	2,500	6,000	750	750	0	10,000
Depreciation of F and F	4	50	25	100	50	25	250
Insurance of plant	3	500	1,200	150	150	0	2,000
Insurance of buildings	1	100	200	150	25	25	500
		11,250	22,175	8,025	6,750	4,300	52,500

Basis of apportionment:

1   floor area
2   effective horsepower
3   plant value
4   fixtures and fittings value

Apportionment of service department overheads to production departments, using the reciprocal method.

	Forming $	Machines $	Assembly $	Maintenance $	General $	Total $
Overheads	11,250	22,175	8,025	6,750	4,300	52,500
	1,350	3,375	1,350	(6,750)	675	
					4,975	
	995	2,985	498	497	(4,975)	
	99	249	99	(497)	50	
	10	30	5	5	(50)	
	1	3	1	(5)		
	13,705	28,817	9,978	0	0	52,500

5 Overhead absorption

5.1 Introduction

FAST FORWARD

Overhead absorption is the process whereby overhead costs allocated and apportioned to production cost centres are added to unit, job or batch costs. Overhead absorption is sometimes called **overhead recovery.**

Having allocated and/or apportioned all overheads, the next stage in the costing treatment of overheads is to add them to, or **absorb them into, cost units.**

Overheads are usually added to cost units using a **predetermined overhead absorption rate**, which is calculated using figures from the budget.

5.2 Calculation of overhead absorption rates

Step 1 Estimate the overhead likely to be incurred during the coming period.

Step 2 Estimate the activity level for the period. This could be total hours, units, or direct costs or whatever it is upon which the overhead absorption rates are to be based.

Step 3 Divide the estimated overhead by the budgeted activity level. This produces the overhead absorption rate.

Step 4 Absorb the overhead into the cost unit by applying the calculated absorption rate.

5.3 Example: The basics of absorption costing

Athena Co makes two products, the Greek and the Roman. Greeks take 2 labour hours each to make and Romans take 5 labour hours. What is the overhead cost per unit for Greeks and Romans respectively if overheads are absorbed on the basis of labour hours?

Solution

Step 1 Estimate the overhead likely to be incurred during the coming period

Athena Co estimates that the total overhead will be $50,000

Step 2 Estimate the activity level for the period

Athena Co estimates that a total of 100,000 direct labour hours will be worked

Step 3 Divide the estimated overhead by the budgeted activity level

$$\text{Absorption rate} = \frac{\$50,000}{100,000 \text{ hrs}} = \$0.50 \text{ per direct labour hour}$$

Step 4 Absorb the overhead into the cost unit by applying the calculated absorption rate

	Greek	Roman
Labour hours per unit	2	5
Absorption rate per labour hour	$0.50	$0.50
Overhead absorbed per unit	$1	$2.50

It should be obvious to you that, even if a company is trying to be 'fair', there is a great lack of precision about the way an absorption base is chosen.

This arbitrariness is one of the main criticisms of absorption costing, and if absorption costing is to be used (because of its other virtues) then it is important that **the methods used are kept under regular**

review. Changes in working conditions should, if necessary, lead to changes in the way in which work is accounted for.

For example, a labour intensive department may become mechanised. If a direct labour hour rate of absorption had been used previous to the mechanisation, it would probably now be more appropriate to change to the use of a machine hour rate.

5.4 Choosing the appropriate absorption base

The different **bases of absorption** (or 'overhead recovery rates') are as follows.

- A percentage of direct materials cost
- A percentage of direct labour cost
- A percentage of prime cost
- A rate per machine hour
- A rate per direct labour hour
- A rate per unit
- A percentage of factory cost (for administration overhead)
- A percentage of sales or factory cost (for selling and distribution overhead)

The choice of an absorption basis is a matter of judgement and common sense, what is required is an **absorption basis** which realistically reflects the characteristics of a given cost centre and which avoids undue anomalies.

Many factories use a **direct labour hour rate** or **machine hour rate** in preference to a rate based on a percentage of direct materials cost, wages or prime cost.

(a)   A **direct labour** hour basis is most appropriate in a **labour intensive** environment.

(b)   A **machine hour** rate would be used in departments where production is controlled or dictated by machines.

(c)   A **rate per unit** would be effective only if all units were identical.

5.5 Example: Overhead absorption

The budgeted production overheads and other budget data of Bridge Cottage Co are as follows.

Budget	Production dept A	Production dept B
Overhead cost	$36,000	$5,000
Direct materials cost	$32,000	
Direct labour cost	$40,000	
Machine hours	10,000	
Direct labour hours	18,000	
Units of production		1,000

Required

Calculate the absorption rate using the various bases of apportionment.

Solution

(a)   Department A

   (i)   Percentage of direct materials cost $\dfrac{\$36,000}{\$32,000} \times 100\% = 112.5\%$

   (ii)   Percentage of direct labour cost $\dfrac{\$36,000}{\$40,000} \times 100\% = 90\%$

(iii) Percentage of prime cost

$$\frac{\$36,000}{\$72,000} \times 100\% = 50\%$$

(iv) Rate per machine hour

$$\frac{\$36,000}{10,000 \text{ hrs}} = \$3.60 \text{ per machine hour}$$

(v) Rate per direct labour hour

$$\frac{\$36,000}{18,000 \text{ hrs}} = \$2 \text{ per direct labour hour}$$

(b) The department B absorption rate will be based on units of output.

$$\frac{\$5,000}{1,000 \text{ units}} = \$5 \text{ per unit produced}$$

5.6 Bases of absorption

The choice of the basis of absorption is significant in determining the cost of individual units, or jobs, produced. Using the previous example, suppose that an individual product has a material cost of $80, a labour cost of $85, and requires 36 labour hours and 23 machine hours to complete. The overhead cost of the product would vary, depending on the basis of absorption used by the company for overhead recovery.

(a) As a percentage of direct material cost, the overhead cost would be

112.5% × $80		= $90.00

(b) As a percentage of direct labour cost, the overhead cost would be

90% × $85		= $76.50

(c) As a percentage of prime cost, the overhead cost would be 50% × $165 = $82.50

(d) Using a machine hour basis of absorption, the overhead cost would be

23 hrs × $3.60		= $82.80

(e) Using a labour hour basis, the overhead cost would be 36 hrs × $2 = $72.00

In theory, each basis of absorption would be possible, but the company should choose a basis for its own costs which seems to be **'fairest'**.

6 Blanket absorption rates and departmental absorption rates

6.1 Introduction

FAST FORWARD

A **blanket overhead absorption rate** is an absorption rate used throughout a factory and for all jobs and units of output irrespective of the department in which they were produced.

For example, if total overheads were $500,000 and there were 250,000 direct machine hours during the period, the **blanket overhead rate** would be $2 per direct machine hour and all jobs passing through the factory would be charged at that rate.

Blanket overhead rates are not appropriate in the following circumstances.

- There is more than one department.
- Jobs do not spend an equal amount of time in each department.

If a single factory overhead absorption rate is used, some products will receive a higher overhead charge than they ought 'fairly' to bear, whereas other products will be under-charged.

If **a separate absorption rate** is used for each department, charging of overheads will be fair and the full cost of production of items will represent the amount of the effort and resources put into making them.

6.2 Example: Separate absorption rates

The Old Grammar School has two production departments, for which the following budgeted information is available.

	Department A	Department B	Total
Budgeted overheads	$360,000	$200,000	$560,000
Budgeted direct labour hours	200,000 hrs	40,000 hrs	240,000 hrs

If a single factory overhead absorption rate is applied, the rate of overhead recovery would be:

$$\frac{\$560,000}{240,000 \text{ hours}} = \$2.33 \text{ per direct labour hour}$$

If separate departmental rates are applied, these would be:

$$Department\ A = \frac{\$360,000}{200,000 \text{ hours}} = \$1.80 \text{ per direct labour hour}$$

$$Department\ B = \frac{\$200,000}{40,000 \text{ hours}} = \$5 \text{ per direct labour hour}$$

Department B has a higher overhead rate of cost per hour worked than department A.

Now let us consider two separate jobs.

Job X has a prime cost of $100, takes 30 hours in department B and does not involve any work in department A.

Job Y has a prime cost of $100, takes 28 hours in department A and 2 hours in department B.

What would be the factory cost of each job, using the following rates of overhead recovery?

(a) A single factory rate of overhead recovery
(b) Separate departmental rates of overhead recovery

Solution

			Job X		Job Y
(a)	**Single factory rate**		$		$
	Prime cost		100		100
	Factory overhead (30 × $2.33)		70		70
	Factory cost		170		170
(b)	**Separate departmental rates**		$		$
	Prime cost		100		100.00
	Factory overhead: department A		0	(28 × $1.80)	50.40
	department B	(30 × $5)	150	(2 × $5)	10.00
	Factory cost		250		160.40

Using a single factory overhead absorption rate, both jobs would cost the same. However, since job X is done entirely within department B where overhead costs are relatively higher, whereas job Y is done mostly within department A, where overhead costs are relatively lower, it is arguable that job X should cost more than job Y. This will occur if separate departmental overhead recovery rates are used to reflect the work done on each job in each department separately.

If all jobs do not spend approximately the same time in each department then, to ensure that all jobs are charged with their fair share of overheads, it is necessary to establish **separate overhead rates for each department**.

Question
Machine hour absorption rate

The following data relate to one year in department A.

Budgeted machine hours	25,000
Actual machine hours	21,875
Budgeted overheads	$350,000
Actual overheads	$350,000

Based on the data above, what is the machine hour absorption rate as conventionally calculated?

A $12   B $14   C $16   D $18

Answer

Don't forget, if your calculations produce a solution which does not correspond with any of the options available, then eliminate the unlikely options and make a guess from the remainder. Never leave out a multiple choice question.

A common pitfall is to think 'we haven't had answer A for a while, so I'll guess that'. The examiner is *not* required to produce an even spread of A, B, C and D answers in the examination. There is no reason why the answer to *every* question cannot be D!

The correct answer in this case is B.

$$\text{Overhead absorption rate} = \frac{\text{Budgeted overheads}}{\text{Budgeted machine hours}} = \frac{\$350,000}{25,000} = \$14 \text{ per machine hour}$$

7 Over and under absorption of overheads

7.1 Introduction

Over and **under absorption** of overheads occurs because the predetermined overhead absorption rates are based on estimates.

The rate of overhead absorption is based on estimates (of both numerator and denominator) and it is quite likely that either one or both of the estimates will not agree with what actually occurs.

(a) **Over absorption** means that the overheads charged to the cost of sales are greater then the overheads actually incurred.

(b) **Under absorption** means that insufficient overheads have been included in the cost of sales.

It is almost inevitable that at the end of the accounting year there will have been an over absorption or under absorption of the overhead actually incurred.

7.2 Example: Over and under absorption

Suppose that the budgeted overhead in a production department is $80,000 and the budgeted activity is 40,000 direct labour hours. The overhead recovery rate (using a direct labour hour basis) would be $2 per direct labour hour.

Actual overheads in the period are, say $84,000 and 45,000 direct labour hours are worked.

	$
Overhead incurred (actual)	84,000
Overhead absorbed (45,000 × $2)	90,000
Over absorption of overhead	6,000

In this example, the cost of produced units or jobs has been charged with $6,000 more than was actually spent. An adjustment to reconcile the overheads charged to the actual overhead is necessary and the over-absorbed overhead will be credited to the profit and loss account at the end of the accounting period.

7.3 The reasons for under-/over-absorbed overhead

The overhead absorption rate is predetermined from budget estimates of overhead cost and the expected volume of activity. Under– or over-recovery of overhead will occur in the following circumstances.

- Actual overhead costs are different from budgeted overheads
- The actual activity level is different from the budgeted activity level
- Actual overhead costs *and* actual activity level differ from the budgeted costs and level

7.4 Example: Reasons for under-/over-absorbed overhead

Pembridge Co has a budgeted production overhead of $50,000 and a budgeted activity of 25,000 direct labour hours and therefore a recovery rate of $2 per direct labour hour.

Required

Calculate the under-/over-absorbed overhead, and the reasons for the under-/over-absorption, in the following circumstances.

(a) Actual overheads cost $47,000 and 25,000 direct labour hours are worked.
(b) Actual overheads cost $50,000 and 21,500 direct labour hours are worked.
(c) Actual overheads cost $47,000 and 21,500 direct labour hours are worked.

Solution

(a)

	$
Actual overhead	47,000
Absorbed overhead (25,000 × $2)	50,000
Over-absorbed overhead	3,000

The reason for the over absorption is that although the actual and budgeted direct labour hours are the same, actual overheads cost less than expected.

(b)

	$
Actual overhead	50,000
Absorbed overhead (21,500 × $2)	43,000
Under-absorbed overhead	7,000

The reason for the under absorption is that although budgeted and actual overhead costs were the same, fewer direct labour hours were worked than expected.

(c)

	$
Actual overhead	47,000
Absorbed overhead (21,500 × $2)	43,000
Under-absorbed overhead	4,000

The reason for the under absorption is a combination of the reasons in (a) and (b).

The distinction between **overheads incurred** (actual overheads) and **overheads absorbed** is an important one which you must learn and understand. The difference between them is known as under– or over-absorbed overheads.

Question

Under-/over-absorbed overhead

The budgeted and actual data for River Arrow Products Co for the year to 31 March 20X5 are as follows.

	Budgeted	Actual
Direct labour hours	9,000	9,900
Direct wages	$34,000	$35,500
Machine hours	10,100	9,750
Direct materials	$55,000	$53,900
Units produced	120,000	122,970
Overheads	$63,000	$61,500

The cost accountant of River Arrow Products Co has decided that overheads should be absorbed on the basis of labour hours.

Required

Calculate the amount of under– or over-absorbed overheads for River Arrow Products Co for the year to 31 March 20X5.

Answer

Overhead absorption rate $= \dfrac{\$63,000}{9,000} = \$7$ per hour

Overheads absorbed by production = 9,900 × $7 = $69,300

	$
Actual overheads	61,500
Overheads absorbed	69,300
Over-absorbed overheads	7,800

xam focus oint

You can always work out whether overheads are under– or over-absorbed by using the following rule.

- If Actual overhead incurred – Absorbed overhead = NEGATIVE (N), then overheads are over-absorbed (O) (NO)

- If Actual overhead incurred – Absorbed overhead = POSITIVE (P), then overheads are under-absorbed (U) (PU)

So, remember the NOPU rule when you go into your examination and you won't have any trouble in deciding whether overheads are under– or over-absorbed!

Question

Budgeted overhead absorption rate

A management consultancy recovers overheads on chargeable consulting hours. Budgeted overheads were $615,000 and actual consulting hours were 32,150. Overheads were under-recovered by $35,000.

If actual overheads were $694,075 what was the budgeted overhead absorption rate per hour?

A $19.13   B $20.50   C $21.59   D $22.68

Answer

	$
Actual overheads	694,075
Under-recoverable overheads	35,000
Overheads recovered for 32,150 hours at budgeted overhead absorption rate (x)	659,075

32,150 x = 659,075

$$x = \frac{659,075}{32,150} = \$20.50$$

The correct option is B.

8 Ledger entries relating to overheads

8.1 Introduction

The bookkeeping entries for overheads are not as straightforward as those for materials and labour. We shall now consider the way in which overheads are dealt with in a cost accounting system.

When an absorption costing system is in use we now know that the amount of overhead included in the cost of an item is absorbed at a predetermined rate. The entries made in the cash book and the nominal ledger, however, are the actual amounts.

You will remember that it is highly unlikely that the actual amount and the predetermined amount will be the same. The difference is called **under– or over-absorbed overhead**. To deal with this in the cost accounting books, therefore, we need to have an account to collect under– or over-absorbed amounts for each type of overhead.

8.2 Example: The under-/over-absorbed overhead account

Mariott's Motorcycles absorbs production overheads at the rate of $0.50 per operating hour and administration overheads at 20% of the production cost of sales. Actual data for one month was as follows.

Administration overheads	$32,000
Production overheads	$46,500
Operating hours	90,000
Production cost of sales	$180,000

What entries need to be made for overheads in the ledgers?

Solution

PRODUCTION OVERHEADS

	DR $		CR $
Cash	46,500	Absorbed into WIP (90,000 × $0.50)	45,000
		Under absorbed overhead	1,500
	46,500		46,500

ADMINISTRATION OVERHEADS

	DR $		CR $
Cash	32,000	To cost of sales (180,000 × 0.2)	36,000
Over-absorbed overhead	4,000		
	36,000		36,000

UNDER-/OVER-ABSORBED OVERHEADS

	DR $		CR $
Production overhead	1,500	Administration overhead	4,000
Balance to profit and loss account	2,500		
	4,000		4,000

Less production overhead has been absorbed than has been spent so there is **under-absorbed overhead** of $1,500. More administration overhead has been absorbed (into cost of sales, note, not into WIP) and so there is **over-absorbed overhead** of $4,000. The net over-absorbed overhead of $2,500 is a credit in the income statement.

9 Non-manufacturing overheads

9.1 Introduction

FAST FORWARD

Non-manufacturing overheads may be allocated by choosing a basis for the overhead absorption rate which most closely matches the non-production overhead, or on the basis of a product's ability to bear the costs.

For **external reporting** (eg statutory accounts) it is not necessary to allocate non-manufacturing overheads to products. This is because many of the overheads are non-manufacturing, and are regarded as **period costs**.

For **internal reporting** purposes and for a number of industries which base the selling price of their product on estimates of **total** cost or even actual cost, a **total cost per unit of output** may be required.

Builders, law firms and garages often charge for their services by adding a **percentage profit margin** to actual cost. For product pricing purposes and for internal management reports it may therefore be appropriate to allocate non-manufacturing overheads to units of output.

9.2 Bases for apportioning non-manufacturing overheads

A number of non-manufacturing overheads such as delivery costs or salespersons' salaries are clearly identified with particular products and can therefore be classified as direct costs. The majority of non-manufacturing overheads, however cannot be directly allocated to particular units of output. Two possible methods of allocating such non-manufacturing overheads are as follows.

Method 1: Choose a basis for the overhead absorption rate which most closely matches the non-manufacturing overhead such as direct labour hours, direct machine hours and so on. The problem with such a method is that most non-manufacturing overheads are unaffected in the short term by changes in the level of output and tend to be fixed costs.

Method 2 : Allocate non-manufacturing overheads on the ability of the products to bear such costs. One possible approach is to use the manufacturing cost as the basis for allocating non-manufacturing costs to products.

Formula to learn

The **overhead absorption rate** is calculated as follows.

$$\text{Overhead absorption rate} = \frac{\text{Estimated non-manufacturing overheads}}{\text{Estimated manufacturing costs}}$$

If, for example, budgeted distribution overheads are $200,000 and budgeted manufacturing costs are $800,000, the predetermined distribution overhead absorption rate will be 25% of manufacturing cost. Other bases for absorbing overheads are as follows.

Type of overhead	Possible absorption base
Selling and marketing	Sales value
Research and development	Consumer cost (= production cost minus cost of direct materials) or added value (= sales value of product minus cost of bought in materials and services)
Distribution	Sales values
Administration	Consumer cost or added value

9.3 Administration overheads

The administration overhead usually consists of the following.

- Executive salaries
- Office rent and rates
- Lighting
- Heating and cleaning the offices

In cost accounting, administration overheads are regarded as periodic charges which are charged against the gross costing profit for the year (as in financial accounting).

9.4 Selling and distribution overheads

Selling and distribution overheads are often considered collectively as one type of overhead but they are actually quite different forms of expense.

(a)   **Selling costs** are incurred in order to obtain sales

(b)   **Distribution costs** begin as soon as the finished goods are put into the warehouse and continue until the goods are despatched or delivered to the customer

Selling overhead is therefore often absorbed on the basis of sales value so that the more profitable product lines take a large proportion of overhead. The normal cost accounting entry for selling overhead is as follows.

DR   Cost of goods sold
CR   Selling overhead control account

Distribution overhead is more closely linked to production than sales and from one point of view could be regarded as an extra cost of production. It is, however, more usual to regard production cost as ending on the factory floor and to deal with distribution overhead separately. It is generally absorbed on a percentage of production cost but special circumstances, such as size and weight of products affecting the delivery charges, may cause a different basis of absorption to be used. The cost accounting entry is as follows.

DR   Cost of goods sold
CR   Distribution overhead control account

Chapter roundup

- **Overhead** is the cost incurred in the course of making a product, providing a service or running a department, but which cannot be traced directly and in full to the product, service or department.

- The **objective of absorption costing** is to include in the total cost of a product an appropriate share of the organisation's total overhead. An appropriate share is generally taken to mean an amount which reflects the amount of time and effort that has gone into producing a unit or completing a job.

- The main reasons for using absorption costing are for **stock valuations, pricing decisions** and **establishing the profitability of different products.**

- The three stages of absorption costing are:
    - Allocation
    - Apportionment
    - Absorption

- **Allocation** is the process by which whole cost items are charged direct to a cost unit or cost centre.

- **Apportionment** is a procedure whereby indirect costs are spread fairly between cost centres. Service cost centre costs may be apportioned to production cost centres by using the reciprocal method.

- The results of the reciprocal method of apportionment may also be obtained by using **algebra** and **simultaneous equations**.

- **Overhead absorption** is the process whereby overhead costs allocated and apportioned to production cost centres are added to unit, job or batch costs. Overhead absorption is sometimes called **overhead recovery**.

- A **blanket overhead absorption rate** is an absorption rate used throughout a factory and for all jobs and units of output irrespective of the department in which they were produced.

- **Over** and **under absorption of overheads** occurs because the predetermined overhead absorption rates are based on estimates.

- **Non-manufacturing overheads** may be allocated by choosing a basis for the overhead absorption rate which most closely matches the non-production overhead, or on the basis of a product's ability to bear the costs.

Quick quiz

1   What is allocation?

2   Name the three stages in charging overheads to units of output.

3   Match the following overheads with the most appropriate basis of apportionment.

Overhead		**Basis of apportionment**	
(a)	Depreciation of equipment	(1)	Direct machine hours
(b)	Heat and light costs	(2)	Number of employees
(c)	Canteen	(3)	Book value of equipment
(d)	Insurance of equipment	(4)	Floor area

4   A direct labour hour basis is most appropriate in which of the following environments?

A   Machine-intensive

B   Labour-intensive

C   When all units produced are identical

D   None of the above

5   What is the problem with using a single factory overhead absorption rate?

6   How is under-/over-absorbed overhead accounted for?

7   Why does under– or over-absorbed overhead occur?

Answers to quick quiz

1   The process whereby whole cost items are charged direct to a cost unit or cost centre.

2   • Allocation
     • Apportionment
     • Absorption

3   (a)   (3)
     (b)   (4)
     (c)   (2)
     (d)   (3)

4   B

5   Because some products will receive a higher overhead charge than they ought 'fairly' to bear and other products will be undercharged.

6   Under-/over-absorbed overhead is written as an adjustment to the income statement at the end of an accounting period.

     • Over-absorbed overhead → credit in income statement
     • Under-absorbed overhead → debit in income statement

7   • Actual overhead costs are different from budgeted overheads
     • The actual activity level is different from the budgeted activity level
     • Actual overhead costs *and* actual activity level differ from the budgeted costs and level

Now try the questions below from the Exam Question Bank

Number	Level	Marks	Time
Q8	MCQ/OTQ	n/a	n/a

Marginal and absorption costing

Topic list	Syllabus reference
1 Marginal cost and marginal costing	D4 (a)
2 The principles of marginal costing	D4 (a)
3 Marginal costing and absorption costing and the calculation of profit	D4 (b), (c)
4 Reconciling profits	D4 (d)
5 Marginal costing versus absorption costing	D4 (e)

Introduction

This chapter defines **marginal costing** and compares it with absorption costing. Whereas absorption costing recognises fixed costs (usually fixed production costs) as part of the cost of a unit of output and hence as product costs, marginal costing treats all fixed costs as period costs. Two such different costing methods obviously each have their supporters and so we will be looking at the arguments both in favour of and against each method. Each costing method, because of the different inventory valuation used, produces a different profit figure and we will be looking at this particular point in detail.

Study guide

		Intellectual level
D4	**Marginal and absorption costing**	
(a)	Explain the importance and apply the concept of contribution	1
(b)	Demonstrate and discuss the effect of absorption and marginal costing on inventory valuation and profit determination	2
(c)	Calculate profit or loss under absorption and marginal costing	2
(d)	Reconcile the profits or losses calculated under absorption and marginal costing	2
(e)	Describe the advantages and disadvantages of absorption and marginal costing	1

Exam guide

Look out for questions in your examination which require you to calculate profit or losses using absorption and marginal costing.

1 Marginal cost and marginal costing

1.1 Introduction

FAST FORWARD

Marginal cost is the variable cost of one unit of product or service.

Key term

Marginal costing is an alternative method of costing to absorption costing. In marginal costing, only variable costs are charged as a cost of sale and a contribution is calculated (sales revenue minus variable cost of sales). Closing inventories of work in progress or finished goods are valued at marginal (variable) production cost. Fixed costs are treated as a period cost, and are charged in full to the profit and loss account of the accounting period in which they are incurred.

The **marginal production cost** per unit of an item usually consists of the following.

- Direct materials
- Direct labour
- Variable production overheads

Direct labour costs might be excluded from marginal costs when the work force is a given number of employees on a fixed wage or salary. Even so, it is not uncommon for direct labour to be treated as a variable cost, even when employees are paid a basic wage for a fixed working week. If in doubt, you should treat direct labour as a variable cost unless given clear indications to the contrary. Direct labour is often a step cost, with sufficiently short steps to make labour costs act in a variable fashion.

The **marginal cost of sales** usually consists of the marginal cost of production adjusted for inventory movements plus the variable selling costs, which would include items such as sales commission, and possibly some variable distribution costs.

1.2 Contribution

FAST FORWARD

Contribution is an important measure in marginal costing, and it is calculated as the difference between sales value and marginal or variable cost of sales.

Contribution is of fundamental importance in marginal costing, and the term 'contribution' is really short for 'contribution towards covering fixed overheads and making a profit'.

2 The principles of marginal costing

The principles of marginal costing are as follows.

(a)   **Period fixed costs are the same, for any volume of sales and production** (provided that the level of activity is within the 'relevant range'). Therefore, by selling an extra item of product or service the following will happen.

- Revenue will increase by the sales value of the item sold.
- Costs will increase by the variable cost per unit.
- Profit will increase by the amount of contribution earned from the extra item.

(b)   Similarly, if the volume of sales falls by one item, the profit will fall by the amount of contribution earned from the item.

(c)   **Profit measurement should therefore be based on an analysis of total contribution**. Since fixed costs relate to a period of time, and do not change with increases or decreases in sales volume, it is misleading to charge units of sale with a share of fixed costs. Absorption costing is therefore misleading, and it is more appropriate to deduct fixed costs from total contribution for the period to derive a profit figure.

(d)   When a unit of product is made, the extra costs incurred in its manufacture are the **variable production costs**. Fixed costs are unaffected, and no extra fixed costs are incurred when output is increased. It is therefore argued that **the valuation of closing inventories should be at variable production cost** (direct materials, direct labour, direct expenses (if any) and variable production overhead) because these are the only costs properly attributable to the product.

2.1 Example: Marginal costing principles

Rain Until September Co makes a product, the Splash, which has a variable production cost of $6 per unit and a sales price of $10 per unit. At the beginning of September 20X0, there were no opening inventories and production during the month was 20,000 units. Fixed costs for the month were $45,000 (production, administration, sales and distribution). There were no variable marketing costs.

Required

Calculate the contribution and profit for September 20X0, using marginal costing principles, if sales were as follows.

(a)   10,000 Splashes
(b)   15,000 Splashes
(c)   20,000 Splashes

Solution

The stages in the profit calculation are as follows.

- To **identify the variable cost of sales, and then the contribution**.
- Deduct fixed costs from the total contribution to derive the profit.
- Value all closing inventories at marginal production cost ($6 per unit).

	10,000 Splashes		15,000 Splashes		20,000 Splashes	
	$	$	$	$	$	$
Sales (at $10)		100,000		150,000		200,000
Opening inventory	0		0		0	
Variable production cost	120,000		120,000			
					120,000	
	120,000		120,000		120,000	
Less value of closing						
inventory (at marginal cost)	60,000		30,000		–	
Variable cost of sales		60,000		90,000		120,000
Contribution		40,000		60,000		80,000
Less fixed costs		45,000		45,000		45,000
Profit/(loss)		(5,000)		15,000		35,000
Profit (loss) per unit		$(0.50)		$1		$1.75
Contribution per unit		$4		$4		$4

The conclusions which may be drawn from this example are as follows.

(a) The **profit per unit varies** at differing levels of sales, because the average fixed overhead cost per unit changes with the volume of output and sales.

(b) The **contribution per unit is constant** at all levels of output and sales. Total contribution, which is the contribution per unit multiplied by the number of units sold, increases in direct proportion to the volume of sales.

(c) Since the **contribution per unit does not change**, the most effective way of calculating the expected profit at any level of output and sales would be as follows.

- First calculate the total contribution.
- Then deduct fixed costs as a period charge in order to find the profit.

(d) In our example the expected profit from the sale of 17,000 Splashes would be as follows.

	$
Total contribution (17,000 × $4)	68,000
Less fixed costs	45,000
Profit	23,000

- If total contribution **exceeds fixed costs**, a profit is made
- If total contribution **exactly equals fixed costs**, no profit or loss is made
- If total contribution is **less than fixed costs**, there will be a loss

Question

Marginal costing principles

Mill Stream makes two products, the Mill and the Stream. Information relating to each of these products for April 20X1 is as follows.

	Mill	Stream
Opening inventory	nil	nil
Production (units)	15,000	6,000
Sales (units)	10,000	5,000
Sales price per unit	$20	$30
Unit costs	$	$
Direct materials	8	14
Direct labour	4	2
Variable production overhead	2	1
Variable sales overhead	2	3

Fixed costs for the month	$
Production costs	40,000
Administration costs	15,000
Sales and distribution costs	25,000

Required

(a) Using marginal costing principles and the method in 2.1(d) above, calculate the profit in April 20X1.

(b) Calculate the profit if sales had been 15,000 units of Mill and 6,000 units of Stream.

Answer

(a)

	$
Contribution from Mills (unit contribution = $20 – $16 = $4 × 10,000)	40,000
Contribution from Streams (unit contribution = $30 – $20 = $10 × 5,000)	50,000
Total contribution	90,000
Fixed costs for the period	80,000
Profit	10,000

(b) At a higher volume of sales, profit would be as follows.

	$
Contribution from sales of 15,000 Mills (× $4)	60,000
Contribution from sales of 6,000 Streams (× $10)	60,000
Total contribution	120,000
Less fixed costs	80,000
Profit	40,000

2.2 Profit or contribution information

The main advantage of **contribution information** (rather than profit information) is that it allows an easy calculation of profit if sales increase or decrease from a certain level. By comparing total contribution with fixed overheads, it is possible to determine whether profits or losses will be made at certain sales levels. **Profit information**, on the other hand, does not lend itself to easy manipulation but note how easy it was to calculate profits using contribution information in the question entitled *Marginal costing principles*. **Contribution information** is more useful for **decision making** than profit information, as we shall see when we go on to study decision making in Section F of this Study Text.

3 Marginal costing and absorption costing and the calculation of profit

3.1 Introduction

FAST FORWARD

In **marginal costing**, fixed production costs are treated as **period costs** and are written off as they are incurred. In **absorption costing**, fixed production costs are absorbed into the cost of units and are carried forward in inventory to be charged against sales for the next period. Inventory values using absorption costing are therefore greater than those calculated using marginal costing.

Marginal costing as a cost accounting system is significantly different from absorption costing. It is an **alternative method** of accounting for costs and profit, which rejects the principles of absorbing fixed overheads into unit costs.

Marginal costing	Absorption costing
Closing inventories are valued at marginal production cost.	Closing inventories are valued at full production cost.
Fixed costs are period costs.	Fixed costs are absorbed into unit costs.
Cost of sales does not include a share of fixed overheads.	Cost of sales does include a share of fixed overheads (see note below).

Note. The share of fixed overheads included in cost of sales are from the previous period (in opening inventory values). Some of the fixed overheads from the current period will be excluded by being carried forward in closing inventory values.

In **marginal costing**, it is necessary to identify the following.

- Variable costs
- Contribution
- Fixed costs

In **absorption costing** (sometimes known as **full costing**), it is not necessary to distinguish variable costs from fixed costs.

3.2 Example: Marginal and absorption costing compared

Look back at the information contained in the question entitled: *Marginal costing principles.* Suppose that the budgeted production for April 20X1 was 15,000 units of Mill and 6,000 units of Stream, and production overhead is absorbed on the basis of budgeted direct labour costs.

Required

Calculate the profit if production was as budgeted, and sales were as follows.

(a)   10,000 units of Mill and 5,000 units of Stream
(b)   15,000 units of Mill and 6,000 units of Stream

Administration, sales and distribution costs should be charged as a period cost.

Solution

Budgeted production overhead is calculated as follows.

		$
Fixed		40,000
Variable:	Mills (15,000 × $2)	30,000
	Streams (6,000 × $1)	6,000
Total		76,000

The **production overhead absorption rate** would be calculated as follows.

$$\frac{\text{Budgeted production overhead}}{\text{Budgeted direct labour cost}} = \frac{\$76,000}{(15,000 \times \$4) + (6,000 \times \$2)} \times 100\%$$

$$= 105.56\% \text{ of direct labour cost}$$

(a)   If sales are 10,000 units of Mill and 5,000 units of Stream, profit would be as follows.

	Absorption costing		
	Mills	Streams	Total
	$	$	$
Costs of production			
Direct materials	120,000	84,000	204,000
Direct labour	60,000	12,000	72,000
Overhead (105.56% of labour)	63,333	12,667	76,000
	243,333	108,667	352,000
Less closing stocks (W1)	81,111	18,111	99,222
Production cost of sales	162,222	90,556	252,778
Administration costs			15,000
Sales and distribution costs			
Variable (W2)			35,000
Fixed			25,000
Total cost of sales			327,778
Sales	200,000	150,000	350,000
Profit			22,222

Note. There is no under-/over-absorption of overhead, since actual production is the same as budgeted production.

The profit derived using absorption costing techniques is different from the profit ($10,000) using marginal costing techniques at this volume of sales (see earlier question).

(b)   If production and sales are exactly the same, (15,000 units of Mill and 6,000 units of Stream) profit would be $40,000.

	$
Sales (300,000 + 180,000)	480,000
Cost of sales (W3)	440,000
Profit	40,000

*   No closing inventory if sales and production are equal.

Workings

1   **Closing inventories**

(a)   If 15,000 units of Mills are produced and only 10,000 units are sold, there will be closing inventories of 5,000 units (15,000 – 10,000).

Therefore, of the production costs of $243,333, 5,000 units of the 15,000 units produced (5,000/15,000 = 1/3) will be carried forward in closing inventory ie 1/3 × $243,333 = $81,111.

(b)   Similarly, if 6,000 units of Streams are produced and only 5,000 units are sold there will be closing inventories of 1,000 units (6,000– 5,000).

Therefore, of the production cost of $108,667, 1,000 units of the 6,000 units produced (1,000/6,000 = 1/6) will be carried forward in closing inventory ie 1/6 × $108,667 = $8,111.

2   **Variable sales and distribution costs**

Mills

Variable sales and distribution costs	= $2 (from Question entitled 'marginal costing principles')
	× 10,000 units
	= $20,000

Streams

Variable sales and distribution costs	= $3 (from Question entitled 'marginal costing principles')
	× 5,000 units

$$= \$15,000$$

∴ Total sales and distribution costs
$$= \$20,000 + \$15,000$$
$$= \$35,000$$

3 **Cost of sales**

	$	$
Costs of production (from part (a))		352,000
Administration costs (from Question entitled 'marginal costing principles')		15,000
Fixed sales and distribution costs (from Question entitled 'marginal costing principles')		25,000
Variable sales overhead		
Mills (15,000 × $2)	30,000	
Streams (6,000 × $3)	18,000	
		48,000
		440,000

This is the same as the profit calculated by marginal costing techniques in the earlier question.

We can draw a number of conclusions from this example.

(a) Marginal costing and absorption costing are different techniques for assessing profit in a period.

(b) If there are **changes in inventories during a period**, so that opening inventory or closing inventory values are different, **marginal costing and absorption costing give different results** for profit obtained.

(c) **If the opening and closing inventory volumes and values are the same, marginal costing and absorption costing will give the same profit figure**. This is because the total cost of sales during the period would be the same, no matter how calculated.

3.3 The long-run effect on profit

In the long run, total profit for a company will be the same whether marginal costing or absorption costing is used. Different accounting conventions merely affect the profit of individual accounting periods.

3.4 Example: Comparison of total profits

To illustrate this point, let us suppose that a company makes and sells a single product. At the beginning of period 1, there are no opening inventories of the product, for which the variable production cost is $4 and the sales price $6 per unit. Fixed costs are $2,000 per period, of which $1,500 are fixed production costs.

	Period 1	Period 2
Sales	1,200 units	1,800 units
Production	1,500 units	1,500 units

Required

Determine the profit in each period using the following methods of costing.

(a) Absorption costing. Assume normal output is 1,500 units per period.
(b) Marginal costing.

Solution

(a) **Absorption costing**: the absorption rate for fixed production overhead is

$$\frac{\$1,500}{1,500\,\text{units}} = \$1\text{ per unit}$$

	Period 1		Period 2		Total	
	$	$	$	$	$	$
Sales		7,200		10,800		18,000
Production costs						
Variable	6,000		6,000		12,000	
Fixed	1,500		1,500		3,000	
	7,500		7,500		15,000	
Add opening inventory b/f	–		1,500			
	7,500		9,000			
Less closing inventory c/f (W1)	1,500		–			
Production cost of sales	6,000		9,000		15,000	
Other costs	500		500		1,000	
Total cost of sales		6,500		9,500		16,000
Unadjusted profit		700		1,300		2,000
(Under-)/over-absorbed overhead		–		–		–
Profit		700		1,300		2,000

(b) **Marginal costing**

	Period 1		Period 2		Total	
	$	$	$	$	$	$
Sales		7,200		10,800		18,000
Variable production cost	6,000		6,000		12,000	
Add opening inventory b/f	–		1,200			
	6,000		7,200			
Less closing inventory c/f (W2)	1,200		–		–	
Variable production cost of sales		4,800		7,200		12,000
Contribution		2,400		3,600		6,000
Fixed costs		2,000		2,000		4,000
Profit		400		1,600		2,000

Workings

1 **Closing inventory – absorption costing**

If 1,500 units are produced in period 1 and only 1,200 units are sold, there will be 300 units left in inventory.

Each unit of the product has a total production cost of $5 per unit using absorption costing.

	$
Variable production cost	4
Fixed production overhead	1
Total production cost	5

∴ Closing inventory valuation = 300 units × $5
= $1,500

2 **Closing inventory – marginal costing**

From (W1) above, there are 300 units of closing inventory.

Each unit of the product has a variable production cost of $4 per unit using marginal costing (there is no fixed production overhead included as there is under the absorption costing method).

$$\therefore \text{Closing inventory valuation} \quad = 300 \text{ units} \times \$4$$
$$= \$1,200$$

Notes

(a) **The total profit over the two periods is the same for each method of costing, but the profit in each period is different**.

(b) In absorption costing, fixed production overhead of $300 is carried forward from period 1 into period 2 in inventory values, and becomes a charge to profit in period 2. In marginal costing all fixed costs are charged in the period they are incurred, therefore the profit in period 1 is $300 lower and in period 2 is $300 higher than the absorption costing profit.

Question   AC versus MC

The overhead absorption rate for product X is $10 per machine hour. Each unit of product X requires five machine hours. Inventory of product X on 1.1.X1 was 150 units and on 31.12.X1 it was 100 units. What is the difference in profit between results reported using absorption costing and results reported using marginal costing?

A   The absorption costing profit would be $2,500 less
B   The absorption costing profit would be $2,500 greater
C   The absorption costing profit would be $5,000 less
D   The absorption costing profit would be $5,000 greater

Answer

Difference in profit = **change** in inventory levels × fixed overhead absorption per unit = $(150 - 100) \times \$10 \times 5 = \$2,500$ **lower** profit, because inventory levels **decreased**. The correct answer is therefore option A.

The key is the change in the volume of inventory. Inventory levels have **decreased** therefore absorption costing will report a **lower** profit. This eliminates options B and D.

Option C is incorrect because it is based on the closing inventory only (100 units × $10 × 5 hours).

4 Reconciling profits

4.1 Introduction

FAST FORWARD

Reported profit figures using marginal costing or absorption costing will differ if there is any change in the level of inventories in the period. If production is equal to sales, there will be no difference in calculated profits using the costing methods.

The difference in profits reported under the two costing systems is due to the different inventory valuation methods used.

If inventory levels increase between the beginning and end of a period, absorption costing will report the higher profit. This is because some of the fixed production overhead incurred during the period will be carried forward in closing inventory (which reduces cost of sales) to be set against sales revenue in the following period instead of being written off in full against profit in the period concerned.

If inventory levels decrease, absorption costing will report the lower profit because as well as the fixed overhead incurred, fixed production overhead which had been carried forward in opening inventory is released and is also included in cost of sales.

4.2 Example: Reconciling profits

The profits reported under absorption costing and marginal costing for period 1 in the example in Paragraph 3.4 would be reconciled as follows.

	$
Marginal costing profit	400
Adjust for fixed overhead in inventory:	
Inventory increase of 300 units × $1 per unit	300
Absorption costing profit	700

Question	Absorption costing profit

When opening inventories were 8,500 litres and closing inventories 6,750 litres, a firm had a profit of $62,100 using marginal costing.

Assuming that the fixed overhead absorption rate was $3 per litre, what would be the profit using absorption costing?

A $41,850   B $56,850   C $67,350   D $82,350

Answer

Difference in profit = (8,500 – 6,750) × $3 = $5,250

Absorption costing profit = $62,100 – $5,250 = $56,850

The correct answer is B.

Since inventory levels reduced, the absorption costing profit will be lower than the marginal costing profit. You can therefore eliminate options C and D.

xam focus oint

The effect on profit of using the two different costing methods can be confusing. You *must* get it straight in your mind before the examination. Remember that if opening inventory values are greater than closing inventory values, marginal costing shows the greater profit.

5 Marginal costing versus absorption costing

FAST FORWARD

In your examination you may be asked to calculate the profit for an accounting period using either of the two methods of accounting. **Absorption costing** is most often used for routine profit reporting and must be used for financial accounting purposes. **Marginal costing** provides better management information for planning and decision making. There are a number of arguments both for and against each of the costing systems.

The following diagram summarises the arguments in favour of both marginal and absorption costing.

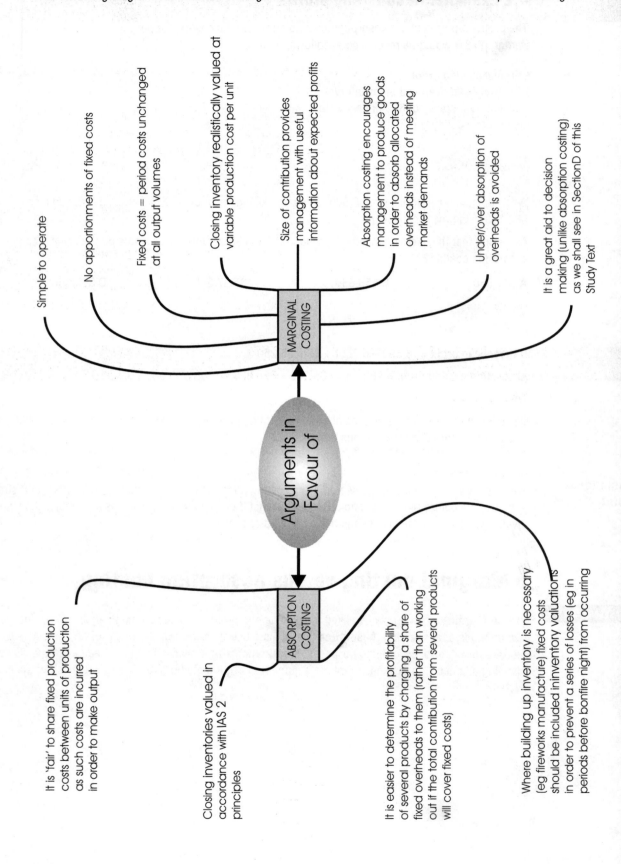

Chapter roundup

- **Marginal cost** is the variable cost of one unit of product or service.

- **Contribution** is an important measure in marginal costing, and it is calculated as the difference between sales value and marginal or variable cost of sales.

- In **marginal costing**, fixed production costs are treated as **period costs** and are written off as they are incurred. In **absorption costing**, fixed production costs are absorbed into the cost of units and are carried forward in inventory to be charged against sales for the next period. Inventory values using absorption costing are therefore greater than those calculated using marginal costing.

- **Reported profit figures using marginal costing or absorption costing will differ if there is any change in the level of inventories in the period**. If production is equal to sales, there will be no difference in calculated profits using these costing methods.

- In your examination you may be asked to calculate the profit for an accounting period using either of the two methods of accounting. **Absorption costing** is most often used for routine profit reporting and must be used for financial accounting purposes. **Marginal costing** provides better management information for planning and decision making. There are a number of arguments both for and against each of the costing systems.

Quick quiz

1   What is marginal costing?

2   What is a period cost in marginal costing?

3   Sales value – marginal cost of sales = ...

4   What is a breakeven point?

5   Marginal costing and absorption costing are different techniques for assessing profit in a period. If there are changes in inventory during a period, marginal costing and absorption costing give different results for profit obtained.

Which of the following statements are true?

I   If inventory levels increase, marginal costing will report the higher profit.

II   If inventory levels decrease, marginal costing will report the lower profit.

III   If inventory levels decrease, marginal costing will report the higher profit.

IV   If the opening and closing inventory volumes are the same, marginal costing and absorption costing will give the same profit figure.

A   All of the above
B   I, II and IV
C   I and IV
D   III and IV

6   Which of the following are arguments in favour of marginal costing?

(a)   Closing stock (inventory) is valued in accordance with IAS 2.
(b)   It is simple to operate.
(c)   There is no under or over absorption of overheads.
(d)   Fixed costs are the same regardless of activity levels.
(e)   The information from this costing method may be used for decision making.

Answers to quick quiz

1   Marginal costing is an alternative method of costing to absorption costing. In marginal costing, only variable costs are charged as a cost of sale and a contribution is calculated (sales revenue – variable cost of sales).

2   A fixed cost

3   Contribution

4   The point at which total contribution exactly equals fixed costs (no profit or loss is made)

5   D

6   (b), (c), (d), (e)

Now try the questions below from the Exam Question Bank

Number	Level	Marks	Time
Q9	MCQ/OTQ	n/a	n/a

BPP
LEARNING MEDIA

Process costing

Topic list	Syllabus reference
1 The basics of process costing	D6 (a), (b), (c)
2 Losses in process costing	D6 (d), (e)
3 Losses with a disposal cost	D6 (i)
4 Valuing closing work in progress	D6 (f), (h)
5 Valuing opening work in progress: FIFO method	D6 (g)
6 Valuing opening work in progress: weighted average cost method	D6 (g)

Introduction

In this chapter we will consider **process costing**. The chapter will consider the topic from basics, looking at how to account for the most simple of processes. We then move on to how to account for any **losses** which might occur, as well as what to do with any **scrapped units** which are sold. We also consider how to deal with any **closing work in progress** and then look at two methods of valuing **opening work in progress**. Valuation of both opening and closing work in progress hinges on the concept of **equivalent units**, which will be explained in detail.

Study guide

		Intellectual level
D6	**Process costing**	
(a)	Describe the characteristics of process costing	1
(b)	Describe situations where the use of process costing would be appropriate	1
(c)	Calculate the cost per unit of process outputs	1
(d)	Explain the concepts of 'normal and abnormal' losses and 'abnormal' gains	1
(e)	Prepare process accounts, involving normal and abnormal losses and abnormal gains	1
(f)	Calculate and explain the concept of equivalent units	1
(g)	Apportion process costs between work remaining in process and transfers out of a process using the weighted average and FIFO methods	2
(h)	Prepare process accounts in situations where work remains incomplete	2
(i)	Prepare process accounts where losses and gains are identified at different stages of the process	1

Note. Situations involving work in process **and** losses in the same process are excluded.

Exam guide

Expect one or two questions on process costing. They will be shorter than the examples and questions in this chapter, but if you have worked through some long questions you will have covered whatever can come up in a short question.

1 The basics of process costing

1.1 Introduction to process costing

Process costing is a costing method used where it is not possible to identify separate units of production, or jobs, usually because of the continuous nature of the production processes involved.

It is common to identify process costing with **continuous production** such as the following.

- Oil refining
- Paper
- Foods and drinks
- Chemicals

Process costing may also be associated with the continuous production of large volumes of low-cost items, such as **cans** or **tins**.

1.2 Features of process costing

(a) The **output** of one process becomes the **input** to the next until the finished product is made in the final process.

(b) The continuous nature of production in many processes means that there will usually be **closing work in progress which must be valued**. In process costing it is not possible to build up cost records of the cost per unit of output or the cost per unit of closing inventory because production in progress is an **indistinguishable homogeneous mass**.

(c) There is often a **loss in process** due to spoilage, wastage, evaporation and so on.

(d) Output from production may be a single product, but there may also be a **by-product** (or by-products) and/or **joint products.**

The aim of this chapter is to describe how cost accountants keep a set of accounts to record the costs of production in a processing industry. The aim of the set of accounts is to derive a cost, or valuation, for output and closing inventory.

1.3 Process accounts

Where a series of separate processes is required to manufacture the finished product, the output of one process becomes the input to the next until the final output is made in the final process. If two processes are required the accounts would look like this.

PROCESS 1 ACCOUNT

	Units	$		Units	$
Direct materials	1,000	50,000	Output to process 2	1,000	90,000
Direct labour		20,000			
Production overhead		20,000			
	1,000	90,000		1,000	90,000

PROCESS 2 ACCOUNT

	Units	$		Units	$
Materials from process 1	1,000	90,000	Output to finished goods	1,000	150,000
Added materials		30,000			
Direct labour		15,000			
Production overhead		15,000			
	1,000	150,000		1,000	150,000

Note that direct labour and production overhead may be treated together in an examination question as **conversion cost**.

Added materials, labour and overhead in process 2 are added gradually throughout the process. Materials from process 1, in contrast, will often be introduced in full at the start of process 2.

The 'units' columns in the process accounts are for **memorandum purposes** only and help you to ensure that you do not miss out any entries.

1.4 Framework for dealing with process costing

FAST FORWARD

Process costing is centred around **four key steps**. The exact work done at each step will depend on whether there are normal losses, scrap, opening and closing work in progress and so on.

Step 1	Determine output and losses
Step 2	Calculate cost per unit of output, losses and WIP
Step 3	Calculate total cost of output, losses and WIP
Step 4	Complete accounts

Let's look at these steps in more detail

Step 1   **Determine output and losses.** This step involves the following.

- Determining expected output
- Calculating normal loss and abnormal loss and gain
- Calculating equivalent units if there is closing or opening work in progress

Step 2   **Calculate cost per unit of output, losses and WIP**. This step involves calculating cost per unit or cost per equivalent unit.

Step 3   **Calculate total cost of output, losses and WIP**. In some examples this will be straightforward; however in cases where there is closing and/or opening work-in-progress a **statement of evaluation** will have to be prepared.

Step 4   **Complete accounts**. This step involves the following.

- Completing the process account
- Writing up the other accounts required by the question

Exam focus point

> In the exam you will only get 2-mark questions, so you will only have to do the equivalent of Step 1, 2 and/or 3. However, you will feel much more confident if you understand all the steps.

2 Losses in process costing

2.1 Introduction

FAST FORWARD

> **Losses** may occur in process. If a certain level of loss is expected, this is known as **normal loss**. If losses are greater than expected, the extra loss is **abnormal loss**. If losses are less than expected, the difference is known as **abnormal gain**.

Key terms

> **Normal loss** is the loss expected during a process. It is not given a cost.
>
> **Abnormal loss** is the extra loss resulting when actual loss is greater than normal or expected loss, and it is given a cost.
>
> **Abnormal gain** is the gain resulting when actual loss is less than the normal or expected loss, and it is given a 'negative cost'.

Since normal loss is not given a cost, the cost of producing these units is borne by the 'good' units of output.

Abnormal loss and gain units are valued at the same unit rate as 'good' units. Abnormal events do not therefore affect the cost of good production. Their costs are **analysed separately** in an **abnormal loss or abnormal gain account**.

2.2 Example: abnormal losses and gains

Suppose that input to a process is 1,000 units at a cost of $4,500. Normal loss is 10% and there are no opening or closing stocks. Determine the accounting entries for the cost of output and the cost of the loss if actual output were as follows.

(a)   860 units (so that actual loss is 140 units)
(b)   920 units (so that actual loss is 80 units)

Solution

Before we demonstrate the use of the 'four-step framework' we will summarise the way that the losses are dealt with.

(a)   Normal loss is given no share of cost.

(b)   The cost of output is therefore based on the **expected** units of output, which in our example amount to 90% of 1,000 = 900 units.

(c) Abnormal loss is given a cost, which is written off to the profit and loss account via an abnormal loss/gain account.

(d) Abnormal gain is treated in the same way, except that being a gain rather than a loss, it appears as a **debit** entry in the process account (whereas a loss appears as a **credit** entry in this account).

(a) **Output is 860 units**

Step 1 Determine output and losses

If actual output is 860 units and the actual loss is 140 units:

	Units
Actual loss	140
Normal loss (10% of 1,000)	100
Abnormal loss	40

Step 2 Calculate cost per unit of output and losses

The cost per unit of output and the cost per unit of abnormal loss are based on expected output.

$$\frac{\text{Costs incurred}}{\text{Expected output}} = \frac{\$4,500}{900 \text{ units}} = \$5 \text{ per unit}$$

Step 3 Calculate total cost of output and losses

Normal loss is not assigned any cost.

	$
Cost of output (860 × $5)	4,300
Normal loss	0
Abnormal loss (40 × $5)	200
	4,500

Step 4 Complete accounts

PROCESS ACCOUNT

	Units	$		Units		$
Cost incurred	1,000	4,500	Normal loss	100		0
			Output (finished goods a/c)	860	(× $5)	4,300
			Abnormal loss	40	(× $5)	200
	1,000	4,500		1,000		4,500

ABNORMAL LOSS ACCOUNT

	Units	$		Units	$
Process a/c	40	200	Income statement	40	200

(b) **Output is 920 units**

Step 1 Determine output and losses

If actual output is 920 units and the actual loss is 80 units:

	Units
Actual loss	80
Normal loss (10% of 1,000)	100
Abnormal gain	20

Step 2 Calculate cost per unit of output and losses

The cost per unit of output and the cost per unit of abnormal gain are based on **expected** output.

$$\frac{\text{Costs incurred}}{\text{Expected output}} = \frac{\$4,500}{900\text{ units}} = \$5 \text{ per unit}$$

(Whether there is abnormal loss or gain does not affect the valuation of units of output. The figure of $5 per unit is exactly the same as in the previous paragraph, when there were 40 units of abnormal loss.)

Step 3   Calculate total cost of output and losses

	$
Cost of output (920 × $5)	4,600
Normal loss	0
Abnormal gain (20 × $5)	(100)
	4,500

Step 4   Complete accounts

PROCESS ACCOUNT

	Units	$		Units	$
Cost incurred	1,000	4,500	Normal loss	100	0
Abnormal gain a/c	20 (x $5)	100	Output	920 (x $5)	4,600
			(finished goods a/c)		
	1,020	4,600		1,020	4,600

ABNORMAL GAIN

	Units	$		Units	$
Income statment	20	100	Process a/c	20	100

2.3 Example: Abnormal losses and gains again

During a four-week period, period 3, costs of input to a process were $29,070. Input was 1,000 units, output was 850 units and normal loss is 10%.

During the next period, period 4, costs of input were again $29,070. Input was again 1,000 units, but output was 950 units.

There were no units of opening or closing inventory.

Required

Prepare the process account and abnormal loss or gain account for each period.

Solution

Step 1   Determine output and losses

Period 3

	Units
Actual output	850
Normal loss (10% × 1,000)	100
Abnormal loss	50
Input	1,000

Period 4

	Units
Actual output	950
Normal loss (10% × 1,000)	100
Abnormal gain	(50)
Input	1,000

Step 2 Calculate cost per unit of output and losses

For each period the cost per unit is based on expected output.

$$\frac{\text{Cost of input}}{\text{Expected units of output}} = \frac{\$29,070}{900} = \$32.30 \text{ per unit}$$

Step 3 Calculate total cost of output and losses

Period 3

	$
Cost of output (850 × $32.30)	27,455
Normal loss	0
Abnormal loss (50 × $32.30)	1,615
	29,070

Period 4

	$
Cost of output (950 × $32.30)	30,685
Normal loss	0
Abnormal gain (50 × $32.30)	1,615
	29,070

Step 4 Complete accounts

PROCESS ACCOUNT

	Units	$		Units	$
Period 3					
Cost of input	1,000	29,070	Normal loss	100	0
			Finished goods a/c	850	27,455
			(× $32.30)		
			Abnormal loss a/c	50	1,615
			(× $32.30)		
	1,000	29,070		1,000	29,070
Period 4					
Cost of input	1,000	29,070	Normal loss	100	0
Abnormal gain a/c	50	1,615	Finished goods a/c	950	30,685
(× $32.30)			(× $32.30)		
	1,050	30,685		1,050	30,685

ABNORMAL LOSS OR GAIN ACCOUNT

	$		$
Period 3		*Period 4*	
Abnormal loss in process a/c	1,615	Abnormal gain in process a/c	1,615

A nil balance on this account will be carried forward into period 5.

If there is a closing balance in the abnormal loss or gain account when the profit for the period is calculated, this balance is taken to the income statement: an abnormal gain will be a credit to the income statement and an abnormal loss will be a debit to the income statement.

Question

3,000 units of material are input to a process. Process costs are as follows.

Material	$11,700
Conversion costs	$6,300

Output is 2,000 units. Normal loss is 20% of input.

Required

Prepare a process account and the appropriate abnormal loss/gain account.

Answer

Step 1 **Determine output and losses**

We are told that output is 2,000 units.
Normal loss = 20% × 3,000 = 600 units
Abnormal loss = (3,000 − 600) − 2,000 = 400 units

Step 2 **Calculate cost per unit of output and losses**

$$\text{Cost per unit} = \frac{\$(11,700 + 6,300)}{2,400} = \$7.50$$

Step 3 **Calculate total cost of output and losses**

		$
Output	(2,000 × $7.50)	15,000
Normal loss		0
Abnormal loss	(400 × $7.50)	3,000
		18,000

Step 4 **Complete accounts**

PROCESS ACCOUNT

	Units	$		Units	$
Material	3,000	11,700	Output	2,000	15,000
Conversion costs		6,300	Normal loss	600	
			Abnormal loss	400	3,000
	3,000	18,000		3,000	18,000

ABNORMAL LOSS ACCOUNT

	$		$
Process a/c	3,000	Income statement	3,000

Question

Charlton Co manufactures a product in a single process operation. Normal loss is 10% of input. Loss occurs at the end of the process. Data for June are as follows.

Opening and closing inventories of work in progress	Nil
Cost of input materials (3,300 units)	$59,100
Direct labour and production overhead	$30,000
Output to finished goods	2,750 units

The full cost of finished output in June was

A $74,250   B $81,000   C $82,500   D $89,100

Answer

Step 1   Determine output and losses

	Units
Actual output	2,750
Normal loss (10% × 3,300)	330
Abnormal loss	220
	3,300

Step 2   Calculate cost per unit of output and losses

$$\frac{\text{Cost of input}}{\text{Expected units of output}} = \frac{\$89,100}{3,300 - 330} = \$30 \text{ per unit}$$

Step 3   Calculate total cost of output and losses

	$
Cost of output (2,750 × $30)	82,500 **(The correct answer is C)**
Normal loss	0
Abnormal loss (220 × $30)	6,600
	89,100

If you were reduced to making a calculated guess, you could have eliminated option D. This is simply the total input cost, with no attempt to apportion some of the cost to the abnormal loss.

Option A is incorrect because it results from allocating a full unit cost to the normal loss: remember that normal loss does not carry any of the process cost.

Option B is incorrect because it results from calculating a 10% normal loss based on *output* of 2,750 units (275 units normal loss), rather than on *input* of 3,300 units.

3 Losses with a disposal cost

3.1 Introduction

You must also be able to deal with losses which have a **disposal cost**.

The basic calculations required in such circumstances are as follows.

(a)   Increase the process costs by the cost of disposing of the units of normal loss and use the resulting cost per unit to value good output and abnormal loss/gain.

(b)   The normal loss is given no value in the process account.

(c)   Include the disposal costs of normal loss on the debit side of the process account.

(d)   Include the disposal costs of abnormal loss in the abnormal loss account and hence in the transfer of the cost of abnormal loss to the income statement.

3.2 Example: Losses with a disposal cost

Suppose that input to a process was 1,000 units at a cost of $4,500. Normal loss is 10% and there are no opening and closing inventories. Actual output was 860 units and loss units had to be disposed of at a cost of $0.90 per unit.

Normal loss = 10% × 1,000 = 100 units. ∴ Abnormal loss = 900 − 860 = 40 units

$$\text{Cost per unit} = \frac{\$4,500 + (100 \times \$0.90)}{900} = \$5.10$$

The relevant accounts would be as follows.

PROCESS ACCOUNT

	Units	$		Units	$
Cost of input	1,000	4,500	Output	860	4,386
Disposal cost of			Normal loss	100	
normal loss		90	Abnormal loss	40	204
	1,000	4,590		1,000	4,590

ABNORMAL LOSS ACCOUNT

	$		$
Process a/c	204	Income statement	240
Disposal cost (40 × $0.90)	36		
	240		240

4 Valuing closing work in progress

4.1 Introduction

FAST FORWARD

When units are partly completed at the end of a period (and hence there is closing work in progress), it is necessary to calculate the **equivalent units of production** in order to determine the cost of a completed unit.

In the examples we have looked at so far we have assumed that opening and closing inventories of work in process have been nil. We must now look at more realistic examples and consider how to allocate the costs incurred in a period between completed output (that is, finished units) and partly completed closing inventory.

Some examples will help to illustrate the problem, and the techniques used to share out (apportion) costs between finished output and closing inventories.

Suppose that we have the following account for Process 2 for period 9.

PROCESS ACCOUNT

	Units	$		Units	$
Materials	1,000	6,200	Finished goods	800	?
Labour and overhead		2,850	Closing WIP	200	?
	1,000	9,050		1,000	9,050

How do we value the finished goods and closing work in process?

With any form of process costing involving closing WIP, we have to apportion costs between output and closing WIP. To apportion costs 'fairly' we make use of the concept of **equivalent units of production**.

4.2 Equivalent units

Key term

Equivalent units are notional whole units which represent incomplete work, and which are used to apportion costs between work in process and completed output.

We will assume that in the example above the degree of completion is as follows.

(a) **Direct materials**. These are added in full at the start of processing, and so any closing WIP will have 100% of their direct material content. (This is not always the case in practice. Materials might be added gradually throughout the process, in which case closing inventory will only be a certain percentage complete as to material content. We will look at this later in the chapter.)

(b) **Direct labour and production overhead.** These are usually assumed to be incurred at an even rate through the production process, so that when we refer to a unit that is 50% complete, we mean that it is half complete for labour and overhead, although it might be 100% complete for materials.

Let us also assume that the closing WIP is 100% complete for materials and 25% complete for labour and overhead.

How would we now put a value to the finished output and the closing WIP?

In **Step 1** of our framework, we have been told what output and losses are. However we also need to calculate **equivalent units**.

STATEMENT OF EQUIVALENT UNITS

		Materials		Labour and overhead	
	Total units	Degree of completion	Equivalent units	Degree of completion	Equivalent units
Finished output	800	100%	800	100%	800
Closing WIP	200	100%	200	25%	50
	1,000		1,000		850

In **Step 2** the important figure is **average cost per equivalent unit**. This can be calculated as follows.

STATEMENT OF COSTS PER EQUIVALENT UNIT

	Materials	Labour and overhead
Costs incurred in the period	$6,200	$2,850
Equivalent units of work done	1,000	850
Cost per equivalent unit (approx)	$6.20	$3.3529

To calculate total costs for **Step 3**, we prepare a statement of evaluation to show how the costs should be apportioned between finished output and closing WIP.

STATEMENT OF EVALUATION

	Materials			Labour and overheads			
Item	Equivalent units	Cost per equivalent units	Cost	Equivalent units	Cost per equivalent units	Cost	Total cost
		$	$		$	$	$
Finished output	800	6.20	4,960	800	3.3529	2,682	7,642
Closing WIP	200	6.20	1,240	50	3.3529	168	1,408
	1,000		6,200	850		2,850	9,050

The process account (work in progress, or work in process account) would be shown as follows.

PROCESS ACCOUNT

	Units	$		Units	$
Materials	1,000	6,200	Finished goods	800	7,642
Labour overhead		2,850	Closing WIP	200	1,408
	1,000	9,050		1,000	9,050

4.3 Different rates of input

In many industries, materials, labour and overhead may be **added at different rates** during the course of production.

(a)   Output from a previous process (for example the output from process 1 to process 2) may be introduced into the subsequent process all at once, so that closing inventory is 100% complete in respect of these materials.

(b)   Further materials may be added gradually during the process, so that closing inventory is only partially complete in respect of these added materials.

(c)   Labour and overhead may be 'added' at yet another different rate. When production overhead is absorbed on a labour hour basis, however, we should expect the degree of completion on overhead to be the same as the degree of completion on labour.

When this situation occurs, **equivalent units**, and a **cost per equivalent unit**, should be calculated separately for each type of material, and also for conversion costs.

4.4 Example: Equivalent units and different degrees of completion

Suppose that Columbine Co is a manufacturer of processed goods, and that results in process 2 for April 20X3 were as follows.

Opening inventory	nil
Material input from process 1	4,000 units

Costs of input:

	$
Material from process 1	6,000
Added materials in process 2	1,080
Conversion costs	1,720

Output is transferred into the next process, process 3.

Closing work in process amounted to 800 units, complete as to:

Process 1 material	100%
Added materials	50%
Conversion costs	30%

Required

Prepare the account for process 2 for April 20X3.

Solution

(a)   STATEMENT OF EQUIVALENT UNITS (OF PRODUCTION IN THE PERIOD)

			Equivalent units of production					
			Process 1 material		Added materials		Labour and overhead	
Input	*Output*	*Total*						
Units		Units	Units	%	Units	%	Units	%
4,000	Completed production	3,200	3,200	100	3,200	100	3,200	100
	Closing inventory	800	800	100	400	50	240	30
4,000		4,000	4,000		3,600		3,440	

(b) STATEMENT OF COST (PER EQUIVALENT UNIT)

Input	Cost $	Equivalent production in units	Cost per unit $
Process 1 material	6,000	4,000	1.50
Added materials	1,080	3,600	0.30
Labour and overhead	1,720	3,440	0.50
	8,800		2.30

(c) STATEMENT OF EVALUATION (OF FINISHED WORK AND CLOSING INVENTORIES)

Production	Cost element	Number of equivalent units	Cost per equivalent unit $	Total $	Cost $
Completed production		3,200	2.30		7,360
Closing inventory:	process 1 material	800	1.50	1,200	
	added material	400	0.30	120	
	labour and overhead	240	0.50	120	
					1,440
					8,800

(d) PROCESS ACCOUNT

	Units	$		Units	$
Process 1 material	4,000	6,000	Process 3 a/c	3,200	7,360
Added material		1,080			
Conversion costs		1,720	Closing inventory c/f	800	1,440
	4,000	8,800		4,000	8,800

5 Valuing opening work in progress: FIFO method

5.1 Introduction

Account can be taken of opening work in progress using either the **FIFO** method or the **weighted average cost method**.

Opening work in progress is partly complete at the beginning of a period and is valued at the cost incurred to date. In the example in Paragraph 4.4, closing work in progress of 800 units at the end of April 20X3 would be carried forward as opening inventory, value $1,440, at the beginning of May 20X3.

It therefore follows that the work required to complete units of opening inventory is 100% minus the work in progress done in the previous period. For example, if 100 units of opening inventory are 70% complete at the beginning of June 20X2, the equivalent units of production would be as follows.

Equivalent units in previous period	(May 20X2) (70%)	=	70
Equivalent units to complete work in current period	(June 20X2) (30%)	=	30
Total work done			100

The FIFO method of valuation deals with production on a first in, first out basis. The assumption is that the first units completed in any period are the units of opening inventory that were held at the beginning of the period.

5.2 Example: WIP and FIFO

Suppose that information relating to process 1 of a two-stage production process is as follows, for August 20X2.

Opening inventory 500 units: degree of completion	60%
Cost to date	$2,800

Costs incurred in August 20X2	$
Direct materials (2,500 units introduced)	13,200
Direct labour	6,600
Production overhead	6,600
	26,400

Closing inventory 300 units: degree of completion	80%

There was no loss in the process.

Required

Prepare the process 1 account for August 20X2.

Solution

As the term implies, first in, first out means that in August 20X2 the first units completed were the units of opening inventory.

Opening inventories: work done to date =	60%
plus work done in August 20X2 =	40%

The cost of the work done up to 1 August 20X2 is known to be $2,800, so that the cost of the units completed will be $2,800 plus the cost of completing the final 40% of the work on the units in August 20X2.

Once the opening inventory has been completed, all other finished output in August 20X2 will be work started as well as finished in the month.

	Units
Total output in August 20X2 *	2,700
Less opening inventory, completed first	500
Work started and finished in August 20X2	2,200

(* Opening inventory plus units introduced minus closing inventory = 500 + 2,500 – 300)

What we are doing here is taking the total output of 2,700 units, and saying that we must divide it into two parts as follows.

(a)   The opening inventory, which was first in and so must be first out.
(b)   The rest of the units, which were 100% worked in the period.

Dividing finished output into two parts in this way is a necessary feature of the FIFO valuation method.

Continuing the example, closing inventory of 300 units will be started in August 20X2, but not yet completed.

The total cost of output to process 2 during 20X2 will be as follows.

		$
Opening stock	cost brought forward	2,800 (60%)
	plus cost incurred during August 20X2,	
	to complete	x (40%)
		2,800 + x
Fully worked 2,200 units		y
Total cost of output to process 2, FIFO basis		2,800 + x + y

Equivalent units will again be used as the basis for apportioning **costs incurred during August 20X2**. Be sure that you understand the treatment of 'opening inventory units completed', and can relate the calculations to the principles of FIFO valuation.

Step 1 Determine output and losses

STATEMENT OF EQUIVALENT UNITS

	Total units		Equivalent units of production in August 20X2
Opening inventory units completed	500	(40%)	200
Fully worked units	2,200	(100%)	2,200
Output to process 2	2,700		2,400
Closing inventory	300	(80%)	240
	3,000		2,640

Step 2 Calculate cost per unit of output and losses

The cost per equivalent unit in August 20X2 can now be calculated.

STATEMENT OF COST PER EQUIVALENT UNIT

$$\frac{\text{Cost incurred}}{\text{Equivalent units}} = \frac{\$26,400}{2,640}$$

Cost per equivalent unit = $10

Step 3 Calculate total costs of output, losses and WIP

STATEMENT OF EVALUATION

	Equivalent units	Valuation $
Opening inventory, work done in August 20X2	200	2,000
Fully worked units	2,200	22,000
Closing inventory	240	2,400
	2,640	26,400

The total value of the completed opening inventory will be $2,800 (brought forward) plus $2,000 added in August before completion = $4,800.

Step 4 Complete accounts

PROCESS 1 ACCOUNT

	Units	$		Units	$
Opening inventory	500	2,800	Output to process 2:		
Direct materials	2,500	13,200	Opening inventory completed	500	4,800
Direct labour		6,600	Fully worked units	2,200	22,000
Production o'hd		6,600		2,700	26,800
			Closing inventory	300	2,400
	3,000	29,200		3,000	29,200

We now know that the value of x is $(4,800 – 2,800) = $2,000 and the value of y is $22,000.

Question   **Closing WIP – FIFO**

The following information relates to process 3 of a three-stage production process for the month of January 20X4.

Opening inventory

		$
300 units complete as to:		
materials from process 2	100%	4,400
added materials	90%	1,150
labour	80%	540
production overhead	80%	810
		6,900

In January 20X4, a further 1,800 units were transferred from process 2 at a valuation of $27,000. Added materials amounted to $6,600 and direct labour to $3,270. Production overhead is absorbed at the rate of 150% of direct labour cost. Closing inventory at 31 January 20X4 amounted to 450 units, complete as to:

process 2 materials	100%
added materials	60%
labour and overhead	50%

Required

Prepare the process 3 account for January 20X4 using FIFO valuation principles.

Answer

Step 1   **Statement of equivalent units**

	Total units	Process 2 materials		Added materials		Conversion costs	
Opening inventory	300	0	(10%)	30	(20%)	60	
Fully worked units *	1,350	1,350		1,350		1,350	
Output to finished goods	1,650	1,350		1,380		1,410	
Closing inventory	450	450	(60%)	270	(50%)	225	
	2,100	1,800		1,650		1,635	

* Transfers from process 2, minus closing inventory.

Step 2   **Statement of costs per equivalent unit**

	Total cost	Equivalent units	Cost per equivalent unit
	$		$
Process 2 materials	27,000	1,800	15.00
Added materials	6,600	1,650	4.00
Direct labour	3,270	1,635	2.00
Production overhead (150% of $3,270)	4,905	1,635	3.00
			24.00

Step 3   **Statement of evaluation**

	Process 2 materials		Additional materials		Labour		Overhead		Total
	$		$		$		$		$
Opening inventory cost b/f	4,400		1,150		540		810		6,900
Added in Jan 20X4	–	(30x$4)	120	(60x$2)	120	(60x$3)	180		420
	4,400		1,270		660		990		7,320
Fully worked units	20,250		5,400		2,700		4,050		32,400
Output to finished Goods	24,650		6,670		3,360		5,040		39,720
Closing inventory (450x$15)	6,750	(270x$4)	1,080	(225x$2)	450	(225x$3)	675		8,955
	31,400		7,750		3,810		5,715		48,675

Step 4 Complete accounts

PROCESS 3 ACCOUNT

	Units	$		Units	$
Opening inventory b/f	300	6,900	Finished goods a/c	1,650	39,720
Process 2 a/c	1,800	27,000			
Stores a/c		6,600			
Wages a/c		3,270			
Production o'hd a/c		4,905	Closing inventory c/f	450	8,955
	2,100	48,675		2,100	48,675

6 Valuing opening work in progress: weighted average cost method

6.1 Introduction

An alternative to FIFO is the **weighted average cost method of inventory valuation** which calculates a weighted average cost of units produced from both opening inventory and units introduced in the current period.

By this method **no distinction is made between units of opening inventory and new units introduced** to the process during the accounting period. The cost of opening inventory is added to costs incurred during the period, and completed units of opening inventory are each given a value of one full equivalent unit of production.

6.2 Example: Weighted average cost method

Magpie produces an item which is manufactured in two consecutive processes. Information relating to process 2 during September 20X3 is as follows.

Opening inventory 800 units
Degree of completion:

		$
process 1 materials	100%	4,700
added materials	40%	600
conversion costs	30%	1,000
		6,300

During September 20X3, 3,000 units were transferred from process 1 at a valuation of $18,100. Added materials cost $9,600 and conversion costs were $11,800.

Closing inventory at 30 September 20X3 amounted to 1,000 units which were 100% complete with respect to process 1 materials and 60% complete with respect to added materials. Conversion cost work was 40% complete.

Magpie uses a weighted average cost system for the valuation of output and closing inventory.

Required

Prepare the process 2 account for September 20X3.

Solution

Step 1
Opening inventory units count as a full equivalent unit of production when the weighted average cost system is applied. Closing inventory equivalent units are assessed in the usual way.

STATEMENT OF EQUIVALENT UNITS

	Total units		Process 1 material		Equivalent units Added material		Conversion costs
Opening inventory	800	(100%)	800		800		800
Fully worked units*	2,000	(100%)	2,000		2,000		2,000
Output to finished goods	2,800		2,800		2,800		2,800
Closing inventory	1,000	(100%)	1,000	(60%)	600	(40%)	400
	3,800		3,800		3,400		3,200

(*3,000 units from process 1 minus closing inventory of 1,000 units)

Step 2   The cost of opening inventory is added to costs incurred in September 20X3, and a cost per equivalent unit is then calculated.

STATEMENT OF COSTS PER EQUIVALENT UNIT

	Process 1 material $	Added materials $	Conversion costs $
Opening inventory	4,700	600	1,000
Added in September 20X3	18,100	9,600	11,800
Total cost	22,800	10,200	12,800
Equivalent units	3,800 units	3,400 units	3,200 units
Cost per equivalent unit	$6	$3	$4

Step 3   STATEMENT OF EVALUATION

	Process 1 material $	Added materials $	Conversion costs $	Total cost $
Output to finished goods (2,800 units)	16,800	8,400	11,200	36,400
Closing inventory	6,000	1,800	1,600	9,400
				45,800

Step 4   PROCESS 2 ACCOUNT

	Units	$		Units	$
Opening inventory b/f	800	6,300	Finished goods a/c	2,800	36,400
Process 1 a/c	3,000	18,100			
Added materials		9,600			
Conversion costs		11,800	Closing inventory c/f	1,000	9,400
	3,800	45,800		3,800	45,800

6.3 Which method should be used?

FIFO inventory valuation is more common than the weighted average method, and should be used unless an indication is given to the contrary. You may find that you are presented with limited information about the opening inventory, which forces you to use either the FIFO or the weighted average method. The rules are as follows.

(a)   If you are told the degree of completion of each element in opening inventory, but not the value of each cost element, then you must use the **FIFO method**.

(b)   If you are not given the degree of completion of each cost element in opening inventory, but you are given the value of each cost element, then you must use the **weighted average method**.

Question

During August, a factory commenced work on 20,000 units. At the start of the month there were no partly finished units but at the end of the month there were 2,000 units which were only 40% complete. Costs in the month were $3,722,400.

(a) How many equivalent units of closing WIP were there in the month?

    A   20,000
    B   2,000
    C   18,000
    D   800

(b) What is the total value of fully completed output which would show in the process account?

    A $3,960,000
    B $3,564,000
    C $3,722,400
    D $3,350,160

Answer

(a) D   Equivalent units of WIP = 40% × 2,000 = 800

(b) B

Total finished output	18,000	units
Total equivalent units =		
18,000 100%	18,000	
2,000 × 40%	800	
	18,800	
Cost per equivalent unit = 3,722,400/18,800 =	$198	
∴ Value of fully completed output:		
18,000 × 198 =	$3,564,000	

Summary of process costing

Chapter roundup

- **Process costing** is a costing method used where it is not possible to identify separate units of production or jobs, usually because of the continuous nature of the production processes involved.

- Process costing is centred around **four key steps**. The exact work done at each step will depend on whether there are normal losses, scrap, opening and closing work in progress and so on.

  Step 1. Determine output and losses
  Step 2. Calculate cost per unit of output, losses and WIP
  Step 3. Calculate total cost of output, losses and WIP
  Step 4. Complete accounts

- **Losses** may occur in process. If a certain level of loss is expected, this is known as **normal loss**. If losses are greater than expected, the extra loss is **abnormal loss**. If losses are less than expected, the difference is known as **abnormal gain**.

- It is conventional for the **scrap value** of normal loss to be deducted from the cost of materials before a cost per equivalent unit is calculated. Abnormal losses and gains never affect the cost of good units of production. The scrap value of abnormal losses is not credited to the process account, and abnormal loss and gain units carry the same full cost as a good unit of production.

- When units are partly completed at the end of a period (and hence there is closing work in progress), it is necessary to calculate the **equivalent units of production** in order to determine the cost of a completed unit.

- Account can be taken of opening work in progress using either the **FIFO** method or the **weighted average cost method**.

Quick quiz

1 Define process costing.

2 Process costing is centred around four key steps.

Step 1. ....

Step 2. ....

Step 3. ....

Step 4. ....

3 Abnormal gains result when actual loss is less than normal or expected loss.

True ☐

False ☐

4

Normal loss (no scrap value) ⎤   ⎡ Same value as good output (positive cost)

Abnormal loss   **?**   No value

Abnormal gain ⎦   ⎣ Same value as good output (negative cost)

5 How is revenue from scrap treated?

A As an addition to sales revenue
B As a reduction in costs of processing
C As a bonus to employees
D Any of the above

6 What is an equivalent unit?

7 When there is closing WIP at the end of a process, what is the first step in the four-step approach to process costing questions and why must it be done?

8 What is the weighted average cost method of inventory valuation?

9 Unless given an indication to the contrary, the weighted average cost method of inventory valuation should be used to value opening WIP.

True ☐

False ☐

Answers to quick quiz

1   **Process costing** is a costing method used where it is not possible to identify separate units of production, or jobs, usually because of the continuous nature of the production processes involved.

2   **Step 1.**   Determine output and losses
    Step 2.   Calculate cost per unit of output, losses and WIP
    Step 3.   Calculate total cost of output, losses and WIP
    Step 4.   Complete accounts

3   True

4

5   B

6   An **equivalent unit** is a notional whole unit which represents incomplete work, and which is used to apportion costs between work in process and completed output.

7   **Step 1.**   It is necessary to calculate the equivalent units of production (by drawing up a statement of equivalent units). Equivalent units of production are notional whole units which represent incomplete work and which are used to apportion costs between work in progress and completed output.

8   A method where no distinction is made between units of opening inventory and new units introduced to the process during the current period.

9   False. FIFO inventory valuation is more common than the weighted average method and should be used unless an indication is given to the contrary.

Now try the questions below from the Exam Question Bank

Number	Level	Marks	Time
Q10	MCQ/OTQ	n/a	n/a

Process costing, joint products and by-products

Topic list	Syllabus reference
1 Joint products and by-products	D6 (a)
2 Dealing with common costs	D6 (b)
3 Joint products in process accounts	D6 (c)
4 Accounting for by-products	D6 (c)

Introduction

You should now be aware of the most simple and the more complex areas of process costing. In this chapter we are going to turn our attention to the methods of accounting for **joint products** and **by-products** which arise as a result of a **continuous process**.

Study guide

		Intellectual level
D6	**Process costing 2**	
(a)	Distinguish between by-products and joint products	1
(b)	Value by-products and joint products at the point of separation	1
(c)	Prepare process accounts in situations where by-products and/or joint products occur	2

Exam guide

The F2 Pilot paper has three questions on process costing, so make sure you understand all the basics here.

1 Joint products and by-products

1.1 Introduction

FAST FORWARD

Joint products are two or more products separated in a process, each of which has a **significant value** compared to the other. A **by-product** is an incidental product from a process which has an **insignificant value** compared to the main product.

Key terms

Joint products are two or more products which are output from the same processing operation, but which are indistinguishable from each other up to their point of separation.

A **by-product** is a supplementary or secondary product (arising as the result of a process) whose value is small relative to that of the principal product.

(a) Joint products have a **substantial sales value**. Often they require further processing before they are ready for sale. Joint products arise, for example, in the oil refining industry where diesel fuel, petrol, paraffin and lubricants are all produced from the same process.

(b) The distinguishing feature of a by-product is its **relatively low sales value** in comparison to the main product. In the timber industry, for example, by-products include sawdust, small offcuts and bark.

What exactly separates a joint product from a by-product?

(a) A **joint product** is regarded as an important saleable item, and so it should be **separately costed**. The profitability of each joint product should be assessed in the cost accounts.

(b) A **by-product** is not important as a saleable item, and whatever revenue it earns is a 'bonus' for the organisation. Because of their relative insignificance, by-products are **not separately costed**.

Exam focus point

The study guide for Paper F2 states that you must be able to 'distinguish between by-products and joint products'.

1.2 Problems in accounting for joint products

The point at which **joint products** and **by-products** become separately identifiable is known as the **split-off point** or **separation point**. Costs incurred up to this point are called **common costs** or **joint costs**.

Costs incurred prior to this point of separation are **common** or **joint costs**, and these need to be allocated (apportioned) in some manner to each of the joint products. In the following sketched example, there are two different split-off points.

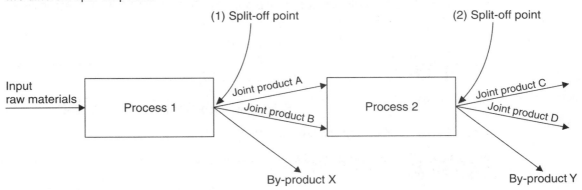

Problems in accounting for joint products are basically of two different sorts.

(a)   How common costs should be apportioned between products, in order to put a value to closing inventories and to the cost of sale (and profit) for each product.

(b)   Whether it is more profitable to sell a joint product at one stage of processing, or to process the product further and sell it at a later stage.

2 Dealing with common costs

2.1 Introduction

The main methods of apportioning joint costs, each of which can produce significantly different results are as follows.

- Physical measurement
- Relative sales value apportionment method; sales value at split-off point

The problem of costing for joint products concerns **common costs**, that is those common processing costs shared between the units of eventual output up to their 'split-off point'. Some method needs to be devised for sharing the common costs between the individual joint products for the following reasons.

(a)   To put a value to closing inventories of each joint product.
(b)   To record the costs and therefore the profit from each joint product.
(c)   Perhaps to assist in pricing decisions.

Here are some examples of the common costs problem.

(a)   How to spread the common costs of oil refining between the joint products made (petrol, naphtha, kerosene and so on).

(b)   How to spread the common costs of running the telephone network between telephone calls in peak and cheap rate times, or between local and long distance calls.

Various methods that might be used to establish a basis for apportioning or allocating common costs to each product are as follows.

- Physical measurement
- Relative sales value apportionment method; sales value at split-off point

2.2 Dealing with common costs: physical measurement

With physical measurement, **the common cost is apportioned to the joint products on the basis of the proportion that the output of each product bears by weight or volume to the total output.** An example of this would be the case where two products, product 1 and product 2, incur common costs to the point of separation of $3,000 and the output of each product is 600 tons and 1,200 tons respectively.

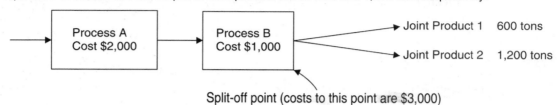

Split-off point (costs to this point are $3,000)

Product 1 sells for $4 per ton and product 2 for $2 per ton.

The division of the common costs ($3,000) between product 1 and product 2 could be based on the tonnage of output.

	Product 1		Product 2	Total
Output	600 tons	+	1,200 tons	1,800 tons
Proportion of common cost	$\dfrac{600}{1,800}$	+	$\dfrac{1,200}{1,800}$	
	$		$	$
Apportioned cost	1,000		2,000	3,000
Sales	2,400		2,400	4,800
Profit	1,400		400	1,800
Profit/sales ratio	58.3%		16.7%	37.5%

Physical measurement has the following limitations.

(a) Where the products separate during the processes into different states, for example where one product is a gas and another is a liquid, this method is unsuitable.

(b) This method does not take into account the relative income-earning potentials of the individual products, with the result that one product might appear very profitable and another appear to be incurring losses.

2.3 Dealing with common costs: sales value at split-off point

FAST FORWARD

The **relative sales value method** is the most widely used method of apportioning joint costs because (ignoring the effect of further processing costs) it assumes that all products achieve the same profit margin.

With relative sales value apportionment of common costs, **the cost is allocated according to the product's ability to produce income**. This method is most widely used because the assumption that some profit margin should be attained for all products under normal marketing conditions is satisfied. The common cost is apportioned to each product in the proportion that the sales (market) value of that product bears to the sales value of the total output from the particular processes concerned. Using the previous example where the sales price per unit is $4 for product 1 and $2 for product 2.

(a)	Common costs of processes to split-off point	$3,000
(b)	Sales value of product 1 at $4 per ton	$2,400
(c)	Sales value of product 2 at $2 per ton	$2,400

	Product 1	Product 2	Total
Sales	$2,400	$2,400	$4,800
Proportion of common cost apportioned	$\left(\dfrac{2,400}{4,800}\right)$	$\left(\dfrac{2,400}{4,800}\right)$	
	$	$	$
Apportioned cost	1,500	1,500	3,000
Sales	2,400	2,400	4,800
Profit	900	900	1,800
Profit/sales ratio	37.5%	37.5%	37.5%

A comparison of the gross profit margin resulting from the application of the above methods for allocating common costs will illustrate the greater acceptability of the relative sales value apportionment method. Physical measurement gives a higher profit margin to product 1, not necessarily because product 1 is highly profitable, but because it has been given a smaller share of common costs.

Question

Joint products

In process costing, a joint product is

A   A product which is produced simultaneously with other products but which is of lesser value than at least one of the other products

B   A product which is produced simultaneously with other products and is of similar value to at least one of the other products

C   A product which is produced simultaneously with other products but which is of greater value than any of the other products

D   A product produced jointly with another organisation

Answer

The correct answer is B, a product which is of similar value to at least one of the other products.

3 Joint products in process accounts

This example illustrates how joint products are incorporated into process accounts.

3.1 Example: joint products and process accounts

Three joint products are manufactured in a common process, which consists of two consecutive stages. Output from process 1 is transferred to process 2, and output from process 2 consists of the three joint products, Hans, Nils and Bumpsydaisies. All joint products are sold as soon as they are produced.

Data for period 2 of 20X6 are as follows.

	Process 1	Process 2
Opening and closing inventory	None	None
Direct material		
(30,000 units at $2 per unit)	$60,000	–
Conversion costs	$76,500	$226,200
Normal loss	10% of input	10% of input
Scrap value of normal loss	$0.50 per unit	$2 per unit
Output	26,000 units	10,000 units of Han
		7,000 units of Nil
		6,000 units of Bumpsydaisy

Selling prices are $18 per unit of Han, $20 per unit of Nil and $30 per unit of Bumpsydaisy.

Required

(a) Prepare the Process 1 account.
(b) Prepare the Process 2 account using the sales value method of apportionment.
(c) Prepare a profit statement for the joint products.

Solution

(a) **Process 1 equivalent units**

	Total units	Equivalent units
Output to process 2	26,000	26,000
Normal loss	3,000	0
Abnormal loss (balance)	1,000	1,000
	30,000	27,000

Costs of process 1

	$
Direct materials	60,000
Conversion costs	76,500
	136,500
Less scrap value of normal loss (3,000 × $0.50)	1,500
	135,000

$$\text{Cost per equivalent unit} = \frac{\$135,000}{27,000} = \$5$$

PROCESS 1 ACCOUNT

	$		$
Direct materials	60,000	Output to process 2 (26,000 × $5)	130,000
Conversion costs	76,500	Normal loss (scrap value)	1,500
		Abnormal loss a/c (1,000 × $5)	5,000
	136,500		136,500

(b) **Process 2 equivalent units**

	Total units	Equivalent units
Units of Hans produced	10,000	10,000
Units of Nils produced	7,000	7,000
Units of Bumpsydaisies produced	6,000	6,000
Normal loss (10% of 26,000)	2,600	0
Abnormal loss (balance)	400	400
	26,000	23,400

Costs of process 2

	$
Material costs – from process 1	130,000
Conversion costs	226,200
	356,200
Less scrap value of normal loss (2,600 × $2)	5,200
	351,000

Cost per equivalent unit $\dfrac{\$351,\!000}{23,\!400} = \$15$

Cost of good output (10,000 + 7,000 + 6,000) = 23,000 units × $15 = $345,000

The sales value of joint products, and the apportionment of the output costs of $345,000, is as follows.

	Sales value		Costs (process 2)
	$	%	$
Hans (10,000 × $18)	180,000	36	124,200
Nils (7,000 × $20)	140,000	28	96,600
Bumpsydaisy (6,000 × $30)	180,000	36	124,200
	500,000	100	345,000

PROCESS 2 ACCOUNT

	$		$
Process 1 materials	130,000	Finished goods accounts	
Conversion costs	226,200	– Hans	124,200
		– Nils	96,600
		– Bumpsydaisies	124,200
		Normal loss (scrap value)	5,200
		Abnormal loss a/c	6,000
	356,200		356,200

(c) PROFIT STATEMENT

	Hans	Nils	Bumpsydaisies
	$'000	$'000	$'000
Sales	180.0	140.0	180.0
Costs	124.2	96.6	124.2
Profit	55.8	43.4	55.8
Profit/ sales ratio	31%	31%	31%

 Question — Unit basis of apportionment

Prepare the Process 2 account and a profit statement for the joint products in the above example using the units basis of apportionment.

Answer

PROCESS 2 ACCOUNT

	$		$
Process 1 materials	130,000	Finished goods accounts	
Conversion costs	226,200	– Hans (10,000 × $15)	150,000
		– Nils (7,000 × $15)	105,000
		– Bumpsydaisies (6,000 × $15)	90,000
		Normal loss (scrap value)	5,200
		Abnormal loss a/c	6,000
	356,200		356,200

PROFIT STATEMENT

	Hans	Nils	Bumpsydaisies
	$'000	$'000	$'000
Sales	180	140	180
Costs	150	105	90
Profit	30	35	90
Profit/ sales ratio	16.7%	25%	50%

4 Accounting for by-products

4.1 Introduction

> The most common method of accounting for by-products is to deduct the **net realisable value** of the by-product from the cost of the main products.

A by-product has some commercial value and any income generated from it may be treated as follows.

(a)   Income (minus any post-separation further processing or selling costs) from the sale of the by-product may be **added to sales of the main product**, thereby increasing sales turnover for the period.

(b)   The sales of the by-product may be **treated as a separate, incidental source of income** against which are set only post-separation costs (if any) of the by-product. The revenue would be recorded in the income statement as 'other income'.

(c)   The sales income of the by-product may be **deducted from the cost of production** or cost of sales of the main product.

(d)   The **net realisable value of the by-product may be deducted from the cost of production of the main product**. The net realisable value is the final saleable value of the by-product minus any post-separation costs. Any closing inventory valuation of the main product or joint products would therefore be reduced.

The choice of method (a), (b), (c) or (d) will be influenced by the circumstances of production and ease of calculation, as much as by conceptual correctness. The method you are most likely to come across in examinations is method (d). An example will help to clarify the distinction between the different methods.

4.2 Example: Methods of accounting for by-products

During November 20X3, Splatter Co recorded the following results.

Opening inventory	main product P, nil
	by-product Z, nil
Cost of production	$120,000

Sales of the main product amounted to 90% of output during the period, and 10% of production was held as closing inventory at 30 November.

Sales revenue from the main product during November 20X2 was $150,000.

A by-product Z is produced, and output had a net sales value of $1,000. Of this output, $700 was sold during the month, and $300 was still in inventory at 30 November.

Required

Calculate the profit for November using the four methods of accounting for by-products.

Solution

The four methods of accounting for by-products are shown below.

(a)   **Income from by-product added to sales of the main product**

	$	$
Sales of main product ($150,000 + $700)		150,700
Opening inventory	0	
Cost of production	120,000	
	120,000	
Less closing inventory (10%)	12,000	
Cost of sales		108,000
Profit, main product		42,700

The closing inventory of the by-product has no recorded value in the cost accounts.

(b)   **By-product income treated as a separate source of income**

	$	$
Sales, main product		150,000
Opening inventory	0	
Cost of production	120,000	
	120,000	
Closing inventory (10%)	12,000	
Cost of sales, main product		108,000
Profit, main product		42,000
Other income		700
Total profit		42,700

The closing inventory of the by-product again has no value in the cost accounts.

(c)   **Sales income of the by-product deducted from the cost of production in the period**

	$	$
Sales, main product		150,000
Opening inventory	0	
Cost of production (120,000 – 700)	119,300	
	119,300	
Less closing inventory (10%)	11,930	
Cost of sales		107,370
Profit, main product		42,630

Although the profit is different from the figure in (a) and (b), the by-product closing inventory again has no value.

(d)   **Net realisable value of the by-product deducted from the cost of production in the period**

	$	$
Sales, main product		150,000
Opening inventory	0	
Cost of production (120,000 – 1,000)	119,000	
	119,000	
Less closing inventory (10%)	11,900	
Cost of sales		107,100
Profit, main product		42,900

As with the other three methods, closing inventory of the by-product has no value in the books of accounting, but the value of the closing inventory ($300) has been used to reduce the cost of production, and in this respect it has been allowed for in deriving the cost of sales and the profit for the period.

Question

Randolph manufactures two joint products, J and K, in a common process. A by-product X is also produced. Data for the month of December 20X2 were as follows.

Opening inventories	nil	
Costs of processing	direct materials	$25,500
	direct labour	$10,000

Production overheads are absorbed at the rate of 300% of direct labour costs.

		Production Units	Sales Units
Output and sales consisted of:	product J	8,000	7,000
	product K	8,000	6,000
	by-product X	1,000	1,000

The sales value per unit of J, K and X is $4, $6 and $0.50 respectively. The saleable value of the by-product is deducted from process costs before apportioning costs to each joint product. Costs of the common processing are apportioned between product J and product K on the basis of sales value of production.

The individual profits for December 20X2 are:

	Product J $	Product K $
A	5,250	6,750
B	6,750	5,250
C	22,750	29,250
D	29,250	22,750

Answer

The sales value of production was $80,000.

	$	
Product J (8,000 × $4)	32,000	(40%)
Product K (8,000 × $6)	48,000	(60%)
	80,000	

The costs of production were as follows.

	$
Direct materials	25,500
Direct labour	10,000
Overhead (300% of $10,000)	30,000
	65,500
Less sales value of by-product (1,000 × 50c)	500
Net production costs	65,000

The profit statement would appear as follows (nil opening inventories).

		Product J $		Product K $	Total $
Production costs	(40%)	26,000	(60%)	39,000	65,000
Less closing inventory	(1,000 units)	3,250	(2,000 units)	9,750	13,000
Cost of sales		22,750		29,250	52,000
Sales	(7,000 units)	28,000	(6,000 units)	36,000	64,000
Profit		5,250		6,750	12,000

The correct answer is therefore A.

If you selected option B, you got the profits for each product mixed up.

If you selected option C or D, you calculated the cost of sales instead of the profit.

Chapter roundup

- **Joint products** are two or more products separated in a process, each of which has a **significant value** compared to the other. A **by-product** is an incidental product from a process which has an **insignificant value** compared to the main product.

- The point at which joint and by-products become separately identifiable is known as the **split-off point** or **separation point**. Costs incurred up to this point are called **common costs** or **joint costs**.

- The main methods of apportioning joint costs, each of which can produce significantly different results are as follows: physical measurement; and relative sales value apportionment method; sales value at split-off point

- The **relative sales value method** is the most widely used method of apportioning joint costs because (ignoring the effect of further processing costs) it assumes that all products achieve the same profit margin.

- The most common method of accounting for by-products is to deduct the **net realisable value** of the by-product from the cost of the main products.

Quick quiz

1   What is the difference between a joint product and a by-product?

2   What is meant by the term 'split-off' point?

3   Name two methods of apportioning common costs to joint products.

4   Describe the four methods of accounting for by-products.

Answers to quick quiz

1   A **joint product** is regarded as an important saleable item whereas a **by-product** is not.

2   The **split-off point** (or the **separation point**) is the point at which joint products become separately identifiable in a processing operation.

3   Physical measurement and sales value at split-off point.

4   See paragraph 4.1.

Now try the questions below from the Exam Question Bank

Number	Level	Marks	Time
Q11	MCQ	n/a	n/a

12

Job, batch and service costing

Topic list	Syllabus reference
1 Costing methods	D5 (a)
2 Job costing	D5 (a), (b), (c), (d)
3 Batch costing	D5 (a), (b), (c), (d)
4 Service costing	D7(a), (b), (c)

Introduction

The first costing method that we shall be looking at is **job costing**. We will see the circumstances in which job costing should be used and how the costs of jobs are calculated. We will look at how the **costing of individual jobs** fits in with the recording of total costs in control accounts and then we will move on to **batch costing**, the procedure for which is similar to job costing.

Service costing deals with **specialist services** supplied to third parties or an **internal service** supplied within an organisation.

Study guide

		Intellectual level
D5	**Job and batch costing**	
(a)	Describe the characteristics of job and batch costing	1
(b)	Describe the situations where the use of job or batch costing would be appropriate	1
(c)	Prepare cost records and accounts in job and batch cost accounting situations	1
(d)	Establish job costs from given information	1
D7	**Service/operation costing**	
(a)	Identify situations where the use of service/operation costing is appropriate	1
(b)	Illustrate suitable unit cost measures that may be used in different service/operation situations	1
(c)	Carry out service cost analysis in simple service industry situations	1

Exam guide

This is a popular topic for MCQs. Make sure that you are able to deal with basic calculations.

1 Costing methods

> **FAST FORWARD**
>
> A **costing method** is designed to suit the way goods are processed or manufactured or the way services are provided.

Each organisation's costing method will therefore have unique features but costing methods of firms in the same line of business will more than likely have common aspects. Organisations involved in completely different activities, such as hospitals and car part manufacturers, will use very different methods.

We will be considering these important costing methods in this chapter.

- Job
- Batch
- Service

2 Job costing

2.1 Introduction

> **FAST FORWARD**
>
> **Job costing** is a costing method applied where work is undertaken to customers' special requirements and each order is of comparatively short duration.

> **Key term**
>
> A **job** is a cost unit which consists of a single order or contract.

The work relating to a job moves through processes and operations as a **continuously identifiable unit**. Job costing is most commonly applied within a factory or workshop, but may also be applied to property repairs and internal capital expenditure.

2.2 Procedure for the performance of jobs

The normal procedure in jobbing concerns involves:

(a) The prospective customer approaches the supplier and indicates the **requirements** of the job.

(b) A representative sees the prospective customer and agrees with him the **precise details** of the items to be supplied. For example the quantity, quality, size and colour of the goods, the date of delivery and any special requirements.

(c) The estimating department of the organisation then **prepares an estimate for the job**. This will be based on the cost of the materials to be used, the labour expense expected, the cost overheads, the cost of any additional equipment needed specially for the job, and finally the supplier's **profit margin**. The total of these items will represent the **quoted selling price**.

(d) If the estimate is accepted the job can be **scheduled**. All materials, labour and equipment required will be 'booked' for the job. In an efficient organisation, the start of the job will be timed to ensure that while it will be ready for the customer by the promised date of delivery it will not be loaded too early, otherwise storage space will have to be found for the product until the date it is required by (and was promised to) the customer.

2.3 Job cost sheets/cards

FAST FORWARD

Costs for each job are collected on a **job cost sheet** or **job card**.

With other methods of costing, it is usual to produce for inventory; this means that management must decide in advance how many units of each type, size, colour, quality and so on will be produced during the coming year, regardless of the identity of the customers who will eventually buy the product. In job costing, because production is usually carried out in accordance with the **special requirements of each customer**, it is **usual for each job to differ in one or more respects from another job.**

A separate record must therefore be maintained to show the details of individual jobs. Such records are often known as **job cost sheets** or **job cost cards**. An example is shown on the next page.

Either the **detail of relatively small jobs** or a **summary** of direct materials, direct labour and so on **for larger jobs** will be shown on a job cost sheet.

2.4 Job cost information

FAST FORWARD

Material costs for each job are determined from **material requisition notes**. **Labour times** on each job are recorded on a **job ticket**, which is then costed and recorded on the job cost sheet. Some labour costs, such as overtime premium or the cost of rectifying sub-standard output, might be charged either directly to a job or else as an overhead cost, depending on the circumstances in which the costs have arisen. **Overhead** is absorbed into the cost of jobs using the predetermined overhead absorption rates.

Information for the direct and indirect costs will be gathered as follows.

2.4.1 Direct material cost

(a) The estimated cost will be calculated by valuing all items on the **bill of materials**. Materials that have to be specially purchased for the job in question will need to be priced by the purchasing department.

(b) The actual cost of materials used will be calculated by valuing materials issues notes for those issues from store for the job and/or from invoices for materials specially purchased. All documentation should indicate the job number to which it relates.

2.4.2 Direct labour cost

(a)   The estimated **labour time requirement** will be calculated from past experience of similar types of work or work study engineers may prepare estimates following detailed specifications. Labour rates will need to take account of any increases, overtime and bonuses.

(b)   The actual labour hours will be available from either time sheets or job tickets/cards, using job numbers where appropriate to indicate the time spent on each job. The actual labour cost will be calculated using the hours information and current labour rates (plus bonuses, overtime payments and so on).

2.4.3 Direct expenses

(a)   The estimated cost of **any expenses likely** to be incurred can be obtained from a supplier.

(b)   The details of actual direct expenses incurred can be taken from invoices.

2.4.4 Production overheads

(a)   The **estimated production overheads** to be included in the job cost will be calculated from **overhead absorption rates** in operation and the estimate of the basis of the absorption rate (for example, direct labour hours). This assumes the job estimate is to include overheads (in a competitive environment management may feel that if overheads are to be incurred irrespective of whether or not the job is taken on, the minimum estimated quotation price should be based on variable costs only).

(b)   The actual production overhead to be included in the job cost will be calculated from the overhead absorption rate and the actual results (such as labour hours coded to the job in question). **Inaccurate overhead absorption rates can seriously harm an organisation**; if jobs are over priced, customers will go elsewhere and if jobs are under priced revenue will fail to cover costs.

2.4.5 Administration, selling and distribution overheads

The organisation may absorb **non-production overheads** using any one of a variety of methods (percentage on full production cost, for example) and estimates of these costs and the actual costs should be included in the estimated and actual job cost.

| JOB COST CARD | | | | | | | | | | | | | | Job No. | B641 | | |

JOB COST CARD					
Customer Mr J White		Customer's Order No.		Vehicle make Peugot 205 GTE	
Job Description Repair damage to offside front door				Vehicle reg. no. G 614 SOX	
Estimate Ref. 2599		Invoice No.		Date to collect 14.6.00	
Quoted price $338.68		Invoice price $355.05			

Material						Labour								Overheads			
				Cost							Bonus	Cost				Cost	
Date	Req. No.	Qty.	Price	$	c	Date	Emp-loyee	Cost Ctre	Hrs.	Rate		$	c	Hrs	OAR	$	c
12.6	36815	1	75.49	75	49	12.6	018	B	1.98	6.50	-	12	87	7.9	2.50	19	75
12.6	36816	1	33.19	33	19	13.6	018	B	5.92	6.50	-	38	48				
12.6	36842	5	6.01	30	05						13.65	13	65				
13.6	36881	5	3.99	19	95												
Total C/F				158	68	Total C/F						65	00	Total C/F		19	75

Expenses						Job Cost Summary	Actual		Estimate	
							$	c	$	c
Date	Ref.	Description	Cost							
			$	c		Direct Materials B/F	158	68	158	68
						Direct Expenses B/F	50	00		
						Direct Labour B/F	65	00	180	00
12.6	-	N. Jolley Panel-beating	50	-		Direct Cost	273	68		
						Overheads B/F	19	75		
							293	43		
						Admin overhead (add 10%)	29	34		
						= Total Cost	322	77	338	68
						Invoice Price	355	05		
Total C/F			50	-		Job Profit/Loss	32	28		

Comments

Job Cost Card Completed by _

2.5 Rectification costs

If the finished output is found to be sub-standard, it may be possible to rectify the fault. The sub-standard output will then be returned to the department or cost centre where the fault arose.

Rectification costs can be treated in two ways.

(a) If rectification work is not a frequent occurrence, but arises on occasions with specific jobs to which it can be traced directly, then the rectification costs should be **charged as a direct cost to the jobs concerned.**

(b) If rectification is regarded as a normal part of the work carried out generally in the department, then the rectification costs should be **treated as production overheads**. This means that they would be included in the total of production overheads for the department and absorbed into the cost of all jobs for the period, using the overhead absorption rate.

2.6 Work in progress

At the year end, the **value of work in progress** is simply the **sum of the costs incurred on incomplete jobs** (provided that the costs are lower than the net realisable value of the customer order).

2.7 Pricing the job

FAST FORWARD

The usual method of fixing prices in a jobbing concern is **cost plus pricing**.

Cost plus pricing means that a desired profit margin is added to total costs to arrive at the selling price.

The estimated profit will depend on the particular circumstance of the job and organisation in question. In competitive situations the profit may be small but if the organisation is sure of securing the job the margin may be greater. In general terms, the profit earned on each job should **conform to the requirements of the organisation's overall business plan**.

The final price quoted will, of course, be affected by what competitors charge and what the customer will be willing to pay.

Exam focus point

An exam question about job costing may ask you to accumulate costs to arrive at a job cost, and then to determine a job price by adding a certain amount of profit. To do this, you need to remember the following crucial formula.

	%
Cost of job	100
+ profit	25
= selling price	125

Profit may be expressed either as a percentage of job cost (such as 25% (25/100) mark up) or as a percentage of selling price (such as 20% (25/125) margin).

2.8 Job costing and computerisation

Job cost sheets exist in manual systems, but it is **increasingly likely** that in large organisations the **job costing system will be computerised**, using accounting software specifically designed to deal with job costing requirements. A computerised job accounting system is likely to contain the following features.

(a) Every job will be given a **job code number**, which will determine how the data relating to the job is stored.

(b) A separate set of **codes will be given for the type of costs** that any job is likely to incur. Thus, 'direct wages', say, will have the same code whichever job they are allocated to.

(c) In a sophisticated system, **costs can be analysed both by job** (for example all costs related to Job 456), **but also by type** (for example direct wages incurred on all jobs). It is thus easy to perform control analysis and to make comparisons between jobs.

(d)   A job costing system might have facilities built into it which incorporate other factors relating to the performance of the job. In complex jobs, sophisticated planning techniques might be employed to ensure that the job is performed in the minimum time possible: time management features may be incorporated into job costing software.

2.9 Example: Job costing

Fateful Morn is a jobbing company. On 1 June 20X2, there was one uncompleted job in the factory. The job card for this work is summarised as follows.

Job Card, Job No 6832

Costs to date	$
Direct materials	630
Direct labour (120 hours)	350
Factory overhead ($2 per direct labour hour)	240
Factory cost to date	1,220

During June, three new jobs were started in the factory, and costs of production were as follows.

Direct materials	$
Issued to: Job 6832	2,390
Job 6833	1,680
Job 6834	3,950
Job 6835	4,420
Damaged inventory written off from stores	2,300

Material transfers	$
Job 6834 to Job 6833	250
Job 6832 to 6834	620

Materials returned to store	$
From Job 6832	870
From Job 6835	170

Direct labour hours recorded	
Job 6832	430 hrs
Job 6833	650 hrs
Job 6834	280 hrs
Job 6835	410 hrs

The cost of labour hours during June 20X2 was $3 per hour, and production overhead is absorbed at the rate of $2 per direct labour hour. Production overheads incurred during the month amounted to $3,800. Completed jobs were delivered to customers as soon as they were completed, and the invoiced amounts were as follows.

Job 6832	$5,500
Job 6834	$8,000
Job 6835	$7,500

Administration and marketing overheads are added to the cost of sales at the rate of 20% of factory cost. Actual costs incurred during June 20X2 amounted to $3,200.

Required

(a)   Prepare the job accounts for each individual job during June 20X2; (the accounts should only show the cost of production, and not the full cost of sale).

(b)   Prepare the summarised job cost cards for each job, and calculate the profit on each completed job.

Solution

(a)   **Job accounts**

JOB 6832

	$		$
Balance b/f	1,220	Job 6834 a/c	620
Materials (stores a/c)	2,390	(materials transfer)	
Labour (wages a/c)	1,290	Stores a/c (materials returned)	870
Production overhead (o'hd a/c)	860	Cost of sales a/c (balance) ●	4,270
	5,760		5,760

JOB 6833

	$		$
Materials (stores a/c)	1,680	Balance c/f	5,180
Labour (wages a/c)	1,950		
Production overhead (o'hd a/c)	1,300		
Job 6834 a/c (materials transfer)	250		
	5,180		5,180

JOB 6834

	$		$
Materials (stores a/c)	3,950	Job 6833 a/c (materials transfer)	250
Labour (wages a/c)	840		
Production overhead (o'hd a/c)	560	Cost of sales a/c (balance) ●	5,720
Job 6832 a/c (materials transfer)	620		
	5,970		5,970

JOB 6835

	$		$
Materials (stores a/c)	4,420	Stores a/c (materials returned)	170
Labour (wages a/c)	1,230		
Production overhead (o'hd a/c)	820	Cost of sales a/c (balance)	6,300
	6,470		6,470

(b)   **Job cards, summarised**

	Job 6832	Job 6833	Job 6834	Job 6835
	$	$	$	$
Materials	1,530*	1,930	4,320**	4,250
Labour	1,640	1,950	840	1,230
Production overhead	1,100	1,300	560	820
Factory cost	4,270	5,180 (c/f)	5,720	6,300
Admin & marketing o'hd (20%)	854		1,144	1,260
Cost of sale	5,124		6,864	7,560
Invoice value	5,500		8,000	7,500
Profit/(loss) on job	376		1,136	(60)

*$(630 + 2,390 − 620 − 870)
**$(3,950 + 620 − 250)

Question
Selling price

The following information relates to job 388886, which is being carried out by Biddy to meet a customer's order.

	Department V	Department Q
Direct materials used	$5,000	$3,000
Direct labour hours	400 hours	200 hours
Direct labour rate per hour	$4	$5
Production overhead per direct labour hour	$4	$4
Administration and other overhead	20% of full production cost	
Profit margin	25% of sales price	

Required

Calculate the selling price of job 388886.

Answer

	Department V $	Department Q $	Total $
Direct materials	5,000	3,000	8,000
Direct labour	1,600	1,000	2,600
Production overhead	1,600	800	2,400
Full production cost			13,000
Other overheads			2,600
Cost of the job			15,600
Profit (25% of sales=33 1/3 % of cost)			5,200
Sales price			20,800

xam focus oint

Job costing is likely to be tested in the exam.

2.10 Job costing for internal services

FAST FORWARD

It is possible to use a job costing system **to control the costs of an internal service department**, such as the maintenance department or the printing department.

If a job costing system is used it is possible to **charge the user departments for the cost of specific jobs carried out, rather than apportioning the total costs of these service departments** to the user departments using an arbitrarily determined apportionment basis.

An internal job costing system for service departments will have the following advantages.

Advantages	Comment
Realistic apportionment	The identification of expenses with jobs and the subsequent charging of these to the department(s) responsible means that costs are borne by those who incurred them.
Increased responsibility and awareness	User departments will be aware that they are charged for the specific services used and may be more careful to use the facility more efficiently. They will also appreciate the true cost of the facilities that they are using and can take decisions accordingly.
Control of service department costs	The service department may be restricted to charging a standard cost to user departments for specific jobs carried out or time spent. It will then be possible to measure the efficiency or inefficiency of the service department by recording the difference between the standard charges and the actual expenditure.
Planning information	This information will ease the planning process, as the purpose and cost of service department expenditure can be separately identified.

Question

Total job cost

A furniture-making business manufactures quality furniture to customers' orders. It has three production departments (A, B and C) which have overhead absorption rates (per direct labour hour) of $12.86, $12.40 and $14.03 respectively.

Two pieces of furniture are to be manufactured for customers. Direct costs are as follows.

	Job XYZ	Job MNO
Direct material	$154	$108
Direct labour	20 hours dept A	16 hours dept A
	12 hours dept B	10 hours dept B
	10 hours dept C	14 hours dept C

Labour rates are as follows: $3.80(A); $3.50 (B); $3.40 (C)

The firm quotes prices to customers that reflect a required profit of 25% on selling price. Calculate the total cost and selling price of each job.

Answer

			Job XYZ		Job MNO
			$		$
Direct material			154.00		108.00
Direct labour:	dept A	(20 × 3.80)	76.00	(16 × 3.80)	60.80
	dept B	(12 × 3.50)	42.00	(10 × 3.50)	35.00
	dept C	(10 × 3.40)	34.00	(14 × 3.40)	47.60
Total direct cost			306.00		251.40
Overhead:	dept A	(20 × 12.86)	257.20	(16 × 12.86)	205.76
	dept B	(12 × 12.40)	148.80	(10 × 12.40)	124.00
	dept C	(10 × 14.03)	140.30	(14 × 14.03)	196.42
Total cost			852.30		777.58
Profit (note)			284.10		259.19
Quoted selling price			1,136.40		1,036.77

(*Note.* If profit is 25% on selling price, this is the same as $33^{1}/_{3}$% (25/75) on cost.)

Question

A firm uses job costing and recovers overheads on direct labour.

Three jobs were worked on during a period, the details of which are as follows.

	Job 1 $	Job 2 $	Job 3 $
Opening work in progress	8,500	0	46,000
Material in period	17,150	29,025	0
Labour for period	12,500	23,000	4,500

The overheads for the period were exactly as budgeted, $140,000.

Jobs 1 and 2 were the only incomplete jobs.

What was the value of closing work in progress?

A $81,900   B $90,175   C $140,675   D $214,425

Answer

Total labour cost = $12,500 + $23,000 + $4,500 = $40,000

Overhead absorption rate = $\dfrac{\$140,000}{\$40,000} \times 100\%$ = 350% of direct labour cost

Closing work in progress valuation

		Job 1 $		Job 2 $	Total $
Costs given in question		38,150		52,025	90,175
Overhead absorbed	(12,500 × 350%)	43,750	(23,000 × 350%)	80,500	124,250
					214,425

Option D is correct.

We can eliminate option B because $90,175 is simply the total of the costs allocated to Jobs 1 and 2, with no absorption of overheads. Option A is an even lower cost figure, therefore it can also be eliminated.

Option C is wrong because it is a simple total of all allocated costs, including Job 3 which is not incomplete.

3 Batch costing

3.1 Introduction

Batch costing is similar to job costing in that each batch of similar articles is separately identifiable. The **cost per unit** manufactured in a batch is the total batch cost divided by the number of units in the batch.

A **batch** is a group of similar articles which maintains its identity during one or more stages of production and is treated as a cost unit.

In general, the **procedures for costing batches are very similar to those for costing jobs**.

(a)   The **batch is treated as a job during production** and the costs are collected in the manner already described in this chapter.

(b)   Once the batch has been completed, the **cost per unit can be calculated as the total batch cost divided into the number of units in the batch**.

3.2 Example: Batch costing

Rio manufactures Brazils to order and has the following budgeted overheads for the year, based on normal activity levels.

Production departments	Budgeted Overheads $	Budgeted activity
Welding	12,000	3,000 labour hours
Assembly	20,000	2,000 labour hours

Selling and administrative overheads are 25% of factory cost. An order for 500 Brazils, made as Batch 38, incurred the following costs.

Materials $24,000

Labour   200 hours in the Welding Department at $5 per hour
400 hours in the Assembly Department at $10 per hour

$1,000 was paid for the hire of x-ray equipment for testing the accuracy of the welds.

Required

Calculate the cost per unit for Batch 38.

Solution

The first step is to calculate the overhead absorption rate for the production departments.

$$\text{Welding} = \frac{\$12,000}{3,000} = \$4 \text{ per labour hour}$$

$$\text{Assembly} = \frac{\$20,000}{2,000} = \$10 \text{ per labour hour}$$

Total cost – Batch 38

	$	$
Direct material		24,000
Direct expense		1,000
Direct labour 200 × $5 =	1,000	
400 × $10 =	4,000	
		5,000
Prime cost		30,000
Overheads 200 × $4 =	800	
400 × $10 =	4,000	
		4,800
Factory cost		34,800
Selling and administrative cost (25% of factory cost)		8,700
Total cost		43,500

$$\text{Cost per unit} = \frac{\$43,500}{500} = \$87$$

4 Service costing

4.1 What is service costing?

Service costing can be used by companies operating in a service industry or by companies wishing to establish the cost of services carried out by some of their departments. Service organisations do not make or sell tangible goods.

Service costing (or **function costing**) is a costing method concerned with establishing the costs, not of items of production, but of services rendered.

Service costing is used in the following circumstances.

(a) A company operating in a service industry will cost its services, for which sales revenue will be earned; examples are electricians, car hire services, road, rail or air transport services and hotels.

(b) A company may wish to establish the cost of services carried out by some of its departments; for example the costs of the vans or lorries used in distribution, the costs of the computer department, or the staff canteen.

4.2 Service costing versus product costing (such as job or process costing)

(a) With many services, the cost of direct materials consumed will be relatively small compared to the labour, direct expenses and overheads cost. In product costing the direct materials are often a greater proportion of the total cost.

(b) Although many services are revenue-earning, others are not (such as the distribution facility or the staff canteen). This means that the purpose of service costing may not be to establish a profit or loss (nor to value closing inventories for the balance sheet) but may rather be to provide management information about the comparative costs or efficiency of the services, with a view to helping managers to budget for their costs using historical data as a basis for estimating costs in the future and to control the costs in the service departments.

(c) The procedures for recording material costs, labour hours and other expenses will vary according to the nature of the service.

4.3 Specific characteristics of services

Specific characteristics of services
- **S**imultaneity
- **H**eterogeneity
- **I**ntangibility
- **P**erishability

Consider the service of providing a haircut.

(a) The production and consumption of a haircut are **simultaneous,** and therefore it cannot be inspected for quality in advance, nor can it be returned if it is not what was required.

(b) A haircut is **heterogeneous** and so the exact service received will vary each time: not only will two hairdressers cut hair differently, but a hairdresser will not consistently deliver the same standard of haircut.

(c)   A haircut is **intangible** in itself, and the performance of the service comprises many other intangible factors, like the music in the salon, the personality of the hairdresser, the quality of the coffee.

(d)   Haircuts are **perishable,** that is, they cannot be stored. You cannot buy them in bulk, and the hairdresser cannot do them in advance and keep them stocked away in case of heavy demand. The incidence of work in progress in service organisations is less frequent than in other types of organisation.

Note the mnemonic **SHIP** for remembering the specific characteristics of services.

4.4 Unit cost measures

The main problem with service costing is the **difficulty in defining a realistic cost unit** that represents a suitable measure of the service provided. Frequently, a composite cost unit may be deemed more appropriate. Hotels, for example, may use the 'occupied bed-night' as an appropriate unit for cost ascertainment and control.

Typical cost units used by companies operating in a service industry are shown below.

Service	Cost unit
Road, rail and air transport services	Passenger/mile or kilometre, ton/mile, tonne/kilometre
Hotels	Occupied bed-night
Education	Full-time student
Hospitals	Patient
Catering establishment	Meal served

Question   Internal services

Can you think of examples of cost units for internal services such as canteens, distribution and maintenance?

Answer

Service	Cost unit
Canteen	Meal served
Vans and lorries used in distribution	Mile or kilometre, ton/mile, tonne/kilometre
Maintenance	Man hour

Each organisation will need to ascertain the **cost unit** most appropriate to its activities. If a number of organisations within an industry use a common cost unit, then valuable comparisons can be made between similar establishments. This is particularly applicable to hospitals, educational establishments and local authorities. Whatever cost unit is decided upon, the calculation of a cost per unit is as follows.

Formula to learn

$$\text{Cost per service unit} = \frac{\text{Total costs for period}}{\text{Number of service units in the period}}$$

4.5 Service cost analysis

Service cost analysis should be performed in a manner which ensures that the following objectives are attained.

(a) Planned costs should be compared with actual costs.

Differences should be investigated and corrective action taken as necessary.

(b) A cost per unit of service should be calculated.

If each service has a number of variations (such as maintenance services provided by plumbers, electricians and carpenters) then the calculation of a cost per unit of each service may be necessary.

(c) The cost per unit of service should be used as part of the control function.

For example, costs per unit of service can be compared, month by month, period by period, year by year and so on and any unusual trends can be investigated.

(d) Prices should be calculated for services being sold to third parties.

The procedure is similar to job costing. A mark-up is added to the cost per unit of service to arrive at a selling price.

(e) Costs should be analysed into fixed, variable and semi-variable costs to help assist management with planning, control and decision making.

4.6 Service cost analysis in internal service situations

FAST FORWARD

Service department costing is also used to establish a specific cost for an internal service which is a service provided by one department for another, rather than sold externally to customers eg canteen, maintenance.

4.6.1 Transport costs

'Transport costs' is a term used here to refer to the costs of the transport services used by a company, rather than the costs of a transport organisation, such as a rail network.

If a company has a fleet of lorries or vans which it uses to distribute its goods, it is useful to know how much the department is costing for a number of reasons.

(a) Management should be able to budget for expected costs, and to control actual expenditure on transport by comparing actual costs with budgeted costs.

(b) The company may charge customers for delivery or 'carriage outwards' costs, and a charge based on the cost of the transport service might be appropriate.

(c) If management knows how much its own transport is costing, a comparison can be made with alternative forms of transport to decide whether a cheaper or better method of delivery can be found.

(d) Similarly, if a company uses, say, a fleet of lorries, knowledge of how much transport by lorry costs should help management to decide whether another type of vehicle, say vans, would be cheaper to use.

Transport costs may be analysed to provide the cost of operating one van or lorry each year, but it is more informative to analyse costs as follows.

(a) The cost per mile or kilometre travelled.

(b) The cost per ton/mile or tonne/kilometre (the cost of carrying one tonne of goods for one kilometre distance) or the cost per kilogram/metre.

For example, suppose that a company lorry makes five deliveries in a week.

Delivery	Tonnes carried	Distance (one way) Kilometres	Tonne/kilometres carried
1	0.4	180	72
2	0.3	360	108
3	1.2	100	120
4	0.8	250	200
5	1.0	60	60
			560

If the costs of operating the lorry during the week are known to be $840, the cost per tonne/kilometre would be:

$$\frac{\$840}{560 \text{ tonne/kilometre}} = \$1.50 \text{ per tonne/kilometre}$$

Transport costs might be collected under five broad headings.

(a) **Running costs** such as petrol, oil, drivers' wages

(b) **Loading costs** (the labour costs of loading the lorries with goods for delivery)

(c) **Servicing, repairs**, spare parts and tyre usage

(d) **Annual direct expenses** such as road tax, insurance and depreciation

(e) **Indirect costs of the distribution department** such as the wages of managers

The role of the cost accountant is to provide a system for **recording and analysing costs**. Just as production costs are recorded by means of material requisition notes, labour time sheets and so on, so too must transport costs be recorded by means of log sheets or time sheets, and material supply notes.

The purpose of a lorry driver's log sheet is to record distance travelled, or the number of tonne/kilometres and the drivers' time.

4.6.2 Canteen costs

Another example of service costing is the cost of a company's **canteen services**. A feature of canteen costing is that some revenue is earned when employees pay for their meals, but the prices paid will be insufficient to cover the costs of the canteen service. The company will subsidise the canteen and a major purpose of canteen costing is to establish the size of the subsidy.

If the costs of the canteen service are recorded by a system of service cost accounting, the likely headings of expense would be as follows.

(a) **Food and drink**: separate canteen stores records may be kept, and the consumption of food and drink recorded by means of 'materials issues' notes.

(b) **Labour costs of the canteen staff**: hourly paid staff will record their time at work on a time card or time sheet. Salaried staff will be a 'fixed' cost each month.

(c) **Consumable stores** such as crockery, cutlery, glassware, table linen and cleaning materials will also be recorded in some form of inventory control system.

(d) **The cost of gas and electricity** may be separately metered; otherwise an apportionment of the total cost of such utilities for the building as a whole will be made to the canteen department.

(e) Asset records will be kept and **depreciation charges** made for major items of equipment like ovens and furniture.

(f) An apportionment of other **overhead costs** of the building (rent and rates, building insurance and maintenance and so on) may be charged against the canteen.

Cash income from canteen sales will also be recorded.

4.6.3 Example: Service cost analysis

Suppose that a canteen recorded the following costs and revenue during the month.

	$
Food and drink	11,250
Labour	11,250
Heating and lighting	1,875
Repairs and consumable stores	1,125
Financing costs	1,000
Depreciation	750
Other apportioned costs	875
Revenue	22,500

The canteen served 37,500 meals in the month.

The size of the subsidy could be easily identified as follows:

	$
The total costs of the canteen	28,125
Revenue	22,500
Loss, to be covered by the company	5,625

The cost per meal averages 75c and the revenue per meal 60c. If the company decided that the canteen should pay its own way, without a subsidy, the average price of a meal would have to be raised by 15 cents.

4.7 The usefulness of costing services that do not earn revenue

4.7.1 Purposes of service costing

The techniques for costing services are similar to the techniques for costing products, but why should we want to establish a cost for 'internal' services, services that are provided by one department for another, rather than sold externally to customers? In other words, what is the purpose of service costing for non-revenue-earning services?

Service costing has two basic purposes.

(a) **To control the costs in the service department**. If we establish a distribution cost per tonne kilometre, a canteen cost per employee, or job costs of repairs, we can establish control measures in the following ways.

  (i) Comparing actual costs against a target or standard
  (ii) Comparing current actual costs against actual costs in previous periods

(b) **To control the costs of the user departments**, and prevent the unnecessary use of services. If the costs of services are charged to the user departments in such a way that the charges reflect the use actually made by each department of the service department's services then the following will occur.

  (i) The overhead costs of user departments will be established more accurately; indeed some service department variable costs might be identified as directly attributable costs of the user department.

  (ii) If the service department's charges for a user department are high, the user department might be encouraged to consider whether it is making an excessively costly and wasteful use of the service department's service.

(iii)   The user department might decide that it can obtain a similar service at a lower cost from an external service company.

4.7.2 Example: costing internal services

(a)   If maintenance costs in a factory are costed as jobs (that is, if each bit of repair work is given a job number and costed accordingly) repair costs can be charged to the departments on the basis of repair jobs actually undertaken, instead of on a more generalised basis, such as apportionment according to machine hour capacity in each department. Departments with high repair costs could then consider their high incidence of repairs, the age and reliability of their machines, or the skills of the machine operatives.

(b)   If IT costs are charged to a user department on the basis of a cost per hour, the user department would assess whether it was getting good value from its use of the IT department and whether it might be better to outsource some if its IT work.

4.8 Service cost analysis in service industry situations

4.8.1 Distribution costs

Example: service cost analysis in the service industry

This example shows how a rate per tonne/kilometre can be calculated for a distribution service.

Rick Shaw operates a small fleet of delivery vehicles. Standard costs have been established as follows.

Loading	1 hour per tonne loaded
Loading costs:	
Labour (casual)	$2 per hour
Equipment depreciation	$80 per week
Supervision	$80 per week
Drivers' wages (fixed)	$100 per man per week
Petrol	10c per kilometre
Repairs	5c per kilometre
Depreciation	$80 per week per vehicle
Supervision	$120 per week
Other general expenses (fixed)	$200 per week

There are two drivers and two vehicles in the fleet.

During a slack week, only six journeys were made.

Journey	Tonnes carried (one way)	One-way distance of journey Kilometres
1	5	100
2	8	20
3	2	60
4	4	50
5	6	200
6	5	300

Required

Calculate the expected average full cost per tonne/kilometre for the week.

Solution

Variable costs	Journey	1	2	3	4	5	6
		$	$	$	$	$	$
Loading labour		10	16	4	8	12	10
Petrol (both ways)		20	4	12	10	40	60
Repairs (both ways)		10	2	6	5	20	30
		40	22	22	23	72	100

Total costs

	$
Variable costs (total for journeys 1 to 6)	279
Loading equipment depreciation	80
Loading supervision	80
Drivers' wages	200
Vehicles depreciation	160
Drivers' supervision	120
Other costs	200
	1,119

Journey	Tonnes	One way distance Kilometres	Tonne/kilometres
1	5	100	500
2	8	20	160
3	2	60	120
4	4	50	200
5	6	200	1,200
6	5	300	1,500
			3,680

Cost per tonne/kilometre $\dfrac{\$1,119}{3,680} = \$0.304$

Note that the large element of fixed costs may distort this measure but that a variable cost per tonne/kilometre of $279/3,680 = $0.076 may be useful for budgetary control.

4.8.2 Education

The techniques described in the preceding paragraphs can be applied, in general, to any service industry situation. Attempt the following question about education.

Question

Suitable cost unit

A university with annual running costs of $3 million has the following students.

Classification	Number	Attendance weeks per annum	Hours per week
3 year	2,700	30	28
4 year	1,500	30	25
Sandwich	1,900	35	20

Required

Calculate a cost per suitable cost unit for the university to the nearest cent.

Answer

We need to begin by establishing a cost unit for the university. Since there are three different categories of students we cannot use 'a student' as the cost unit. Attendance hours would seem to be the most appropriate cost unit. The next step is to calculate the number of units.

Number of students		Weeks		Hours		Total hours per annum
2,700	×	30	×	28	=	2,268,000
1,500	×	30	×	25	=	1,125,000
1,900	×	35	×	20	=	1,330,000
						4,723,000

The cost per unit is calculated as follows.

$$\text{Cost per unit} = \frac{\text{Total cost}}{\text{Number of units}} = \$\left(\frac{3,000,000}{4,723,000}\right) = \$0.64$$

Question

Service costing

State which of the following are characteristics of service costing.

(i)   High levels of indirect costs as a proportion of total costs
(ii)   Use of composite cost units
(iii)   Use of equivalent units

A   (i) only
B   (i) and (ii) only
C   (ii) only
D   (ii) and (iii) only

Answer

B   In service costing it is difficult to identify many attributable direct costs. Many costs must be shared over several cost units, therefore characteristic (i) does apply. Composite cost units such as tonne-mile or room-night are often used, therefore characteristic (ii) does apply. Equivalent units are more often used in costing for tangible products, therefore characteristic (iii) does not apply. The correct answer is therefore B.

Chapter roundup

- A **costing method** is designed to suit the way goods are processed or manufactured or the way services are provided.

- **Job costing** is a costing method applied where work is undertaken to customers' special requirements and each order is of comparatively short duration.

- Costs for each job are collected on a **job cost sheet** or **job card.**

- **Material costs** for each job are determined from **material requisition notes**. **Labour times** on each job are recorded on a **job ticket**, which is then costed and recorded on the job cost sheet. Some labour costs, such as overtime premium or the cost of rectifying sub-standard output, might be charged either directly to a job or else as an overhead cost, depending on the circumstances in which the costs have arisen. **Overhead** is absorbed into the cost of jobs using the predetermined overhead absorption rates.

- The usual method of fixing prices within a jobbing concern is **cost plus pricing**.

- It is possible to use a job costing system **to control the costs of an internal service department**, such as the maintenance department or the printing department.

- **Batch costing** is similar to job costing in that each batch of similar articles is separately identifiable. The **cost per unit** manufactured in a batch is the total batch cost divided by the number of units in the batch.

- Service costing can be used by companies operating in a service industry or by companies wishing to establish the cost of services carried out by some of their departments. Service organisations do not make or sell tangible goods.

- Specific characteristics of services

    - **S**imultaneity
    - **H**eterogeneity
    - **I**ntangibility
    - **P**erishability

- The main problem with service costing is the difficulty in **defining a realistic cost unit** that represents a suitable measure of the service provided. Frequently, a composite cost unit may be deemed more appropriate. Hotels, for example, may use the 'occupied bed-night' as an appropriate cost unit for ascertainment and control.

- Cost per service unit = $\dfrac{\text{Total costs for period}}{\text{Number of service units in the period}}$

- Service department costing is also used to establish a specific cost for an internal service which is a service provided by one department for another, rather than sold externally to customers eg canteen, maintenance.

Quick quiz

1 How are the material costs for each job determined?

2 Which of the following are not characteristics of job costing?

   I Customer driven production
   II Complete production possible within a single accounting period
   III Homogeneous products

   A I and II only
   B I and III only
   C II and III only
   D III only

3 The cost of a job is $100,000

   (a) If profit is 25% of the job cost, the price of the job = $.................

   (b) If there is a 25% margin, the price of the job = $....................

4 What is a batch?

5 How would you calculate the cost per unit of a completed batch?

6 Define service costing

7 Match up the following services with their typical cost units

Service		Cost unit
Hotels		Patient-day
Education	?	Meal served
Hospitals		Full-time student
Catering organisations		Occupied bed-night

8 What is the advantage of organisations within an industry using a common cost unit?

9 Cost per service unit = ...

10 Service department costing is used to establish a specific cost for an 'internal service' which is a service provided by one department for another.

   True ☐

   False ☐

Answers to quick quiz

1   From materials requisition notes, or from suppliers' invoices if materials are purchased specifically for a particular job.

2   D

3   (a) $100,000 + (25% × $100,000) = $100,000 + $25,000 = $125,000

(b)   Let price of job = x

$$\therefore \text{Profit} = 25\% \times x \text{ (selling price)}$$
$$\text{If profit} = 0.25x$$
$$x - 0.25x = \text{cost of job}$$
$$0.75x = \$100,000$$
$$x = \frac{\$100,000}{0.75}$$
$$= \$133,333$$

4   A group of similar articles which maintains its identity during one or more stages of production and is treated as a cost unit.

5    $$\frac{\text{Total batch cost}}{\text{Number of units in the batch}}$$

6   Cost accounting for services or functions eg canteens, maintenance, personnel (service centres/functions).

7   **Service**   **Cost unit**

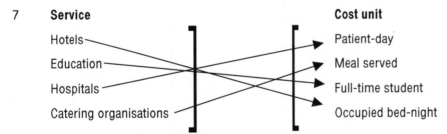

Service	Cost unit
Hotels	Patient-day
Education	Meal served
Hospitals	Full-time student
Catering organisations	Occupied bed-night

8   It is easier to make comparisons.

9   Cost per service unit = $\dfrac{\text{Total costs for period}}{\text{Number of service units in the period}}$

10   True

Now try the questions below from the Exam Question Bank

Number	Level	Marks	Time
Q12	MCQ/OTQ	n/a	n/a

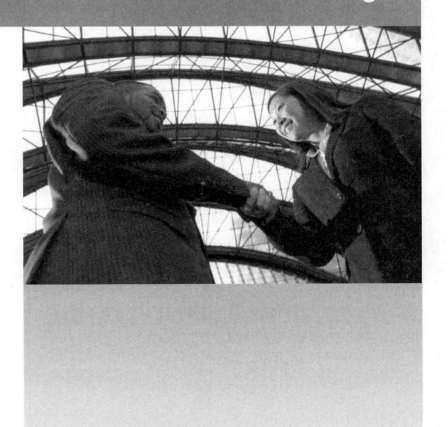

Part E
Budgeting and standard costing

Budgeting

Topic list	Syllabus reference
1 Budgetary planning and control systems	E1 (a)
2 The preparation of budgets	E1 (b), (c) E2 (a)
3 The sales budget	E2 (b)
4 Production and related budgets	E2 (b)
5 Fixed and flexible budgets	E3 (a)
6 Preparing flexible budgets	E3 (a)
7 Flexible budgets and budgetary control	E3 (a) E5 (a)

Introduction

This chapter begins a new topic, **budgeting**. You will meet the topic at all stages of your future examination studies and so it is vital that you get a firm grasp of it now.

The chapter begins by explaining the **reasons for operating a budgetary planning and control system** (**Section 1**), explains some of the **key terms** associated with budgeting and reminds you of the steps in the preparation of a master budget (**Section 2**).

Study guide

		Intellectual level
E1	**Nature and purpose of budgeting**	
(a)	Explain why organisations use budgeting	1
(b)	Explain the administrative procedures used in the budgeting process	1
(c)	Describe the stages in the budgeting process	1
E2	**Functional budgets**	
(a)	Explain the term 'principal budget factor'	1
(b)	Prepare budgets for sales production, materials (usage and purchase), labour and overheads	1
E3	**Flexible budgets and standard costing**	
(a)	Explain and prepare fixed, flexible and flexed budgets	1
E5	**Reconciliation of budgeted profit and actual profit**	
(a)	Reconcile budgeted profit with actual profit under standard absorption costing	1

Exam guide

This topic was not in the previous syllabus but has been brought into this one – so expect it to be tested.

1 Budgetary planning and control systems

FAST FORWARD

A **budget** is a quantified plan of action for a forthcoming accounting period. A **budget** is a plan of what the organisation is aiming to achieve and what is has set as a target whereas a **forecast** is an estimate of what is likely to occur in the future

Key term

The **budget** is 'a quantitative statement for a defined period of time, which may include planned revenues, expenses, assets, liabilities and cash flows. A budget facilitates planning'.

There is, however, little point in an organisation simply preparing a budget for the sake of preparing a budget. A beautifully laid out budgeted income statement filed in the cost accountant's file and never looked at again is worthless. The organisation should gain from both the actual preparation process and from the budget once it has been prepared.

FAST FORWARD

The **objectives** of a budgetary planning and control system are as follows.

- To ensure the achievement of the organisation's objectives
- To compel planning
- To communicate ideas and plans
- To coordinate activities
- To provide a framework for responsibility accounting
- To establish a system of control
- To motivate employees to improve their performance

Budgets are therefore not prepared in isolation and then filed away but are the fundamental components of what is known as the **budgetary planning and control system**. A budgetary planning and control system is essentially a system for ensuring **communication**, **coordination** and **control** within an organisation. Communication, coordination and control are general objectives: more information is provided by an inspection of the specific objectives of a budgetary planning and control system.

Objective	Comment
Ensure the achievement of the organisation's objectives	Objectives are set for the organisation as a whole, and for individual departments and operations within the organisation. Quantified expressions of these objectives are then drawn up as targets to be achieved within the timescale of the budget plan.
Compel planning	This is probably the most important feature of a budgetary planning and control system. Planning forces management to look ahead, to set out detailed plans for achieving the targets for each department, operation and (ideally) each manager and to anticipate problems. It thus prevents management from relying on ad hoc or uncoordinated planning which may be detrimental to the performance of the organisation. It also helps managers to **foresee potential threats or opportunities**, so that they may **take action now** to avoid or minimise the effect of the threats and to take full advantage of the opportunities.
Communicate ideas and plans	A formal system is necessary to ensure that each person affected by the plans is aware of what he or she is supposed to be doing. Communication might be one-way, with managers giving orders to subordinates, or there might be a two-way dialogue and exchange of ideas.
Coordinate activities	The activities of different departments or sub-units of the organisation need to be coordinated to ensure maximum integration of effort towards common goals. This concept of coordination implies, for example, that the purchasing department should base its budget on production requirements and that the production budget should in turn be based on sales expectations. Although straightforward in concept, coordination is remarkably difficult to achieve, and there is often **'sub-optimality'** and conflict between departmental plans in the budget so that the efforts of each department are not fully integrated into a combined plan to achieve the company's best targets.
Provide a framework for responsibility accounting	Budgetary planning and control systems require that managers of **budget centres** are made responsible for the achievement of budget targets for the operations under their personal control.
Establish a system of control	A budget is a **yardstick** against which actual performance is monitored and assessed. Control over actual performance is provided by the comparisons of actual results against the budget plan. Departures from budget can then be investigated and the reasons for the departures can be divided into **controllable** and **uncontrollable** factors.
Motivate employees to improve their performance	The interest and commitment of employees can be retained via a system of feedback of actual results, which lets them know how well or badly they are performing. The identification of controllable reasons for departures from budget with managers responsible provides an incentive for improving future performance.

Objective	Comment
Provide a framework for authorisation	Once the budget has been agreed by the directors and senior managers it acts as an authorisation for each budget holder to incur the costs included in the budget centre's budget. **As long as the expenditure is included in the formalised budget** the budget holder can carry out day to day operations without needing to seek separate authorisation for each item of expenditure.
Provide a basis for performance evaluation	As well as providing a yardstick for control by comparison, the monitoring of actual results compared with the budget can provide a basis for **evaluating the performance of the budget holder.** As a result of this evaluation the manager might be rewarded, perhaps with a financial bonus or promotion. Alternatively the evaluation process might highlight the need for more investment in staff development and training.

2 The preparation of budgets

Having seen why organisations prepare budgets, we will now turn our attention to the mechanics of budget preparation. We will begin by defining and explaining a number of terms.

2.1 Planning

Key term

Planning is the establishment of objectives, and the formulation of the policies, strategies and tactics required to achieve them. Planning comprises long-term/strategic planning, and short-term operation planning.

2.1.1 The value of long-term planning

A **budgetary planning and control system** operating in **isolation** without any form of long-term planning as a framework is **unlikely to produce maximum potential benefits** for an organisation.

(a) **Without stated long-term objectives**, managers **do not know what they should be trying to achieve** and so there are **no criteria against which to assess possible courses of action**.

(b) Without long-term planning, budgets may simply be based on a sales forecast. Performance can therefore only be judged in terms of previous years' results, **no analysis of the organisation's potential** having been carried out.

(c) Many business **decisions need to be taken on a long-term basis**. For instance, **new products** cannot simply be introduced when sales of existing products begin to decline. Likewise, **capital equipment** cannot necessarily be purchased and installed in the short term if production volumes start to increase.

(d) With long-term planning, **limiting factors** (other than sales) which might arise can possibly be anticipated, and avoided or overcome.

2.2 The budget period

Except for capital expenditure budgets, the budget period is commonly the accounting year (sub-divided into 12 or 13 control periods).

2.3 The budget manual

> The **budget manual** is a collection of instructions governing the responsibilities of persons and the procedures, forms and records relating to the preparation and use of budgetary data.

Likely contents of a budget manual	Examples
An explanation of the objectives of the budgetary process	• The purpose of budgetary planning and control • The objectives of the various stages of the budgetary process • The importance of budgets in the long-term planning and administration of the enterprise
Organisational structures	• An organisation chart • A list of individuals holding budget responsibilities
Principal budgets	• An outline of each • The relationship between them
Administrative details of budget preparation	• Membership and terms of reference of the budget committee • The sequence in which budgets are to be prepared • A timetable
Procedural matters	• Specimen forms and instructions for their completion • Specimen reports • Account codes (or a chart of accounts) • The name of the budget officer to whom enquiries must be sent

2.4 The responsibility for preparing budgets

The initial responsibility for preparing the budget will normally be with the managers (and their subordinates) who will be carrying out the budget, selling goods or services and authorising expenditure. However, the budget is normally set as part of a longer process, involving the authorisation of set targets by senior management and the negotiation process with the budget holders. Depending on the size of the organisation there may be a large number of **budget centres** and a separate **budget holder** would be responsible for setting and achieving the budget for the centre.

Examples of the functional budgets that would be prepared and **the managers responsible for their preparation** are as follows.

(a) The **sales manager** should draft the **sales budget** and **selling overhead** cost centre budgets.

(b) The **purchasing manager** should draft the **material purchases** budget.

(c) The **production manager** should draft the **direct production** cost budgets.

(d) Various **cost centre managers** should prepare the individual production, administration and distribution cost centre budgets for their own cost centre.

(e) The **cost accountant** will **analyse** the budgeted overheads to determine the overhead absorption rates for the next budget period.

2.5 Budget committee

> The **budget committee** is the coordinating body in the preparation and administration of budgets.

The **coordination** and **administration** of budgets is usually the responsibility of a **budget committee** (with the managing director as chairman).

(a)   The budget committee is assisted by a **budget officer** who is usually an accountant. Every part of the organisation should be represented on the committee, so there should be a representative from sales, production, marketing and so on.

(b)   **Functions of the budget committee**

- **Coordination** of the preparation of budgets, which includes the issue of the budget manual

- **Issuing of timetables** for the preparation of functional budgets

- **Allocation of responsibilities** for the preparation of functional budgets

- **Provision of information** to assist in the preparation of budgets

- **Communication of final budgets** to the appropriate managers

- **Comparison** of actual results with budget and the investigation of variances

- **Continuous assessment** of the budgeting and planning process, in order to improve the planning and control function

2.6 Budget preparation

Let us now look at the steps involved in the preparation of a budget. The procedures will differ from organisation to organisation, but the step-by-step approach described in this chapter is indicative of the steps followed by many organisations. The preparation of a budget may take weeks or months, and the budget committee may meet several times before the functional budgets are co-ordinated and the master budget is finally agreed.

2.7 The principal budget factor

> The **principal budget factor** should be identified at the beginning of the budgetary process, and the budget for this is prepared before all the others.

The first task in the budgetary process is to identify the **principal budget factor**. This is also known as the **key** budget factor or **limiting** budget factor.

Key term

> The **principal budget factor** is the factor which limits the activities of an organisation.

Likely principal budget factors

(a)   The **principal budget factor** is usually **sales demand**: a company is usually restricted from making and selling more of its products because there would be no sales demand for the increased output at a price which would be acceptable/profitable to the company.

(b)   Other possible factors

- Machine capacity
- Distribution and selling resources

- The availability of key raw materials
- The availability of cash.

Once this factor is defined then the remainder of the budgets can be prepared. For example, if sales are the principal budget factor then the production manager can only prepare his budget after the sales budget is complete.

Management may not know what the limiting budget factor is until a draft budget has been attempted. The first draft budget will therefore usually begin with the preparation of a draft sales budget.

Question   Budgets

A company that manufactures and sells a range of products, with sales potential limited by market share, is considering introducing a system of budgeting.

Required

(a)   List (in order of preparation) the functional budgets that need to be prepared.

(b)   State which budgets will comprise the master budget.

(c)   Consider how the work outlined in (a) and (b) can be coordinated in order for the budgeting process to be successful.

Answer

(a)   The **sequence of budget preparation** will be roughly as follows.

- Sales budget. (The market share limits demand and so sales is the principal budget factor. All other activities will depend upon this forecast.)
- Finished goods inventory budget (in units)
- Production budget (in units)
- Production resources budgets (materials, machine hours, labour)
- Overhead budgets for production, administration, selling and distribution, research and development and so on

Other budgets required will be the capital expenditure budget, the working capital budget (receivables and payables) and, very importantly, the cash budget.

(b)   The **master budget** is the summary of all the functional budgets. It often includes a summary income statement and balance sheet.

(c)   Procedures for preparing budgets can be contained in a **budget manual** which shows which budgets must be prepared when and by whom, what each functional budget should contain and detailed directions on how to prepare budgets including, for example, expected price increases, rates of interest, rates of depreciation and so on.

The formulation of budgets can be coordinated by a **budget committee** comprising the senior executives of the departments responsible for carrying out the budgets: sales, production, purchasing, personnel and so on.

The budgeting process may also be assisted by the use of a **spreadsheet/computer budgeting package**.

3 The sales budget

We have already established that, for many organisations, the principal budget factor is sales volume. The sales budget is therefore **often the primary budget** from which the majority of the other budgets are derived.

Before the sales budget can be prepared a sales forecast has to be made. A **forecast** is an estimate of what is likely to occur in the future. A budget, in contrast, is a plan of what the organisation is aiming to achieve and what it has set as a target.

On the basis of the sales forecast and the production capacity of the organisation, a sales budget will be prepared. This may be subdivided, possible subdivisions being by product, by sales area, by management responsibility and so on.

Once the sales budget has been agreed, related budgets can be prepared.

4 Production and related budgets

If the principal budget factor was production capacity then the production budget would be the first to be prepared. To assess whether production is the principal budget factor, the **production capacity available** must be determined, taking account of a number of factors.

- **Available labour**, including idle time, overtime and standard output rates per hour
- **Availability of raw materials** including allowances for losses during production
- **Maximum machine hours available**, including expected idle time and expected output rates per machine hour

It is, however, normally sales volume that is the constraint and therefore the production budget is usually prepared after the sales budget and the finished goods inventory budget.

The production budget will show the quantities and costs for each product and product group and will tie in with the sales and inventory budgets. This co-ordinating process is likely to show any shortfalls or excesses in capacity at various times over the budget period.

If there is likely to be a **shortfall** then consideration should be given to how this can be avoided. Possible **options** include the following.

- Overtime working
- Subcontracting
- Machine hire
- New sources of raw materials

A significant shortfall means that production capacity is, in fact, the limiting factor.

If **capacity exceeds sales volume** for a length of time then consideration should be given to **product diversification**, a **reduction in selling price** (if demand is price elastic) and so on.

Once the production budget has been finalised, the labour, materials and machine budgets can be drawn up. These budgets will be based on budgeted activity levels, planned inventory positions and projected labour and material costs.

4.1 Example: the production budget and direct labour budget

Landy manufactures two products, A and B, and is preparing its budget for 20X3. Both products are made by the same grade of labour, grade Q. The company currently holds 800 units of A and 1,200 units of B in inventory, but 250 of these units of B have just been discovered to have deteriorated in quality, and must therefore be scrapped. Budgeted sales of A are 3,000 units and of B 4,000 units, provided that the company maintains finished goods inventories at a level equal to three months' sales.

Grade Q labour was originally expected to produce one unit of A in two hours and one unit of B in three hours, at an hourly rate of $2.50 per hour. In discussions with trade union negotiators, however, it has been agreed that the hourly wage rate should be raised by 50c per hour, provided that the times to produce A and B are reduced by 20%.

Required

Prepare the production budget and direct labour budget for 20X3.

Solution

The expected time to produce a unit of A will now be 80% of 2 hours = 1.6 hours, and the time for a unit of B will be 2.4 hours. The hourly wage rate will be $3, so that the direct labour cost will be $4.80 for A and $7.20 for B (thus achieving a saving for the company of 20c per unit of A produced and 30c per unit of B).

(a)   **Production budget**

		Product A			Product B	
		Units	Units		Units	Units
Budgeted sales			3,000			4,000
Closing inventories	($^3/_{12}$ of 3,000)	750		($^3/_{12}$ of 4,000)	1,000	
Opening inventories (minus inventories scrapped)		800			950	
(Decrease)/increase in inventories						50
			(50)			
Production			2,950			4,050

(b)   **Direct labour budget**

	Grade Q	Cost
	Hours	$
2,950 units of product A	4,720	14,160
4,050 units of product B	9,720	29,160
Total	14,440	43,320

It is assumed that there will be no idle time among grade Q labour which, if it existed, would have to be paid for at the rate of $3 per hour.

4.2 The standard hour

ey term

A **standard hour** or standard minute is the amount of work achievable at standard efficiency levels in that time period.

This is a useful concept in budgeting for labour requirements. For example, budgeted **output of different products or jobs** in a period could be converted into standard hours of production, and a labour budget constructed accordingly.

Standard hours are particularly useful when management wants to monitor the production levels of a variety of dissimilar units. For example product A may take five hours to produce and product B, seven hours. If four units of each product are produced, instead of saying that total output is eight units, we could state the production level as (4 × 5) + (4 × 7) standard hours = 48 standard hours.

4.3 Example: direct labour budget based on standard hours

Truro manufactures a single product, Q, with a single grade of labour. Its sales budget and finished goods inventory budget for period 3 are as follows.

Sales	700 units
Opening inventories, finished goods	50 units
Closing inventories, finished goods	70 units

The goods are inspected only when production work is completed, and it is budgeted that 10% of finished work will be scrapped.

The standard direct labour hour content of product Q is three hours. The budgeted productivity ratio for direct labour is only 80% (which means that labour is only working at 80% efficiency).

The company employs 18 direct operatives, who are expected to average 144 working hours each in period 3.

Required

(a)   Prepare a production budget.

(b)   Prepare a direct labour budget.

(c)   Comment on the problem that your direct labour budget reveals, and suggest how this problem might be overcome.

Solution

(a)   **Production budget**

	Units
Sales	700
Add closing inventory	70
	770
Less opening inventory	50
Production required of 'good' output	720
Wastage rate	10%

Total production required $720 \times \dfrac{100 *}{90} = 800$ units

(* Note that the required adjustment is 100/90, not 110/100, since the waste is assumed to be 10% of total production, not 10% of good production.)

(b)   Now we can prepare the **direct labour budget**.

Standard hours per unit	3
Total standard hours required = 800 units × 3 hours	2,400 hours
Productivity ratio	80%

Actual hours required $2,400 \times \dfrac{100}{80} = 3,000$ hours

(c)   If we look at the **direct labour budget** against the information provided, we can identify the problem.

	Hours
Budgeted hours available (18 operatives × 144 hours)	2,592
Actual hours required	3,000
Shortfall in labour hours	408

The (draft) budget indicates that there will not be enough direct labour hours to meet the production requirements.

(d)   **Overcoming insufficient labour hours**

(i)   **Reduce the closing inventory** requirement below 70 units. This would reduce the number of production units required.

(ii)   Persuade the workforce to do some **overtime** working.

(iii)   Perhaps **recruit** more direct labour if long-term prospects are for higher production volumes.

(iv)   **Improve** the **productivity** ratio, and so reduce the number of hours required to produce the output.

(v)   If possible, **reduce** the **wastage** rate below 10%.

4.4 Example: the material purchases budget

Tremor manufactures two products, S and T, which use the same raw materials, D and E. One unit of S uses 3 litres of D and 4 kilograms of E. One unit of T uses 5 litres of D and 2 kilograms of E. A litre of D is expected to cost $3 and a kilogram of E $7.

Budgeted sales for 20X2 are 8,000 units of S and 6,000 units of T; finished goods in inventory at 1 January 20X2 are 1,500 units of S and 300 units of T, and the company plans to hold inventories of 600 units of each product at 31 December 20X2.

Inventories of raw material are 6,000 litres of D and 2,800 kilograms of E at 1 January, and the company plans to hold 5,000 litres and 3,500 kilograms respectively at 31 December 20X2.

The warehouse and stores managers have suggested that a provision should be made for damages and deterioration of items held in store, as follows.

Product S :   loss of 50 units
Product T :   loss of 100 units
Material D :   loss of 500 litres
Material E :   loss of 200 kilograms

Required

Prepare a material purchases budget for the year 20X2.

Solution

To calculate material purchase requirements, it is first of all necessary to calculate the budgeted production volumes and material usage requirements.

	Product S		*Product T*	
	Units	Units	Units	Units
Sales		8,000		6,000
Provision for losses		50		100
Closing inventory	600		600	
Opening inventory	1,500		300	
(Decrease)/increase in inventory		(900)		300
Production budget		7,150		6,400

	Material D		*Material E*	
	Litres	Litres	Kg	Kg
Usage requirements				
To produce 7,150 units of S		21,450		28,600
To produce 6,400 units of T		32,000		12,800
Usage budget		53,450		41,400
Provision for losses		500		200
		53,950		41,600
Closing inventory	5,000		3,500	
Opening inventory	6,000		2,800	
(Decrease)/increase in inventory		(1,000)		700
Material purchases budget		52,950		42,300

	Material D	Material E
Cost per unit	$3 per litre	$7 per kg
Cost of material purchases	$158,850	$296,100
Total purchases cost		$454,950

Question   **Material purchases budget**

J purchases a basic commodity and then refines it for resale. Budgeted sales of the refined product are as follows.

	April	May	June
Sales in kg	9,000	8,000	7,000

- The basic raw material costs $3 per kg.

- Material losses are 10% of finished output.

- The target month-end raw material inventory level is 5,000 kg plus 25% of the raw material required for next month's budgeted production.

- The target month-end inventory level for finished goods is 6,000 kg plus 25% of next month's budgeted sales.

What are the budgeted raw material purchases for April?

A   8,500 kg
B   9,350 kg
C   9,444.25 kg
D   9,831.25 kg

Answer

The correct answer is B.

	March	April	May
Required finished inventory:	kg	kg	kg
Base inventory	6,000	6,000	6,000
+ 25% of next month's sales	2,250	2,000	1,750
= Required inventory	8,250	8,000	7,750
Sales for month		9,000	8,000
		17,000	15,750
Less: opening inventory		8,250	8,000
Required finished production		8,750	7,750
+ 10% losses = raw material required		9,625	8,525
Required material inventory:			
Base inventory	5,000.00	5,000.00	
+ 25% of material for next month's production	2,406.25	2,131.25	
= Required closing material inventory	7,406.25	7,131.25	
Production requirements		9,625.00	
		16,756.25	
Less: opening inventory		7,406.25	
Required material purchases		9,350.00	

4.5 Non-production overheads

In the modern business environment, an increasing proportion of overheads are not directly related to the volume of production, such as administration overheads and research and development costs.

4.6 Key decisions in the budgeting process for non-production overheads

Deciding which fixed costs are committed (will be incurred no matter what) and which fixed costs will depend on management decisions.

Deciding what factors will influence the level of variable costs. Administration costs for example may be partly governed by the number of orders received.

5 Fixed and flexible budgets

AST FORWARD

Fixed budgets remain unchanged regardless of the level of activity; **flexible budgets** are designed to flex with the level of activity.

Flexible budgets are prepared using marginal costing and so mixed costs must be split into their fixed and variable components (possibly using the **high/low method**).

5.1 Fixed budgets

The master budget prepared before the beginning of the budget period is known as the **fixed** budget. By the term 'fixed', we do not mean that the budget is kept unchanged. Revisions to a fixed master budget will be made if the situation so demands. The term 'fixed' means the following.

(a)   The budget is prepared on the basis of an estimated volume of production and an estimated volume of sales, but no plans are made for the event that actual volumes of production and sales may differ from budgeted volumes.

(b)   When actual volumes of production and sales during a control period (month or four weeks or quarter) are achieved, a fixed budget is not adjusted (in retrospect) to represent a new target for the new levels of activity.

The major purpose of a fixed budget lies in its use at the planning stage, when it seeks to define the broad objectives of the organisation.

> **y term**
>
> A **fixed budget** is a budget which is normally set prior to the start of an accounting period, and which is not changed in response to changes in activity or costs/revenues.

Fixed budgets (in terms of a **pre-set expenditure limit**) are also useful for **controlling any fixed cost**, and **particularly non-production fixed costs** such as advertising, because such costs should be unaffected by changes in activity level (within a certain range).

5.2 Flexed budgets

ST FORWARD

Comparison of a fixed budget with the actual results for a different level of activity is of little use for **budgetary control purposes**. Flexible budgets should be used to show what cost and revenues should have been for the actual level of activity. Differences between the flexible budget figures and actual results are **variances**.

> **y term**
>
> A **flexible budget** is a budget which is designed to change as volume of activity changes.

Two uses of flexible budgets

(a)   **At the planning stage**. For example, suppose that a company expects to sell 10,000 units of output during the next year. A master budget (the fixed budget) would be prepared on the basis of these expected volumes. However, if the company thinks that output and sales might be as low as 8,000 units or as high as 12,000 units, it may prepare **contingency** flexible budgets, at volumes of, say 8,000, 9,000, 11,000 and 12,000 units, and then assess the possible outcomes.

(b)   **Retrospectively.** At the end of each control period, flexible budgets can be used to compare actual results achieved with what results should have been under the circumstances. Flexible budgets are an essential factor in budgetary control.

(i)   Management needs to know about how good or bad actual performance has been. To provide a measure of performance, there must be a yardstick (budget/ standard) against which actual performance can be measured.

(ii)   Every business is dynamic, and actual volumes of output cannot be expected to conform exactly to the fixed budget. Comparing actual costs directly with the fixed budget costs is meaningless.

(iii)   For useful control information, it is necessary to compare actual results at the actual level of activity achieved against the results that should have been expected at this level of activity, which are shown by the flexible budget.

6 Preparing flexible budgets

6.1 Example: fixed and flexible budgets

Suppose that Gemma expects production and sales during the next year to be 90% of the company's output capacity, that is, 9,000 units of a single product. Cost estimates will be made using the high-low method and the following historical records of cost.

Units of output/sales	Cost of sales
	$
9,800	44,400
7,700	38,100

The company's management is not certain that the estimate of sales is correct, and has asked for flexible budgets to be prepared at output and sales levels of 8,000 and 10,000 units. The sales price per unit has been fixed at $5 .

Required

Prepare appropriate budgets.

Solution

If we assume that within the range 8,000 to 10,000 units of sales, all costs are fixed, variable or mixed (in other words there are no stepped costs, material discounts, overtime premiums, bonus payments and so on) the fixed and flexible budgets would be based on the estimate of fixed and variable cost.

		$
Total cost of 9,800 units	=	44,400
Total cost of 7,700 units	=	38,100
Variable cost of 2,100 units	=	6,300

The variable cost per unit is $3.

		$
Total cost of 9,800 units	=	44,400
Variable cost of 9,800 units (9,800 × $3)	=	29,400
Fixed costs (all levels of output and sales)	=	15,000

The fixed budgets and flexible budgets can now be prepared as follows.

	Flexible budget 8,000 units	Fixed budget 9,000 units	Flexible budget 10,000 units
	$	$	$
Sales (× $5)	40,000	45,000	50,000
Variable costs (× $3)	24,000	27,000	30,000
Contribution	16,000	18,000	20,000
Fixed costs	15,000	15,000	15,000
Profit	1,000	3,000	5,000

6.2 The need for flexible budgets

We have seen that flexible budgets may be prepared in order to plan for variations in the level of activity above or below the level set in the fixed budget. It has been suggested, however, that since many cost items in modern industry are fixed costs, the value of flexible budgets in planning is dwindling.

(a) In many manufacturing industries, plant costs (depreciation, rent and so on) are a very large proportion of total costs, and these tend to be fixed costs.

(b) Wage costs also tend to be fixed, because employees are generally guaranteed a basic wage for a working week of an agreed number of hours.

(c) With the growth of service industries, labour (wages or fixed salaries) and overheads will account for most of the costs of a business, and direct materials will be a relatively small proportion of total costs.

Flexible budgets are nevertheless necessary, and even if they are not used at the planning stage, they must be used for budgetary control variance analysis.

7 Flexible budgets and budgetary control

AST FORWARD

> Budgetary control is based around a system of **budget centres**. Each centre has its own budget which is the responsibility of the **budget holder**.

In other words, individual managers are held responsible for investigating differences between budgeted and actual results, and are then expected to take corrective action or amend the plan in the light of actual events.

It is therefore vital to ensure that valid comparisons are being made. Consider the following example.

7.1 Example

Penny manufactures a single product, the Darcy. Budgeted results and actual results for May are as follows.

	Budget	Actual	Variance
Production and sales of the Darcy (units)	7,500	8,200	
	$	$	$
Sales revenue	75,000	81,000	6,000 (F)
Direct materials	22,500	23,500	1,000 (A)
Direct labour	15,000	15,500	500 (A)
Production overhead	22,500	22,800	300 (A)
Administration overhead	10,000	11,000	1,000 (A)
	70,000	72,800	2,800 (A)
Profit	5,000	8,200	3,200 (F)

Note. (F) denotes a favourable variance and (A) an unfavourable or adverse variance.

In this example, the variances are meaningless for the purposes of control. All costs were higher than budgeted but the volume of output was also higher; it is to be expected that actual variable costs would be greater those included in the fixed budget. However, it is not possible to tell how much of the increase is due to **poor cost control** and how much is due to the **increase in activity**.

Similarly it is not possible to tell how much of the increase in sales revenue is due to the increase in activity. Some of the difference may be due to a difference between budgeted and actual selling price but we are unable to tell from the analysis above.

For control purposes we need to know the answers to questions such as the following.

- Were actual costs higher than they should have been to produce and sell 8,200 Darcys?
- Was actual revenue satisfactory from the sale of 8,200 Darcys?

Instead of comparing actual results with a fixed budget which is based on a different level of activity to that actually achieved, the correct approach to budgetary control is to compare actual results with a budget which has been **flexed** to the actual activity level achieved.

Suppose that we have the following estimates of the behaviour of Penny's costs.

(a)   Direct materials and direct labour are variable costs.

(b)   Production overhead is a semi-variable cost, the budgeted cost for an activity level of 10,000 units being $25,000.

(c)   Administration overhead is a fixed cost.

(d)   Selling prices are constant at all levels of sales.

Solution

The **budgetary control analysis** should therefore be as follows.

	Fixed budget	Flexible budget	Actual results	Variance
Production and sales (units)	7,500	8,200	8,200	
	$	$	$	$
Sales revenue	75,000	82,000 (W1)	81,000	1,000 (A)
Direct materials	22,500	24,600 (W2)	23,500	1,100 (F)
Direct labour	15,000	16,400 (W3)	15,500	900 (F)
Production overhead	22,500	23,200 (W4)	22,800	400 (F)
Administration overhead	10,000	10,000 (W5)	11,000	1,000 (A)
	70,000	74,200	72,800	1,400 (F)
Profit	5,000	7,800	8,200	400 (F)

Workings

1   Selling price per unit = $75,000 ÷ 7,500 = $10 per unit
    Flexible budget sales revenue = $10 × 8,200 = $82,000

2   Direct materials cost per unit = $22,500 ÷ 7,500 = $3
    Budget cost allowance = $3 × 8,200 = $24,600

3   Direct labour cost per unit = $15,000 ÷ 7,500 = $2
    Budget cost allowance = $2 × 8,200 = $16,400

4   Variable production overhead cost per unit = $(25,000 − 22,500)/(10,000 − 7,500)
    = $2,500/2,500 = $1 per unit

    ∴ Fixed production overhead cost = $22,500 − (7,500 × $1) = $15,000
    ∴ Budget cost allowance = $15,000 + (8,200 × $1) = $23,200

5   Administration overhead is a fixed cost and hence budget cost allowance = $10,000

Comment

(a)   In selling 8,200 units, the expected profit should have been, not the fixed budget profit of $5,000, but the flexible budget profit of $7,800. Instead actual profit was $8,200 ie $400 more than we should have expected.

One of the reasons for this improvement is that, given output and sales of 8,200 units, the cost of resources (material, labour etc) was $1,400 lower than expected. (A comparison of the fixed budget and the actual costs in Example 7.1 appeared to indicate that costs were not being controlled since all of the variances were adverse).

Total cost variances can be analysed to reveal how much of the variance is due to lower resource prices and how much is due to efficient resource usage.

(b)   The sales revenue was, however, $1,000 less than expected because a lower price was charged than budgeted.

We know this because flexing the budget has eliminated the effect of changes in the volume sold, which is the only other factor that can affect sales revenue. You have probably already realised that this variance of $1,000 (A) is a **selling price variance**.

The lower selling price could have been caused by the increase in the volume sold (to sell the additional 700 units the selling price had to fall below $10 per unit). We do not know if this is the case but without flexing the budget we could not know that a different selling price to that budgeted had been charged. Our initial analysis above had appeared to indicate that sales revenue was ahead of budget.

The difference of $400 between the flexible budget profit of $7,800 at a production level of 8,200 units and the actual profit of $8,200 is due to the net effect of cost savings of $1,400 and lower than expected sales revenue (by $1,000).

The difference between the original budgeted profit of $5,000 and the actual profit of $8,200 is the total of the following.

(a)   The savings in resource costs/lower than expected sales revenue (a net total of $400 as indicated by the difference between the flexible budget and the actual results).

(b)   The effect of producing and selling 8,200 units instead of 7,500 units (a gain of $2,800 as indicated by the difference between the fixed budget and the flexible budget). This is the **sales volume contribution variance**.

A **full variance analysis statement** would be as follows.

	$	$
Fixed budget profit		5,000
Variances		
Sales volume	2,800 (F)	
Selling price	1,000 (A)	
Direct materials cost	1,100 (F)	
Direct labour cost	900 (F)	
Production overhead cost	400 (F)	
Administration overhead cost	1,000 (A)	
		3,200 (F)
Actual profit		8,200

If management believes that any of the variances are large enough to justify it, they will investigate the reasons for their occurrence to see whether any corrective action is necessary.

Flexible budget

Flower budgeted to sell 200 units and produced the following budget.

	$	$
Sales		71,400
Variable costs		
Labour	31,600	
Material	12,600	
		44,200
Contribution		27,200
Fixed costs		18,900
Profit		8,300

Actual sales turned out to be 230 units, which were sold for $69,000. Actual expenditure on labour was $27,000 and on material $24,000. Fixed costs totalled $10,000.

Required

Prepare a flexible budget that will be useful for management control purposes.

Answer

	Budget 200 units $	Budget per unit $	Flexed budget 230 units $	Actual 230 units $	Variance $
Sales	71,400	357	82,110	69,000	13,110 (A)
Variable costs					
Labour	31,600	158	36,340	27,000	9,340 (F)
Material	12,600	63	14,490	24,000	9,510 (A)
	44,200	221	50,830	51,000	
Contribution	27,200	136	31,280	18,000	13,280 (A)
Fixed costs	18,900		18,900	10,000	8,900 (F)
Profit	8,300		12,380	8,000	4,380 (A)

7.2 Flexible budgets, control and computers

The production of flexible budget control reports is an area in which computers can provide invaluable assistance to the cost accountant, calculating flexed budget figures using fixed budget and actual results data and hence providing detailed variance analysis. For control information to be of any value it must be produced quickly: speed is one of the many advantages of computers.

7.3 The link between standard costing and budget flexing

The calculation of standard cost variances and the use of a flexed budget to control costs and revenues are **very similar in concept**.

For example, a direct material total variance in a standard costing system is calculated by **comparing the material cost that should have been incurred for the output achieved, with the actual cost that was incurred**.

Exactly the same process is undertaken when a budget is flexed to provide a basis for comparison with the actual cost: **the flexible budget cost allowance for material cost is the same as the cost that should have been incurred for the activity level achieved**. In the same way as for standard costing, this is then compared with the actual cost incurred in order to practice control by comparison.

However, there are differences between the two techniques.

(a) **Standard costing variance analysis is more detailed**. The total material cost variance is analysed further to determine how much of the total variance is caused by a difference in the price paid for materials (the material price variance) and how much is caused by the usage of material being different from the standard (the material usage variance). In flexible budget comparisons only total cost variances are derived.

(b) **For a standard costing system to operate it is necessary to determine a standard unit cost for all items of output**. All that is required to operate a flexible budgeting system is an understanding of the cost behaviour patterns and a measure of activity to use to flex the budget cost allowance for each cost element.

**xam focus
int**

Make sure you understand the **principal budget factor** and the difference between **fixed** and **flexible** budgets.

Chapter Roundup

- A **budget** is a quantified plan of action for a forthcoming accounting period. A **budget** is a plan of what the organisation is aiming to achieve and what is has set as a target, whereas a **forecast** is an estimate of what is **likely** to occur in the future

- The **objectives** of a budgetary planning and control system are as follows.
    - To ensure the achievement of the organisation's objectives
    - To compel planning
    - To communicate ideas and plans
    - To coordinate activities
    - To provide a framework for responsibility accounting
    - To establish a system of control
    - To motivate employees to improve their performance

- The **budget committee** is the coordinating body in the preparation and administration of budgets.

- The **principal budget factor** should be identified at the beginning of the budgetary process, and the budget for this is prepared before all the others.

- **Fixed budgets** remain unchanged regardless of the level of activity; **flexible budgets** are designed to flex with the level of activity.

- **Flexible budgets** are prepared using marginal costing and so mixed costs must be split into their fixed and variable component.

- Comparison of a fixed budget with the actual results for a different level of activity is of little use for **budgeting control purposes**. Flexible budgets should be used to show what cost and revenues should have been for the actual level of activity. Differences between the flexible budget figures and actual results are **variances.**

- Budgetary control is based around a system of **budget centres**. Each centre has its own budget which is the responsibility of the **budget holder**.

Quick Quiz

1   Which of the following is not an objective of a system of budgetary planning and control?

   A   To establish a system of control
   B   To coordinate activities
   C   To compel planning
   D   To motivate employees to maintain current performance levels

2   Sales is always the principal budget factor and so it is always the first budget to be prepared. *True or false?*

3   *Choose the appropriate words from those highlighted.*

   A **forecast/budget** is an **estimate/guarantee** of what is **likely to occur in the future/has happened in the past.**

   A **forecast/budget** is a **quantified plan/unquantified plan/guess** of what the organisation is aiming to **achieve/spend**.

4   *Fill in the blanks.*

   When preparing a production budget, the quantity to be produced is equal to sales ....
   opening inventory .... closing inventory.

Answers to Quick Quiz

1   D. The objective is to motivate employees to *improve* their performance.

2   False. The budget for the principal budget factor must be prepared first, but sales is not always the principal budget factor.

3   A forecast is an estimate of what is likely to occur in the future.

   A budget is a quantified plan of what the organisation is aiming to achieve.

4   When preparing a production budget, the quantity to be produced is equal to sales minus opening inventory plus closing inventory.

Now try the questions below from the Exam Question Bank			
Number	**Level**	**Marks**	**Time**
Q13	MCQ/OTQ	n/a	n/a

Standard costing

Introduction

Just as there are **standards** for most things in our daily lives (cleanliness in hamburger restaurants, educational achievement of nine year olds, number of trains running on time), there are standards for the costs of products and services. Moreover, just as the standards in our daily lives are not always met, the standards for the costs of products and services are not always met. We will not, however, be considering the standards of cleanliness of hamburger restaurants in this chapter but we will be looking at standards for **costs**, what they are used for and how they are set.

In the next chapter we will see how **standard costing** forms the basis of a process called **variance analysis**, a vital management control tool.

Study guide

		Intellectual level
E3	**Flexible budgets and standard costing**	
(a)	Explain the purpose and principles of standard costing	1
(b)	Establish the standard cost per unit under absorption and marginal costing	1

Exam guide

Standard costing can be applied under both absorption and marginal costing and is important in calculating variances, which we look at in the next chapter. You may be given the standard cost and required to calculate the variance.

1 What is standard costing?

1.1 Introduction

> **FAST FORWARD**
>
> A **standard cost** is a **predetermined estimated unit cost**, used for inventory valuation and control.

The building blocks of standard costing are standard costs and so before we look at standard costing in any detail you really need to know what a standard cost is.

1.2 Standard cost card

> **FAST FORWARD**
>
> A **standard cost card** shows full details of the standard cost of each product.

The standard cost card of product 1234 is set out below.

STANDARD COST CARD – PRODUCT 1234

	$	$
Direct materials		
Material X – 3 kg at $4 per kg	12	
Material Y – 9 litres at $2 per litre	18	
		30
Direct labour		
Grade A – 6 hours at $1.50 per hour	9	
Grade B – 8 hours at $2 per hour	16	
		25
Standard direct cost		55
Variable production overhead – 14 hours at $0.50 per hour		7
Standard variable cost of production		62
Fixed production overhead – 14 hours at $4.50 per hour		63
Standard full production cost		125
Administration and marketing overhead		15
Standard cost of sale		140
Standard profit		20
Standard sales price		160

Notice how the total standard cost is built up from standards for each cost element: standard quantities of materials at standard prices, standard quantities of labour time at standard rates and so on. It is therefore determined by management's estimates of the following.

- The expected prices of materials, labour and expenses
- Efficiency levels in the use of materials and labour
- Budgeted overhead costs and budgeted volumes of activity

We will see how management arrives at these estimates in Section 2.

But why should management want to prepare standard costs? Obviously to assist with standard costing, but what is the point of standard costing?

1.3 The uses of standard costing

Standard costing has a variety of uses but its two principal ones are as follows.

(a) To **value inventories** and **cost production** for cost accounting purposes.

(b) To act as a **control device** by establishing standards (planned costs), highlighting (via **variance analysis** which we will cover in the next chapter) activities that are not conforming to plan and thus **alerting management** to areas which may be out of control and in need of corrective action.

Question   Standard cost card

Bloggs makes one product, the joe. Two types of labour are involved in the preparation of a joe, skilled and semi-skilled. Skilled labour is paid $10 per hour and semi-skilled $5 per hour. Twice as many skilled labour hours as semi-skilled labour hours are needed to produce a joe, four semi-skilled labour hours being needed.

A joe is made up of three different direct materials. Seven kilograms of direct material A, four litres of direct material B and three metres of direct material C are needed. Direct material A costs $1 per kilogram, direct material B $2 per litre and direct material C $3 per metre.

Variable production overheads are incurred at Bloggs Co at the rate of $2.50 per direct labour (skilled) hour.

A system of absorption costing is in operation at Bloggs Co. The basis of absorption is direct labour (skilled) hours. For the forthcoming accounting period, budgeted fixed production overheads are $250,000 and budgeted production of the joe is 5,000 units.

Administration, selling and distribution overheads are added to products at the rate of $10 per unit.

A mark-up of 25% is made on the joe.

Required

Using the above information draw up a standard cost card for the joe.

Answer

STANDARD COST CARD – PRODUCT JOE

	$	$
Direct materials		
A – 7 kgs × $1	7	
B – 4 litres × $2	8	
C – 3 m × $3	9	
		24
Direct labour		
Skilled – 8 × $10	80	
Semi-skilled – 4 × $5	20	
		100
Standard direct cost		124
Variable production overhead – 8 × $2.50		20
Standard variable cost of production		144
Fixed production overhead – 8 × $6.25 (W)		50
Standard full production cost		194
Administration, selling and distribution overhead		10
Standard cost of sale		204
Standard profit (25% × 204)		51
Standard sales price		255

Working

Overhead absorption rate = $\dfrac{\$250,000}{5,000 \times 8}$ = \$6.25 per skilled labour hour

Question   Marginal costing system

What would a standard cost card for product joe show under a marginal system?

Answer

STANDARD COST CARD – PRODUCT JOE

	$
Direct materials	24
Direct labour	100
Standard direct cost	124
Variable production overhead	20
Standard variable production cost	144
Standard sales price	255
Standard contribution	111

Although the use of standard costs to simplify the keeping of cost accounting records should not be overlooked, we will be concentrating on the **control** and **variance analysis** aspect of standard costing.

Key term

> **Standard costing** is a control technique which compares standard costs and revenues with actual results to obtain variances which are used to improve performance.

Notice that the above definition highlights the control aspects of standard costing.

1.4 Standard costing as a control technique

FAST FORWARD

> Differences between actual and standard costs are called **variances**.

Standard costing therefore involves the following.

- The establishment of predetermined estimates of the costs of products or services
- The collection of actual costs
- The comparison of the actual costs with the predetermined estimates.

The predetermined costs are known as **standard costs** and the difference between standard and actual cost is known as a **variance**. The process by which the total difference between standard and actual results is analysed is known as **variance analysis**.

Although standard costing can be used in a variety of costing situations (batch and mass production, process manufacture, jobbing manufacture (where there is standardisation of parts) and service industries (if a realistic cost unit can be established)), the greatest benefit from its use can be gained if there is a **degree of repetition** in the production process. It is therefore most suited to **mass production** and **repetitive assembly work**.

2 Setting standards

2.1 Introduction

Standard costs may be used in both absorption costing and in marginal costing systems. We shall, however, confine our description to standard costs in absorption costing systems.

As we noted earlier, the standard cost of a product (or service) is made up of a number of different standards, one for each cost element, each of which has to be set by management. We have divided this section into two: the first part looks at setting the monetary part of each standard, whereas the second part looks at setting the resources requirement part of each standard.

2.2 Direct material prices

Direct material prices will be estimated by the purchasing department from their knowledge of the following.

- Purchase contracts already agreed
- Pricing discussions with regular suppliers
- The forecast movement of prices in the market
- The availability of bulk purchase discounts

Price inflation can cause difficulties in setting realistic standard prices. Suppose that a material costs $10 per kilogram at the moment and during the course of the next twelve months it is expected to go up in price by 20% to $12 per kilogram. What standard price should be selected?

- The current price of $10 per kilogram
- The average expected price for the year, say $11 per kilogram

Either would be possible, but neither would be entirely satisfactory.

(a) If the **current price** were used in the standard, the reported price variance will become adverse as soon as prices go up, which might be very early in the year. If prices go up gradually rather than in one big jump, it would be difficult to select an appropriate time for revising the standard.

(b) If an **estimated mid-year price** were used, price variances should be favourable in the first half of the year and adverse in the second half of the year, again assuming that prices go up gradually throughout the year. Management could only really check that in any month, the price variance did not become excessively adverse (or favourable) and that the price variance switched from being favourable to adverse around month six or seven and not sooner.

2.3 Direct labour rates

Direct labour rates per hour will be set by discussion with the personnel department and by reference to the payroll and to any agreements on pay rises with trade union representatives of the employees.

(a) A separate hourly rate or weekly wage will be set for each different labour grade/type of employee.

(b) An average hourly rate will be applied for each grade (even though individual rates of pay may vary according to age and experience).

Similar problems when dealing with inflation to those described for material prices can be met when setting labour standards.

2.4 Overhead absorption rates

When standard costs are fully absorbed costs, the **absorption rate** of fixed production overheads will be **predetermined**, usually each year when the budget is prepared, and based in the usual manner on budgeted fixed production overhead expenditure and budgeted production.

For selling and distribution costs, standard costs might be absorbed as a percentage of the standard selling price.

Standard costs under marginal costing will, of course, not include any element of absorbed overheads.

2.5 Standard resource requirements

To estimate the materials required to make each product (**material usage**) and also the labour hours required (**labour efficiency**), **technical specifications** must be prepared for each product by production experts (either in the production department or the work study department).

(a)   The **'standard product specification'** for materials must list the quantities required per unit of each material in the product. These standard input quantities must be made known to the operators in the production department so that control action by management to deal with **excess material wastage** will be understood by them.

(b)   The **'standard operation sheet'** for labour will specify the expected hours required by each grade of labour in each department to make one unit of product. These standard times must be carefully set (for example by work study) and must be understood by the labour force. Where necessary, **standard procedures** or **operating methods** should be stated.

Exam focus point

> An exam question may give you actual costs and variances and require you to calculate the standard cost.

Chapter roundup

- A **standard cost** is a **predetermined estimated unit cost**, used for inventory valuation and control.
- A **standard cost card** shows full details of the standard cost of each product.
- Differences between actual and standard cost are called **variances**.

Quick quiz

1   A standard cost is ....

2   What are two main uses of standard costing?

3   A control technique which compares standard costs and revenues with actual results to obtain variances which are used to stimulate improved performance is known as:

    A   Standard costing
    B   Variance analysis
    C   Budgetary control
    D   Budgeting

4   Standard costs may only be used in absorption costing.

    True   ☐

    False   ☐

5   Two types of performance standard are

    (a)   ....

    (b)   ....

Answers to quick quiz

1   A planned unit cost.

2   (a)   To value inventories and cost production for cost accounting purposes.

    (b)   To act as a control device by establishing standards and highlighting activities that are not conforming to plan and bringing these to the attention of management.

3   A

4   False. They may be used in a marginal costing system as well.

5   (a)   Attainable

    (b)   Ideal

Now try the questions below from the Exam Question Bank

Number	Level	Marks	Time
Q14	MCQ/OTQ	n/a	n/a

15

Basic variance analysis

Topic list	Syllabus reference
1 Variances	E4 (a)
2 Direct material cost variances	E4 (a)
3 Direct labour cost variances	E4 (a)
4 Variable production overhead variances	E4 (a)
5 Fixed production overhead variances	E4 (a)
6 The reasons for cost variances	E4 (b), (c)
7 The significance of cost variances	E4 (d)

Introduction

The actual results achieved by an organisation during a reporting period (week, month, quarter, year) will, more than likely, be different from the expected results (the expected results being the standard costs and revenues which we looked at in the previous chapter). Such differences may occur between individual items, such as the cost of labour and the volume of sales, and between the total expected profit/contribution and the total actual profit/contribution.

Management will have spent considerable time and trouble setting standards. Actual results have differed from the standards. The wise manager will consider the differences that have occurred and use the results of these considerations to assist in attempts to attain the standards. The wise manager will use **variance analysis** as a method of **control**.

This chapter examines **variance analysis** and sets out the method of calculating the variances stated below in the Study Guide.
We will then go on to look at the reasons for and significance of cost variances.

Chapter 16 of this **Management Accounting** Study Text will build on the basics set down in this chapter by introducing **sales variances** and **operating statements**.

Study guide

		Intellectual level
E4	**Basic variance analysis under absorption and marginal costing**	
(a)	Calculate the following variances (i) Materials total, price and usage (ii) Labour total, rate and efficiency (iii) Variable overhead total, expenditure and efficiency (iv) Fixed overhead total, expenditure and, where appropriate, volume capacity and efficiency	1
(b)	Interpret all the variances above	1
(c)	Explain possible causes of all the variances above	1
(d)	Describe the interrelationships between the variances above	1

Exam guide

Variance calculation is a very important part of your Management Accounting studies and it is vital that you are able to calculate all of the different types of variance included in the syllabus.

1 Variances

FAST FORWARD

A **variance** is the difference between a planned, budgeted, or standard cost and the actual cost incurred. The same comparisons may be made for revenues. The process by which the **total** difference between standard and actual results is analysed is known as **variance analysis**.

When actual results are better than expected results, we have a **favourable variance** (F). If, on the other hand, actual results are worse than expected results, we have an **adverse variance** (A).

Variances can be divided into three main groups.

- Variable cost variances
- Sales variances
- Fixed production overhead variances.

In the remainder of this chapter we will consider, in detail, variable cost variances and fixed production overhead variances.

2 Direct material cost variances

2.1 Introduction

FAST FORWARD

The direct material total variance can be subdivided into the **direct material price** variance and the **direct material usage** variance.

y terms

The **direct material total variance** is the difference between what the output actually cost and what it should have cost, in terms of material.

The **direct material price variance.** This is the **difference between the standard cost and the actual cost for the actual quantity of material used or purchased.** In other words, it is the difference between what the material did cost and what it should have cost.

The **direct material usage variance.** This is the **difference between the standard quantity of materials that should have been used for the number of units actually produced, and the actual quantity of materials used, valued at the standard cost per unit of material.** In other words, it is the difference between how much material should have been used and how much material was used, valued at standard cost.

2.2 Example: Direct material variances

Product X has a standard direct material cost as follows.

> 10 kilograms of material Y at $10 per kilogram = $100 per unit of X.

During period 4, 1,000 units of X were manufactured, using 11,700 kilograms of material Y which cost $98,600.

Required

Calculate the following variances.

(a)   The direct material total variance
(b)   The direct material price variance
(c)   The direct material usage variance

Solution

(a)   **The direct material total variance**

This is the difference between what 1,000 units should have cost and what they did cost.

	$
1,000 units should have cost (× $100)	100,000
but did cost	98,600
Direct material total variance	1,400 (F)

The variance is **favourable** because the units cost less than they should have cost.

Now we can break down the direct material total variance into its two constituent parts: the direct material **price** variance and the direct material **usage** variance.

(b)   **The direct material price variance**

This is the difference between what 11,700 kgs should have cost and what 11,700 kgs did cost.

	$
11,700 kgs of Y should have cost (× $10)	117,000
but did cost	98,600
Material Y price variance	18,400 (F)

The variance is **favourable** because the material cost less than it should have.

(c)   **The direct material usage variance**

This is the difference between how many kilograms of Y should have been used to produce 1,000 units of X and how many kilograms were used, valued at the standard cost per kilogram.

1,000 units should have used (× 10 kgs)	10,000 kgs
but did use	11,700 kgs
Usage variance in kgs	1,700 kgs (A)
× standard cost per kilogram	× $10
Usage variance in $	$17,000 (A)

The variance is **adverse** because more material than should have been used was used.

(d) **Summary**

	$
Price variance	18,400 (F)
Usage variance	17,000 (A)
Total variance	1,400 (F)

2.3 Materials variances and opening and closing inventory

FAST FORWARD ▶

Direct material price variances are usually extracted at the time of the **receipt** of the materials rather than at the time of usage.

Suppose that a company uses raw material P in production, and that this raw material has a standard price of $3 per metre. During one month 6,000 metres are bought for $18,600, and 5,000 metres are used in production. At the end of the month, inventory will have been increased by 1,000 metres. In variance analysis, the problem is to decide the **material price variance**. Should it be calculated on the basis of **materials purchased** (6,000 metres) or on the basis of **materials used** (5,000 metres)?

The answer to this problem depends on how **closing inventories** of the raw materials will be valued.

(a) If they are valued at **standard cost**, (1,000 units at $3 per unit) the price variance is calculated on material **purchases** in the period.

(b) If they are valued at **actual cost (**FIFO**)** (1,000 units at $3.10 per unit) the price variance is calculated on materials **used in production** in the period.

A **full standard costing system** is usually in operation and therefore the price variance is usually calculated on **purchases** in the period. The variance on the full 6,000 metres will be written off to the costing profit and loss account, even though only 5,000 metres are included in the cost of production.

There are two main advantages in extracting the material price variance at the time of **receipt**.

(a) If variances are extracted at the time of receipt they will be **brought to the attention of managers earlier** than if they are extracted as the material is used. If it is necessary to correct any variances then management action can be more timely.

(b) Since variances are extracted at the time of receipt, **all inventories will be valued at standard price**. This is administratively easier and it means that all issues from inventory can be made at standard price. If inventories are held at actual cost it is necessary to calculate a separate price variance on each batch as it is issued. Since issues are usually made in a number of small batches this can be a time-consuming task, especially with a manual system.

The price variance would be calculated as follows.

	$
6,000 metres of material P purchased should cost (× $3)	18,000
but did cost	18,600
Price variance	600 (A)

BPP
LEARNING MEDIA

3 Direct labour cost variances

3.1 Introduction

The direct labour total variance can be subdivided into the **direct labour rate** variance and the **direct labour efficiency** variance.

The **direct labour total variance** is the difference between what the output should have cost and what it did cost, in terms of labour.

The **direct labour rate variance**. This is similar to the direct material price variance. It is the **difference between the standard cost and the actual cost for the actual number of hours paid for.**

In other words, it is the difference between what the labour did cost and what it should have cost.

The **direct labour efficiency variance** is similar to the direct material usage variance. It is the **difference between the hours that should have been worked for the number of units actually produced, and the actual number of hours worked, valued at the standard rate per hour.**

In other words, it is the difference between how many hours should have been worked and how many hours were worked, valued at the standard rate per hour.

The calculation of **direct labour variances** is very similar to the calculation of direct material variances.

3.2 Example: Direct labour variances

The standard direct labour cost of product X is as follows.

> 2 hours of grade Z labour at $5 per hour = $10 per unit of product X.

During period 4, 1,000 units of product X were made, and the direct labour cost of grade Z labour was $8,900 for 2,300 hours of work.

Required

Calculate the following variances.

(a)   The direct labour total variance
(b)   The direct labour rate variance
(c)   The direct labour efficiency (productivity) variance

Solution

(a)   **The direct labour total variance**

This is the difference between what 1,000 units should have cost and what they did cost.

	$
1,000 units should have cost (× $10)	10,000
but did cost	8,900
Direct labour total variance	1,100 (F)

The variance is **favourable** because the units cost less than they should have done.

Again we can analyse this total variance into its two constituent parts.

(b)   **The direct labour rate variance**

This is the difference between what 2,300 hours should have cost and what 2,300 hours did cost.

	$
2,300 hours of work should have cost (× $5 per hr)	11,500
but did cost	8,900
Direct labour rate variance	2,600 (F)

The variance is **favourable** because the labour cost less than it should have cost.

(c)   **The direct labour efficiency variance**

1,000 units of X should have taken (× 2 hrs)	2,000 hrs
but did take	2,300 hrs
Efficiency variance in hours	300 hrs (A)
× standard rate per hour	× $5
Efficiency variance in $	$1,500 (A)

The variance is **adverse** because more hours were worked than should have been worked.

(d)   **Summary**

	$
Rate variance	2,600 (F)
Efficiency variance	1,500 (A)
Total variance	1,100 (F)

4 Variable production overhead variances

FAST FORWARD

> The variable production overhead total variance can be subdivided into the variable production overhead **expenditure** variance and the variable production overhead **efficiency** variance (**based on actual hours**).

4.1 Example: Variable production overhead variances

Suppose that the variable production overhead cost of product X is as follows.

   2 hours at $1.50 = $3 per unit

During period 6, 400 units of product X were made. The labour force worked 820 hours, of which 60 hours were recorded as idle time. The variable overhead cost was $1,230.

Calculate the following variances.

(a)   The variable overhead total variance
(b)   The variable production overhead expenditure variance
(c)   The variable production overhead efficiency variance

Since this example relates to variable production costs, the total variance is based on actual units of production. (If the overhead had been a variable selling cost, the variance would be based on sales volumes.)

	$
400 units of product X should cost (× $3)	1,200
but did cost	1,230
Variable production overhead total variance	30 (A)

In many variance reporting systems, the variance analysis goes no further, and expenditure and efficiency variances are not calculated. However, the adverse variance of $30 may be explained as the sum of two factors.

(a)   The hourly rate of spending on variable production overheads was higher than it should have been, that is there is an expenditure variance.

(b)   The labour force worked inefficiently, and took longer to make the output than it should have done. This means that spending on variable production overhead was higher than it should have been, in other words there is an efficiency (productivity) variance. The variable production overhead efficiency variance is exactly the same, in hours, as the direct labour efficiency variance, and occurs for the same reasons.

It is usually assumed that **variable overheads are incurred during active working hours**, but are not incurred during idle time (for example the machines are not running, therefore power is not being consumed, and no indirect materials are being used). This means in our example that although the labour force was paid for 820 hours, they were actively working for only 760 of those hours and so variable production overhead spending occurred during 760 hours.

ey term

> The **variable production overhead expenditure variance** is the difference between the amount of variable production overhead that should have been incurred in the actual hours actively worked, and the actual amount of variable production overhead incurred.

(a)

	$
760 hours of variable production overhead should cost (× $1.50)	1,140
but did cost	1,230
Variable production overhead expenditure variance	90 (A)

ey term

> The **variable production overhead efficiency variance**. If you already know the direct labour efficiency variance, the variable production overhead efficiency variance is exactly the same in hours, but priced at the variable production overhead rate per hour.

(b)   In our example, the efficiency variance would be as follows.

400 units of product X should take (× 2hrs)	800 hrs
but did take (active hours)	760 hrs
Variable production overhead efficiency variance in hours	40 hrs (F)
× standard rate per hour	× $1.50
Variable production overhead efficiency variance in $	$60 (F)

(c)   **Summary**

	$
Variable production overhead expenditure variance	90 (A)
Variable production overhead efficiency variance	60 (F)
Variable production overhead total variance	30 (A)

5 Fixed production overhead variances

5.1 Introduction

FAST FORWARD

> The fixed production overhead total variance can be subdivided into an **expenditure** variance and a **volume** variance. The fixed production overhead volume variance can be further subdivided into an efficiency and capacity variance.

You may have noticed that the method of calculating cost variances for variable cost items is essentially the same for labour, materials and variable overheads. Fixed production overhead variances are very different. In an **absorption costing system**, they are an attempt to explain the **under– or over-absorption of fixed production overheads** in production costs. We looked at under/over absorption of fixed overheads in Chapter 8.

The fixed production overhead total variance (ie the under– or over-absorbed fixed production overhead) may be broken down into two parts as usual.

- An **expenditure** variance
- A **volume** variance. This in turn may be split into two parts
  - A **volume efficiency variance**
  - A **volume capacity variance**

You will find it easier to calculate and understand **fixed overhead variances**, if you keep in mind the whole time that you are trying to 'explain' (put a name and value to) any under– or over-absorbed overhead.

<table>
<tr><td>**Exam focus point**</td><td>You will need to be able to distinguish between marginal and absorption costing. The variances introduced above and discussed below relate to an absorption costing system. Marginal costing is dealt with in Chapter 16. In the marginal costing system the only fixed overhead variance is an expenditure variance.</td></tr>
</table>

5.2 Under/over absorption

Remember that the **absorption rate** is calculated as follows.

$$\text{Overhead absorption rate} = \frac{\text{Budgeted fixed overhead}}{\text{Budgeted activity level}}$$

Remember that the budgeted fixed overhead is the **planned** or **expected** fixed overhead and the budgeted activity level is the **planned** or **expected** activity level.

If either of the following are incorrect, then we will have an under– or over-absorption of overhead.

- The numerator (number on top) = Budgeted fixed overhead
- The denominator (number on bottom) = Budgeted activity level

5.3 The fixed overhead expenditure variance

The fixed overhead expenditure variance occurs if the numerator is incorrect. It measures the under– or over-absorbed overhead caused by the **actual total overhead** being different from the budgeted total overhead.

Therefore, fixed overhead expenditure variance = **Budgeted (planned) expenditure – Actual Expenditure.**

5.4 The fixed overhead volume variance

As we have already stated, the fixed overhead volume variance is made up of the following sub-variances.

- Fixed overhead efficiency variance
- Fixed overhead capacity variance

These variances arise if the denominator (ie the budgeted activity level) is incorrect.

The fixed overhead efficiency and capacity variances measure the under– or over-absorbed overhead caused by the **actual activity level** being different from the budgeted activity level used in calculating the absorption rate.

There are two reasons why the **actual activity** level may be different from the **budgeted activity level** used in calculating the absorption rate.

(a) The workforce may have worked more or less efficiently than the standard set. This deviation is measured by the **fixed overhead efficiency variance.**

(b) The hours worked by the workforce could have been different to the budgeted hours (regardless of the level of efficiency of the workforce) because of overtime and strikes etc. This deviation from the standard is measured by the **fixed overhead capacity variance.**

5.5 How to calculate the variances

In order to clarify the overhead variances which we have encountered in this section, consider the following definitions which are expressed in terms of how each overhead variance should be calculated.

> **Fixed overhead total variance** is the difference between fixed overhead incurred and fixed overhead absorbed. In other words, it is the under– or over-absorbed fixed overhead.
>
> **Fixed overhead expenditure variance** is the difference between the budgeted fixed overhead expenditure and actual fixed overhead expenditure.
>
> **Fixed overhead volume variance** is the difference between actual and budgeted (planned) volume multiplied by the standard absorption rate per *unit*.
>
> **Fixed overhead volume efficiency variance** is the difference between the number of hours that actual production should have taken, and the number of hours actually taken (that is, worked) multiplied by the standard absorption rate per *hour*.
>
> **Fixed overhead volume capacity variance** is the difference between budgeted (planned) hours of work and the actual hours worked, multiplied by the standard absorption rate per *hour*.

You should now be ready to work through an example to demonstrate all of the fixed overhead variances.

5.6 Example: Fixed overhead variances

Suppose that a company plans to produce 1,000 units of product E during August 20X3. The expected time to produce a unit of E is five hours, and the budgeted fixed overhead is $20,000. The standard fixed overhead cost per unit of product E will therefore be as follows.

5 hours at $4 per hour = $20 per unit

Actual fixed overhead expenditure in August 20X3 turns out to be $20,450. The labour force manages to produce 1,100 units of product E in 5,400 hours of work.

Task

Calculate the following variances.

(a) The fixed overhead total variance
(b) The fixed overhead expenditure variance
(c) The fixed overhead volume variance
(d) The fixed overhead volume efficiency variance
(e) The fixed overhead volume capacity variance

Solution

All of the variances help to assess the under– or over-absorption of fixed overheads, some in greater detail than others.

(a)   **Fixed overhead total variance**

	$
Fixed overhead incurred	20,450
Fixed overhead absorbed (1,100 units × $20 per unit)	22,000
Fixed overhead total variance	1,550 (F)
(= under-/over-absorbed overhead)	

The variance is favourable because more overheads were absorbed than budgeted.

(b)   **Fixed overhead expenditure variance**

	$
Budgeted fixed overhead expenditure	20,000
Actual fixed overhead expenditure	20,450
Fixed overhead expenditure variance	450 (A)

The variance is adverse because actual expenditure was greater than budgeted expenditure.

(c)   **Fixed overhead volume variance**

The production volume achieved was greater than expected. The fixed overhead volume variance measures the difference at the standard rate.

	$
Actual production at standard rate (1,100 × $20 per unit)	22,000
Budgeted production at standard rate (1,000 × $20 per unit)	20,000
Fixed overhead volume variance	2,000 (F)

The variance is **favourable** because output was greater than expected.

(i)   The labour force may have worked efficiently, and produced output at a faster rate than expected. Since overheads are absorbed at the rate of $20 per unit, more will be absorbed if units are produced more quickly. This **efficiency variance** is exactly the same in hours as the direct labour efficiency variance, but is valued in $ at the standard absorption rate for fixed overhead.

(ii)   The labour force may have worked longer hours than budgeted, and therefore produced more output, so there may be a **capacity variance**.

(d)   **Fixed overhead volume efficiency variance**

The volume efficiency variance is calculated in the same way as the labour efficiency variance.

1,100 units of product E should take (× 5 hrs)	5,500 hrs
but did take	5,400 hrs
Fixed overhead volume efficiency variance in hours	100 hrs (F)
× standard fixed overhead absorption rate per hour	× $4
Fixed overhead volume efficiency variance in $	$400 (F)

The labour force has produced 5,500 standard hours of work in 5,400 actual hours and so output is 100 standard hours (or 20 units of product E) higher than budgeted for this reason and the variance is **favourable**.

(e) **Fixed overhead volume capacity variance**

The volume capacity variance is the difference between the budgeted hours of work and the actual active hours of work (excluding any idle time).

Budgeted hours of work	5,000 hrs
Actual hours of work	5,400 hrs
Fixed overhead volume capacity variance	400 hrs (F)
× standard fixed overhead absorption rate per hour	× $4
Fixed overhead volume capacity variance in $	$1,600 (F)

Since the labour force worked 400 hours longer than planned, we should expect output to be 400 standard hours (or 80 units of product E) higher than budgeted and hence the variance is **favourable**.

The variances may be summarised as follows.

	$
Expenditure variance	450 (A)
Efficiency variance	400 (F)
Capacity variance	1,600 (F)
Over-absorbed overhead (total variance)	$1,550 (F)

**xam focus
oint**

In general, a favourable cost variance will arise if actual results are less than expected results. Be aware, however, of the **fixed overhead volume variance** and the **fixed overhead volume capacity variance** which give rise to favourable and adverse variances in the following situations.

- A favourable fixed overhead volume variance occurs when actual production is **greater than** budgeted (planned) production

- An adverse fixed overhead volume variance occurs when actual production is **less than budgeted** (planned) production

- A favourable fixed overhead volume capacity variance occurs when actual hours of work are **greater than** budgeted (planned) hours of work

- An adverse fixed overhead volume capacity variance occurs when actual hours of work are **less than** budgeted (planned) hours of work

Do not worry if you find fixed production overhead variances more difficult to grasp than the other variances we have covered. Most students do. Read over this section again and then try the following practice questions.

The following information relates to the questions shown below

Barbados has prepared the following standard cost information for one unit of Product Zeta.

Direct materials	4kg @ $10/kg	$40.00
Direct labour	2 hours @ $4/hour	$8.00
Fixed overheads	3 hours @ $2.50	$7.50

The fixed overheads are based on a budgeted expenditure of $75,000 and budgeted activity of 30,000 hours.

Actual results for the period were recorded as follows.

Production	9,000 units
Materials – 33,600 kg	$336,000
Labour – 16,500 hours	$68,500
Fixed overheads	$70,000

Question

The direct material price and usage variances are:

	Material price	Material usage
	$	$
A	–	24,000 (F)
B	–	24,000 (A)
C	24,000 (F)	–
D	24,000 (A)	–

Answer

Material price variance

	$
33,600 kg should have cost (× $10/kg)	336,000
and did cost	336,000
	–

Material usage variance

9,000 units should have used (× 4kg)	36,000 kg
but did use	33,600 kg
	2,400 kg (F)
× standard cost per kg	× $10
	24,000 (F)

The correct answer is therefore A.

Question

The direct labour rate and efficiency variances are:

	Labour rate	Labour efficiency
	$	$
A	6,000 (F)	2,500 (A)
B	6,000 (A)	2,500 (F)
C	2,500 (A)	6,000 (F)
D	2,500 (F)	6,000 (A)

Answer

Direct labour rate variance

	$
16,500 hrs should have cost (× $4)	66,000
but did cost	68,500
	2,500 (A)

Direct labour efficiency variance

9,000 units should have taken (× 2 hrs)	18,000 hrs
but did take	16,500 hrs
	1,500 (F)
× standard rate per hour (× $4)	× $4
	6,000 (F)

The correct answer is therefore C.

Question

The total fixed production overhead variance is:

A $5,000 (A)
B $5,000 (F)
C $2,500 (A)
D $2,500 (F)

Answer

	$
Fixed production overhead absorbed ($7.50 × 9,000)	67,500
Fixed production overhead incurred	70,000
	2,500 (A)

The correct answer is therefore C.

6 The reasons for cost variances

There are many possible reasons for cost variances arising, as you will see from the following list of possible causes.

Variance	Favourable	Adverse
(a) Material price	Unforeseen discounts received More care taken in purchasing Change in material standard	Price increase Careless purchasing Change in material standard
(b) Material usage	Material used of higher quality than standard More effective use made of material Errors in allocating material to jobs	Defective material Excessive waste Theft Stricter quality control Errors in allocating material to jobs
(c) Labour rate	Use of apprentices or other workers at a rate of pay lower than standard	Wage rate increase Use of higher grade labour
(d) Idle time	The idle time variance is always adverse	Machine breakdown Non-availability of material Illness or injury to worker
(e) Labour efficiency	Output produced more quickly than expected because of work motivation, better quality of equipment or materials, or better methods. Errors in allocating time to jobs	Lost time in excess of standard allowed Output lower than standard set because of deliberate restriction, lack of training, or sub-standard material used Errors in allocating time to jobs

Variance		Favourable	Adverse
(f)	Overhead expenditure	Savings in costs incurred More economical use of services	Increase in cost of services used Excessive use of services Change in type of services used
(g)	Overhead volume efficiency	Labour force working more efficiently (favourable labour efficiency variance)	Labour force working less efficiently (adverse labour efficiency variance)
(h)	Overhead volume capacity	Labour force working overtime	Machine breakdown, strikes, labour shortages

7 The significance of cost variances

7.1 Introduction

FAST FORWARD

Materiality, controllability, the type of standard being used, the interdependence of variances and the cost of an investigation should be taken into account when deciding whether to investigate reported variances.

Once variances have been calculated, management have to decide whether or not to investigate their causes. It would be extremely time consuming and expensive to investigate every variance therefore managers have to decide which variances are worthy of investigation.

There are a number of factors which can be taken into account when deciding whether or not a variance should be investigated.

(a)   **Materiality.** A standard cost is really only an **average** expected cost and is not a rigid specification. Small variations either side of this average are therefore bound to occur. The problem is to decide whether a variation from standard should be considered **significant** and worthy of investigation. **Tolerance limits** can be set and only variances which exceed such limits would require investigating.

(b)   **Controllability.** Some types of variance may not be controllable even once their cause is discovered. For example, if there is a general worldwide increase in the price of a raw material there is nothing that can be done internally to control the effect of this. If a central decision is made to award all employees a 10% increase in salary, staff costs in division A will increase by this amount and the variance is not controllable by division A's manager. Uncontrollable variances call for a change in the plan, not an investigation into the past.

(c)   **The type of standard being used.**

(i)   The efficiency variance reported in any control period, whether for materials or labour, will depend on the **efficiency level** set. If, for example, an **ideal standard** is used, variances will always be **adverse**.

(ii)   A similar problem arises if **average price levels** are used as standards. If inflation exists, favourable price variances are likely to be reported at the beginning of a period, to be offset by adverse price variances later in the period as inflation pushes prices up.

(d)   **Interdependence between variances**. Quite possibly, individual variances should not be looked at in isolation. One variance might be inter-related with another, and much of it might have occurred only because the other, inter-related, variance occurred too. We will investigate this issue further in a moment.

(e)   **Costs of investigation.** The costs of an investigation should be weighed against the benefits of correcting the cause of a variance.

7.2 Interdependence between variances

When two variances are interdependent (interrelated) one will usually be adverse and the other one favourable.

7.3 Interdependence – materials price and usage variances

It may be decided to purchase cheaper materials for a job in order to obtain a favourable **price variance**. This may lead to higher materials wastage than expected and therefore, **adverse usage variances occur**. If the cheaper materials are more difficult to handle, there might be some **adverse labour efficiency variance** too.

If a decision is made to purchase more expensive materials, which perhaps have a longer service life, the price variance will be adverse but the usage variance might be favourable.

7.4 Interdependence – labour rate and efficiency variances

If employees in a workforce are paid higher rates for experience and skill, using a highly skilled team should incur an **adverse rate variance** at the same time as a **favourable efficiency variance**. In contrast, a **favourable rate variance** might indicate a high proportion of inexperienced workers in the workforce, which could result in an **adverse labour efficiency variance** and possibly an **adverse materials usage variance** (due to high rates of rejects).

Chapter roundup

- A **variance** is the difference between a planned, budgeted, or standard cost and the actual cost incurred. The same comparisons can be made for revenues. The process by which the **total** difference between standard and actual results is analysed is known as the **variance analysis**.

- The direct material total variance can be subdivided into the **direct material price** variance and the **direct material usage** variance.

- Direct material price variances are usually extracted at the time of **receipt** of the materials, rather than at the time of usage.

- The direct labour total variance can be subdivided into the **direct labour rate** variance and the **direct labour efficiency** variance.

- If **idle time** arises, it is usual to calculate a separate idle time variance, and to base the calculation of the efficiency variance on **active hours** (when labour actually worked) only. It is always an **adverse** variance.

- The variable production overhead total variance can be subdivided into the variable production overhead **expenditure** variance and the variable production overhead **efficiency** variance **(based on active hours).**

- The fixed production overhead total variance can be subdivided into an **expenditure** variance and a **volume** variance. The fixed production overhead volume variance can be further subdivided into an **efficiency** and a **capacity** variance.

- Materiality, controllability, the type of standard being used, the interdependence of variances and the cost of an investigation should be taken into account when deciding whether to investigate reported variances.

Quick quiz

1   Subdivide the following variances.

    (a)   Direct materials cost variance

    (b)   Direct labour cost variance

    (c)   Variable production overhead variance

2   What are the two main advantages in calculating the material price variance at the time of receipt of materials?

3   Idle time variances are always adverse.

    True

    False

4   Adverse material usage variances might occur for the following reasons.

    I   Defective material
    II   Excessive waste
    III   Theft
    IV   Unforeseen discounts received

    A   I
    B   I and II
    C   I, II and III
    D   I, II, III and IV

5   List the factors which should be taken into account when deciding whether or not a variance should be investigated.

Answers to quick quiz

1 (a) Price

Usage

(b) Rate

Efficiency

(c) Expenditure

Efficiency

2 (a) The earlier variances are extracted, the sooner they will be brought to the attention of managers.

(b) All inventories will be valued at standard price which requires less administration effort.

3 True

4 C

5 • Materiality
• Controllability
• Type of standard being used
• Interdependence between variances
• Costs of investigation

Now try the questions below from the Exam Question Bank

Number	Level	Marks	Time
Q15	MCQ/OTQ	n/a	n/a

Further
variance analysis

Topic list	Syllabus reference
1 Sales variances	E4 (a)
2 Operating statements	E5 (a), (b)
3 Variances in a standard marginal costing system	E4 (b)
4 Deriving actual data from standard cost details and variances	E4 (b)

Introduction

The objective of cost variance analysis, which we looked at in the previous chapter, is to assist management in the **control of costs**. Costs are, however, only one factor which contribute to the achievement of planned profit. **Sales** are another important factor and sales variances can be calculated to aid management's control of their business. We will therefore begin this chapter by examining **sales variances**.

Having discussed the variances you need to know about, we will be looking in Section 2 at the **ways in which variances should be presented to management** to aid their control of the organisation.

We then consider in Section 3 how **marginal cost variances** differ from absorption cost variances and how marginal costing information should be presented.

Finally we will consider **how actual data can be derived from standard cost details and variances**.

Study guide

		Intellectual level
E4	**Basic variance analysis under absorption and marginal costing**	
(a)	Calculate interpret and explain sales price and volume variance	1
(b)	Calculate actual or standard figures where the following variances are given: (i) Sales price and volume (ii) Materials total, price and usage (iii) Labour total, rate and efficiency (iv) Variable overhead total, expenditure and efficiency (v) Fixed overhead total, expenditure and, where appropriate, volume, capacity and efficiency	1
E5	**Reconciliation of budgeted profit and actual profit**	
(a)	Reconcile budgeted profit with actual profit under standard absorption costing	1
(b)	Reconcile budgeted profit or contribution with actual profit or contribution under standard marginal costing	1

Exam guide

Variance analysis is traditionally a very popular exam topic. Make sure that you are able to prepare operating statements and explain why calculated variances have occurred.

1 Sales variances

1.1 Selling price variance

> **FAST FORWARD**
>
> The **selling price variance** is a measure of the effect on expected profit of a different selling price to standard selling price. It is calculated as the difference between what the sales revenue should have been for the actual quantity sold, and what it was.

1.2 Example: Selling price variance

Suppose that the standard selling price of product X is $15. Actual sales in 20X3 were 2,000 units at $15.30 per unit. The selling price variance is calculated as follows.

	$
Sales revenue from 2,000 units should have been (× $15)	30,000
but was (× $15.30)	30,600
Selling price variance	600 (F)

The variance calculated is **favourable** because the price was higher than expected.

1.3 Sales volume profit variance

> **FAST FORWARD**
>
> The **sales volume profit variance** is the difference between the actual units sold and the budgeted (planned) quantity, valued at the standard profit per unit. In other words, it measures the increase or decrease in standard profit as a result of the sales volume being higher or lower than budgeted (planned).

1.4 Example: Sales volume profit variance

Suppose that a company budgets to sell 8,000 units of product J for $12 per unit. The standard full cost per unit is $7. Actual sales were 7,700 units, at $12.50 per unit.

The **sales volume profit variance** is calculated as follows.

Budgeted sales volume	8,000 units
Actual sales volume	7,700 units
Sales volume variance in units	300 units (A)
× standard profit per unit ($(12–7))	× $5
Sales volume variance	$1,500 (A)

The variance calculated above is **adverse** because actual sales were less than budgeted (planned).

Question	Selling price variance

Jasper Ltd has the following budget and actual figures for 20X4.

	Budget	Actual
Sales units	600	620
Selling price per unit	$30	$29

Standard full cost of production = $28 per unit.

Required

Calculate the selling price variance and the sales volume profit variance.

Answer

Sales revenue for 620 units should have been (× $30)	18,600
but was (× $29)	17,980
Selling price variance	620 (A)
Budgeted sales volume	600 units
Actual sales volume	620 units
Sales volume variance in units	20 units (F)
× standard profit per unit ($(30 – 28))	× $2
Sales volume profit variance	$40 (F)

1.5 The significance of sales variances

The possible **interdependence** between sales price and sales volume variances should be obvious to you. A reduction in the sales price might stimulate bigger sales demand, so that an adverse sales price variance might be counterbalanced by a favourable sales volume variance. Similarly, a price rise would give a favourable price variance, but possibly at the cost of a fall in demand and an adverse sales volume variance.

It is therefore important in analysing an unfavourable sales variance that the overall consequence should be considered, that is, has there been a counterbalancing favourable variance as a direct result of the unfavourable one?

2 Operating statements

2.1 Introduction

Operating statements show how the combination of variances reconcile budgeted profit and actual profit.

So far, we have considered how variances are calculated without considering how they combine to reconcile the difference between budgeted profit and actual profit during a period. This reconciliation is usually presented as a report to senior management at the end of each control period. The report is called an **operating statement** or **statement of variances**.

Key term

An **operating statement** is a regular report for management of actual costs and revenues, usually showing variances from budget.

An extensive example will now be introduced, both to revise the variance calculations already described, and also to show how to combine them into an operating statement.

2.2 Example: Variances and operating statements

Sydney manufactures one product, and the entire product is sold as soon as it is produced. There are no opening or closing inventories and work in progress is negligible. The company operates a standard costing system and analysis of variances is made every month. The standard cost card for the product, a boomerang, is as follows.

STANDARD COST CARD – BOOMERANG

		$
Direct materials	0.5 kilos at $4 per kilo	2.00
Direct wages	2 hours at $2.00 per hour	4.00
Variable overheads	2 hours at $0.30 per hour	0.60
Fixed overhead	2 hours at $3.70 per hour	7.40
Standard cost		14.00
Standard profit		6.00
Standing selling price		20.00

Selling and administration expenses are not included in the standard cost, and are deducted from profit as a period charge.

Budgeted (planned) output for the month of June 20X7 was 5,100 units. Actual results for June 20X7 were as follows.

Production of 4,850 units was sold for $95,600.
Materials consumed in production amounted to 2,300 kgs at a total cost of $9,800.
Labour hours paid for amounted to 8,500 hours at a cost of $16,800.
Actual operating hours amounted to 8,000 hours.
Variable overheads amounted to $2,600.
Fixed overheads amounted to $42,300.
Selling and administration expenses amounted to $18,000.

Required

Calculate all variances and prepare an operating statement for the month ended 30 June 20X7.

Solution

		$
(a)		
	2,300 kg of material should cost (× $4)	9,200
	but did cost	9,800
	Material price variance	600 (A)

(b)	4,850 boomerangs should use (× 0.5 kgs)	2,425 kg
	but did use	2,300 kg
	Material usage variance in kgs	125 kg (F)
	× standard cost per kg	× $4
	Material usage variance in $	$ 500 (F)

		$
(c)		
	8,500 hours of labour should cost (× $2)	17,000
	but did cost	16,800
	Labour rate variance	200 (F)

(d)	4,850 boomerangs should take (× 2 hrs)	9,700 hrs
	but did take (active hours)	8,000 hrs
	Labour efficiency variance in hours	1,700 hrs (F)
	× standard cost per hour	× $2
	Labour efficiency variance in $	$3,400 (F)

(e)	Idle time variance 500 hours (A) × $2	$1,000 (A)

		$
(f)		
	8,000 hours incurring variable o/hd expenditure should cost (× $0.30)	2,400
	but did cost	2,600
	Variable overhead expenditure variance	200 (A)

(g)	Variable overhead efficiency variance in hours is the same as the labour efficiency variance:	
	1,700 hours (F) × $0.30 per hour	$ 510 (F)

		$
(h)		
	Budgeted fixed overhead (5,100 units × 2 hrs × $3.70)	37,740
	Actual fixed overhead	42,300
	Fixed overhead expenditure variance	4,560 (A)

		$
(i)		
	4,850 boomerangs should take (× 2 hrs)	9,700 hrs
	but did take (active hours)	8,000 hrs
	Fixed overhead volume efficiency variance in hrs	1,700 hrs (F)
	× standard fixed overhead absorption rate per hour	× $3.70
	Fixed overhead volume efficiency variance in $	6,290 (F)

		$
(j)		
	Budgeted hours of work (5,100 × 2 hrs)	10,200 hrs
	Actual hours of work	8,000 hrs
	Fixed overhead volume capacity variance in hrs	2,200 hrs (A)
	× standard fixed overhead absorption rate per hour	× $3.70
	Fixed overhead volume capacity variance in $	8,140 (A)

(k)

	$
Revenue from 4,850 boomerangs should be (× $20)	97,000
but was	95,600
Selling price variance	1,400 (A)

(l)

Budgeted sales volume	5,100 units
Actual sales volume	4,850 units
Sales volume profit variance in units	250 units
× standard profit per unit	× $6 (A)
Sales volume profit variance in $	$1,500 (A)

There are several ways in which an operating statement may be presented. Perhaps the most common format is one which **reconciles budgeted profit to actual profit**. In this example, sales and administration costs will be introduced at the end of the statement, so that we shall begin with 'budgeted profit before sales and administration costs'.

Sales variances are reported first, and the total of the budgeted profit and the two sales variances results in a figure for 'actual sales minus the standard cost of sales'. The cost variances are then reported, and an actual profit (before sales and administration costs) calculated. Sales and administration costs are then deducted to reach the actual profit for June 20X7.

SYDNEY – OPERATING STATEMENT JUNE 20X7

		$	$
Budgeted (planned) profit before sales and administration costs			30,600
Sales variances:	price	1,400 (A)	
	volume	1,500 (A)	
			2,900 (A)
Actual sales minus the standard cost of sales			27,700

	(F)	(A)	
Cost variances	$	$	
Material price		600	
Material usage	500		
Labour rate	200		
Labour efficiency	3,400		
Labour idle time		1,000	
Variable overhead expenditure		200	
Variable overhead efficiency	510		
Fixed overhead expenditure		4,560	
Fixed overhead volume efficiency	6,290		
Fixed overhead volume capacity		8,140	
	10,900	14,500	3,600 (A)
Actual profit before sales and administration costs			24,100
Sales and administration costs			18,000
Actual profit, June 20X7			6,100

Check	$	$
Sales		95,600
Materials	9,800	
Labour	16,800	
Variable overhead	2,600	
Fixed overhead	42,300	
Sales and administration	18,000	
		89,500
Actual profit		6,100

3 Variances in a standard marginal costing system

3.1 Introduction

There are two main differences between the variances calculated in an absorption costing system and the variances calculated in a marginal costing system.

- In the marginal costing system **the only fixed overhead variance is an expenditure variance**.
- The sales volume variance is **valued at standard contribution margin**, not standard profit margin.

In all of the examples we have worked through so far, a system of standard absorption costing has been in operation. If an organisation uses **standard marginal costing** instead of standard absorption costing, there will be two differences in the way the variances are calculated.

(a) In marginal costing, fixed costs are not absorbed into product costs and so there are no fixed cost variances to explain any under or over absorption of overheads. There will, therefore, be **no fixed overhead volume variance**. There will be a fixed overhead expenditure variance which is calculated in exactly the same way as for absorption costing systems.

(b) The **sales volume variance** will be valued at **standard contribution margin** (sales price per unit minus variable costs of sale per unit), **not** standard **profit** margin.

3.2 Preparing a marginal costing operating statement

Returning once again to the example of Sydney, the variances in a system of standard marginal costing would be as follows.

(a) There is **no fixed overhead volume variance** (and therefore no fixed overhead volume efficiency and volume capacity variances).

(b) The standard contribution per unit of boomerang is $(20 - 6.60) = $13.40, therefore the **sales volume contribution variance** of 250 units (A) is valued at ($\times$ $13.40) = $3,350 (A).

The other variances are unchanged. However, this operating statement differs from an absorption costing operating statement in the following ways.

(a) It begins with the budgeted **contribution** ($30,600 + budgeted fixed production costs $37,740 = $68,340).

(b) The subtotal before the analysis of cost variances is actual sales ($95,600) less the standard **variable** cost of sales ($4,850 $\times$ $6.60) = $63,590.

(c) **Actual contribution** is highlighted in the statement.

(d) Budgeted (planned) fixed production overhead is adjusted by the fixed overhead expenditure variance to show the **actual** fixed production overhead expenditure.

Therefore a marginal costing operating statement might look like this.

SYDNEY – OPERATING STATEMENT JUNE 20X7

	$	$	$
Budgeted (planned) contribution			68,340
Sales variances: volume		3,350 (A)	
price		1,400 (A)	
			4,750 (A)
Actual sales minus the standard variable cost of sales			63,590

	(F)	(A)	
	$	$	
Variable cost variances			
Material price		600	
Material usage	500		
Labour rate	200		
Labour efficiency	3,400		
Labour idle time		1,000	
Variable overhead expenditure		200	
Variable overhead efficiency	510		
	4,610	1,800	
			2,810 (F)
Actual contribution			66,400
Budgeted (planned) fixed production overhead		37,740	
Expenditure variance		4,560 (A)	
Actual fixed production overhead			42,300
Actual profit before sales and administration costs			24,100
Sales and administration costs			18,000
Actual profit			6,100

Notice that the actual profit is the same as the profit calculated by standard absorption costing because there were no changes in inventory levels. Absorption costing and marginal costing do not always produce an identical profit figure.

Question

Variances

Piglet, a manufacturing firm, operates a standard marginal costing system. It makes a single product, PIG, using a single raw material LET.

Standard costs relating to PIG have been calculated as follows.

Standard cost schedule – PIG

	Per unit
	$
Direct material, LET, 100 kg at $5 per kg	500
Direct labour, 10 hours at $8 per hour	80
Variable production overhead, 10 hours at $2 per hour	20
	600

The standard selling price of a PIG is $900 and Piglet Co produce 1,020 units a month.

During December 20X0, 1,000 units of PIG were produced. Relevant details of this production are as follows.

Direct material LET

90,000 kgs costing $720,000 were bought and used.

Direct labour

8,200 hours were worked during the month and total wages were $63,000.

Variable production overhead

The actual cost for the month was $25,000.

Inventories of the direct material LET are valued at the standard price of $5 per kg.

Each PIG was sold for $975.

Required

Calculate the following for the month of December 20X0.

(a) Variable production cost variance
(b) Direct labour cost variance, analysed into rate and efficiency variances
(c) Direct material cost variance, analysed into price and usage variances
(d) Variable production overhead variance, analysed into expenditure and efficiency variances
(e) Selling price variance
(f) Sales volume contribution variance

Answer

(a) This is simply a 'total' variance.

	$
1,000 units should have cost (× $600)	600,000
but did cost (see working)	808,000
Variable production cost variance	208,000 (A)

(b) **Direct labour cost variances**

	$
8,200 hours should cost (× $8)	65,600
but did cost	63,000
Direct labour rate variance	2,600 (F)

1,000 units should take (× 10 hours)	10,000 hrs
but did take	8,200 hrs
Direct labour efficiency variance in hrs	1,800 hrs (F)
× standard rate per hour	× $8
Direct labour efficiency variance in $	$14,400 (F)

Summary	$
Rate	2,600 (F)
Efficiency	14,400 (F)
Total	17,000 (F)

(c) **Direct material cost variances**

	$
90,000 kg should cost (× $5)	450,000
but did cost	720,000
Direct material price variance	270,000 (A)

1,000 units should use (× 100 kg)	100,000 kg
but did use	90,000 kg
Direct material usage variance in kgs	10,000 kg (F)
× standard cost per kg	× $5
Direct material usage variance in $	$50,000 (F)

	$
Summary	
Price	270,000 (A)
Usage	50,000 (F)
Total	220,000 (A)

(d)   **Variable production overhead variances**

	$
8,200 hours incurring o/hd should cost (× $2)	16,400
but did cost	25,000
Variable production overhead expenditure variance	8,600 (A)

Efficiency variance in hrs (from (b))	1,800 hrs (F)
× standard rate per hour	× $2
Variable production overhead efficiency variance	$3,600 (F)

Summary

	$
Expenditure	8,600 (A)
Efficiency	3,600 (F)
Total	5,000 (A)

(e)   **Selling price variance**

	$
Revenue from 1,000 units should have been (× $900)	900,000
but was (× $975)	975,000
Selling price variance	75,000 (F)

(f)   **Sales volume contribution variance**

Budgeted sales	1,020 units
Actual sales	1,000 units
Sales volume variance in units	20 units (A)
× standard contribution margin ($(900 – 600))	× $300
Sales volume contribution variance in $	$6,000 (A)

Workings

	$
Direct material	720,000
Total wages	63,000
Variable production overhead	25,000
	808,000

Exam focus point

> This question is much longer than what will appear in your exam, but any one of these variances, individually, may be the subject of a 2-mark question.

The summary diagram on the next page summarises how the different variances are calculated and how they interrelate with each other.

SUMMARY DIAGRAM

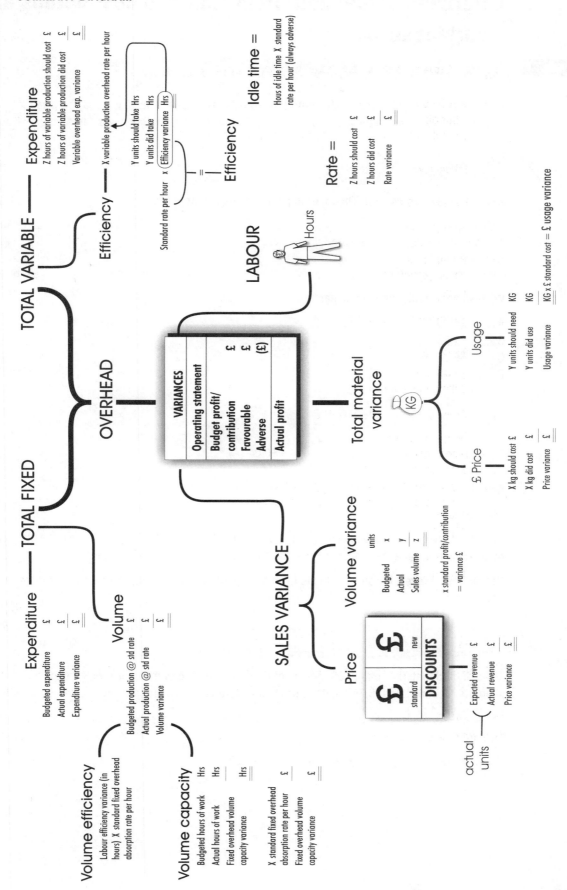

4 Deriving actual data from standard cost details and variances

Variances can be used to derive actual data from standard cost details.

Rather than being given actual data and asked to calculate the variances, you may be given the variances and required to calculate the actual data on which they were based. See if you can do these two questions.

Question

Rate of pay

XYZ uses standard costing. The following data relates to labour grade II.

Actual hours worked	10,400 hours
Standard allowance for actual production	8,320 hours
Standard rate per hour	$5
Rate variance (adverse)	$416

What was the actual rate of pay per hour?

A $4.95
B $4.96
C $5.04
D $5.05

Answer

Rate variance per hour worked = $\dfrac{\$416}{10,400}$ = $0.04 (A)

Actual rate per hour = $(5.00 + 0.04) = $5.04.

The correct answer is C.

You should have been able to eliminate options A and B because they are both below the standard rate per hour. If the rate variance is adverse then the actual rate must be above standard.

Option D is incorrect because it results from basing the calculations on standard hours rather than actual hours.

Question

Quantity of material

The standard material content of one unit of product A is 10kg of material X which should cost $10 per kilogram. In June 20X4, 5,750 units of product A were produced and there was an adverse material usage variance of $1,500.

Required

Calculate the quantity of material X used in June 20X4.

Answer

Let the quantity of material X used = Y

5,750 units should have used (× 10kg)	57,500 kg
but did use	Y kg
Usage variance in kg	(Y − 57,500) kg
× standard price per kg	× $10
Usage variance in $	$1,500 (A)

$$\therefore \quad 10(Y - 57,500) = 1,500$$
$$Y - 57,500 = 150$$
$$\therefore \quad Y = 57,650 \text{ kg}$$

am focus
int

One way that the examiner can test your understanding of variance analysis is to provide information about variances from which you have to 'work backwards' to determine the actual results.

Make sure that you understand the questions covering this technique that we have provided. This type of question **really** tests your understanding of the subject. If you simply memorise variance formulae you will have difficulty in answering such questions.

Chapter roundup

- The **selling price variance** is a measure of the effect on expected profit of a different selling price to standard selling price. It is calculated as the difference between what the sales revenue should have been for the actual quantity sold.

- The **sales volume profit variance** is the difference between the actual units sold and the budgeted (planned) quantity, valued at the standard profit per unit. In other words, it measures the increase or decrease in standard profit as a result of the sales volume being higher or lower than budgeted (planned).

- **Operating statements** show how the combination of variances reconcile budgeted profit and actual profit.

- There are two main differences between the variances calculated in an absorption costing system and the variances calculated in a marginal costing system.

  - In a marginal costing system **the only fixed overhead variance is an expenditure variance.**
  - The sales volume variance is **valued at standard contribution margin**, not standard profit margin.

- Variances can be used to derive actual data from standard cost details.

Quick quiz

1   What is the sales volume profit variance?

2   A regular report for management of actual cost, and revenue, and usually comparing actual results with budgeted (planned) results (and showing variances) is known as

    A   Bank statement
    B   Variance statement
    C   Budget statement
    D   Operating statement

3   If an organisation uses standard marginal costing instead of standard absorption costing, which two variances are calculated differently?

Answers to quick quiz

1   It is a measure of the increase or decrease in standard profit as a result of the sales volume being higher or lower than budgeted (planned).

2   D

3   (a)   In marginal costing there is no fixed overhead volume variance (because fixed costs are not absorbed into product costs).

    (b)   In marginal costing, the sales volume variance will be valued at standard contribution margin and not standard profit margin.

Now try the questions below from the Exam Question Bank

Number	Level	Marks	Time
Q16	MCQ	n/a	n/a

BPP
LEARNING MEDIA

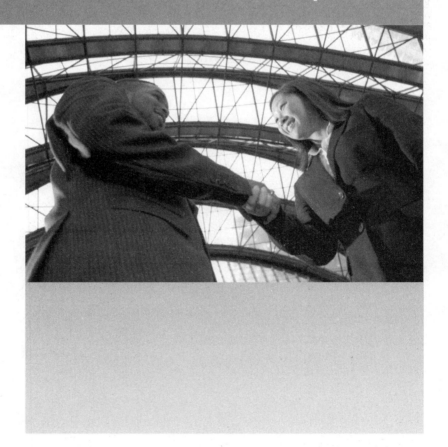

Part F
Short-term decision-making techniques

17

Cost-volume-profit (CVP) analysis

Topic list	Syllabus reference
1 CVP analysis and breakeven point	F1 (a)
2 The contribution to sales (C/S) ratio	F1 (b)
3 The margin of safety	F1 (a)
4 Breakeven arithmetic and profit targets	F1 (d)
5 Breakeven charts, contribution charts and profit/volume charts	F1 (c)
6 Limitations of CVP analysis	F1 (d)

Introduction

You should by now realise that the cost accountant needs estimates of **fixed** and **variable costs**, and **revenues**, at various output levels. The cost accountant, must also be fully aware of **cost behaviour** because, to be able to estimate costs, he must know what a particular cost will do given particular conditions.

An understanding of cost behaviour is not all that you may need to know, however. The application of **cost-volume-profit analysis**, which is based on the cost behaviour principles and marginal costing ideas, is sometimes necessary so that the appropriate decision-making information can be provided. As you may have guessed, this chapter is going to look at that very topic, **cost-volume-profit analysis** or **breakeven analysis**.

Study guide

		Intellectual level
F1	**Cost-volume-profit (CVP) analysis**	
(a)	Calculate and interpret a breakeven point and a margin of safety	2
(b)	Understand and use the concepts of a target profit or revenue and a contribution to sales ratio	2
(c)	Identify the elements in traditional and contribution breakeven charts and profit/volume charts	1
(d)	Apply CVP analysis to single product situations	2

Note. Multi-product breakeven charts and profit/volume charts are excluded.

Exam guide

A question on this topic may give you a breakeven chart and ask you to extract data from it.

1 CVP analysis and breakeven point

1.1 Introduction

FAST FORWARD

Cost-volume-profit (CVP)/breakeven analysis is the study of the interrelationships between costs, volume and profit at various levels of activity.

The management of an organisation usually wishes to know the profit likely to be made if the aimed-for production and sales for the year are achieved. Management may also be interested to know the following.

(a)   The **breakeven** point which is the activity level at which there is neither profit nor loss.

(b)   The **amount** by which actual **sales can fall** below anticipated sales, **without** a **loss** being incurred.

1.2 Breakeven point

FAST FORWARD

$$\text{Breakeven point} = \frac{\text{Total fixed costs}}{\text{Contribution per unit}} = \frac{\text{Contribution required to break even}}{\text{Contribution per unit}}$$

$$= \text{Number of units of sale required to break even.}$$

1.3 Example: breakeven point

Expected sales	10,000 units at $8 = $80,000
Variable cost	$5 per unit
Fixed costs	$21,000

Required

Compute the breakeven point.

Solution

The contribution per unit is $(8–5)$ = $3
Contribution required to break even   =   fixed costs = $21,000
Breakeven point (BEP)   =   21,000 ÷ 3
  =   7,000 units
In revenue, BEP   =   (7,000 × $8) = $56,000

Sales above $56,000 will result in profit of $3 per unit of additional sales and sales below $56,000 will mean a loss of $3 per unit for each unit by which sales fall short of 7,000 units. In other words, profit will improve or worsen by the amount of contribution per unit.

	7,000 units	7,001 units
	$	$
Revenue	56,000	56,008
Less variable costs	35,000	35,005
Contribution	21,000	21,003
Less fixed costs	21,000	21,000
Profit	0 (= breakeven)	3

2 The contribution to sales (C/S) ratio

ST FORWARD

$$\frac{\text{Contribution required to breakeven}}{\text{C/S ratio}} = \frac{\text{Fixed costs}}{\text{C/S ratio}}$$

(The contribution/sales (C/S) ratio is also sometimes called a **profit/volume** or **P/V ratio**).

An alternative way of calculating the breakeven point to give an answer in terms of sales revenue.

In the example in Paragraph 1.3 the C/S ratio is $\dfrac{\$3}{\$8} = 37.5\%$

Breakeven is where sales revenue equals $\dfrac{\$21,000}{37.5\%} = \$56,000$

At a price of $8 per unit, this represents 7,000 units of sales.

AST FORWARD

The C/S ratio (or P/V ratio) is a measure of how much contribution is earned from each $1 of sales.

The C/S ratio of 37.5% in the above example means that for every $1 of sales, a contribution of 37.5c is earned. Thus, in order to earn a total contribution of $21,000 and if contribution increases by 37.5c per $1 of sales, sales must be:

$$\frac{\$1}{37.5c} \times \$21,000 = \$56,000$$

Question

Breakeven point

The C/S ratio of product W is 20%. IB, the manufacturer of product W, wishes to make a contribution of $50,000 towards fixed costs. How many units of product W must be sold if the selling price is $10 per unit?

Answer

$$\frac{\text{Required contribution}}{\text{C/S ratio}} = \frac{\$50,000}{20\%} = \$250,000$$

∴ Number of units = $250,000 ÷ $10 = 25,000.

A company manufactures a single product with a variable cost of $44. The contribution to sales ratio is 45%. Monthly fixed costs are $396,000. What is the breakeven point in units?

Answer

Contribution per unit = $44/0.55 × 0.45
                       = $36

Breakeven point = Fixed costs/contribution per unit
                 =– $396,000/$36
                 = 11,000 units

3 The margin of safety

The **margin of safety** is the difference in units between the **budgeted sales volume** and the **breakeven sales volume**. It is sometimes expressed as a percentage of the budgeted sales volume. The margin of safety may also be expressed as the difference between the **budgeted sales revenue** and **breakeven sales revenue** expressed as a percentage of the budgeted sales revenue.

3.1 Example: margin of safety

Mal de Mer makes and sells a product which has a variable cost of $30 and which sells for $40. Budgeted fixed costs are $70,000 and budgeted sales are 8,000 units.

Required

Calculate the breakeven point and the margin of safety.

Solution

(a)   Breakeven point $= \dfrac{\text{Total fixed costs}}{\text{Contribution per unit}} = \dfrac{\$70,000}{\$(40-30)}$

                        =   7,000 units

(b)   Margin of safety   =   8,000 – 7,000 units = 1,000 units

      which may be expressed as $\dfrac{1,000 \text{ units}}{8,000 \text{ units}} \times 100\% \times 100\% = 12\frac{1}{2}\%$ of budget

(c)   The margin of safety indicates to management that actual sales can fall short of budget by 1,000 units or 12½% before the breakeven point is reached and no profit at all is made.

4 Breakeven arithmetic and profit targets

At the **breakeven point**, sales revenue equals total costs and there is no profit. At the breakeven point **total contribution = fixed costs**.

rmula to
arn

> S   = V + F
>
> where S   = Sales revenue
>
>   V   = Total variable costs
>
>   F   = Total fixed costs
>
> Subtracting V from each side of the equation, we get:
>
>   S − V = F, that is, **total contribution = fixed costs**

4.1 Example: breakeven arithmetic

Butterfingers makes a product which has a variable cost of $7 per unit.

Required

If fixed costs are $63,000 per annum, calculate the selling price per unit if the company wishes to break even with a sales volume of 12,000 units.

Solution

			$
Contribution required to break even (= Fixed costs)	=	$63,000	
Volume of sales	=	12,000 units	
Required contribution per unit (S − V)	=	$63,000 ÷ 12,000 =	5.25
Variable cost per unit (V)	=		7.00
Required sales price per unit (S)	=		12.25

4.2 Target profits

AST FORWARD

The **target profit** is achieved when S = V + F + P. Therefore the total contribution required for a target profit = **fixed costs + required profit.**

A similar formula may be applied where a company wishes to achieve a certain profit during a period. To achieve this profit, sales must cover all costs and leave the required profit.

rmula to
arn

> The **target profit** is achieved when: S = V + F + P,
>
>   where   P = required profit
>
> Subtracting V from each side of the equation, we get:
>
>   S − V   = F + P, so
>
> Total contribution required   = F + P

4.3 Example: target profits

Riding Breeches makes and sells a single product, for which variable costs are as follows.

	$
Direct materials	10
Direct labour	8
Variable production overhead	6
	24

The sales price is $30 per unit, and fixed costs per annum are $68,000. The company wishes to make a profit of $16,000 per annum.

Required

Determine the sales required to achieve this profit.

Solution

Required contribution = fixed costs + profit = $68,000 + $16,000 = $84,000

Required sales can be calculated in one of two ways.

(a) $\dfrac{\text{Required contribution}}{\text{Contribution per unit}}$ = $\dfrac{\$84,000}{\$(30-24)}$ = 14,000 units, or $420,000 in revenue

(b) $\dfrac{\text{Required contribution}}{\text{C/S ratio}}$ = $\dfrac{\$84,000}{20\%^{*}}$ = $420,000 of revenue, or 14,000 units.

* C/S ratio = $\dfrac{\$30-\$24}{\$30}$ = $\dfrac{\$6}{\$30}$ = 0.2 = 20%.

Question	Target profits

Seven League Boots wishes to sell 14,000 units of its product, which has a variable cost of $15 to make and sell. Fixed costs are $47,000 and the required profit is $23,000.

Required

Calculate the sales price per unit.

Answer

Required contribution	=	fixed costs plus profit
	=	$47,000 + $23,000
	=	$70,000
Required sales		14,000 units

	$
Required contribution per unit sold	5
Variable cost per unit	15
Required sales price per unit	20

4.4 Decisions to change sales price or costs

You may come across a problem in which you have to work out the effect of altering the selling price, variable cost per unit or fixed cost. Such problems are slight variations on basic breakeven arithmetic.

4.5 Example: Change in selling price

Stomer Cakes bake and sell a single type of cake. The variable cost of production is 15c and the current sales price is 25c. Fixed costs are $2,600 per month, and the annual profit for the company at current sales volume is $36,000. The volume of sales demand is constant throughout the year.

The sales manager, Ian Digestion, wishes to raise the sales price to 29c per cake, but considers that a price rise will result in some loss of sales.

Required

Ascertain the minimum volume of sales required each month to raise the price to 29c.

Solution

The minimum volume of demand which would justify a price of 29c is one which would leave total profit at least the same as before, ie $3,000 per month. Required profit should be converted into required contribution, as follows.

	$
Monthly fixed costs	2,600
Monthly profit, minimum required	3,000
Current monthly contribution	5,600
Contribution per unit (25c − 15c)	10c
Current monthly sales	56,000 cakes

The minimum volume of sales required after the price rise will be an amount which earns a contribution of $5,600 per month, no worse than at the moment. The contribution per cake at a sales price of 29c would be 14c.

$$\text{Required sales} = \frac{\text{required contribution}}{\text{contribution per unit}} = \frac{\$5,600}{14c} = 40,000 \text{ cakes per month.}$$

4.6 Example: Change in production costs

Close Brickett makes a product which has a variable production cost of $8 and a variable sales cost of $2 per unit. Fixed costs are $40,000 per annum, the sales price per unit is $18, and the current volume of output and sales is 6,000 units.

The company is considering whether to have an improved machine for production. Annual hire costs would be $10,000 and it is expected that the variable cost of production would fall to $6 per unit.

Required

(a)   Determine the number of units that must be produced and sold to achieve the same profit as is currently earned, if the machine is hired.

(b)   Calculate the annual profit with the machine if output and sales remain at 6,000 units per annum.

Solution

The current unit contribution is $(18 − (8+2)) = $8

(a)

	$
Current contribution (6,000 × $8)	48,000
Less current fixed costs	40,000
Current profit	8,000

With the new machine fixed costs will go up by $10,000 to $50,000 per annum. The variable cost per unit will fall to $(6 + 2) = $8, and the contribution per unit will be $10.

	$
Required profit (as currently earned)	8,000
Fixed costs	50,000
Required contribution	58,000
Contribution per unit	$10
Sales required to earn $8,000 profit	5,800 units

(b) **If sales are 6,000 units**

	$	$
Sales (6,000 × $18)		108,000
Variable costs: production (6,000 × $6)	36,000	
sales (6,000 × $2)	12,000	
		48,000
Contribution (6,000 × $10)		60,000
Less fixed costs		50,000
Profit		10,000

Alternative calculation

	$
Profit at 5,800 units of sale (see (a))	8,000
Contribution from sale of extra 200 units (× $10)	2,000
Profit at 6,000 units of sale	10,000

4.7 Sales price and sales volume

It may be clear by now that, given no change in fixed costs, **total profit is maximised when the total contribution is at its maximum**. Total contribution in turn depends on the unit contribution and on the sales volume.

An increase in the sales price will increase unit contribution, but sales volume is likely to fall because fewer customers will be prepared to pay the higher price. A decrease in sales price will reduce the unit contribution, but sales volume may increase because the goods on offer are now cheaper. The **optimum combination** of sales price and sales volume is arguably the one which **maximises total contribution**.

4.8 Example: Profit maximisation

C has developed a new product which is about to be launched on to the market. The variable cost of selling the product is $12 per unit. The marketing department has estimated that at a sales price of $20, annual demand would be 10,000 units.

However, if the sales price is set above $20, sales demand would fall by 500 units for each 50c increase above $20. Similarly, if the price is set below $20, demand would increase by 500 units for each 50c stepped reduction in price below $20.

Required

Determine the price which would maximise C's profit in the next year.

Solution

At a price of $20 per unit, the unit contribution would be $(20 − 12) = $8. Each 50c increase (or decrease) in price would raise (or lower) the unit contribution by 50c. The total contribution is calculated at each sales price by multiplying the unit contribution by the expected sales volume.

	Unit price $	Unit contribution $	Sales volume Units	Total contribution $
	20.00	8.00	10,000	80,000
(a) **Reduce price**				
	19.50	7.50	10,500	78,750
	19.00	7.00	11,000	77,000

(b)   Increase price

20.50	8.50	9,500	80,750
21.00	9.00	9,000	81,000
21.50	9.50	8,500	80,750
22.00	10.00	8,000	80,000
22.50	10.50	7,500	78,750

The total contribution would be maximised, and therefore profit maximised, at a sales price of $21 per unit, and sales demand of 9,000 units.

Question   Breakeven output level

Betty Battle manufactures a product which has a selling price of $20 and a variable cost of $10 per unit. The company incurs annual fixed costs of $29,000. Annual sales demand is 9,000 units.

New production methods are under consideration, which would cause a $1,000 increase in fixed costs and a reduction in variable cost to $9 per unit. The new production methods would result in a superior product and would enable sales to be increased to 9,750 units per annum at a price of $21 each.

If the change in production methods were to take place, the breakeven output level would be:

A   400 units higher
B   400 units lower
C   100 units higher
D   100 units lower

Answer

	Current	Revised	Difference
	$	$	
Selling price	20	21	
Variable costs	10	9	
Contribution per unit	10	12	
Fixed costs	$29,000	$30,000	
Breakeven point (units)	2,900	2,500	**400 lower**

$$\text{Breakeven point} = \frac{\text{Total fixed costs}}{\text{Contribution per unit}}$$

$$\text{Current BEP} = \frac{\$29,000}{\$10} = 2,900 \text{ units}$$

$$\text{Revised BEP} = \frac{\$30,000}{\$12} = 2,500 \text{ units}$$

The correct answer is therefore B.

5 Breakeven charts, contribution charts and profit/volume charts

5.1 Breakeven charts

The breakeven point can also be determined graphically using a breakeven chart or a contribution breakeven chart. These charts show approximate levels of profit or loss at different sales volume levels within a limited range.

A breakeven chart has the following axes.

- A **horizontal** axis showing the **sales/output** (in value or units)
- A **vertical axis** showing $ for **sales revenues** and **costs**

The following lines are drawn on the breakeven chart.

(a) The **sales line**

- Starts at the origin
- Ends at the point signifying expected sales

(b) The **fixed costs line**

- Runs parallel to the horizontal axis
- Meets the vertical axis at a point which represents total fixed costs

(c) The **total costs line**

- Starts where the fixed costs line meets the vertical axis

- Ends at the point which represents anticipated sales on the horizontal axis and total costs of anticipated sales on the vertical axis

The **breakeven point** is the **intersection** of the **sales line** and the **total costs line**.

The distance between the **breakeven point** and the **expected (or budgeted) sales**, in units, indicates the **margin of safety**.

5.2 Example: A breakeven chart

The budgeted annual output of a factory is 120,000 units. The fixed overheads amount to $40,000 and the variable costs are 50c per unit. The sales price is $1 per unit.

Required

Construct a breakeven chart showing the current breakeven point and profit earned up to the present maximum capacity.

Solution

We begin by calculating the profit at the budgeted annual output.

	$
Sales (120,000 units)	120,000
Variable costs	60,000
Contribution	60,000
Fixed costs	40,000
Profit	20,000

Breakeven chart (1) is shown on the following page.

The chart is drawn as follows.

(a)   The **vertical axis** represents **money** (costs and revenue) and the **horizontal axis** represents the **level of activity** (production and sales).

(b)   The fixed costs are represented by a **straight line parallel to the horizontal axis** (in our example, at $40,000).

(c)   The **variable costs** are added 'on top of' fixed costs, to give **total costs**. It is assumed that fixed costs are the same in total and variable costs are the same per unit at all levels of output.

The line of costs is therefore a straight line and only two points need to be plotted and joined up. Perhaps the two most convenient points to plot are total costs at zero output, and total costs at the budgeted output and sales.

•   At zero output, costs are equal to the amount of fixed costs only, $40,000, since there are no variable costs.

•   At the budgeted output of 120,000 units, costs are $100,000.

	$
Fixed costs	40,000
Variable costs 120,000 × 50c	60,000
Total costs	100,000

(d)   The sales line is also drawn by plotting two points and joining them up.

        •   At zero sales, revenue is nil.
        •   At the budgeted output and sales of 120,000 units, revenue is $120,000.

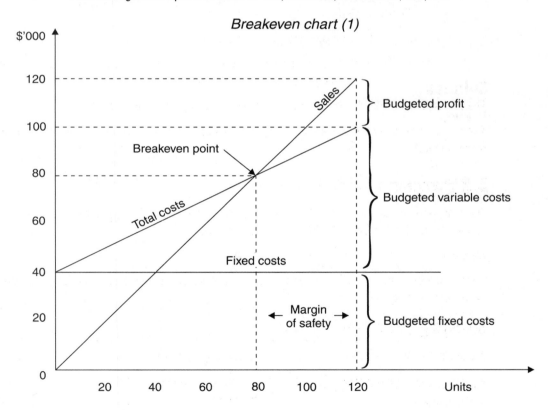

Breakeven chart (1)

The breakeven point is where total costs are matched exactly by total revenue. From the chart, this can be seen to occur at output and sales of 80,000 units, when revenue and costs are both $80,000. This breakeven point can be proved mathematically as:

$$\frac{\text{Required contribution (= fixed costs)}}{\text{Contribution per unit}} = \frac{\$40,000}{50\text{c per unit}} = 80,000 \text{ units}$$

The margin of safety can be seen on the chart as the difference between the budgeted level of activity and the breakeven level.

5.3 The value of breakeven charts

Breakeven charts are used as follows.

- To **plan** the production of a company's products
- To **market** a company's products
- To give a **visual display** of breakeven arithmetic

5.4 Example: Variations in the use of breakeven charts

Breakeven charts can be used to **show variations** in the possible **sales price**, **variable costs** or **fixed costs**. Suppose that a company sells a product which has a variable cost of $2 per unit. Fixed costs are $15,000. It has been estimated that if the sales price is set at $4.40 per unit, the expected sales volume would be 7,500 units; whereas if the sales price is lower, at $4 per unit, the expected sales volume would be 10,000 units.

Required

Draw a breakeven chart to show the budgeted profit, the breakeven point and the margin of safety at each of the possible sales prices.

Solution

Workings

	Sales price $4.40 per unit			Sales price $4 per unit
	$			$
Fixed costs	15,000			15,000
Variable costs (7,500 × $2.00)	15,000	(10,000 × $2.00)		20,000
Total costs	30,000			35,000
Budgeted revenue (7,500 × $4.40)	33,000	(10,000 × $4.00)		40,000

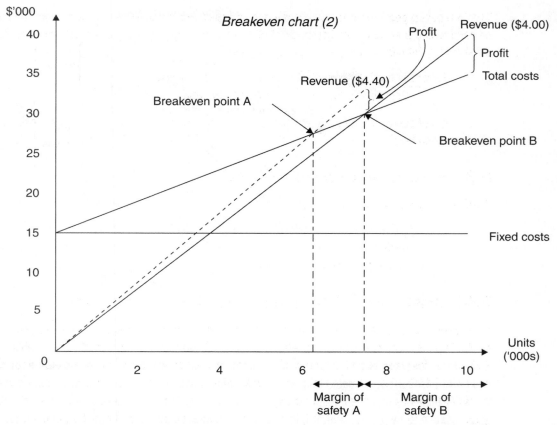

Breakeven chart (2)

(a)   **Breakeven point A** is the breakeven point at a sales price of $4.40 per unit, which is 6,250 units or
      $27,500 in costs and revenues.

$$\text{(check: } \frac{\text{Required contribution to breakeven}}{\text{Contribution per unit}} \quad \frac{\$15,000}{\$2.40 \text{ per unit}} = 6{,}250 \text{ units)}$$

The margin of safety (A) is 7,500 units − 6,250 units = 1,250 units or 16.7% of expected sales.

(b)   **Breakeven point B** is the breakeven point at a sales price of $4 per unit which is 7,500 units or
      $30,000 in costs and revenues.

$$\text{(check: } \frac{\text{Required contribution to breakeven}}{\text{Contribution per unit}} \quad \frac{\$15,000}{\$2 \text{ per unit}} = 7{,}500 \text{ units)}$$

The margin of safety (B) = 10,000 units − 7,500 units = 2,500 units or 25% of expected sales.

Since a price of $4 per unit gives a higher expected profit and a wider margin of safety, this price will
probably be preferred even though the breakeven point is higher than at a sales price of $4.40 per unit.

Contribution (or contribution breakeven) charts

As an alternative to drawing the fixed cost line first, it is possible to start with that for variable costs. This is
known as a **contribution chart**. An example is shown below using the example in Paragraphs 5.2 and 5.4.

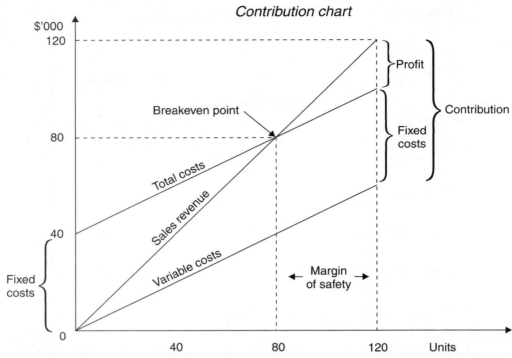

Contribution chart

One of the **advantages** of the contribution chart is that is shows clearly the **contribution** for **different levels of production** (indicated here at 120,000 units, the budgeted level of output) as the 'wedge' shape between the sales revenue line and the variable costs line. At the **breakeven point**, the **contribution equals fixed costs** exactly. At levels of output **above** the **breakeven** point, the **contribution** is **larger**, and not only covers fixed costs, but also leaves a profit. **Below** the **breakeven** point, the **loss** is the amount by which contribution fails to cover fixed costs.

5.5 The Profit/Volume (P/V) chart

FAST FORWARD ➤➤

The **profit/volume (P/V) chart** is a variation of the breakeven chart which illustrates the relationship of costs and profits to sales and the margin of safety.

A P/V chart is constructed as follows (look at the chart in the example that follows as you read the explanation).

(a)   'P' is on the y axis and actually comprises not only 'profit' but contribution to profit (in monetary value), extending above and below the x axis with a zero point at the intersection of the two axes, and the negative section below the x axis representing fixed costs. This means that at zero production, the firm is incurring a loss equal to the fixed costs.

(b)   'V' is on the x axis and comprises either volume of sales or value of sales (revenue).

(c)   The profit-volume line is a straight line drawn with its starting point (at zero production) at the intercept on the y axis representing the level of fixed costs, and with a gradient of contribution/unit (or the P/V ratio if sales value is used rather than units). The P/V line will cut the x axis at the breakeven point of sales volume. Any point on the P/V line above the x axis represents the profit to the firm (as measured on the vertical axis) for that particular level of sales.

5.6 Example: P/V chart

Let us draw a P/V chart for our example. At sales of 120,000 units, total contribution will be 120,000 × $(1 − 0.5) = $60,000 and total profit will be $20,000.

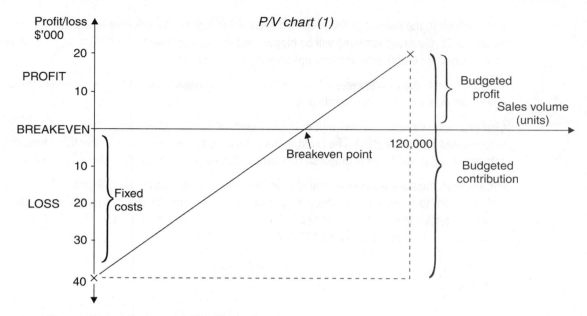

P/V chart (1)

5.7 The advantage of the P/V chart

The P/V chart shows clearly the effect on profit and breakeven point of any changes in selling price, variable cost, fixed cost and/or sales demand.

If the budgeted selling price of the product in our example is increased to $1.20, with the result that demand drops to 105,000 units despite additional fixed costs of $10,000 being spent on advertising, we could add a line representing this situation to our P/V chart.

At sales of 105,000 units, contribution will be 105,000 × $(1.20 − 0.50) = $73,500 and total profit will be $23,500 (fixed costs being $50,000).

P/V chart (2)

The diagram shows that if the selling price is increased, the breakeven point occurs at a lower level of sales revenue (71,429 units instead of 80,000 units), although this is not a particularly large increase when viewed in the context of the projected sales volume. It is also possible to see that for sales above 50,000 units, the profit achieved will be higher (and the loss achieved lower) if the price is $1.20. For sales volumes below 50,000 units the first option will yield lower losses.

The P/V chart is the clearest way of presenting such information; two conventional breakeven charts on one set of axes would be very confusing.

Changes in the variable cost per unit or in fixed costs at certain activity levels can also be easily incorporated into a P/V chart. The profit or loss at each point where the cost structure changes should be calculated and plotted on the graph so that the profit/volume line becomes a series of straight lines.

For example, suppose that in our example, at sales levels in excess of 120,000 units the variable cost per unit increases to $0.60 (perhaps because of overtime premiums that are incurred when production exceeds a certain level). At sales of 130,000 units, contribution would therefore be 130,000 × $(1 – 0.60) = $52,000 and total profit would be $12,000.

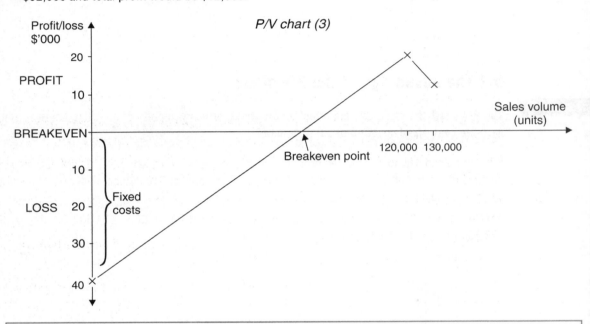

P/V chart (3)

> You may be given a breakeven or PV chart and required to extract the information from it.

6 Limitations of CVP analysis

FAST FORWARD

> Breakeven analysis is a useful technique for managers as it can provide **simple** and **quick** estimates. **Breakeven charts** provide a **graphical representation** of breakeven arithmetic. Breakeven analysis does, however, have number of limitations.

- It **can only apply to a single product** or a single mix of a group of products
- A breakeven chart may be **time-consuming** to prepare
- It **assumes** fixed costs are constant at all levels of output.
- It **assumes** that **variable costs** are the **same** per unit at all levels of output
- It **assumes** that **sales prices** are **constant** at all levels of output
- It assumes **production** and **sales** are the **same** (inventory levels are ignored)
- It **ignores** the **uncertainty** in the estimates of fixed costs and variable cost per unit

Chapter roundup

- **Cost-volume– profit (CVP)/breakeven analysis** is the study of the interrelationships between costs, volume and profits at various levels of activity.

- **Breakeven point** = **Number of units of sale** required to breakeven

  $$= \frac{\text{Fixed costs}}{\text{Contribution per unit}}$$

  $$= \frac{\text{Contribution required to break even}}{\text{Contribution per unit}}$$

- **Breakeven point** = **Sales revenue** required to break even

  $$= \frac{\text{Contribution required to break even}}{\text{C/S ratio}}$$

  $$= \frac{\text{Fixed costs}}{\text{C/S ratio}}$$

- The **C/S ratio** (or **P/V ratio**) is a measure of how much contribution is earned from each $1 of sales.

- The **margin of safety** is the difference in units between the **budgeted sales volume** and the **breakeven sales volume**. It is sometimes expressed as a percentage of the budgeted sales volume. The **margin of safety** may also be expressed as the difference between the **budgeted sales revenue** and the **breakeven sales revenue** expressed as a percentage of the budgeted sales revenue.

- At the **breakeven point**, sales revenue = total costs and there is no profit. At the breakeven point **total contribution = fixed costs.**

- The **target profit** is achieved when S = V + F + P. Therefore the **total contribution required** for a target profit = **fixed costs + required profit.**

- The breakeven point can also be determined graphically using a **breakeven chart** or a **contribution breakeven chart**. These charts show approximate levels of profit or loss at different sales volume levels within a limited range.

- The **profit/volume (PV) chart** is a variation of the breakeven chart which illustrates the relationship of costs and profits to sales and the margin of safety.

- The **P/V chart** shows clearly the effect on profit and breakeven point of any changes in selling price, variable cost, fixed cost and/or sales demand.

- **Breakeven analysis** is a useful technique for managers as it can provide simple and quick estimates. **Breakeven charts** provide a graphical representation of breakeven arithmetic. Breakeven analysis does, however, have a number of **limitations.**

Quick quiz

1 What does CVP analysis study?

2 The **breakeven point** is the ………………………………..………..
or……..………………………………… ………………… .

3 Use the following to make up three formulae which can be used to calculate the breakeven point.

Contribution per unit
Contribution per unit
Fixed costs
Fixed costs
Contribution required to breakeven
Contribution required to breakeven
C/S ratio
C/S ratio

(a) Breakeven point (sales units) = [_____]

or [_____]

(b) Breakeven point (sales revenue) = [_____]

or [_____]

4 The C/S ratio is a measure of how much profit is earned from each $1 of sales.

True [_____]

False [_____]

5 The **margin of safety** is the difference in units between the budgeted sales volume and the breakeven sales volume. How is it sometimes expressed?

6 Profits are maximised at the breakeven point.

True [_____]

False [_____]

7 At the breakeven point, total contribution = ……………………………………… .

8 The total contribution required for a **target profit** = ………………………………………………….. .

9 Give three uses of breakeven charts.

10   Breakeven charts show approximate levels of profit or loss at different sales volume levels within a limited range. Which of the following are true?

I   The sales line starts at the origin
II   The fixed costs line runs parallel to the vertical axis
III   Breakeven charts have a horizontal axis showing the sales/output (in value or units)
IV   Breakeven charts have a vertical axis showing $ for revenues and costs
V   The breakeven point is the intersection of the sales line and the fixed cost line

A   I and II
B   I and III
C   I, III and IV
D   I, III, IV, and V

11   On a breakeven chart, the distance between the breakeven point and the expected (or budgeted) sales, in units, indicates the ....

12   Give seven limitations of CVP analysis.

- ....

- ....

- ....

- ....

- ....

- ....

- ....

Answers to quick quiz

1   The interrelations between **costs, volume** and **profits** of a product at various activity levels.

2   The **breakeven point** is the number of units of sale required to breakeven or the sales revenue required to breakeven.

3   (a)   Breakeven point (sales units) $=$ $\dfrac{\text{Fixed costs}}{\text{Contribution per unit}}$

                or $\dfrac{\text{Contribution required to breakeven}}{\text{Contribution per unit}}$

   (b)   Breakeven point (sales revenue) $=$ $\dfrac{\text{Fixed costs}}{\text{C/S ratio}}$

                or $\dfrac{\text{Contribution required to breakeven}}{\text{C/S ratio}}$

4   False. The C/S ratio is a measure of how much **contribution** is earned from each $1 of sales.

5   As a **percentage** of the budgeted sales volume.

6   False. At the breakeven point there is no profit.

7   At the breakeven point, total contribution = fixed costs

8   Fixed costs + required profit

9
- To plan the production of a company's products
- To market a company's products
- To give a visual display of breakeven arithmetic

10   C

11   Margin of safety

12
- It **can only apply to a single product** or a single mix of a group of products.
- A breakeven chart may be **time-consuming** to prepare.
- It **assumes** fixed costs are constant at all levels of output.
- It **assumes** that **variable costs** are the **same** per unit at all levels of output.
- It **assumes** that **sales prices** are **constant** at all levels of output.
- It assumes **production** and **sales** are the **same** (inventory levels are ignored).
- It **ignores** the **uncertainty** in the estimates of fixed costs and variable cost per unit.

Now try the questions below from the Exam Question Bank

Number	Level	Marks	Time
Q17	MCQ	n/a	n/a

Relevant costing and decision making

18

Topic list	Syllabus reference
1 Relevant costs	F2 (a)-(d)
2 Choice of product (product mix) decisions	F3 (a), (b)

Introduction

Management at all levels within an organisation take decisions. The overriding requirement of the information that should be supplied by the cost accountant to aid decision making is that of **relevance.** This chapter therefore begins by looking at the costing technique required in decision-making situations, that of **relevant costing**, and explains how to decide which costs need taking into account when a decision is being made and which costs do not.

We then go on to see how to apply relevant costing to product mix decisions.

Study guide

		Intellectual level
F2	**Relevant costing**	
(a)	Explain the concept of relevant costing	1
(b)	Calculate the relevant costs for materials, labour and overheads	2
(c)	Calculate the relevant costs associated with non-current assets	1
(d)	Explain and apply the concept of opportunity cost	1
F3	**Limiting factors**	
(a)	Identify a single limiting factor	1
(b)	Determine the optimal production plan where an organisation is restricted by a single limiting factor	2

Exam guide

Relevant costing is one of the key syllabus topics for Paper F2. Make sure that you can calculate relevant costs for materials and labour and the deprival value of an asset. Multiple choice questions are a good way of testing your understanding of this subject.

1 Relevant costs

1.1 Relevant costs

FAST FORWARD

Relevant costs are future cash flows arising as a direct consequence of a decision.

- Relevant costs are **future costs**
- Relevant costs are **cash flows**
- Relevant costs are **incremental costs**

Decision making should be based on relevant costs.

(a) **Relevant costs are future costs**. A decision is about the future and it cannot alter what has been done already. Costs that have been incurred in the past are totally irrelevant to any decision that is being made 'now'. Such costs are **past costs** or **sunk costs**.

Costs that have been incurred include not only costs that have already been paid, but also costs that have been **committed**. A **committed cost** is a future cash flow that will be incurred anyway, regardless of the decision taken now.

(b) **Relevant costs are cash flows**. Only cash flow information is required. This means that costs or charges which do not reflect **additional cash spending** (such as depreciation and notional costs) should be ignored for the purpose of decision making.

(c) **Relevant costs are incremental costs**. For example, if an employee is expected to have no other work to do during the next week, but will be paid his basic wage (of, say, $100 per week) for attending work and doing nothing, his manager might decide to give him a job which earns the organisation $40. The net gain is $40 and the $100 is irrelevant to the decision because although it is a future cash flow, it will be incurred anyway whether the employee is given work or not.

Other terms are sometimes used to describe relevant costs.

1.2 Avoidable costs

> **Avoidable costs** are costs which would not be incurred if the activity to which they relate did not exist.

One of the situations in which it is necessary to identify the avoidable costs is in deciding whether or not to **discontinue a product**. The only costs which would be saved are the **avoidable costs** which are usually the variable costs and sometimes some specific costs. Costs which would be incurred whether or not the product is discontinued are known as **unavoidable costs**.

1.3 Differential costs and opportunity costs

Relevant costs are also **differential costs** and **opportunity costs**.

- **Differential cost** is the difference in total cost between alternatives.
- An **opportunity cost** is the value of the benefit sacrificed when one course of action is chosen in preference to an alternative.

For example, if decision option A costs $300 and decision option B costs $360, the **differential cost** is $60.

1.3.1 Example: Differential costs and opportunity costs

Suppose for example that there are three options, A, B and C, only one of which can be chosen. The net profit from each would be $80, $100 and $70 respectively.

Since only one option can be selected option B would be chosen because it offers the biggest benefit.

	$
Profit from option B	100
Less opportunity cost (ie the benefit from the most profitable alternative, A)	80
Differential benefit of option B	20

The decision to choose option B would not be taken simply because it offers a profit of $100, but because it offers a differential profit of $20 in excess of the next best alternative.

1.4 Controllable and uncontrollable costs

We came across the term **controllable costs** at the beginning of this study text. **Controllable costs** are items of expenditure which can be directly influenced by a given manager within a given time span.

As a general rule, **committed fixed costs** such as those costs arising from the possession of plant, equipment and buildings (giving rise to depreciation and rent) are largely **uncontrollable** in the short term because they have been committed by longer-term decisions.

Discretionary fixed costs, for example, advertising and research and development costs can be thought of as being **controllable** because they are incurred as a result of decisions made by management and can be raised or lowered at fairly short notice.

1.5 Sunk costs

> A **sunk cost** is a past cost which is not directly relevant in decision making.

The principle underlying decision accounting is that management decisions can only affect the future. In decision making, managers therefore require information about **future costs and revenues** which would be affected by the decision under review. They must not be misled by events, costs and revenues in the past, about which they can do nothing.

Sunk costs, which have been charged already as a cost of sales in a previous accounting period or will be charged in a future accounting period although the expenditure has already been incurred, are irrelevant to decision making.

1.5.1 Example: Sunk costs

An example of a sunk cost is development costs which have already been incurred. Suppose that a company has spent $250,000 in developing a new service for customers, but the marketing department's most recent findings are that the service might not gain customer acceptance and could be a commercial failure. The decision whether or not to abandon the development of the new service would have to be taken, but the $250,000 spent so far should be ignored by the decision makers because it is a **sunk cost**.

1.6 Fixed and variable costs

FAST FORWARD

In general, variable costs will be relevant costs and fixed costs will be irrelevant to a decision.

Exam focus point

Unless you are given an indication to the contrary, you should assume the following.

- Variable costs will be relevant costs.
- Fixed costs are irrelevant to a decision.

This need not be the case, however, and you should analyse variable and fixed cost data carefully. Do not forget that 'fixed' costs may only be fixed in the short term.

1.6.1 Non-relevant variable costs

There might be occasions when a variable cost is in fact a sunk cost (and therefore a **non-relevant variable cost**). For example, suppose that a company has some units of raw material in inventory. They have been paid for already, and originally cost $2,000. They are now obsolete and are no longer used in regular production, and they have no scrap value. However, they could be used in a special job which the company is trying to decide whether to undertake. The special job is a 'one-off' customer order, and would use up all these materials in inventory.

(a)   In deciding whether the job should be undertaken, the relevant cost of the materials to the special job is nil. Their original cost of $2,000 is a **sunk cost**, and should be ignored in the decision.

(b)   However, if the materials did have a scrap value of, say, $300, then their relevant cost to the job would be the **opportunity cost** of being unable to sell them for scrap, ie $300.

1.6.2 Attributable fixed costs

There might be occasions when a fixed cost is a relevant cost, and you must be aware of the distinction between **'specific'** or **'directly attributable' fixed costs**, and general fixed overheads.

Directly attributable fixed costs are those costs which, although fixed within a relevant range of activity level are relevant to a decision for either of the following reasons.

(a)   They could increase if certain extra activities were undertaken. For example, it may be necessary to employ an extra supervisor if a particular order is accepted. The extra salary would be an **attributable fixed cost**.

(b)   They would decrease or be eliminated entirely if a decision were taken either to reduce the scale of operations or shut down entirely.

General fixed overheads are those fixed overheads which will be unaffected by decisions to increase or decrease the scale of operations, perhaps because they are an apportioned share of the fixed costs of items which would be completely unaffected by the decisions. General fixed overheads are not relevant in decision making.

1.6.3 Absorbed overhead

Absorbed overhead is a **notional** accounting cost and hence should be ignored for decision-making purposes. **It is overhead incurred which may be relevant to a decision**.

1.7 The relevant cost of materials

The relevant cost of raw materials is generally their **current replacement cost**, *unless* the materials have already been purchased and would not be replaced once used. In this case the relevant cost of using them is the **higher** of the following.

- Their current resale value
- The value they would obtain if they were put to an alternative use

If the materials have no resale value and no other possible use, then the relevant cost of using them for the opportunity under consideration would be nil.

Question	Relevant cost of materials

O'Reilly has been approached by a customer who would like a special job to be done for him, and who is willing to pay $22,000 for it. The job would require the following materials.

Material	Total units required	Units already in inventory	Book value of units in inventory $/unit	Realisable value $/unit	Replacement cost $/unit
A	1,000	0	-	-	6
B	1,000	600	2	2.50	5
C	1,000	700	3	2.50	4
D	200	200	4	6.00	9

Material B is used regularly by O'Reilly, and if units of B are required for this job, they would need to be replaced to meet other production demand.

Materials C and D are in inventory as the result of previous over-buying, and they have a restricted use. No other use could be found for material C, but the units of material D could be used in another job as substitute for 300 units of material E, which currently costs $5 per unit (of which the company has no units in inventory at the moment).

Required

Calculate the relevant costs of material for deciding whether or not to accept the contract.

Answer

(a) **Material A** is not yet owned. It would have to be bought in full at the replacement cost of $6 per unit.

(b) **Material B** is used regularly by the company. There are existing inventories (600 units) but if these are used on the contract under review a further 600 units would be bought to replace them. Relevant costs are therefore 1,000 units at the replacement cost of $5 per unit.

(c) 1,000 units of **material C** are needed and 700 are already in inventory. If used for the contract, a further 300 units must be bought at $4 each. The existing inventories of 700 will not be replaced. If they are used for the contract, they could not be sold at $2.50 each. The realisable value of these 700 units is an opportunity cost of sales revenue forgone.

(d) The required units of **material D** are already in inventory and will not be replaced. There is an opportunity cost of using D in the contract because there are alternative opportunities either to sell the existing inventories for $6 per unit ($1,200 in total) or avoid other purchases (of material E), which would cost 300 × $5 = $1,500. Since substitution for E is more beneficial, $1,500 is the opportunity cost.

(e) **Summary of relevant costs**

	$
Material A (1,000 × $6)	6,000
Material B (1,000 × $5)	5,000
Material C (300 × $4) plus (700 × $2.50)	2,950
Material D	1,500
Total	15,450

Question

A company regularly uses a material. It currently has 100kg in inventory for which it paid $200. If it were sold it could be sold for $3 per kg. The market price is now $4 per kg. A customer has placed an order that will use 200kg of the material. The relevant cost of the 200kg is:

A $500
B $600
C $700
D $300 $800

Answer

The material is in regular use and so 200kg will be purchased. The relevant cost is therefore 200 × $4 = $800. Answer D.

1.8 The relevant cost of labour

The relevant cost of labour, in different situations, is best explained by means of an example.

1.8.1 Example: Relevant cost of labour

LW is currently deciding whether to undertake a new contract. 15 hours of labour will be required for the contract. LW currently produces product L, the standard cost details of which are shown below.

STANDARD COST CARD
PRODUCT L

	$/unit
Direct materials (10kg @ $2)	20
Direct labour (5 hrs @ $6)	30
	50
Selling price	72
Contribution	22

(a)   What is the relevant cost of labour if the labour must be hired from outside the organisation?
(b)   What is the relevant cost of labour if LW expects to have 5 hours spare capacity?
(c)   What is the relevant cost of labour if labour is in short supply?

Solution

(a)   Where labour must be hired from outside the organisation, the relevant cost of labour will be the variable costs incurred.

Relevant cost of labour on new contract = 15 hours @ $6 = $90

(b)   It is assumed that the 5 hours spare capacity will be paid anyway, and so if these 5 hours are used on another contract, there is no additional cost to LW.

Relevant cost of labour on new contract

	$
Direct labour (10 hours @ $6)	60
Spare capacity (5 hours @ $0)	0
	60

(c)   Contribution earned per unit of Product L produced = $22

If it requires 5 hours of labour to make one unit of product L, the contribution earned per labour hour = $22/5 = $4.40.

Relevant cost of labour on new contract

	$
Direct labour (15 hours @ $6)	90
Contribution lost by not making product L ($4.40 × 15 hours)	66
	156

It is important that you should be able to identify the relevant costs which are appropriate to a decision. In many cases, this is a fairly straightforward problem, but there are cases where great care should be taken. Attempt the following question.

Question   Customer order

A company has been making a machine to order for a customer, but the customer has since gone into liquidation, and there is no prospect that any money will be obtained from the winding up of the company.

Costs incurred to date in manufacturing the machine are $50,000 and progress payments of $15,000 had been received from the customer prior to the liquidation.

The sales department has found another company willing to buy the machine for $34,000 once it has been completed.

To complete the work, the following costs would be incurred.

(a)   Materials: these have been bought at a cost of $6,000. They have no other use, and if the machine is not finished, they would be sold for scrap for $2,000.

(b)   Further labour costs would be $8,000. Labour is in short supply, and if the machine is not finished, the work force would be switched to another job, which would earn $30,000 in revenue, and incur direct costs of $12,000 and absorbed (fixed) overhead of $8,000.

(c)   Consultancy fees $4,000. If the work is not completed, the consultant's contract would be cancelled at a cost of $1,500.

(d)   General overheads of $8,000 would be added to the cost of the additional work.

Required

Assess whether the new customer's offer should be accepted.

Answer

(a)   Costs incurred in the past, or revenue received in the past are not relevant because they cannot affect a decision about what is best for the future. Costs incurred to date of $50,000 and revenue received of $15,000 are 'water under the bridge' and should be ignored.

(b)   Similarly, the price paid in the past for the materials is **irrelevant**. The only relevant cost of materials affecting the decision is the opportunity cost of the revenue from scrap which would be forgone – $2,000.

(c)   **Labour costs**

	$
Labour costs required to complete work	8,000
Opportunity costs: contribution forgone by losing other work $(30,000 – 12,000)	18,000
Relevant cost of labour	26,000

(d)   The **incremental cost** of consultancy from completing the work is $2,500.

	$
Cost of completing work	4,000
Cost of cancelling contract	1,500
Incremental cost of completing work	2,500

(e)   **Absorbed overhead is a notional accounting cost** and should be ignored. Actual overhead incurred is the only overhead cost to consider. General overhead costs (and the absorbed overhead of the alternative work for the labour force) should be ignored.

(f)   **Relevant costs may be summarised as follows.**

	$	$
Revenue from completing work		34,000
Relevant costs		
Materials: opportunity cost	2,000	
Labour: basic pay	8,000	
opportunity cost	18,000	
Incremental cost of consultant	2,500	
		30,500
Extra profit to be earned by accepting the order		3,500

1.9 The relevant cost of an asset

FAST FORWARD

The **relevant cost** of an asset represents the amount of money that a company would have to receive if it were deprived of an asset in order to be no worse off than it already is. We can call this the **deprival value**.

Exam focus point

The study guide for Paper F2 states that candidates must be able to calculate the relevant costs associated with non-current assets.

The deprival value of an asset is best demonstrated by means of an example.

1.9.1 Example: Deprival value of an asset

A machine cost $14,000 ten years ago. It is expected that the machine will generate future revenues of $10,000. Alternatively, the machine could be scrapped for $8,000. An equivalent machine in the same condition would cost $9,000 to buy now. What is the deprival value of the machine?

Solution

Firstly, let us think about the relevance of the costs given to us in the question.

Cost of machine = $14,000 = past/sunk cost
Future revenues = $10,000 = revenue expected to be generated
Net realisable value = $8,000 = scrap proceeds
Replacement cost = $9,000

When calculating the **deprival value** of an asset, use the following diagram.

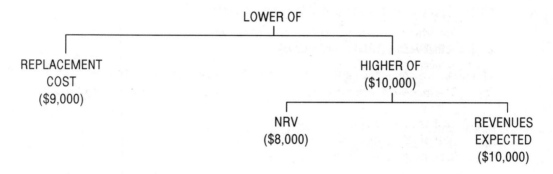

Therefore, the deprival value of the machine is the lower of the replacement cost and $10,000. The deprival value is therefore $9,000.

am focus
int

> Your exam will use the term 'relevant cost' rather than 'deprival value', but you may find that 'deprival value' is a useful concept to bear in mind when considering a non-current asset.

2 Choice of product (product mix) decisions

2.1 The limiting factor

ST FORWARD

A **limiting factor** is a factor which limits the organisation's activities. In a **limiting factor situation**, contribution will be maximised by earning the biggest possible contribution per unit of limiting factor.

A limiting factor is anything which limits the activity of the entity. This could be the level of demand for its product or it could be one or more scarce resources which limit production to below that level.

Possible limiting factors are:

(a) **Sales**. There may be a limit to sales demand

(b) **Labour**. There may be a limit to total quantity of labour available or to labour having particular skills

(c) **Materials**. There may be insufficient available materials to produce enough units to satisfy sales demand

(d) **Manufacturing capacity**. There may not be sufficient machine capacity for the production required to meet sales demand

One of the more common decision-making problems is a situation where there are not enough resources to meet the potential sales demand, and so a decision has to be made about what mix of products to produce, using what resources there are as effectively as possible.

A **limiting factor** could be sales if there is a limit to sales demand but any one of the organisation's resources (labour, materials and so on) may be insufficient to meet the level of production demanded.

It is assumed in limiting factor accounting that management wishes to maximise profit and that **profit will be maximised when contribution is maximised** (given no change in fixed cost expenditure incurred). In other words, **marginal costing ideas are applied**.

Contribution will be maximised by earning the biggest possible contribution from each unit of limiting factor. For example if grade A labour is the limiting factor, contribution will be maximised by earning the biggest contribution from each hour of grade A labour worked.

The limiting factor decision therefore involves the determination of the contribution earned by each different product from each unit of the limiting factor.

2.2 Example: Limiting factor

AB makes two products, the Ay and the Be. Unit variable costs are as follows.

	Ay $	Be $
Direct materials	1	3
Direct labour ($3 per hour)	6	3
Variable overhead	1	1
	8	7

The sales price per unit is $14 per Ay and $11 per Be. During July 20X2 the available direct labour is limited to 8,000 hours. Sales demand in July is expected to be 3,000 units for Ays and 5,000 units for Bes.

Required

Determine the profit-maximising production mix, assuming that monthly fixed costs are $20,000, and that opening inventories of finished goods and work in progress are nil.

Solution

Step 1 Confirm that the limiting factor is something other than sales demand.

	Ays	Bes	Total
Labour hours per unit	2 hrs	1 hr	
Sales demand	3,000 units	5,000 units	
Labour hours needed	6,000 hrs	5,000 hrs	11,000 hrs
Labour hours available			8,000 hrs
Shortfall			3,000 hrs

Labour is the limiting factor on production.

Step 2 Identify the contribution earned by each product per unit of limiting factor, that is per labour hour worked.

	Ays $	Bes $
Sales price	14	11
Variable cost	8	7
Unit contribution	6	4
Labour hours per unit	2 hrs	1 hr
Contribution per labour hour (= unit of limiting factor)	$3	$4

Although Ays have a higher unit contribution than Bes, two Bes can be made in the time it takes to make one Ay. Because labour is in short supply it is more profitable to make Bes than Ays.

Step 3 Determine the **optimum production plan**. Sufficient Bes will be made to meet the full sales demand, and the remaining labour hours available will then be used to make Ays.

(a)

Product	Demand	Hours required	Hours available	Priority of manufacture
Bes	5,000	5,000	5,000	1st
Ays	3,000	6,000	3,000 (bal)	2nd
		11,000	8,000	

(b)

Product	Units	Hours needed	Contribution per unit $	Total $
Bes	5,000	5,000	4	20,000
Ays	1,500	3,000	6	9,000
		8,000		29,000
Less fixed costs				20,000
Profit				9,000

In conclusion

(a) Unit contribution is **not** the correct way to decide priorities.

(b) Labour hours are the scarce resource, and therefore contribution **per labour hour** is the correct way to decide priorities.

(c) The Be earns $4 contribution per labour hour, and the Ay earns $3 contribution per labour hour. Bes therefore make more profitable use of the scarce resource, and should be manufactured first.

Question
Limiting factor 1

The following details relate to three products made by DSF Co.

	V $ per unit	A $ per unit	L $ per unit
Selling price	120	170	176
Direct materials	30	40	60
Direct labour	20	30	20
Variable overhead	10	16	20
Fixed overhead	20	32	40
	80	118	140
Profit	40	52	36

All three products use the same direct labour and direct materials, but in different quantities.

In a period when the labour used on these products is in short supply, the most and least profitable use of the labour is

	Most profitable	Least profitable
A	L	V
B	L	A
C	V	A
D	A	L

Answer

The correct answer is B.

	V	A	L
	$	$	$
Selling price per unit	120	170	176
Variable cost per unit	60	86	100
Contribution per unit	60	84	76
Labour cost per unit	$20	$30	$20
Contribution per $ of labour	$3	$2.80	$3.80
Ranking	2	3	1

Question

Limiting factor 2

Jam Co makes two products, the K and the L. The K sells for $50 per unit, the L for $70 per unit. The variable cost per unit of the K is $35, that of the L $40. Each unit of K uses 2 kg of raw material. Each unit of L uses 3 kg of material.

In the forthcoming period the availability of raw material is limited to 2,000 kg. Jam Co is contracted to supply 500 units of K. Maximum demand for the L is 250 units. Demand for the K is unlimited.

What is the profit-maximising product mix?

	K	L
A	250 units	625 units
B	1,250 units	750 units
C	625 units	250 units
D	750 units	1,250 units

Answer

The correct answer is C.

	K	L
Contribution per unit	$15	$30
Contribution per unit of limiting factor	$15/2 = $7.50	$30/3 = $10
Ranking	2	1

Production plan	Raw material used
	kg
Contracted supply of K (500 x 2 kg)	1,000
Meet demand for L (250 x 3 kg)	750
Remainder of resource for K (125 x 2 kg)	250
	2,000

Chapter roundup

- **Relevant costs** are future cash flows arising as a direct consequence of a decision.

  - Relevant costs are **future costs**
  - Relevant costs are **cashflows**
  - Relevant costs are **incremental costs**

- Relevant costs are also **differential costs** and **opportunity costs.**

  - **Differential cost** is the difference in total cost between alternatives.

  - An **opportunity cost** is the value of the benefit sacrificed when one course of action is chosen in preference to an alternative.

- A **sunk cost** is a past cost which is not directly relevant in decision making.

- **In general**, variable costs will be relevant costs and fixed costs will be irrelevant to a decision.

- The **relevant cost** of an asset represents the amount of money that a company would have to receive if it were deprived of an asset in order to be no worse off than it already is. We can call this the **deprival value**.

- A **limiting factor** is a factor which limits the organisation's activities. In a **limiting factor situation**, contribution will be maximised by earning the biggest possible contribution per unit of limiting factor.

Quick quiz

1   Relevant costs are:

(a)

(b)

(c)

(d)

(e)

2   Sunk costs are directly relevant in decision making.

True   ☐

False   ☐

3   The following information relates to machine Z.

Purchase price = $7,000

Expected future revenues = $5,000

Scrap value = $4,000

Replacement cost = $4,500

Complete the following diagram in order to calculate the relevant cost of machine Z.

The relevant cost of machine Z is ....

4   A limiting factor is a factor which ....

5   A sunk cost is:

A   a cost committed to be spent in the current period
B   a cost which is irrelevant for decision making
C   a cost connected with oil exploration in the North Sea
D   a cost unaffected by fluctuations in the level of activity

Answers to quick quiz

1   (a)   Future costs
    (b)   Cash flows
    (c)   Incremental costs
    (d)   Differential costs
    (e)   Opportunity costs

2   False

3

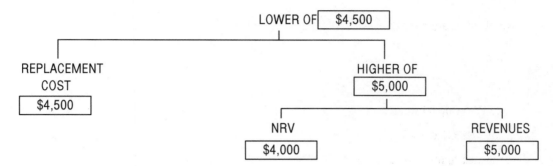

The relevant cost of machine Z is **$4,500**.

4   Limits the organisation's activities.

5   B

Now try the questions below from the Exam Question Bank

Number	Level	Marks	Time
Q18	MCQ/OTQ	n/a	n/a

19

Linear programming

Topic list	Syllabus reference
1 The problem	F3 (a), (b)
2 Formulating the problem	F3 (c)
3 Graphing the model	F3 (d)
4 Finding the best solution	F3 (c)
5 The graphical method using simultaneous equations	F3 (e)

Introduction

We are now going to look at a decision-making technique which involves **allocating resources in order to achieve the best results**. The name '**linear programming**' sounds rather formidable and the technique *can* get very complicated. Don't worry though: you are only expected to be able to analyse the simplest examples.

Study guide

		Intellectual level
F3	**Limiting factors**	
(a)	Identify a single limiting factor	1
(b)	Determine the optimal production plan where an organisation is restricted by a single limiting factor	2
(c)	Formulate a linear programming problem involving two variables	1
(d)	Determine the optimal solution to a linear programming problem using a graphical approach	1
(e)	Use simultaneous equations where appropriate, in the solution of a linear programming problem	1

Exam guide

The Pilot paper has four questions on this part of the syllabus. Make sure you understand both the graphical approach and the method using simultaneous equations.

1 The problem

FAST FORWARD

A **limiting factor** limits the organisation's production. It could be a limited supply of labour, inventory, machine hours or some other factor. The production plan must aim to maximise the **contribution per unit of limiting factor.**

A typical business problem is to decide how a company should **divide up its production among the various types of product** it manufactures in order to obtain the **maximum possible profit**. A business cannot simply aim to produce as much as possible because there will be **limitations** or **constraints** within which the production must operate. Such constraints could be one or more of the following.

- Limited quantities of raw materials available
- A fixed number of man-hours per week for each type of worker
- Limited machine hours

Moreover, since the profits generated by different products vary, it may be better not to produce any of a less profitable line, but to concentrate all resources on producing the more profitable ones. On the other hand limitations in market demand could mean that some of the products produced may not be sold.

Refer back to Chapter 18 for simple production planning. In this chapter we look at the approach using linear programming.

2 Formulating the problem

AST FORWARD

Linear programming is a technique for solving problems of profit maximisation or cost minimisation and resource allocation. 'Programming' has nothing to do with computers: the word is simply used to denote a series of events.

Linear programming, at least at this fairly simple level, is a technique that can be carried out in a fairly 'handle turning' manner once you have got the basic ideas sorted out. The steps involved are as follows.

1   Define variables
2   Establish constraints
3   Construct objective function
4   Graph constraints
5   Establish feasible region
6   Add iso-profit/contribution line
7   Determine optimal solution

Let us imagine that B makes just two models, the Super and the Deluxe, and that the **only constraint** faced by the company is that **monthly machine capacity is restricted to 400 hours**. The Super requires 5 hours of machine time per unit and the Deluxe 1.5 hours. Government restrictions mean that the maximum number of units that can be sold each month is 150, that number being made up of any combination of the Super and the Deluxe.

Let us now work through the steps involved in setting up a linear programming model.

Step 1   Define variables

What are the quantities that the company can vary? Obviously not the number of machine hours or the maximum sales, which are fixed by external circumstances beyond the company's control. The only things which it can determine are the number of each type of unit to manufacture. It is these numbers which have to be determined in such a way as to get the maximum possible profit. Our variables will therefore be as follows.

Let x = the number of units of the Super manufactured.
Let y = the number of units of the Deluxe manufactured.

Step 2   Establish constraints

Having defined these two variables we can now translate the two constraints into inequalities involving the variables.

Let us first consider the machine hours constraint. Each Super requires 5 hours of machine time. Producing five Supers therefore requires $5 \times 5 = 25$ hours of machine time and, more generally, producing x Supers will require 5x hours. Likewise producing y Deluxes will require 1.5y hours. The total machine hours needed to make x Supers and y Deluxes is 5x + 1.5y. We know that this cannot be greater than 400 hours so we arrive at the following inequality.

$5x + 1.5y \leq 400$

We can obtain the other inequality more easily. The total number of Supers and Deluxes made each month is x + y but this has to be less than 150 due to government restrictions. The sales order constraint is therefore as follows.

$x + y \leq 150$

Non-negativity

The variables in linear programming models should usually be non-negative in value. In this example, for instance, you cannot make a negative number of units and so we need the following constraints.

$x \geq 0$; $y \geq 0$

Do not forget these non-negativity constraints when formulating a linear programming model.

Step 3   **Construct objective function**

We have yet to introduce the question of profits. Let us assume that the profit on each model is as follows.

	$
Super	100
Deluxe	200

The **objective** of B is to **maximise profit** and so the **function** to be maximised is as follows.

Profit (P) = 100x + 200y

The problem has now been reduced to the following four inequalities and one equation.

$$5x + 1.5y \leq 400$$
$$x + y \leq 150$$
$$x \geq 0$$
$$y \geq 0$$
$$P = 100x + 200y$$

Have you noticed that **the inequalities are all linear expressions**? If plotted on a graph, they would all give **straight lines**. This explains why the technique is called **linear programming** and also gives a hint as to how we should proceed with trying to find the solution to the problem.

Question   Constraints

Patel manufactures two products, X and Y, in quantities x and y units per week respectively. The contribution is $60 per X and $70 per Y. For practical reasons, no more than 100 Xs can be produced per week. If Patel plc uses linear programming to determine a profit-maximising production policy and on the basis of this information, which one of the following constraints is correct?

A $x \leq 60$
B $y \leq 100$
C $x \leq 100$
D $60x + 70y \leq 100$

Answer

The correct answer is C because the question states that the number of Xs produced cannot exceed 100 and so $x \leq 100$.

Option A has no immediate bearing on the number of units of X produced which must be ≤ 100. ($60 represents the contribution per unit of X).

We have no information on the production volume of Product Y and option B is therefore incorrect.

The contribution earned per week is given by 60x + 70y but we have no reason to suppose that this must be less than or equal to 100. Option D is therefore incorrect.

Students often have problems with constraints of the style 'the quantity of one type must not exceed twice that of the other'. This can be interpreted as follows: the quantity of one type (say X) must not exceed (must be less than or equal to) twice that of the other (2Y) (ie $X \le 2Y$).

We have looked at how to **formulate a problem** and in the next section we will look at solving a problem using graphs.

3 Graphing the model

AST FORWARD

A graphical solution is only possible when there are two variables in the problem. One variable is represented by the x axis and one by the y axis of the graph. Since non-negative values are not usually allowed, the graph shows only zero and positive values of x and y.

A linear equation with one or two variables is shown as a straight line on a graph. Thus y = 6 would be shown as follows.

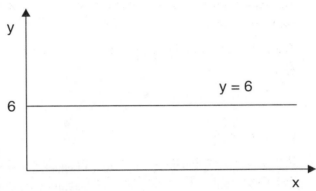

If the problem included a constraint that y could not exceed 6, the **inequality** $y \le 6$ would be represented by the shaded area of the graph below.

The equation 4x + 3y = 24 is also a straight line on a graph. To draw any straight line, we need only to plot two points and join them up. The easiest points to plot are the following.

(a)   x = 0 (in this example, if x = 0, 3y = 24, y = 8)
(b)   y = 0 (in this example, if y = 0, 4x = 24, x = 6)

By plotting the points, (0, 8) and (6, 0) on a graph, and joining them up, we have the line for 4x + 3y = 24.

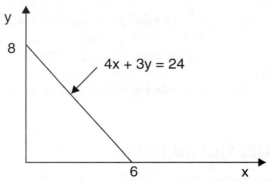

If we had a constraint 4x + 3y ≤ 24, any combined value of x and y within the shaded area below (on or below the line) would satisfy the constraint.

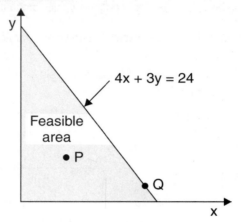

For example, at point P where (x = 2, y = 2) 4x + 3y = 14 which is less than 24; and at point Q where x = 5.5, y = 2/3, 4x + 3y = 24. Both P and Q lie within the **feasible area** (the area where the inequality is satisfied, also called the feasible region). A **feasible area** enclosed on all sides may also be called a **feasible polygon**.

The inequalities y ≥ 6, x ≥ 6 and 4x + 3y ≥ 24, would be shown graphically as follows.

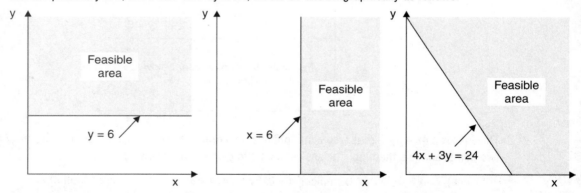

When there are several constraints, the feasible area of combinations of values of x and y must be an area where all the inequalities are satisfied.

Thus, if y ≤ 6 *and* 4x + 3y ≤ 24 the feasible area would be the shaded area in the graph following.

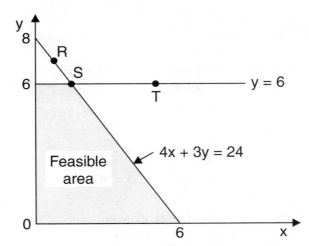

(a) Point R (x = 0.75, y = 7) is not in the feasible area because although it satisfies the inequality 4x + 3y ≤ 24, it does not satisfy y ≤ 6.

(b) Point T (x = 5, y = 6) is not in the feasible area, because although it satisfies the inequality y ≤ 6, it does not satisfy 4x + 3y ≤ 24.

(c) Point S (x = 1.5, y = 6) satisfies both inequalities and lies just on the boundary of the feasible area since y = 6 exactly, and 4x + 3y = 24. Point S is thus at the intersection of the two equation lines.

Similarly, if y ≥ 6 and 4x + 3y ≥ 24 but x ≤ 6, the feasible area would be the shaded area in the graph below.

Question   Feasible region

Draw the feasible region which arises from the constraints facing B Co (see Section 2).

Answer

If 5x + 1.5y = 400, then if x = 0, y = 267 and if y = 0, x = 80.
If x + y = 150, then if x = 0, y = 150 and if y = 0, x = 150

 ### Question

In a linear programming problem, one of the constraints is given by 2x ≤ 3y. Which of the following statements about the graphical presentation of this constraint is correct?

I   The constraint line passes through the point x = 2, y = 3.
II   The constraint line passes through the origin.
III   The constraint line passes through the point x = 3, y = 2.
IV   The region below the constraint line is part of the feasible area.

A   I and II only
B   I and III only
C   II and III only
D   II, III and IV only

Answer

When x = 0 then y must also equal 0, therefore statement II is correct.

When x = 3, 6 = 3y and hence y = 2, therefore statement III is correct.

Statements II and III are correct and therefore option C is the right answer.

Statement I is incorrect since when x = 2, 4 = 3y and y = 1.33 and y does not equal 3 when x = 2.

Statement IV is incorrect since 3y is greater than 2x above the line, not below it.

4 Finding the best solution

4.1 Introduction

Having found the **feasible region** (which includes all the possible solutions to the problem) we need to find which of these possible solutions is **'best'** in the sense that it yields the **maximum possible profit**. We could do this by finding out what profit each of the possible solutions would give, and then choosing as our 'best' combination the one for which the profit is greatest.

Consider, however, the feasible region of the problem faced by B Co (see the solution to the question entitled Feasible region). Even in such a simple problem as this, there are a great many possible solution points within the feasible area. Even to write them all down would be a time consuming process and also an unnecessary one, as we shall see.

4.2 Example: Finding the best solution

Let us look again at the graph of B's problem.

Consider, for example, the point A at which 40 Supers and 80 Deluxes are being manufactured. This will yield a profit of $((40 \times 100) + (80 \times 200)) = \$20,000$. We would clearly get more profit at point B, where the same number of Deluxes are being manufactured but where the number of Supers being manufactured has increased by five, or from point C where the same number of Supers but 10 more Deluxes are manufactured. This argument suggests that **the 'best' solution is going to be a point on the edge of the feasible area rather than in the middle of it**.

This still leaves us with quite a few points to look at but there is a way we can narrow down the candidates for the best solution still further. Suppose that B Co wish to make a profit of $10,000. The company could sell the following combinations of Supers and Deluxes.

(a)   100 Super, no Deluxe

(b)   No Super, 50 Deluxe

(c)   A proportionate mix of Super and Deluxe, such as 80 Super and 10 Deluxe or 50 Super and 25 Deluxe

The possible combinations of Supers and Deluxes required to earn a profit of $10,000 could be shown by the straight line $100x + 200y = 10,000$.

For a total profit of $15,000, a similar line $100x + 200y = 15,000$ could be drawn to show the various combinations of Supers and Deluxes which would achieve the total of $15,000.

Similarly a line $100x + 200y = 8,000$ would show the various combinations of Supers and Deluxes which would earn a total profit of $8,000.

These profit lines are all parallel. (They are called **iso-profit lines**, 'iso' meaning equal.) A similar line drawn for any other total profit would also be parallel to the three lines shown here. This means that if we wish to know the slope or gradient of the profit line, for any value of total profit, we can simply draw one line for any convenient value of profit, and we will know that all the other lines will be parallel to the one drawn: they will have the same slope.

Bigger profits are shown by lines further from the origin ($100x + 200y = 15,000$), **smaller profits by lines closer to the origin** ($100x + 200y = 8,000$). As B Co try to **increase possible profit** we need to **slide the profit line outwards from the origin**, while always keeping it **parallel** to the other profit lines.

As we do this there will come a point at which, if we were to move the profit line out any further, it would cease to lie in the feasible region and therefore larger profits could not be achieved in practice because of the constraints. In our example concerning B Co this will happen, as you should test for yourself, where the profit line is just passing through the intersection of $x + y = 150$ with the y axis (at (0, 150)). The point (0, 150) will therefore give us the best production combination of the Super and the Deluxe, that is, to produce 150 Deluxe models and no Super models.

4.3 Example: A maximisation problem

Brunel manufactures plastic-covered steel fencing in two qualities, standard and heavy gauge. Both products pass through the same processes, involving steel-forming and plastic bonding.

Standard gauge fencing sells at $18 a roll and heavy gauge fencing at $24 a roll. Variable costs per roll are $16 and $21 respectively. There is an unlimited market for the standard gauge, but demand for the heavy gauge is limited to 1,300 rolls a year. Factory operations are limited to 2,400 hours a year in each of the two production processes.

	Processing hours per roll	
Gauge	Steel-forming	Plastic-bonding
Standard	0.6	0.4
Heavy	0.8	1.2

What is the production mix which will maximise total contribution and what would be the total contribution?

Solution

(a) Let S be the number of standard gauge rolls per year.

Let H be the number of heavy gauge rolls per year.

The objective is to maximise 2S + 3H (contribution) subject to the following constraints.

$$0.6S + 0.8H \leq 2,400 \quad \text{(steel-forming hours)}$$
$$0.4S + 1.2H \leq 2,400 \quad \text{(plastic-bonding hours)}$$
$$H \leq 1,300 \quad \text{(sales demand)}$$
$$S, H \geq 0$$

Note that **the constraints are inequalities**, and are not equations. There is no requirement to use up the total hours available in each process, nor to satisfy all the demand for heavy gauge rolls.

(b) If we take the production constraint of 2,400 hours in the steel-forming process

$$0.6S + 0.8H \leq 2,400$$

it means that since there are only 2,400 hours available in the process, output must be limited to a maximum of:

(i) $\dfrac{2,400}{0.6}$ = 4,000 rolls of standard gauge;

(ii) $\dfrac{2,400}{0.8}$ = 3,000 rolls of heavy gauge; or

(iii) a proportionate combination of each.

This maximum output represents the boundary line of the constraint, where the inequality becomes the equation

$$0.6S + 0.8H = 2,400.$$

(c) The line for this equation may be drawn on a graph by joining up two points on the line (such as S = 0, H = 3,000; H = 0, S = 4,000).

(d) The other constraints may be drawn in a similar way with lines for the following equations.

$$0.4S + 1.2H = 2,400 \text{ (plastic-bonding)}$$
$$H = 1,300 \text{ (sales demand)}$$

(e)

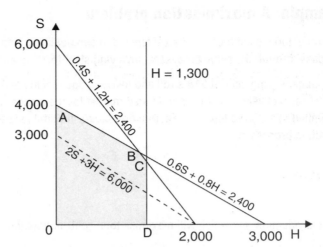

To satisfy all the constraints simultaneously, the values of S and H must lie on or below each constraint line. The outer limits of the feasible polygon are the lines, but all combined values of S and H within the shaded area are feasible solutions.

(f) The next step is to find the optimal solution, which maximises the objective function. Since the objective is to maximise contribution, the solution to the problem must involve relatively high values (within the feasible polygon) for S, or H or a combination of both.

If, as is likely, there is only one combination of S and H which provides the optimal solution, this combination will be one of the outer corners of the feasible polygon. There are four such corners, A, B, C and D. However, it is possible that any combination of values for S and H on the boundary line between two of these corners might provide solutions with the same total contribution.

(g) To solve the problem we establish the slope of the iso-contribution lines, by drawing a line for any one level of contribution. In our solution, a line 2S + 3H = 6,000 has been drawn. (6,000 was chosen as a convenient multiple of 2 and 3). This line has no significance except to indicate the slope, or gradient, of every iso-contribution line for 2S + 3H.

Using a ruler to judge at which corner of the feasible polygon we can draw an iso– contribution line which is as far to the right as possible, (away from the origin) but which still touches the feasible polygon.

(h) This occurs at corner B where the constraint line 0.4S + 1.2H = 2,400 crosses with the constraint line 0.6S + 0.8H = 2,400. At this point, there are simultaneous equations, from which the exact values of S and H may be calculated.

0.4S +	1.2H	=	2,400	(1)
0.6S +	0.8H	=	2,400	(2)
1.2S +	3.6H	=	7,200	(3) ((1) × 3)
1.2S +	1.6H	=	4,800	(4) ((2) × 2)
	2H	=	2,400	(5) ((3) − (4))
	H	=	1,200	(6)

Substituting 1,200 for H in either equation, we can calculate that S = 2,400.

The contribution is maximised where H = 1,200, and S = 2,400.

	Units	Contribution per unit $	Total contribution $
Standard gauge	2,400	2	4,800
Heavy gauge	1,200	3	3,600
			8,400

Question

The Dervish Chemical Company operates a small plant. Operating the plant requires two raw materials, A and B, which cost $5 and $8 per litre respectively. The maximum available supply per week is 2,700 litres of A and 2,000 litres of B.

The plant can operate using either of two processes, which have differing contributions and raw materials requirements, as follows.

Process	Raw materials consumed (litres per processing hour)		Contribution per hour
	A	B	$
1	20	10	70
2	30	20	60

The plant can run for 120 hours a week in total, but for safety reasons, process 2 cannot be operated for more than 80 hours a week.

Formulate a linear programming model, and then solve it, to determine how many hours process 1 should be operated each week and how many hours process 2 should be operated each week.

Answer

The decision variables are processing hours in each process. If we let the processing hours per week for process 1 be P_1 and the processing hours per week for process 2 be P_2 we can formulate an objective and constraints as follows.

The objective is to maximise $70P_1 + 60P_2$, subject to the following constraints.

$$\begin{aligned} 20P_1 + 30P_2 &\leq 2,700 && \text{(material A supply)} \\ 10P_1 + 20P_2 &\leq 2,000 && \text{(material B supply)} \\ P_2 &\leq 80 && \text{(maximum time for } P_2) \\ P_1 + P_2 &\leq 120 && \text{(total maximum time)} \\ P_1, P_2 &\geq 0 && \text{(non-negativity)} \end{aligned}$$

The feasible area is ABCDO. The optimal solution, found by moving the iso-contribution line outwards, is at point A, where $P_1 = 120$ and $P_2 = 0$. Total contribution would be $120 \times 70 = \$8,400$ a week.

4.4 Multiple solutions

It is possible that the optimum position might lie, not at a particular corner, but all along the length of one of the sides of the feasibility polygon. This will occur if the iso-contribution line is exactly parallel to one of the constraint lines.

If this happens then there is no one optimum solution but a **range of optimum solutions**. All of these will maximise the objective function at the same level. However, *any* value of the decision variables that happens to satisfy the constraint between the points where the constraint line forms part of the feasibility region would produce this optimum level of contribution.

4.5 Minimisation problems in linear programming

Although decision problems with limiting factors usually involve the maximisation of contribution, there may be a requirement to **minimise costs**. A graphical solution, involving two variables, is very similar to that for a maximisation problem, with the exception that instead of finding a contribution line touching the feasible area as far away from the origin as possible, we look for a **total cost line touching the feasible area as close to the origin as possible**.

4.5.1 Example: A minimisation problem

Claire Speke Co has undertaken a contract to supply a customer with at least 260 units in total of two products, X and Y, during the next month. At least 50% of the total output must be units of X. The products are each made by two grades of labour, as follows.

	X Hours	Y Hours
Grade A labour	4	6
Grade B labour	4	2
Total	8	8

Although additional labour can be made available at short notice, the company wishes to make use of 1,200 hours of Grade A labour and 800 hours of Grade B labour which has already been assigned to working on the contract next month. The total variable cost per unit is $120 for X and $100 for Y.

Claire Speke Ltd wishes to minimise expenditure on the contract next month. How much of X and Y should be supplied in order to meet the terms of the contract?

Solution

(a) Let the number of units of X supplied be x, and the number of units of Y supplied be y.

The objective is to minimise 120x + 100y (costs), subject to the following constraints.

$x + y$	$\geq$	260	(supply total)
x	$\geq$	$0.5 (x + y)$	(proportion of x in total)
$4x + 6y$	$\geq$	1,200	(Grade A labour)
$4x + 2y$	$\geq$	800	(Grade B labour)
x, y	$\geq$	0	

The constraint $x \geq 0.5 (x + y)$ needs simplifying further.

$$x \geq 0.5 (x + y)$$
$$2x \geq x + y$$
$$x \geq y$$

In a graphical solution, the line will be x = y. Check this carefully in the following diagram.

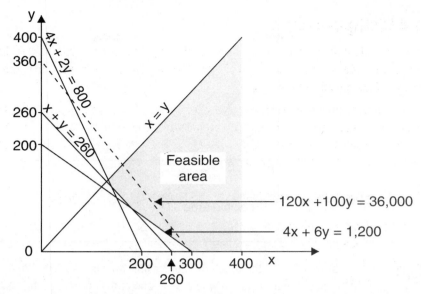

(b) The cost line 120x + 100y = 36,000 has been drawn to show the slope of every cost line 120x + 100 y. **Costs are minimised where a cost line touches the feasible area as close as possible to the origin of the graph**. This occurs where the constraint line 4x + 2y = 800 crosses the constraint line x + y = 260. This point is found as follows.

$$
\begin{aligned}
x + y &= 260 \quad (1) \\
4x + 2y &= 800 \quad (2) \\
2x + y &= 400 \quad (3)\ ((2) \div 2) \\
x &= 140 \quad (4)\ ((3) - (1)) \\
y &= 120 \quad (5)
\end{aligned}
$$

(c) Costs will be minimised by supplying the following.

	Unit cost	Total cost
	$	$
140 units of X	120	16,800
120 units of Y	100	12,000
		28,800

The proportion of units of X in the total would exceed 50%, and demand for Grade A labour would exceed the 1,200 hours minimum.

4.6 The use of simultaneous equations

You might think that a lot of time could be saved if we started by solving the simultaneous equations in a linear programming problem and did not bother to draw the graph.

Certainly, this procedure may give the right answer, but in general, it is *not* recommended until you have shown graphically which constraints are effective in determining the optimal solution. To illustrate this point, consider the following graph.

No figures have been given on the graph but the feasible area is OABCDE. When solving this problem, we would know that the optimum solution would be at one of the corners of the feasible area. We need to work out the profit at each of the corners of the feasible area and pick the one where the profit is greatest.

Once the optimum point has been determined graphically, simultaneous equations can be applied to find the exact values of x and y at this point.

5 The graphical method using simultaneous equations

FAST FORWARD

The optimal solution can also be found using **simultaneous equations**.

5.1 Example: using simultaneous equations

An organisation manufactures plastic-covered steel fencing in two qualities: standard and heavy gauge. Both products pass through the same processes involving steel forming and plastic bonding.

The standard gauge sells at $15 a roll and the heavy gauge at $20 a roll. There is an unlimited market for the standard gauge but outlets for the heavy gauge are limited to 13,000 rolls a year. The factory operations of each process are limited to 2,400 hours a year. Other relevant data is given below.

Variable costs per roll

	Direct material	*Direct wages*	*Direct expense*
	$	$	$
Standard	5	7	1
Heavy	7	8	2

Processing hours per 100 rolls

	Steel forming Hours	*Plastic bonding* Hours
Standard	6	4
Heavy	8	12

Required

Calculate the allocation of resources and hence the production mix which will maximise total contribution.

Solution

Step 1 **Define variables**

Let the number of rolls of standard gauge to be produced be x and the number of rolls of heavy gauge be y.

Step 2 **Establish objective function**

Standard gauge produces a contribution of $2 per roll ($15 − $(5 + 7 + 1)) and heavy gauge a contribution of $3 ($20 − $(7 + 8 + 2)).

Therefore the objective is to maximise contribution (C) = 2x + 3y subject to the constraints below.

Step 3 **Establish constraints**

The constraints are as follows.

$$0.06x + 0.08y \leq 2,400 \quad \text{(steel forming hours)}$$
$$0.04x + 0.12y \leq 2,400 \quad \text{(plastic bonding hours)}$$
$$y \leq 13,000 \quad \text{(demand for heavy gauge)}$$
$$x, y \geq 0 \quad \text{(non-negativity)}$$

Step 4 **Graph problem**

The graph of the problem can now be drawn.

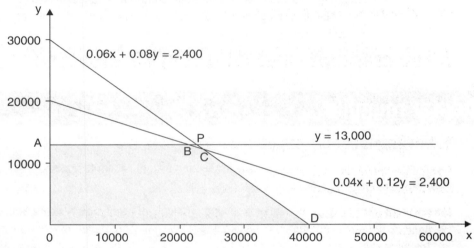

Step 5 **Define feasible area**

The combinations of x and y that satisfy all three constraints are represented by the area OABCD.

Step 6 **Determine optimal solution**

Which combination will maximise contribution? Obviously, the more units of x and y, the bigger the contribution will be, and the optimal solution will be at point B, C or D. It will not be at A, since at A, y = 13,000 and x = 0, whereas at B, y = 13,000 (the same) and x is greater than zero.

Using **simultaneous equations** to calculate the value of x and y at each of points B, C and D, and then working out total contribution at each point from this, we can establish the contribution-maximising product mix.

Point B

$$y = 13,000 \, (1)$$
$$0.04x + 0.12y = 2,400 \quad (2) \text{ (Plastic forming hours)}$$
$$0.12y = 1,560 \quad (3) \, ((1) \times 0.12) \, (13,000 \times 0.12)$$
$$0.04x = 840 \quad (4) \, ((2) - (3)) \, (2,400 - 1,560)$$
$$x = 21,000 \, (5) \, (840 \div 0.04)$$

Total contribution = (21,000 × $2) + (13,000 × $3) = $81,000.

Note. At **Point B** we can see from the graph that y =13,000, so we only need to find x. At **Point C** we have to find x and y.

Point C

0.06x + 0.08y	=	2,400	(1) (Steel forming hours)
0.04x + 0.12y	=	2,400	(2) (Plastic bonding hours)
0.12x + 0.16y	=	4,800	(3) ((1) × 2)
0.12x + 0.36y	=	7,200	(4) ((2) × 3)
0.2y	=	2,400	(5) ((4) − (3))
y	=	12,000	(6)
0.06x + 960	=	2,400	(7) (substitute in (1)) (960 = 0.08y)
x	=	24,000	(8)

← Here we produce two equations in which the value of X is the same. This enables us to calculate Y

Total contribution = (24,000 × $2) + (12,000 × $3) = $84,000.

Point D

Total contribution = 40,000 × $2 = $80,000.

Comparing B, C and D, we can see that contribution is maximised at C, by making 24,000 rolls of standard gauge and 12,000 rolls of heavy gauge, to earn a contribution of $84,000.

Exam focus point

In any exam question involving the graphical method, you will be given the graph.

Chapter roundup

- A **limiting factor** limits the organisation's production, It could be a limited supply of labour, inventory, machine hours or some other factor. The production plan must aim to maximise the **contribution per unit of limiting factor.**

- **Linear programming** is a technique for solving problems of profit maximisation or cost minimisation and resource allocation. 'Programming' has nothing to do with computers: the word is simply used to denote a series of events.

- **Linear programming**, at least at this fairly simple level, is a technique that can be carried out in a fairly 'handle-turning' manner once you have got the basic ideas sorted out. The steps involved are as follows.

  1   Define variables
  2   Establish constraints
  3   Construct objective function
  4   Graph constraints
  5   Establish feasible region
  6   Add iso-profit/contribution line
  7   Determine optimal solution

- A graphical solution is only possible when there are two variables in the problem. One variable is represented by the x axis and one by the y axis of the graph. Since non-negative values are not usually allowed, the graph only shows zero and positive values of x and y.

- The optimal solution can also be found using **simultaneous** equations.

Quick quiz

1   What are the three main steps involved in setting up a linear programming model?

   Step 1.   ....

   Step 2.   ....

   Step 3.   ....

2   Draw the inequality $4x + 3y \leq 24$ on the graph below.

3   A feasible area enclosed on all sides may also be called a ....

4   How does the graphical solution of minimisation problems differ from that of maximisation problems?

5   The graphical method cannot be used when there are more than two decision variables.

   True   ☐

   False   ☐

Answers to quick quiz

1 **Step 1.** Define variables

   Step 2. Establish constraints

   Step 3. Establish objective function

2

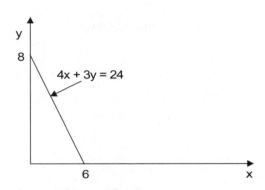

3 Feasible polygon.

4 Instead of finding a contribution line touching the feasible area as far away from the origin as possible, we look for a total cost line touching the feasible area **as close to the origin as possible**.

5 True

Now try the questions below from the Exam Question Bank

Number	Level	Marks	Time
Q19	MCQ	n/a	N/a

Appendix
Basic maths

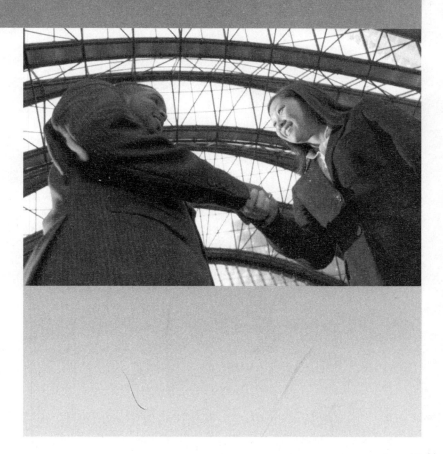

Appendix

1 Using this appendix

The **Management Accounting** syllabus assumes that you have some knowledge of basic mathematics and statistics. The purpose of this appendix is to provide the knowledge required in this area if you haven't studied it before, or to provide a means of reminding you of basic maths and statistics if you are feeling a little rusty in one or two areas!

Accordingly, this appendix sets out from first principles a good deal of the knowledge that you are assumed to possess in the main body of the Study Text. You may wish to work right through it now. You may prefer to dip into it as and when you need to. You may just like to try a few questions to sharpen up your knowledge. Don't feel obliged to learn everything in the following pages: they are intended as an extra resource to be used in whatever way best suits you.

2 Integers, fractions and decimals

2.1 Integers, fractions and decimals

An **integer** is a whole number and can be either positive or negative. The integers are therefore as follows.

.....,-5, -4, -3, -2, -1, 0, 1, 2, 3, 4, 5..... .

Fractions (such as $\frac{1}{2}$, $\frac{1}{4}$, $\frac{19}{35}$, $\frac{101}{377}$, ...) and **decimals** (0.1, 0.25, 0.3135 .....) are both ways of showing parts of a whole. Fractions can be turned into decimals by dividing the numerator by the denominator (in other words, the top line by the bottom line). To turn decimals into fractions, all you have to do is remember that places after the decimal point stand for tenths, hundredths, thousandths and so on.

2.2 Significant digits

Sometimes a decimal number has too many digits in it for practical use. This problem can be overcome by rounding the decimal number to a specific number of **significant digits** by discarding digits using the following rule.

If the first digit to be discarded is greater than or equal to five then add one to the previous digit. Otherwise the previous digit is unchanged.

2.3 Example: Significant digits

(a)   187.392 correct to five significant digits is 187.39

Discarding a 2 causes nothing to be added to the 9.

(b)   187.392 correct to four significant digits is 187.4

Discarding the 9 causes one to be added to the 3.

(c)   187.392 correct to three significant digits is 187

Discarding a 3 causes nothing to be added to the 7.

Question

What is 17.385 correct to four significant digits?

Answer

17.39

3 Mathematical notation

3.1 Brackets

Brackets are commonly used to indicate which parts of a mathematical expression should be grouped together, and calculated before other parts. In other words, brackets can indicate a priority, or an order in which calculations should be made. The rule is as follows.

(a)   Do things in brackets before doing things outside them.

(b)   Subject to rule (a), do things in this order.

(i)   Powers and roots
(ii)   Multiplications and divisions, working from left to right
(iii)   Additions and subtractions, working from left to right

Thus brackets are used for the sake of **clarity**. Here are some examples.

(a) $3 + 6 \times 8 = 51$. This is the same as writing $3 + (6 \times 8) = 51$.
(b) $(3 + 6) \times 8 = 72$. The brackets indicate that we wish to multiply the sum of 3 and 6 by 8.
(c) $12 - 4 \div 2 = 10$. This is the same as writing $12 - (4 \div 2) = 10$ or $12 - (4/2) = 10$.
(d) $(12 - 4) \div 2 = 4$. The brackets tell us to do the subtraction first.

A figure outside a bracket may be multiplied by two or more figures inside a bracket, linked by addition or subtraction signs. Here is an example.

$5(6 + 8) = 5 \times (6 + 8) = 5 \times 6 + 5 \times 8 = 70$

This is the same as $5(14) = 5 \times 14 = 70$

The multiplication sign after the 5 can be omitted, as shown here $(5(6 + 8))$, but there is no harm in putting it in $(5 \times (6 + 8))$ if you want to.

Similarly:

$5(8 - 6) = 5(2) = 10$; or
$5 \times 8 - 5 \times 6 = 10$

When two sets of figures linked by addition or subtraction signs within brackets are multiplied together, each figure in one bracket is multiplied in turn by every figure in the second bracket. Thus:

$(8 + 4)(7 + 2) = (12)(9) = 108$ or
$8 \times 7 + 8 \times 2 + 4 \times 7 + 4 \times 2 =$
$56 + 16 + 28 + 8 = 108$

3.2 Negative numbers

When a negative number (–p) is added to another number (q), the net effect is to subtract p from q.

    (a) $10 + (-6) = 10 - 6 = 4$

    (b) $-10 + (-6) = -10 - 6 = -16$

When a negative number (-p) is subtracted from another number (q), the net effect is to add p to q.

    (a) $12 - (-8) = 12 + 8 = 20$

    (b) $-12 - (-8) = -12 + 8 = -4$

When a negative number is multiplied or divided by another negative number, the result is a positive number.

    $-8 \times (-4) = +32$

    $-18/(-3) = +6$

If there is only one negative number in a multiplication or division, the result is negative.

    $-8 \times 4 \quad = -32$

    $3 \times (-2) \quad = -6$

    $12/(-4) \quad = -3$

    $-20/5 \quad = -4$

Question

Negative numbers

Work out the following.

(a) $(72 - 8) - (-3 + 1)$

(b) $\dfrac{88 + 8}{12} + \dfrac{(29 - 11)}{-2}$

(c) $8(2 - 5) - (4 - (-8))$

(d) $\dfrac{-36}{9 - 3} - \dfrac{84}{3 - 10} - \dfrac{-81}{3}$

Answer

(a) $64 - (-2) = 64 + 2 = 66$

(b) $8 + (-9) = -1$

(c) $-24 - (12) = -36$

(d) $-6 - (-12) - (-27) = -6 + 12 + 27 = 33$

3.3 Reciprocals

The **reciprocal** of a number is just 1 divided by that number. For example, the reciprocal of 2 is 1 divided by 2, ie ½.

3.4 Extra symbols

You will come across several mathematical signs in this book and there are five which you should learn right away.

(a)   > means 'greater than'. So 46 > 29 is true, but 40 > 86 is false.

(b)   ≥ means 'is greater than or equal to'. So 4 ≥ 3 and 4 ≥ 4.

(c)   < means ' is less than'. So 29 < 46 is true, but 86 < 40 is false.

(d)   ≤ means ' is less than or equal to'. So 7 ≤ 8 and 7 ≤ 7.

(e)   ≠ means 'is not equal to'. So we could write 100.004 ≠ 100.

4 Percentages and ratios

4.1 Percentages and ratios

Percentages are used to indicate the **relative size** or **proportion** of items, rather than their absolute size. For example, if one office employs ten accountants, six secretaries and four supervisors, the **absolute** values of staff numbers and the *percentage* of the total work force in each type would be as follows.

	Accountants	Secretaries	Supervisors	Total
Absolute numbers	10	6	4	20
Percentages	50%	30%	20%	100%

The idea of percentages is that the whole of something can be thought of as 100%. The whole of a cake, for example, is 100%. If you share it out equally with a friend, you will get half each, or $^{100\%}/_2$ = 50% each.

To turn a percentage into a fraction or decimal you divide by 100. To turn a fraction or decimal back into a percentage you multiply by 100%. Consider the following.

(a) $0.16 = 0.16 \times 100\% = 16\%$

(b) $^4/_5 = {}^4/_5 \times 100\% = {}^{400}/_5\% = 80\%$

(c) $40\% = {}^{40}/_{100} = {}^2/_5 = 0.4$

There are two main types of situations involving percentages.

(a)   You may be required to calculate a percentage of a figure, having been given the percentage.

       Question: What is 40% of $64?

       Answer: 40% of $64 = 0.4 × $64 = $25.60.

(b)   You may be required to state what percentage one figure is of another, so that you have to work out the percentage yourself.

       Question: What is $16 as a percentage of $64?

       Answer: $16 as a percentage of $64 $= \dfrac{16}{64} \times 100\% = \dfrac{1}{4} \times 100\% = 25\%$

       In other words, put the $16 as a fraction of the $64, and then multiply by 100%.

4.2 Proportions

A **proportion** means writing a percentage as a proportion of 1 (that is, as a decimal).

100% can be thought of as the whole, or 1. 50% is half of that, or 0.5. Consider the following.

       Question: There are 14 women in an audience of 70. What proportion of the audience are men?

       Answer: Number of men   =   70 − 14 = 56

               Proportion of men $= \dfrac{56}{70} = \dfrac{8}{10} = 80\% = 0.8$

(a) $^8/_{10}$ or $^4/_5$ is the **fraction** of the audience made up by men.

(b)   80% is the **percentage** of the audience made up by men.

(c)   0.8 is the **proportion** of the audience made up by men.

4.3 Ratios

Suppose Tom has $12 and Dick has $8. The **ratio** of Tom's cash to Dick's cash is 12:8. This can be cancelled down, just like a fraction, to 3:2.

Usually an examination question will pose the problem the other way around: Tom and Dick wish to share $20 out in the ratio 3:2. How much will each receive?

Because 3 + 2 = 5, we must divide the whole up into five equal parts, then give Tom three parts and Dick two parts.

(a) $20 ÷ 5 = $4 (so each part is $4)

(b)   Tom's share = 3 × $4 = $12

(c)   Dick's share = 2 × $4 = $8

(d)   **Check:** $12 + $8 = $20 (adding up the two shares in the answer gets us back to the $20 in the question).

This method of calculating ratios as amounts works no matter how many ratios are involved. Here is another example.

Question: A, B, C and D wish to share $600 in the ratio 6:1:2:3. How much will each receive?

Answer: (a)   Number of parts   =   6 + 1 + 2 + 3 = 12.

(b)   Value of each part   = $600 ÷ 12 = $50

(c)   A: 6 × $50   = $300
B: 1 × $50   = $50
C: 2 × $50   = $100
D   3 × $50   = $150

(d)   *Check:* $300 + $50 + $100 + $150 = $600.

Question   Ratios

(a)   Peter and Paul wish to share $60 in the ratio 7 : 5. How much will each receive?

(b)   Bill and Ben own 300 and 180 flower pots respectively. What is the ratio of Ben's pots: Bill's pots?

(c)   Tom, Dick and Harry wish to share out $800. Calculate how much each would receive if the ratio used was:

(i)   3 : 2 : 5;

(ii)   5 : 3 : 2;

(iii)   3 : 1 : 1.

(d)   Lynn and Laura share out a certain sum of money in the ratio 4 : 5, and Laura ends up with $6.

(i)   How much was shared out in the first place?

(ii)   How much would have been shared out if Laura had got $6 and the ratio had been 5 : 4 instead of 4 : 5?

Answer

(a)   There are 7 + 5 = 12 parts
       Each part is worth $60 ÷ 12 = $5
       Peter receives 7 × $5 = $35
       Paul receives 5 × $5 = $25

(b)   Ben's pots : Bill's pots = 180 : 300 = 3 : 5

(c)   (i)   Total parts = 10
           Each part is worth $800 ÷ 10 = $80
           Tom gets   3 × $80 = $240
           Dick gets   2 × $80 = $160
           Harry gets   5 × $80 = $400

      (ii)   Same parts as (i) but in a different order.
           Tom gets $400
           Dick gets $240
           Harry gets $160

      (iii) Total parts = 5
           Each part is worth $800 ÷ 5 = $160
           Therefore Tom gets $480
           Dick and Harry each get $160

(d)   (i)   Laura's share = $6 = 5 parts
           Therefore one part is worth $6 ÷ 5 = $1.20
           Total of 9 parts shared out originally
           Therefore total was 9 × $1.20 = = $10.80

      (ii)   Laura's share = $6 = 4 parts
           Therefore one part is worth $6 ÷ 4 = $1.50
           Therefore original total was 9 × $1.50 = $13.50

5 Roots and powers

5.1 Square roots

The square root of a number is a value which, when multiplied by itself, equals the original number.

$$\sqrt{9} = 3, \text{ since } 3 \times 3 = 9$$

Similarly, the cube root of a number is the value which, when multiplied by itself twice, equals the original number.

$$\sqrt[3]{64} = 4, \text{ since } 4 \times 4 \times 4 = 64$$

The nth root of a number is a value which, when multiplied by itself (n – 1) times, equals the original number.

5.2 Powers

Powers work the other way round.
Thus the 6th power of $2 = 2^6 = 2 \times 2 \times 2 \times 2 \times 2 \times 2 = 64$.

Similarly, $3^4 = 3 \times 3 \times 3 \times 3 = 81$.

Since $\sqrt{9} = 3$, it also follows that $3^2 = 9$, and since $\sqrt[3]{64} = 4$, $4^3 = 64$.

When a number with an index (a 'to the power of' value) is multiplied by the *same* number with the same or a different index, the result is that number to the power of the sum of the indices.

(a) $5^2 \times 5 = 5^2 \times 5^1 = 5^{(2+1)} = 5^3 = 125$

(b) $4^3 \times 4^3 = 4^{(3+3)} = 4^6 = 4,096$

Similarly, when a number with an index is divided by the *same* number with the same or a different index, the result is that number to the power of the first index minus the second index.

(a) $6^4 \div 6^3 = 6^{(4-3)} = 6^1 = 6$

(b) $7^8 \div 7^6 = 7^{(8-6)} = 7^2 = 49$

Any figure to the power of zero equals one. $1^0 = 1$, $2^0 = 1$, $3^0 = 1$, $4^0 = 1$ and so on.

Similarly, $8^2 \div 8^2 = 8^{(2-2)} = 8^0 = 1$

An index can be a fraction, as in $16^{\frac{1}{2}}$. What $16^{\frac{1}{2}}$ means is the square root of $16(\sqrt{16}$ or 4). If we multiply $16^{\frac{1}{2}}$ by $16^{\frac{1}{2}}$ we get $16^{(\frac{1}{2}+\frac{1}{2})}$ which equals 16^1 and thus 16.

Similarly, $216^{\frac{1}{3}}$ is the cube root of 216 (which is 6) because $216^{\frac{1}{3}} \times 216^{\frac{1}{3}} \times 216^{\frac{1}{3}} = 216^{(\frac{1}{3}+\frac{1}{3}+\frac{1}{3})}$ $= 216^1 = 216$.

An index can be a negative value. The negative sign represents a reciprocal. Thus 2^{-1} is the reciprocal of, or one over, 2^1

$= \dfrac{1}{2^1} = \dfrac{1}{2}$

5.3 Example: Roots and powers

(a) $2^{-2} = \dfrac{1}{2^2} = \dfrac{1}{4}$ and $2^{-3} = \dfrac{1}{2^3} = \dfrac{1}{8}$

(b) $5^{-6} = \dfrac{1}{5^6} = \dfrac{1}{15,625}$

(c) $4^5 \times 4^{-2} = 4^5 \times \dfrac{1}{4^2} = 4^{5-2} = 4^3 = 64$

When we multiply or divide by a number with a negative index, the rules previously stated still apply.

(a) $9^2 \times 9^{-2} = 9^{(2+(-2))} = 9^0 = 1$ (That is, $9^2 \times \dfrac{1}{9^2} = 1$)

(b) $4^5 \div 4^{-2} = 4^{(5-(-2))} = 4^7 = 16,384$

(c) $3^8 \times 3^{-5} = 3^{(8-5)} = 3^3 = 27$

(d) $3^{-5} \div 3^{-2} = 3^{-5-(-2)} = 3^{-3} = \dfrac{1}{3^3} = \dfrac{1}{27}$. (This could be re-expressed as $\dfrac{1}{3^5} \div \dfrac{1}{3^2} = \dfrac{1}{3^5} \times 3^2 = \dfrac{1}{3^3}$.)

Question   Calculations

Work out the following, using your calculator as necessary.

(a) $(18.6)^{2.6}$

(b) $(18.6)^{-2.6}$

(c) $\sqrt[2.6]{18.6}$

(d) $(14.2)^4 \times (14.2)^{\frac{1}{4}}$

(e) $(14.2)^4 + (14.2)^{\frac{1}{4}}$

Answer

(a) $(18.6)^{2.6} = 1,998.64$

(b) $(18.6)^{-2.6} = (\frac{1}{18.6})^{2.6} = 0.0005$

(c) $\sqrt[2.6]{18.6} = 3.078$

(d) $(14.2)^4 \times (14.2)^{\frac{1}{4}} = (14.2)^{4.25} = 78,926.98$

(e) $(14.2)^4 + (14.2)^{\frac{1}{4}} = 40,658.69 + 1.9412 = 40,660.6312$

6 Equations

6.1 Introduction

So far all our problems have been formulated entirely in terms of specific numbers. However, think back to when you were calculating powers with your calculator earlier in this chapter. You probably used the x^y key on your calculator. x and y stood for whichever numbers we happened to have in our problem, for example, 3 and 4 if we wanted to work out 3^4. When we use letters like this to stand for any numbers we call them **variables**. Today when we work out 3^4, x stands for 3. Tomorrow, when we work out 7^2, x will stand for 7: its value can vary.

The use of variables enables us to state general truths about mathematics.

For example:

$$x = x$$
$$x^2 = x \times x$$

If $y = 0.5 \times x$, then $x = 2 \times y$

These will be true **whatever** values x and y have. For example, let $y = 0.5 \times x$

If $y = 3$, $x = 2 \times y = 6$
If $y = 7$, $x = 2 \times y = 14$
If $y = 1$, $x = 2 \times y = 2$, and so on for any other choice of a value for y.

We can use variables to build up useful **formulae**. We can then put in values for the variables, and get out a value for something we are interested in.

Let us consider an example. For a business, profit = revenue – costs. Since revenue = selling price $\times$ units sold, we can say that

profit = selling price $\times$ units sold – costs.

'Selling price $\times$ units sold – costs' is a **formula** for profit.

We can then use single letters to make the formula quicker to write.

Let   x = profit
        p = selling price
        u = units sold
        c = cost

Then $x = p \times u - c$.

If we are then told that in a particular month, p = \$5, u = 30 and c = \$118, we can find out the month's profit.

Profit   = $x = p \times u - c = \$5 \times 30 - \$118$
          = $\$150 - \$118 = \$32$.

It is usual when writing formulae to leave out multiplication signs between letters. Thus $p \times u - c$ can be written as $pu - c$. We will also write (for example) 2x instead of $2 \times x$.

6.2 Equations

In the above example, $pu - c$ was a formula for profit. If we write $x = pu - c$, we have written an equation. It says that one thing (profit, x) is equal to another ($pu - c$).

Sometimes, we are given an equation with numbers filled in for all but one of the variables. The problem is then to find the number which should be filled in for the last variable. This is called **solving** the equation.

(a)   Returning to $x = pu - c$, we could be told that for a particular month p = \$4, u = 60 and c = \$208. We would then have the **equation** $x = \$4 \times 60 - \$208$. We can solve this easily by working out $\$4 \times 60 - \$208 = \$240 - \$208 = \$32$. Thus x = \$32.

(b)   On the other hand, we might have been told that in a month when profits were \$172, 50 units were sold and the selling price was \$7. The thing we have not been told is the month's costs, c. We can work out c by writing out the equation.

$\$172 = \$7 \times 50 - c$
$\$172 = \$350 - c$

We need c to be such that when it is taken away from \$350 we have \$172 left. With a bit of trial and error, we can get to c = \$178.

Trial and error takes far too long in more complicated cases, however, and we will now go on to look at a rule for solving equations, which will take us directly to the answers we want.

6.3 The rule for solving equations

To solve an equation, we need to get it into the form:

Unknown variable = something with just numbers in it, which we can work out.

We therefore want to get the unknown variable on one side of the = sign, and everything else on the other side.

The rule is that you can do what you like to one side of an equation, so long as you do the same thing to the other side straightaway. The two sides are equal, and they will stay equal so long as you treat them in the same way.

For example, you can do any of the following.

       Add 37 to both sides.
       Subtract 3x from both sides.
       Multiply both sides by –4.329.
       Divide both sides by (x + 2).
       Take the reciprocal of both sides.
       Square both sides.
       Take the cube root of both sides.

We can do any of these things to an equation either before or after filling in numbers for the variables for which we have values.

(a)   In Paragraph 6.2, we had

$$\$172 = \$350 - c.$$

We can then get

$\$172 + c = \$350$	(add c to each side)
$c = \$350 - \$172$	(subtract $172 from each side)
$c = \$178$	(work out the right hand side).

(b)
$450 = 3x + 72$	(initial equation: x unknown)
$450 - 72 = 3x$	(subtract 72 from each side)
$\dfrac{450 - 72}{3} = x$	(divide each side by 3)
$126 = x$	(work out the left hand side).

(c)
$3y + 2 = 5y - 7$	(initial equation: y unknown)
$3y + 9 = 5y$	(add 7 to each side)
$9 = 2y$	(subtract 3y from each side)
$4.5 = y$	(divide each side by 2).

(d)
$\dfrac{\sqrt{3x^2 + x}}{2\sqrt{x}} = 7$		(initial equation: x unknown)
$\dfrac{3x^2 + x}{4x} =$	49	(square each side)
$(3x + 1)/4 =$	49	(cancel x in the numerator and the denominator of the left hand side: this does not affect the value of the left hand side, so we do not need to change the right hand side)
$3x + 1 =$	196	(multiply each side by 4)
$3x =$	195	(subtract 1 from each side)
$x =$	65	(divide each side by 3).

(e)   Our example in Paragraph 6.1 was $x = pu - c$. We could change this, so as to give a formula for p.

$x = pu - c$	
$x + c = pu$	(add c to each side)
$\dfrac{x + c}{u} = p$	(divide each side by u)
$p = \dfrac{x + c}{u}$	(swap the sides for ease of reading).

Given values for x, c and u we can now find p. We have *re-arrange*d the equation to give p *in terms of* x, c and u.

(f)   Given that $y = \sqrt{3x + 7}$, we can get an equation giving x in terms of y.

$y = \sqrt{3x + 7}$	
$y^2 = 3x + 7$	(square each side)
$y^2 - 7 = 3x$	(subtract 7 from each side)
$x = \dfrac{y^2 - 7}{3}$	(divide each side by 3, and swap the sides for ease of reading).

(g) Given that $7 + g = \dfrac{5}{3\sqrt{h}}$, we can get an equation giving h in terms of g.

$$7 + g = \frac{5}{3\sqrt{h}}$$

$$\frac{1}{7+g} = \frac{3\sqrt{h}}{5} \qquad \text{(take the reciprocal of each side)}$$

$$\frac{5}{7+g} = 3\sqrt{h} \qquad \text{(multiply each side by 5)}$$

$$\frac{5}{3(7+g)} = \sqrt{h} \qquad \text{(divide each side by 3)}$$

$$h = \frac{25}{9(7+g)^2} \qquad \text{(square each side, and swap the sides for ease of reading).}$$

In equations, you may come across expressions like $3(x + 4y - 2)$ (that is, $3 \times (x + 4y - 2)$). These can be re-written in separate bits without the brackets, simply by multiplying the number outside the brackets by each item inside them. Thus $3(x + 4y - 2) = 3x + 12y - 6$.

Question

Find the value of x in each of the following equations.

(a) $47x + 256 = 52x$

(b) $4\sqrt{x} + 32 = 40.6718$

(c) $\dfrac{1}{3x + 4} = \dfrac{5}{2.7x - 2}$

(d) $x^3 = 4.913$

(e) $34x - 7.6 = (17x - 3.8) \times (x + 12.5)$

Answer

(a)
$$\begin{aligned}
47x + 256 &= 52x \\
256 &= 5x \qquad \text{(subtract 47x from each side)} \\
51.2 &= x \qquad \text{(divide each side by 5).}
\end{aligned}$$

(b)
$$\begin{aligned}
4\sqrt{x} + 32 &= 40.6718 \\
4\sqrt{x} &= 8.6718 \qquad \text{(subtract 32 from each side)} \\
\sqrt{x} &= 2.16795 \qquad \text{(divide each side by 4)} \\
x &= 4.7 \qquad \text{(square each side).}
\end{aligned}$$

(c)
$$\frac{1}{3x + 4} = \frac{5}{2.7x - 2}$$

$$3x + 4 = \frac{2.7x - 2}{5} \qquad \text{(take the reciprocal of each side)}$$

$$\begin{aligned}
15x + 20 &= 2.7x - 2 \qquad \text{(multiply each side by 5)} \\
12.3x &= -22 \qquad \text{(subtract 20 and subtract 2.7x from each side)} \\
x &= -1.789 \qquad \text{(divide each side by 12.3).}
\end{aligned}$$

(d)
$$\begin{aligned}
x^3 &= 4.913 \\
x &= 1.7 \qquad \text{(take the cube root of each side).}
\end{aligned}$$

(e) $34x - 7.6 = (17x - 3.8) \times (x + 12.5)$

This one is easy if you realise that $17 \times 2 = 34$ and $3.8 \times 2 = 7.6$, so

$2 \times (17x - 3.8) = 34x - 7.6.$

We can then divide each side by $17x - 3.8$ to get

$$2 = x + 12.5$$
$$-10.5 = x \text{ (subtract 12.5 from each side).}$$

Question

Re-arrange

(a) Re-arrange $x = (3y - 20)^2$ to get an expression for y in terms of x.

(b) Re-arrange $2(y - 4) - 4(x^2 + 3) = 0$ to get an expression for x in terms of y.

Answer

(a) $x = (3y - 20)^2$

$\sqrt{x} = 3y - 20$ (take the square root of each side)

$20 + \sqrt{x} = 3y$ (add 20 to each side)

$y = \dfrac{20 + \sqrt{x}}{3}$ (divide each side by 3, and swap the sides for ease of reading).

(b) $2(y - 4) - 4(x^2 + 3) = 0$

$2(y - 4) = 4(x^2 + 3)$ (add $4(x^2 + 3)$ to each side)

$0.5(y - 4) = x^2 + 3$ (divide each side by 4)

$0.5(y - 4) - 3 = x^2$ (subtract 3 from each side)

$x = \sqrt{0.5(y - 4) - 3}$ (take the square root of each side, and swap the sides for ease of reading)

$x = \sqrt{0.5y - 5}$ (simplify $0.5(y-4) - 3$: this is an optional last step).

---

7 Linear equations

7.1 Introduction

A linear equation has the general form $y = a + bx$

where   y   is the dependent variable whose value depends upon the value of x;

       x   is the independent variable whose value helps to determine the corresponding value of y;

       a   is a constant, that is, a fixed amount;

       b   is also a constant, being the coefficient of x (that is, the number by which the value of x should be multiplied to derive the value of y).

Let us establish some basic linear equations. Suppose that it takes Joe Bloggs 15 minutes to walk one mile. How long does it take Joe to walk two miles? Obviously it takes him 30 minutes. How did you calculate the time? You probably thought that if the distance is doubled then the time must be doubled. How do you explain (in words) the relationships between the distance walked and the time taken? One explanation would be that every mile walked takes 15 minutes.

That is an explanation in words. Can you explain the relationship with an equation?

First you must decide which is the dependent variable and which is the independent variable. In other words, does the time taken depend on the number of miles walked or does the number of miles walked depend on the time it takes to walk a mile? Obviously the time depends on the distance. We can therefore let y be the dependent variable (time taken in minutes) and x be the independent variable (distance walked in miles).

We now need to determine the constants a and b. There is no fixed amount so a = 0. To ascertain b, we need to establish the number of times by which the value of x should be multiplied to derive the value of y. Obviously y = 15x where y is in minutes. If y were in hours then y = $^x/_4$.

7.2 Example: Deriving a linear equation

A salesman's weekly wage is made up of a basic weekly wage of $100 and commission of $5 for every item he sells. Derive an equation which describes this scenario.

Solution

$$
\begin{aligned}
x &= \text{number of items sold} \\
y &= \text{weekly wage} \\
a &= \$100 \\
b &= \$5 \\
\therefore \quad y &= 5x + 100
\end{aligned}
$$

Note that the letters used in an equation do not have to be x and y. It may be sensible to use other letters, for example we could use p and q if we are describing the relationship between the price of an item and the quantity demanded.

8 Linear equations and graphs

8.1 The rules for drawing graphs

One of the clearest ways of presenting the relationship between two variables is by plotting a linear equation as a straight line on a graph.

A graph has a horizontal axis, the x axis and a vertical axis, the y axis. The x axis is used to represent the independent variable and the y axis is used to represent the dependent variable.

If calendar time is one variable, it is always treated as the independent variable. When time is represented on the x axis of a graph, we have a time series.

(a)   If the data to be plotted are derived from calculations, rather than given in the question, make sure that there is a neat table in your working papers.

(b)   The scales on each axis should be selected so as to use as much of the graph paper as possible. Do not cramp a graph into one corner.

(c)   In some cases it is best not to start a scale at zero so as to avoid having a large area of wasted paper. This is perfectly acceptable as long as the scale adopted is clearly shown on the axis. One way of avoiding confusion is to break the axis concerned, as follows.

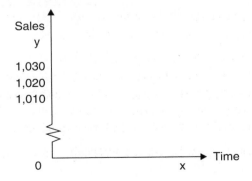

(d)   The scales on the x axis and the y axis should be marked. For example, if the y axis relates to amounts of money, the axis should be marked at every $1, or $100 or $1,000 interval or at whatever other interval is appropriate. The axes must be marked with values to give the reader an idea of how big the values on the graph are.

(e)   A graph should not be overcrowded with too many lines. Graphs should always give a clear, neat impression.

(f)   A graph must always be given a title, and where appropriate, a reference should be made to the source of data.

8.2 Example: Drawing graphs

Plot the graphs for the following relationships.

(a) $y = 4x + 5$
(b) $y = 10 - x$

In each case consider the range of values from $x = 0$ to $x = 10$

Solution

The first step is to draw up a table for each equation. Although the problem mentions $x = 0$ to $x = 10$, it is not necessary to calculate values of y for $x = 1, 2, 3$ etc. A graph of a linear equation can actually be drawn from just two (x, y) values but it is always best to calculate a number of values in case you make an arithmetical error. We have calculated six values. You could settle for three or four.

(a)		(b)	
x	y	x	y
0	5	0	10
2	13	2	8
4	21	4	6
6	29	6	4
8	37	8	2
10	45	10	0

(a)

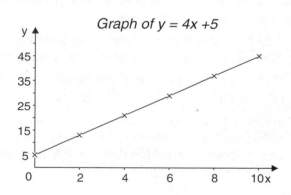

Graph of y = 4x +5

BPP
LEARNING MEDIA

(b)

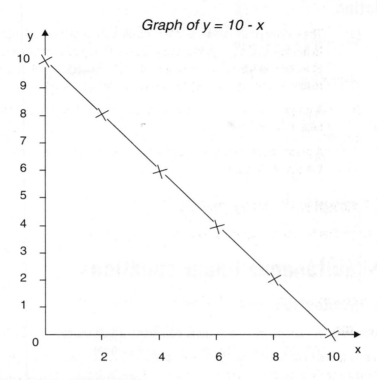

Graph of y = 10 - x

8.3 The intercept and the slope

The graph of a linear equation is determined by two things, the gradient (or slope) of the straight line and the point at which the straight line crosses the y axis.

The point at which the straight line crosses the y axis is known as the intercept. Look back at Paragraph 8.2(a). The intercept of $y = 4x + 5$ is $(0, 5)$ and the intercept of $y = 10 - x$ is $(0, 10)$. It is no coincidence that the intercept is the same as the constant represented by a in the general form of the equation $y = a + bx$. a is the value y takes when $x = 0$, in other words a constant, and so is represented on a graph by the point $(0, a)$.

The gradient of the graph of a linear equation is $(y_2 - y_1)/(x_2 - x_1)$ where (x_1, y_1) and (x_1, x_2) are two points on the straight line.

The slope of $y = 4x + 5 = (21 - 13)/(4-2) = 8/2 = 4$ where $(x_1, y_1) = (2, 13)$ and $(x_2, y_2) = (4,21)$

The slope of $y = 10 - x = (6 - 8)/(4 - 2) = -2/2 = -1$.

Note that the gradient of $y = 4x + 5$ is positive whereas the gradient of $y = 10 - x$ is negative. A positive gradient slopes upwards from left to right whereas a negative gradient slopes downwards from right to left. The greater the value of the gradient, the steeper the slope.

Just as the intercept can be found by inspection of the linear equation, so can the gradient. It is represented by the coefficient of x (b in the general form of the equation). The slope of the graph $y = 7x - 3$ in therefore 7 and the slope of the graph $y = 3,597 - 263 x$ is -263.

8.4 Example: intercept and slope

Find the intercept and slope of the graphs of the following linear equations.

(a) $y = \dfrac{x}{10} - \dfrac{1}{3}$

(b) $4y = 16x - 12$

Solution

(a)   Intercept $= a = -\dfrac{1}{3}$ ie $(0, -\dfrac{1}{3})$

Slope $= b = \dfrac{1}{10}$

(b) $4y = 16x - 12$

Equation must be form $y = a + bx$

$y = -\dfrac{12}{4} + \dfrac{16}{4} \, x = -3 + 4x$

Intercept $= a = -3$ ie $(0, -3)$

Slope $= 4$

9 Simultaneous linear equations

9.1 Introduction

Simultaneous equations are two or more equations which are satisfied by the same variable values. For example, we might have the following two linear equations.

$y = 3x + 16$
$2y = x + 72$

There are two unknown values, x and y, and there are two different equations which both involve x and y. There are as many equations as there are unknowns and so we can find the values of x and y.

9.2 Graphical solution

One way of finding a solution is by a graph. If both equations are satisfied together, the values of x and y must be those where the straight line graphs of the two equations intersect.

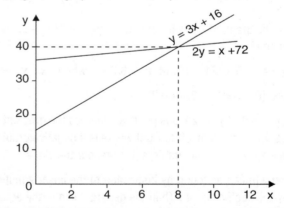

Since both equations are satisfied, the values of x and y must lie on both the lines. Since this happens only once, at the intersection of the lines, the value of x must be 8, and of y 40.

9.3 Algebraic solution

A more common method of solving simultaneous equations is by algebra.

(a)   Returning to the original equations, we have:

$y = 3x + 16$ (1)
$2y = x + 72$ (2)

BPP
LEARNING MEDIA

(b)　Rearranging these, we have:

$y - 3x = 16$ .... (3)
$2y - x = 72$ .... (4)

(c)　If we now multiply equation (4) by 3, so that the coefficient for x becomes the same as in equation (3) we get:

$6y - 3x = 216$ .... (5)
$y - 3x = 16$ .... (3)

(d)　Subtracting (3) from (5) means that we lose x and we get:

$5y = 200$
$y = 40$

(e)　Substituting 40 for y in any equation, we can derive a value for x. Thus substituting in equation (4) we get:

$2(40) - x = 72$
$80 - 72 = x$
$8 = x$

(f)　The solution is y = 40, x = 8.

9.4 Example: Simultaneous equations

Solve the following simultaneous equations using algebra.

$5x + 2y = 34$
$x + 3y = 25$

Solution

$5x + 2y = 34$	(1)	
$x + 3y = 25$	(2)	
$5x + 15y = 125$	(3)	$5 \times (2)$
$13y = 91$	(4)	$(3) - (1)$
$y = 7$		
$x + 21 = 25$		Substitute into (2)
$x = 25 - 21$		
$x = 4$		

The solution is x = 4, y = 7.

Question ▮▮▮▮▮▮▮▮▮▮▮▮▮▮▮▮▮▮▮▮▮▮▮▮▮▮▮▮　　　　　　　Simultaneous equations

Solve the following simultaneous equations to derive values for x and y.

$4x + 3y = 23$ .... (1)
$5x - 4y = -10$ .... (2)

Answer

(a)   If we multiply equation (1) by 4 and equation (2) by 3, we will obtain coefficients of +12 and −12 for y in our two products.

$16x + 12y = 92$ (3)
$15x − 12y = −30$ (4)

(b)   Add (3) and (4).

$31x = 62$
$x = 2$

(c)   Substitute $x = 2$ into (1)

$$4(2) + 3y = 23$$
$$3y = 23 − 8 = 15$$
$$y = 5$$

(d)   The solution is $x = 2$, $y = 5$.

Appendix
Exam formulae

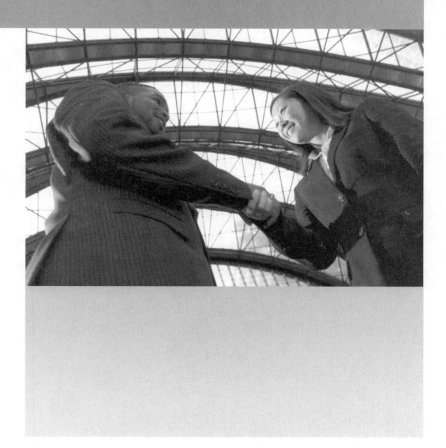

Regression analysis

$$a = \frac{\sum y}{n} - \frac{b\sum x}{n}$$

$$b = \frac{n\sum xy - \sum x \sum y}{n\sum x^2 - (\sum x)^2}$$

$$r = \frac{n\sum xy - \sum x \sum y}{\sqrt{[n\sum x^2 - (\sum x)^2][n\sum y^2 - (\sum y)^2]}}$$

Economic order quantity $= \sqrt{\dfrac{2C_0 D}{C_h}}$

Economic batch quantity $= \sqrt{\dfrac{2C_0 D}{C_h \left(1 - \dfrac{D}{R}\right)}}$

Exam question bank

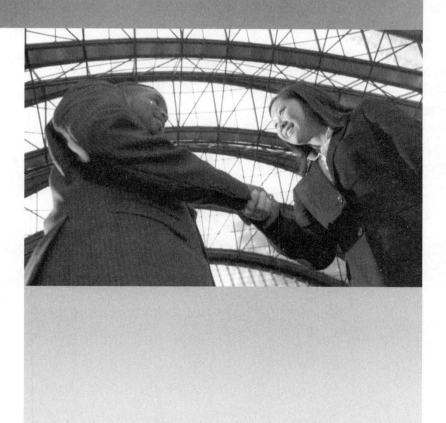

1 Information for management

(a)   Which of the following statements is/are true?

      I   Information is the raw material for data processing
      II   External sources of information include an organisation's financial accounting records
      III   The main objective of a non-profit making organisation is usually to provide goods and services

      A   I and III only
      B   I, II and III
      C   II and III only
      D   III only   **(2 marks)**

(b)   Which of the following statements is not true?

      A   Management accounts detail the performance of an organisation over a defined period and the state of affairs at the end of that period

      B   There is no legal requirement to prepare management accounts

      C   The format of management accounts is entirely at management discretion   **(1 mark)**

(c)   Which of the following could higher level management carry out?

      A   taking long-term decisions
      B   taking short-term decisions
      C   taking long-term and short-term decisions   **(1 mark)**

(d)   Which of the following statements is not correct?

      A   Financial accounting information can be used for internal reporting purposes

      B   Routine information can be used to make decisions regarding both the long term and the short term

      C   Management accounting provides information relevant to decision making, planning, control and evaluation of performances

      D   Cost accounting can only be used to provide inventory valuations for internal reporting
      (2 marks)

2 Cost classification

(a)   Which of the following items might be a suitable cost unit within the accounts payable department of a company?

      (i)   Postage cost
      (ii)   Invoice processed
      (iii)   Supplier account

      A   Item (i) only
      B   Item (ii) only
      C   Item (iii) only
      D   Items (ii) and (iii) only   **(2 marks)**

(b)   Which of the following are direct expenses?

      (i)   The cost of special designs, drawing or layouts
      (ii)   The hire of tools or equipment for a particular job
      (iii)   Salesman's wages
      (iv)   Rent, rates and insurance of a factory

A   (i) and (ii)
B   (i) and (iii)
C   (i) and (iv)
D   (iii) and (iv)   **(2 marks)**

(c)   Which of the following would be appropriate cost units for a passenger coach company?

	Appropriate	Not appropriate
(a) Vehicle cost per passenger-kilometre		
(b) Fuel cost for each vehicle per kilometre		
(c) Fixed cost per kilometre		

(2 marks)

3 Cost behaviour

(a)   Variable costs are conventionally deemed to

A   be constant per unit of output
B   vary per unit of output as production volume changes
C   be constant in total when production volume changes   **(1 mark)**

(b)   The following is a graph of total cost against level of activity.

To which one of the following costs does the graph correspond?

A   Photocopier rental costs, where a fixed rental is payable up to a certain number of copies each period. If the number of copies exceeds this amount, a constant charge per copy is made for all subsequent copies during that period.

B   Vehicle hire costs, where a constant rate is charged per mile travelled, up to a maximum monthly payment regardless of the miles travelled.

C   Supervisor salary costs, where one supervisor is needed for every five employees added to the staff.

D   The cost of direct materials, where the unit rate per kg purchased reduces when the level of purchases reaches a certain amount.

(c)   Identify which type of cost is being described in (a)-(d) below.

VARIABLE COST	FIXED COST	STEPPED FIXED COST	SEMI-VARIABLE COST

(a)   This type of cost stays the same, no matter how many products you produce

(b)   This type of cost increases as you produce more products. The sum of these costs are also known as the marginal cost of a product

(c)   This type of cost is fixed but only within certain levels of activity

(d)   This type of cost contains both fixed and variable elements

(2 marks)

4 Correlation and regression

(a)   A company's weekly costs ($C) were plotted against production level (P) for the last 50 weeks and a regression line calculated to be C = 1,000 + 250P. Which statement about the breakdown of weekly costs is true?

A   Fixed costs are $1,000. Variable costs per unit are $5.
B   Fixed costs are $250. Variable costs per unit are $4.
C   Fixed costs are $250. Variable costs per unit are $1,000.
D   Fixed costs are $1,000. Variable costs per unit are $250.   **(2 marks)**

(b)   The value of the correlation coefficient between x and y is 0.9. Which of the following is correct?

A   There is a weak relationship between x and y

B   x is 90% of y

C   If the values of x and y were plotted on a graph, the line relating them would have a slope of 0.9

D   There is a very strong relationship between x and y   **(2 marks)**

5 Spreadsheets

(a)   A chart wizard can be used to generate graphs. Which type of chart would be best used to track a trend over time?

A   A pie chart
B   A line graph
C   A multiple bar chart
D   A radar chart   **(2 marks)**

(b)   **A macro** is used for occasional complicated tasks in spreadsheets.

True

False   **(1 mark)**

(c)   The following statements relate to spreadsheet formulae

I   Absolute cell references (B3) change when you copy formulae to other locations
II   The F4 key is used to change cell references from absolute to relative
III   Relative cell references ($B$3) stay the same when you copy formulae to other locations

Which statements are correct?

A   I and II only
B   I and III only
C   II and III only
D   II only   **(2 marks)**

Questions (d) to (f) refer to the spreadsheet shown below.

	A	B	C	D
1	Unit selling price	$65	Annual volume	10,000
2				
3	Seasonal variations			
4	Quarter 1	-20%		
5	Quarter 2	-35%		
6	Quarter 3	10%		
7	Quarter 4	45%		
8				
9	**Sales budgets**	Seasonal variations (units)	Quarterly volume	Quarterly turnover
10	Quarter 1			
11	Quarter 2			
12	Quarter 3			
13	Quarter 4			
14				

(d)   The cell B10 shows the seasonal variation in units for quarter 1. Which of the following would be a suitable formula for this cell?

A   =$D$1/4*B4
B   =(D1/4)*B4
C   =$D$1/4*B1
D   =D1/4*$B$4   **(2 marks)**

(e)   The cell C10 shows the sales volume in units for quarter 1. Which of the following would be a suitable formula for this cell?

A   =$D$1/4+B10
B   =D1/4+$B$10
C   =D1+B10
D   =($D$1/4)+B10   **(2 marks)**

(f)   The cell D10 shows the turnover in Quarter 1 Which of the following would be a suitable formula for this cell?

A   =D1*$B$1
B   =C10-B10
C   =C10*$B$1
D   =(C10+B10)*$B$1   **(2 marks)**

6 Material costs

(a) The following data relates to an item of raw material

Unit cost of raw material	$20
Usage per week	250 units
Cost of ordering material, per order	$400
Annual cost of holding inventory, as a % of cost	10%
Number of weeks in a year	48

What is the economic order quantity, to the nearest unit?

A   316 units
B   693 units
C   1,549 units
D   2,191 units   **(2 marks)**

(b) The following data relates to the stores ledger control account of Duckboard, a manufacturing company, for the month of October.

	$
Opening inventory	18,500
Closing inventory	16,100
Deliveries from suppliers	142,000
Returns to suppliers	2,300
Cost of indirect materials issued	25,200

The issue of direct materials would have been recorded in the cost accounts as follows.

			$	$
A	Debit	Stores ledger control account	119,200	
	Credit	Work in progress control account		119,200
B	Debit	Work in progress control account	119,200	
	Credit	Stores ledger control account		119,200
C	Debit	Stores ledger control account	116,900	
	Credit	Work in progress control account		116,900
D	Debit	Work in progress control account	116,900	
	Credit	Stores ledger control account		116,900

(2 marks)

7 Labour costs

(a) Gross wages incurred in department 1 in June were $54,000. The wages analysis shows the following summary breakdown of the gross pay.

	Paid to direct labour	Paid to indirect labour
	$	$
Ordinary time	25,185	11,900
Overtime: basic pay	5,440	3,500
premium	1,360	875
Shift allowance	2,700	1,360
Sick pay	1,380	300
	36,065	17,935

What is the direct wages cost for department 1 in June?

A $25,185
B $30,625
C $34,685
D $36,065   (2 marks)

(b)   The wages control account for A Co for February is shown below.

WAGES CONTROL ACCOUNT

	$		$
Bank	128,400	Work in progress control	79,400
Balance c/d	12,000	Production overhead control	61,000
	140,400		140,400
		Balance b/d	12,000

Which of the following statements about wages for February is *not* correct?

A   Wages paid during February amounted to $128,400
B   Wages for February were prepaid by $12,000
C   Direct wages cost incurred during February amounted to $79,400
D   Indirect wages cost incurred during February amounted to $61,000   (2 marks)

8 Overheads and absorption costing

A company absorbs overheads based on labour hours. Data for the latest period are as follows.

Budgeted labour hours	8,500
Budgeted overheads	$148,750
Actual labour hours	7,928
Actual overheads	$146,200

(a)   Based on the data given above, what is the labour hour overhead absorption rate?

A $17.20 per hour
B $17.50 per hour
C $18.44 per hour
D $18.76 per hour   (2 marks)

(b)   Based on the data given above, what is the amount of under-/over-absorbed overhead?

A $2,550 under-absorbed overhead
B $2,550 over-absorbed overhead
C $7,460 over-absorbed overhead
D $7,460 under-absorbed overhead   (2 marks)

(c)   The budgeted production overheads and other budget data of Eiffel Co are as follows.

	Production
Budget	dept X
Overhead cost	$36,000
Direct materials cost	$32,000
Direct labour cost	$40,000
Machine hours	10,000
Direct labour hours	18,000

What would be the absorption rate for Department X using the various bases of apportionment?

(a) % of direct material cost =

(b) % of direct labour cost =

(c) % of total direct cost =

(d) Rate per machine hour =

(e) Rate per direct labour hour =   **(2 marks)**

9 Marginal and absorption costing

(a) The overhead absorption rate for product Y is $2.50 per direct labour hour. Each unit of Y requires 3 direct labour hours. Stock of product Y at the beginning of the month was 200 units and at the end of the month was 250 units. What is the difference in the profits reported for the month using absorption costing compared with marginal costing?

A   The absorption costing profit would be $375 less
B   The absorption costing profit would be $125 greater
C   The absorption costing profit would be $375 greater
D   The absorption costing profit would be $1,875 greater   **(2 marks)**

(b) B Company makes a product which has a variable production cost of $21 per unit and a sales price of $39 per unit. At the beginning of 20X5, there was no opening inventory and sales during the year were 50,000 units. Fixed costs (production, administration, sales and distribution) totalled $328,000. Production was 70,000 units.

(a) The contribution per unit is $ [   ].   **(2 marks)**

(b) The profit per unit is $ [   ].   **(2 marks)**

10 Process costing

The following data relates to questions (a) and (b)

A chemical is manufactured in two processes, X and Y. Data for process Y for last month are as follows.

Material transferred from process X	2,000 litres @ $4 per litre
Conversion costs incurred	$12,250
Output transferred to finished goods	1,600 litres
Closing work in progress	100 litres

Normal loss is 10% of input. All losses are fully processed and have a scrap value of $4 per litre.

Closing work in progress is fully complete for material, but is only 50 per cent processed.

(a) What is the value of the completed output (to the nearest $)?

A $15,808
B $17,289
C $17,244
D $17,600   **(2 marks)**

(b) What is the value of the closing work in progress (to the nearest $)?

A $674
B $728
C $750
D $1,100   **(2 marks)**

(c)   20,000 litres of liquid were put into a process at the beginning of the month at a cost of $4,400. The output of finished product was 17,000 litres. The normal level of waste in this process is 20% and the waste which is identified at the end of the process can be sold at $0.50 per litre. Use this information to complete the process account below.

PROCESS ACCOUNT

	Litres	$		Litres	$
Materials			Normal waste		
Abnormal gains	_____	_____	Finished goods	_____	_____
	=====	=====		=====	=====

(2 marks)

(d)   A food manufacturing process has a normal wastage of 10% of input. In a period, 3,000 kg of material was input and there was an abnormal loss of 75 kg. No inventories are held at the beginning or end of the process.

The quantity of good production achieved was [   ] kg.   **(2 marks)**

(e)   A company makes a product, which passes through a single process.

Details of the process for the last period are as follows.

Materials	5,000 kg at 50c per kg
Labour	$700
Production overheads	200% of labour

Normal losses are 10% of input in the process, and without further processing any losses can be sold as scrap for 20c per kg.

The output for the period was 4,200 kg from the process.

There was no work in progress at the beginning or end of the period.

The value of the abnormal loss for the period is $ [   ]   **(2 marks)**

11 Joint products and by-products

(a)   SH Ltd manufactures three joint products and one by-product from a single process.

Data for May are as follows.

Opening and closing inventories	Nil
Raw materials input	$90,000
Conversion costs	$70,000

Output

		Units	Sales price $ per unit
Joint product	J	2,500	36
	K	3,500	40
	L	2,000	35
By-product M		4,000	1

By-product sales revenue is credited to the process account. Joint costs are apportioned on a physical units basis.

What were the full production costs of product K in May?

A $45,500
B $46,667
C $68,250
D $70,000   **(2 marks)**

(b)   Samakand Preparations operates a continuous process producing three products and one by-product. Output from the process for one month was as follows.

	Selling price per unit	Output
Joint product	$	Units
A	38	20,000
B	54	40,000
C	40	35,000
By-product		
D	4	20,000

Total output costs were $4,040,000.

The saleable value of the by-product is deducted from process costs before apportioning costs to each joint product. Using the sales revenue basis for allocating joint costs, the unit valuation for joint product B was (to 2 decimal places):

A $49.50
B $45.00
C $50.00
D $100.00   **(2 marks)**

12 Job, batch and service costing

(a)   Which of the following would be appropriate cost units for a transport business?

(i)   Cost per tonne-kilometre
(ii)   Fixed cost per kilometre
(iii)   Maintenance cost of each vehicle per kilometre

A   (i) only
B   (i) and (ii) only
C   (i) and (iii) only
D   All of them   **(2 marks)**

(b)   JC Co operates a job costing system. The company's standard net profit margin is 20 per cent of sales value.

The estimated costs for job B124 are as follows.

Direct materials   3 kg @ $5 per kg
Direct labour   4 hours @ $9 per hour

Production overheads are budgeted to be $240,000 for the period, to be recovered on the basis of a total of 30,000 labour hours.

Other overheads, related to selling, distribution and administration, are budgeted to be $150,000 for the period. They are to be recovered on the basis of the total budgeted production cost of $750,000 for the period.

The price to be quoted for job B124 is $ ☐   **(2 marks)**

(c)   In which of the following situation(s) will job costing normally be used?

☐   Production is continuous

☐   Production of the product can be completed in a single accounting period

☐   Production relates to a single special order   **(1 mark)**

(d) Consider the following features and identify whether they relate to job costing, contract costing, service costing or none of these costing methods.

J = Job costing
C = Contract costing
S = Service costing
N = None of these costing methods

(i) Production is carried out in accordance with the wishes of the customer

(ii) Work is usually of a relatively long duration

(iii) Work is usually undertaken on the contractor's premises

(iv) Costs are averaged over the units produced in the period

(v) It establishes the costs of services rendered

(2 marks)

(e) Ali Pali Ltd is a small jobbing company. Budgeted direct labour hours for the current year were 45,000 hours and budgeted direct wages costs were $180,000.

Job number 34679, a rush job for which overtime had to be worked by skilled employees, had the following production costs.

	$	$
Direct materials		2,000
Direct wages		
Normal rate (400 hrs)	2,000	
Overtime premium	500	
		2,500
Production overhead		4,000
		8,500

Production overhead is based on a direct labour hour rate

If production overhead had been based on a percentage of direct wages costs instead, the production cost of job number 34679 would have been:

A $5,500
B $9,000
C $10,250
D $10,750

(2 marks)

13 Budgeting

(a) What does the statement 'sales is the principal budget factor' mean?

A   The level of sales will determine the level of cash at the end of the period
B   The level of sales will determine the level of profit at the end of the period
C   The company's activities are limited by the level of sales it can achieve   **(1 mark)**

(b) When preparing a production budget, the quantity to be produced equals

A   sales quantity + opening inventory of finished goods + closing inventory of finished goods
B   sales quantity – opening inventory of finished goods + closing inventory of finished goods
C   sales quantity – opening inventory of finished goods – closing inventory of finished goods
D   sales quantity + opening inventory of finished goods – closing inventory of finished goods

(2 marks)

(c)   PQ Co plans to sell 24,000 units of product R next year. Opening inventory of R is expected to be 2,000 units and PQ Co plans to increase inventory by 25 per cent by the end of the year. How many units of product R should be produced next year?

A   23,500 units
B   24,000 units
C   24,500 units
D   30,000 units   **(2 marks)**

(d)   Each unit of product Alpha requires 3 kg of raw material. Next month's production budget for product Alpha is as follows.

Opening inventories:

Raw materials	15,000 kg
Finished units of Alpha	2,000 units
Budgeted sales of Alpha	60,000 units

Planned closing inventories:

Raw materials	7,000 kg
Finished units of Alpha	3,000 units

The number of kilograms of raw materials that should be purchased next month is:

A   172,000
B   175,000
C   183,000
D   191,000   **(2 marks)**

(e)   Budgeted sales of X for December are 18,000 units. At the end of the production process for X, 10% of production units are scrapped as defective. Opening inventories of X for December are budgeted to be 15,000 units and closing inventories will be 11,400 units. All inventories of finished goods must have successfully passed the quality control check. The production budget for X for December, in units is

A   12,960
B   14,400
C   15,840
D   16,000   **(2 marks)**

(f)   In a situation where there are no production resource limitations, which of the following must be available for the material usage budget to be completed? Tick all that apply.

(a)   Production volume from the production budget

(b)   Budgeted change in materials inventory

(c)   Standard material usage per unit   **(2 marks)**

(g)   If a company has no production resource limitations, in which order would the following budgets be prepared?

	Order
Material usage budget	
Sales budget	
Material purchase budget	
Finished goods inventory budget	
Production budget	
Material inventory budget	

(2 marks)

(h)

		True	False
(a)	Budgetary control procedures are useful only to maintain control over an organisation's expenditure		
(b)	A prerequisite of flexible budgeting is a knowledge of cost behaviour patterns		
(c)	Fixed budgets are not useful for control purposes		

(2 marks)

14 Standard costing

(a) Which of the following would *not* be used to estimate standard direct material prices?

A   The availability of bulk purchase discounts
B   Purchase contracts already agreed
C   The forecast movement of prices in the market
D   Performance standards in operation **(2 marks)**

(b) JC Co operates a bottling plant. The liquid content of a filled bottle of product T is 2 litres. During the filling process there is a 30% loss of liquid input due to spillage and evaporation. The standard price of the liquid is $1.20 per litre. The standard cost of the liquid per bottle of product T, to the nearest penny, is

A $2.40
B $2.86
C $3.12
D $3.43 **(2 marks)**

(c) Standard costing provides which of the following? Tick all that apply.

(a)   Targets and measures of performance

(b)   Information for budgeting

(c)   Simplification of inventory control systems

(d)   Actual future costs **(2 marks)**

(d) Calculate the standard cost of producing 100 wheels for a toy car using the information given below. Fill in the shaded box.

	Bending	Cutting	Assembly
Standard labour rates of pay per hour $	4	6	5
Standard labour rates per 100 wheels (hours)	0.8	0.5	1.2

STANDARD COST CARD			
Toy car wheels	Part number 5917B - 100 wheels		Date:
	Quantity	*Rate/price*	*Total* $
Direct materials Tyres Steel strip Wire	100 50 1000	10c each $10.40 per 100 2c each	
Direct labour Bending Cutting Assembly	hours	$	
STANDARD COST			

(2 marks)

15 Basic variance analysis

(a) The standard cost information for SC's single product shows the standard direct material content to be 4 litres at $3 per litre.

Actual results for May were:

Production   1,270 units
Material used 5,000 litres at a cost of $16,000

All of the materials were purchased and used during the period. The direct material price and usage variances for May are:

	Material price	*Material usage*
A	$1,000 (F)	$240 (F)
B	$1,000 (A)	$240 (F)
C	$1,000 (F)	$240 (A)
D	$1,000 (A)	$256 (F)

(2 marks)

The following information relates to questions (b) and (c)

The standard variable production overhead cost of product B is as follows.

4 hours at $1.70 per hour = $6.80 per unit

During period 3 the production of B amounted to 400 units. The labour force worked 1,690 hours, of which 30 hours were recorded as idle time. The variable overhead cost incurred was $2,950.

(b) The variable production overhead expenditure variance for period 3 was

 A $77 adverse
 B $128 adverse
 C $128 favourable
 D $230 adverse   **(2 marks)**

(c)   The variable production overhead efficiency variance for period 3 was

A $102 favourable
B $102 adverse
C $105 adverse
D $153 adverse   **(2 marks)**

(d)   Which of the following would help to explain a favourable direct material price variance?

		Would help to explain variance	Would not help to explain variance
(a)	The standard price per unit of direct material was unrealistically high		
(b)	Output quantity was greater than budgeted and it was possible to obtain bulk purchase discounts		
(c)	The material purchased was of a higher quality than standard		

(2 marks)

16 Further variance analysis

(a)   W uses a standard absorption costing system. The following data relates to one of its products.

	$ per unit	$ per unit
Selling price		27.00
Variable costs	12.00	
Fixed costs	9.00	
		21.00
Profit		6.00

Budgeted sales for control period 7 were 2,400 units, but actual sales were 2,550 units. The revenue earned from these sales was $67,320.

Profit reconciliation statements are drawn up using absorption costing principles. What sales variances would be included in such a statement for period 7?

	Price	Volume
A	$1,530 (F)	$900 (F)
B	$1,530 (A)	$900 (F)
C	$1,530 (F)	$900 (A)
D	$1,530 (A)	$900 (A)

(2 marks)

(b)   A standard marginal costing system:

(i)   calculates fixed overhead variances using the budgeted absorption rate per unit
(ii)   calculates sales volume variances using the standard contribution per unit
(iii)   values finished goods stock at the standard variable cost of production

Which of the above statements is/are correct?

A   (i), (ii) and (iii)
B   (i) and (ii) only
C   (ii) and (iii) only
D   (i) and (iii) only   **(2 marks)**

17 Cost-volume profit analysis

(a)   A company manufactures a single product for which cost and selling price data are as follows.

Selling price per unit $12
Variable cost per unit $8
Fixed costs per month $96,000
Budgeted monthly sales   30,000 units

The margin of safety, expressed as a percentage of budgeted monthly sales, is (to the nearest whole number):

A   20%
B   25%
C   73%
D   125%   **(2 marks)**

(b)

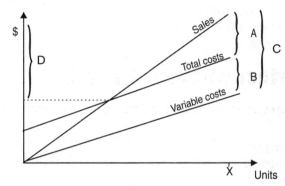

In the above breakeven chart, the contribution at level of activity x can be read as:

A   distance A
B   distance B
C   distance C
D   distance D   **(2 marks)**

18 Relevant costing and decision making

(a)   Sue is considering starting a new business and she has already spent $5,000 on market research and intends to spend a further $2,000.

In the assessment of the relevant costs of the decision to set up the business, market research costs are:

A   a sunk cost of $7,000
B   a sunk cost of $5,000 and an incremental cost of $2,000
C   a sunk cost of $2,000 and an incremental cost of $5,000
D   an opportunity cost of $7,000   **(2 marks)**

(b)   ABC Ltd is in the process of deciding whether or not to accept a special order. The order will require 100 litres of liquid X. ABC Ltd has 85 litres of liquid X in inventory but no longer produces the product which required liquid X. It could therefore sell the 85 litres for $2 per litre if it rejected the special order. The liquid was purchased three years ago at a price of $8 per litre but its replacement cost is $10 per litre. What is the relevant cost of liquid X to include in the decision-making process?

A $200
B $320
C $800
D $1,000   **(2 marks)**

(c)   V Co manufactures three products which have the following selling prices and costs per unit.

	V1	V2	V3
	$	$	$
Selling price	30.00	36.00	34.00
Costs per unit			
Direct materials	8.00	10.00	20.00
Direct labour	4.00	8.00	3.60
Overhead			
Variable	2.00	4.00	1.80
Fixed	9.00	6.00	2.70
	23.00	28.00	28.10
Profit per unit	7.00	8.00	5.90

All three products use the same type of labour.

In a period in which labour is in short supply, the rank order of production is:

V1   ....

V2   ....

V3   ....   **(2 marks)**

(d)   S Co manufactures a single product, V. Data for the product are as follows.

	$ per unit
Selling price	40
Direct material cost	8
Direct labour cost	6
Variable production overhead cost	4
Variable selling overhead cost	2
Fixed overhead cost	10
Profit per unit	10

The profit/volume ratio for product V is [   ]   **(2 marks)**

(e)   Fast Fandango Co manufactures a single product, the FF, which sells for $10. At 75% capacity, which is the normal level of activity for the factory, sales are $600,000 per period.

The cost of these sales are as follows.

Direct cost per unit $3
Production overhead $156,000 (including variable costs of $30,000)
Sales costs $ 80,000
Distribution costs $ 60,000 (including variable costs of $15,000)
Administration overhead $ 40,000 (including variable costs of $9,000)

The sales costs are fixed with the exception of sales commission which is 5% of sales value.

(a)   The contribution per unit of product FF is $ _____   **(2 marks)**

(b)   The fixed cost per period is $ _____   **(2 marks)**

(c)   The breakeven volume of sales per period is _____ units   **(2 marks)**

19 Linear programming

(a)   A company produces two types of orange juice, ordinary (X cartons per year) and premium (Y cartons per year). Which of the following inequalities represents the fact that the amount of ordinary orange juice produced must be no more than twice the amount of premium orange juice produced.

A $X \geq 2Y$
B $2X \geq Y$
C $2X \leq Y$
D $X \leq 2Y$ **(2 marks)**

(b)   In a linear programming problem, the constraints are $X \leq 41$ and $Y \geq 19$. Describe the feasible region, assuming where appropriate that the axes also constitute boundaries.

A   A rectangle to the left of X = 41 and below Y = 19
B   An infinite rectangle to the right of X = 41 and below Y = 19
C   An infinite region above Y = 19 and to the right of X = 41
D   An infinite rectangle to the left of X = 41 and above Y = 19   **(2 marks)**

Exam answer bank

1 Information for management

(a)　D　**Data** is the raw material for data processing. **Information** is data that has been processed in such a way as to be meaningful to the person who receives it. Statement I is therefore incorrect.

An organisation's financial accounting records are an example of an **internal** source of information. Statement II is therefore incorrect.

The main objective of a non-profit making organisation is usually to provide goods and services. Statement III is therefore correct.

(b)　A　**Financial accounts** (not management accounts) detail the performance of an organisation over a defined period and the state of affairs at the end of that period. **Management accounts** are used to aid management record, plan and control the organisation's activities and to help the decision-making process.

(c)　C　Higher level management are likely to be involved with taking decisions at all levels within an organisation.

(d)　D　Cost accounting can also be used to provide inventory valuations for external reporting.

2 Cost classification

(a)　D　It would be appropriate to use the cost per invoice processed and the cost per supplier account for control purposes. Therefore items (ii) and (iii) are suitable cost units and the correct answer is D.

Postage cost, item (i), is an expense of the department, therefore option A is not a suitable cost unit.

If you selected option B or option C you were probably rushing ahead and not taking care to read all the options. Items (ii) and (iii) *are* suitable cost units, but neither of them are the *only* suitable suggestions.

(b)　A　Special designs, and the hire of tools etc for a particular job can be traced to a specific cost unit. Therefore they are direct expenses and the correct answer is A.

Item (iii) is a selling and distribution overhead and item (iv) describes production overheads.

			Appropriate	Not appropriate
(c)	(a)	Vehicle cost per passenger - kilometre	✓	
	(b)	Fuel cost for each vehicle per kilometre	✓	
	(c)	Fixed cost per kilometre		✓

3 Cost behaviour

(a)   A   Variable costs are conventionally deemed to increase or decrease in direct proportion to changes in output. Therefore the correct answer is A. Description B implies a changing unit rate, which does not comply with this convention. Description C relates to a fixed cost.

(b)   B   The cost depicted begins as a linear variable cost, increasing at a constant rate in line with activity. At a certain point the cost becomes fixed regardless of the level of activity. The vehicle hire costs follow this pattern.

Graphs for the other options would look like this.

(c)   (a) | FIXED COST |
       (b) | VARIABLE COST |
       (c) | STEPPED FIXED COST |
       (d) | SEMI-VARIABLE COST |

4 Correlation and regression

(a)   D   If C = 1,000 + 250P, then fixed costs are $1,000 and variable costs are $250 per unit.

(b)   D   The correlation coefficient of 0.9 is very close to 1 and so there is a very strong relationship between x and y.

5 Spreadsheets

(a)   A   A line graph is the best way of illustrating a trend over time.

(b) | False |

A macro is used for automating frequently repeated tasks

(c)   D   II only

Relative cell references (B3) change when you copy formulae to other locations. Absolute cell references ($B$3) stay the same when you copy formulae to other locations.

(d)   A   =$D$1/4*B4

This formula will divide the annual turnover by 4 and multiply the result by the seasonal variation. The $ signs show that the cell reference for D1 is absolute so the reference will stay the same when the formula is copied into the cells below.

(e)   D   =($D$1/4)+B10

This formula will divide the annual turnover by 4 and add the result to the seasonal variation found in cell B10. The $ signs show that the cell reference for D1 is absolute so the reference will stay the same when the formula is copied into the cells below. Brackets are needed so that Excel does the multiplication before the addition.

(f)   C   =C10*$B$1

This formula will multiply the quarterly volume in units from cell C10 by the unit selling price in cell B1. The $ signs show that the cell reference for B1 is absolute so the reference will stay the same when the formula is copied into the cells below

6 Material costs

(a)   D $EOQ = \sqrt{\dfrac{2 \times \$400 \times (250 \times 48)}{\$20 \times 10\%}} = 2,191$

Therefore the correct answer is D.

If you selected option A you used **weekly** usage in the calculations instead of the annual usage.

If you selected option B you did not take ten per cent of the material cost as the annual inventory holding cost.

If you selected option C you omitted the 2.

(b)   D   The easiest way to solve this question is to draw up a stores ledger control account.

STORES LEDGER CONTROL ACCOUNT

	$		$
Opening stock b/f	18,500	Payables (returns)	2,300
Payables/cash (deliveries)	142,000	Overhead account (indirect materials)	25,200
		WIP (balancing figure)	116,900
		Closing inventory c/f	16,100
	160,500		160,500

If you selected option C you determined the correct value of the direct materials issued but you **reversed the entries**.

If you selected options A or B you placed the figure for returns on the **wrong side of your account**, and in option A you **reversed the entries** for the issue of direct materials from stores.

7 Labour costs

(a)   B   The only direct costs are the wages paid to direct workers for ordinary time, plus the basic pay for overtime.

$25,185 + $5,440 = $30,625.

If you selected option A you forgot to include the basic pay for overtime of direct workers, which is always classified as a direct labour cost.

If you selected option C you have included overtime premium and shift allowances, which are usually treated as indirect costs. However, if overtime and shiftwork are incurred specifically for a particular cost unit, then they are classified as direct costs of that cost unit. There is no mention of such a situation here.

Option D includes sick pay, which is classified as an indirect labour cost.

(b)   B   The credit balance on the wages control account indicates that the amount of wages incurred and analysed between direct wages and indirect wages was **higher** than the wages paid through the bank. Therefore there was a $12,000 balance of **wages owing** at the end of February and statement B is not correct. Therefore the correct option is B.

Statement A is correct. $128,400 of wages was paid from the bank account.

Statement C is correct. $79,400 of direct wages was transferred to the work in progress control account.

Statement D is correct. $61,000 of indirect wages was transferred to the production overhead control account.

8 Overheads and absorption costing

(a)   B   Overhead absorption rate $= \dfrac{\text{budgeted overheads}}{\text{budgeted labour hours}} = \dfrac{\$148,750}{8,500} = \$17.50$ per hr

If you selected option A you divided the actual overheads by the budgeted labour hours. Option C is based on the actual overheads and actual labour hours. If you selected option D you divided the budgeted overheads by the actual hours.

(b)   D

	$
Overhead absorbed = $17.50 × 7,928 =	138,740
Overhead incurred =	146,200
Under-absorbed overhead =	7,460

If you selected options A or B you calculated the difference between the budgeted and actual overheads and interpreted it as an under or over absorption. If you selected option C you performed the calculations correctly but misinterpreted the result as an over absorption.

(c)

(a)	% of direct material cost =	112.5%
(b)	% of direct labour cost =	90%
(c)	% of total direct cost =	50%
(d)	Rate per machine hour =	$3.60
(e)	Rate per direct labour hour =	$2

Workings

(a) % of direct materials cost $\dfrac{\$36,000}{\$32,000} \times 100\% = 112.5\%$

(b) % of direct labour cost $\dfrac{\$36,000}{\$40,000} \times 100\% = 90\%$

(c) % of total direct cost $\dfrac{\$36,000}{\$72,000} \times 100\% = 50\%$

(d) Rate per machine hour $\dfrac{\$36,000}{10,000\,hrs} = \$3.60$ per machine hour

(e) Rate per direct labour hour $\dfrac{\$36,000}{18,000\,hrs} = \$2$ per direct labour hour

9 Marginal and absorption costing

(a) C Difference in profit = change in inventory level × fixed overhead per unit
= (200 − 250) × ($2.50 × 3)
= $375

The absorption costing profit will be greater because inventories have increased.

If you selected option A you calculated the correct profit difference but the absorption costing profit would be greater because fixed overheads are carried forward in the increasing inventory levels.

If you selected option B you multiplied the inventory difference by the direct labour-hour rate instead of by the total overhead cost per unit, which takes three hours.

If you selected option D you based the profit difference on the closing inventory only (250 units × $2.50 × 3).

(b) (a) The contribution per unit is $900,000/50,000 = $18

(b) The profit per unit is $572,000/50,000 = $11.44

	$'000	$'000
Sales (at $39 per unit)		1,950
Opening inventory	–	
Variable production cost ($21 × 70,000)	1,470	
Less closing inventory ($21 × 20,000)	420	
Variable cost of sales		1,050
Contribution		900
Less fixed costs		328
Profit		572

10 Process costing

(a)   D   **Step 1. Determine output and losses**

			Equivalent units of production			
Input	Output	Total	Process X		Conversion costs	
Units		Units	Units	%	Units	%
2,000	Finished units	1,600	1,600	100	1,600	100
	Normal loss	200				
	Abnormal loss (balance)	100	100	100	100	100
	Closing inventory	100	100	100	50	50
2,000		2,000	1,800		1,750	

Step 2. Calculate cost per unit of output, losses and WIP

Input	Cost	Equivalent units	Cost per equivalent unit
	$		$
Process X material ($8,000 – 800)	7,200	1,800	4
Conversion costs	12,250	1,750	7
			11

Step 3. Calculate total cost of output

Cost of completed production = $11 × 1,600 litres = $17,600

If you selected option A you included the normal loss in your equivalent units calculation, but these units do not carry any of the process costs. If you selected option B you did not allow for the fact that the work in progress units were incomplete as regards conversion costs. If you selected option C you reduced the process costs by the scrap value of all lost units, instead of the normal loss units only.

(b)   C   Using the unit rates from answer (a) step 2, we can proceed again to step 3.

Calculate the total cost of work in progress

	Cost element	Number of equivalent units	Cost per equivalent unit	Total
			$	$
Work in progress	Process X material	100	4	400
	Conversion costs	50	7	350
				750

If you selected option A you included the normal loss in your equivalent units calculation. If you selected option B you reduced the process costs by the scrap value of all lost units, instead of the normal loss units only. Option D does not allow for the fact that the work in progress (WIP) is incomplete when calculating the total cost of WIP.

(c)

PROCESS ACCOUNT

	Litres	$		Litres	$
Materials	20,000	4,400	Normal waste		
			(4,000 × $0.50)	4,000	2,000
			Finished goods	17,000	2,550
Abnormal gain	1,000	150			
	21,000	4,550		21,000	4,550

Workings

Normal loss = 20% × 20,000 litres = 4,000 litres

Expected output = 20,000 – 4,000 = 16,000 litres

Cost per unit $= \dfrac{\text{Process costs - scrap proceeds of normal loss}}{\text{Expected output}}$

$= \dfrac{\$4,400 - (4,000 \times \$0.50)}{16,000 \text{ litres}}$

$= \dfrac{\$4,400 - \$2,000}{16,000 \text{ litres}}$

$= \dfrac{\$2,400}{16,000 \text{ litres}}$

$= \$0.15$

(d)   The quantity of good production achieved was ⬚ 2,625 ⬚ kg.

Good production   = input – normal loss – abnormal loss
                   = 3,000 – (10% × 3,000) – 75
                   = 3,000 – 300 – 75
                   = 2,635 kg

(e)   The value of the abnormal loss for the period is $ ⬚ 300 ⬚ .

	kg
Input	5,000
Normal loss (10% × 5,000 kg)	(500)
Abnormal loss	(300)
Output	4,200

Cost per kg $= \dfrac{\text{Input costs} - \text{scrap value of normal loss}}{\text{Expected output}}$

$= \dfrac{\$4,600^{*} - \$100}{5,000 - 500}$

$= \dfrac{\$4,500}{4,500} = \$1.00$

Value of abnormal loss = 300 × $1.00 = $300

	$
*Materials (5,000 kg × 0.5)	2,500
Labour	700
Production overhead	1,400
	4,600

11 Joint products and by-products

(a) C   Net process costs

	$
Raw materials	90,000
Conversion costs	70,000
Less by-product revenue	(4,000)
Net process costs	156,000

Apportionment of net process costs

		Units		Apportioned costs
			$	$
Product	J	2,500	$156,000 × (2,500/8,000)	48,750
	K	3,500	$156,000 × (3,500/8,000)	68,250
	L	2,000	$156,000 × (2,000/8,000)	39,000
		8,000		156,000

If you selected option A or B you apportioned a share of the process costs to the by-product, and with option B or D you did not deduct the by-product revenue from the process costs.

(b) A   *Workings*

	Sales revenue	
Joint product	$	
A	760,000	($38 × 20,000)
B	2,160,000	($54 × 40,000)
C	1,400,000	($40 × 35,000)
Total sales revenues	4,320,000	

Joint costs to be allocated = Total output costs − sales revenue from by-product D

= $4,040,000 − $80,000 ($4 × 20,000)
= $3,960,000

$$\text{Costs allocated to joint product B} = \frac{\$2,160,000}{\$4,320,000} \times \$3,960,000$$

$$= \$1,980,000$$

$$\text{Unit valuation (joint product B)} = \frac{\$1,980,000}{40,000}$$

$$= \$49.50 \text{ (to 2 decimal places)}$$

If you selected option B, you forgot to deduct the sales revenue (from by-product D) from the joint costs to be allocated.

If you selected option C, you excluded by-product D from your calculations completely.

If you selected option D, you divided the total sales revenue (instead of the joint costs to be allocated) by the number of units of joint product D.

12 Job, batch and service costing

(a) C Cost per tonne – kilometre (i) is appropriate for cost control purposes because it combines the distance travelled and the load carried, **both of which affect cost**.

The fixed cost per kilometre (ii) is not particularly useful for control purposes because it **varies with the number of kilometres travelled**.

The maintenance cost of each vehicle per kilometre (iii) can be useful for control purposes because it **focuses on a particular aspect** of the cost of operating each vehicle. Therefore the correct answer is C.

(b) The price to be quoted for job B124 is $ | 124.50 |

Production overhead absorption rate = $240,000/30,000 = $8 per labour hour

Other overhead absorption rate = ($150,000/$750,000) × 100% = 20% of total production cost

Job B124	$
Direct materials (3 kg × $5)	15.00
Direct labour (4 hours × $9)	36.00
Production overhead (4 hours × $8)	32.00
Total production cost	83.00
Other overhead (20% × $83)	16.60
Total cost	99.60
Profit margin: 20% of sales (× $^{20}/_{80}$)	24.90
Price to be quoted	124.50

(c) ✓ Production of the product can be completed in a single accounting period

✓ Production relates to a single special order

Job costing is appropriate where each cost unit is **separately identifiable** and is of relatively **short duration**.

(d) (i) Production is carried out in accordance with the wishes of the customer — J

(ii) Work is usually of a relatively long duration — C

(iii) Work is usually undertaken on the contractor's premises — N

(iv) Costs are averaged over the units produced in the period — S

(v) It establishes the costs of services rendered — S

(e) D

Hours for job 34679	= 400 hours
Production overhead cost	$4,000
∴ Overhead absorption rate ($4,000 ÷ 400)	$10 per direct labour hour
Budgeted direct labour hours	45,000
∴ Total budgeted production overheads	$450,000
Budgeted direct wages cost	$180,000
∴ Absorption rate as % of wages cost	= $450,000/$180,000 × 100%
	= 250%

Cost of job 34679

	$
Direct materials	2,000
Direct labour, including overtime premium *	2,500
Overhead (250% × $2,500)	6,250
Total production cost	10,750

* The overtime premium is a direct labour cost because the overtime was worked specifically for this job.

If you selected option A you got your calculation of the overhead absorption rate 'upside down' and derived a percentage rate of 40 per cent in error. If you selected option B you did not include the overtime premium and the corresponding overhead. If you selected option C you did not include the overtime premium in the direct labour costs.

13 Budgeting

(a) C   The **principal budget factor** is the factor which limits the activities of an organisation.

Although cash and profit are affected by the level of sales (options A and B), sales is not the only factor which determines the level of cash and profit.

(b) B   Any opening inventory available at the beginning of a period will **reduce** the additional quantity required from production in order to satisfy a given sales volume. Any closing inventory required at the end of a period will **increase** the quantity required from production in order to satisfy sales and leave a sufficient volume in inventory. Therefore we need to **deduct** the opening inventory and **add** the required closing inventory.

(c) C

	Units
Required for sales	24,000
Required to increase inventory (2,000 × 0.25)	500
	24,500

If you selected option A you subtracted the change in inventory from the budgeted sales. However, if inventories are to be increased then **extra units must be made for inventory**.

Option B is the budgeted sales volume which would only be equal to budgeted production if there were no planned changes to inventory volume.

If you selected option D you increased the sales volume by 25 per cent, instead of adjusting inventory by this percentage.

(d) B

	Units
Required increase in finished goods inventory	1,000
Budgeted sales of Alpha	60,000
Required production	61,000

	kg
Raw materials usage budget (× 3 kg)	183,000
Budgeted decrease in raw materials inventory	(8,000)
Raw material purchase budget	175,000

If you selected option A you made no allowance for the increase in finished goods inventory. If you selected option C you did not adjust for the budgeted decrease in raw materials inventory and option D adjusts for an increase in raw material inventory, rather than a decrease.

(e) D

	Units
Budgeted sales	18,000
Budgeted reduction in finished goods	(3,600)
Budgeted production of completed units	14,400
Allowance for defective units (10% of output = 1/9 of input)	1,600
Production budget	16,000

If you selected option A you deducted a ten per cent allowance for defective units, instead of adding it, and option B makes no allowance for defective units at all. If you selected option C you added ten per cent to the required completed units to allow for the defective units, but the ten per cent **should be based on the total number of units output**, ie ten per cent of 16,000 = 1,600 units.

(f) (a) Production volume from the production budget   ✓

     (b) Budgeted change in materials inventory

     (c) Standard material usage per unit   ✓

Since there are no production resource limitations, the production budget would be prepared before the material usage budget (a). The standard material usage per unit (c) would then indicate the total material usage required to produce the budgeted production volume.

It would not be necessary to know the budgeted change in materials inventory (b) since this would affect the material purchases, rather than the material usage.

(g)

	Order
Material usage budget	4
Sales budget	1
Material purchase budget	6
Finished goods inventory budget	2
Production budget	3
Material inventory budget	5

(h)

		True	False
(a)	Budgetary control procedures are useful only to maintain control over an organisation's expenditure		✓
(b)	A prerequisite of flexible budgeting is a knowledge of cost behaviour patterns	✓	
(c)	Fixed budgets are not useful for control purposes		✓

Comments

(a) Budgetary control procedures can also be useful to maintain control over an organisation's revenue.

(b) A knowledge of cost behaviour patterns is necessary so that the variable cost allowance can be flexed in line with changes in activity.

(c) Fixed budgets may be useful for control purposes when:

    (i) Variable costs are negligible or non-existent
    (ii) Activity levels are not subject to change

475

14 Standard costing

(a)   D   Performance standards would be taken into account when estimating **material usage**, they would not have a direct effect on material price. Therefore the correct answer is D.

All of the other factors would be used to estimate standard material prices for a forthcoming period.

(b)   D   Required liquid input = 2 litres $\times \dfrac{100}{70}$ = 2.86 litres

Standard cost of liquid input = 2.86 × $1.20 = $3.43 (to the nearest cent)

If you selected option A you made no allowance for spillage and evaporation. Option B is the figure for the quantity of material input, not its cost. If you selected option C you simply added an extra 30 per cent to the finished volume. However, the wastage is 30 per cent of the liquid **input**, not 30 per cent of output.

(c)

(a)	Targets and measures of performance	✓
(b)	Information for budgeting	✓
(c)	Simplification of inventory control systems	✓
(d)	Actual future costs	

Standard costing provides targets for achievement, and yardsticks against which actual performance can be monitored (**item (a)**). It also provides the unit cost information for evaluating the volume figures contained in a budget (**item (b)**). Inventory control systems are simplified with standard costing. Once the variances have been eliminated, all inventory units are evaluated at standard price (**item (c)**).

Item (d) is incorrect because standard costs are an estimate of what will happen in the future, and a unit cost target that the organisation is aiming to achieve.

(d)

STANDARD COST CARD			
Toy car wheels	Part number 5917B - 100 wheels		Date:
	Quantity	Rate/price	Total $
Direct materials			
Tyres	100	10c each	10.00
Steel strip	50	$10.40 per 100	5.20
Wire	1000	2c each	20.00
			35.20
Direct labour	hours	$	
Bending	4	0.8	3.20
Cutting	6	0.5	3.00
Assembly	5	1.2	6.00
			12.20
STANDARD COST			47.40

15 Basic variance analysis

(a)   B $

Material price variance

5,000 litres did cost	16,000
But should have cost (× $3)	15,000
	1,000 (A)

Material usage variance

1,270 units did use	5,000 litres
But should have used (× 4 litres)	5,080 litres
Usage variance in litres	80 (F)
× standard cost per litre	$3
	240 (F)

If you selected options A or C you calculated the money values of the variances correctly but misinterpreted their direction.

If you selected option D you valued the usage variance in litres at the actual cost per litre instead of the standard cost per litre.

(b)   B

	$
1,660 hours of variable production overhead should cost (× $1.70)	2,822
But did cost	2,950
	128 (A)

If you selected option A you based your expenditure allowance on all of the labour hours worked. However, it is usually assumed that **variable overheads are incurred during active working hours**, but are not incurred during idle time.

If you selected option C you calculated the correct money value of the variance but you misinterpreted its direction.

Option D is the variable production overhead total variance.

(c)   B

400 units of Product B should take (× 4 hours)	1,600 hours
But did take (active hours)	1,660 hours
Efficiency variance in hours	60 hours (A)
× standard rate per hour	× $1.70
	102 (A)

If you selected option A you calculated the correct money value of the variance but you misinterpreted its direction.

If you selected option C you valued the efficiency variance in hours at the actual variable production overhead rate per hour. Option D bases the calculation on all of the hours worked, instead of only the active hours.

(d)

		Would help to explain variance	Would not help to explain variance
(a)	The standard price per unit of direct material was unrealistically high	✓	
(b)	Output quantity was greater than budgeted and it was possible to obtain bulk purchase discounts	✓	
(c)	The material purchased was of a higher quality than standard		✓

Statement (a) is consistent with a favourable material price variance. If the standard is high then actual prices are likely to be below the standard.

Statement (b) is consistent with a favourable material price variance. Bulk purchase discounts would not have been allowed at the same level in the standard, because purchases were greater than expected.

Statement (c) is not consistent with a favourable material price variance. Higher quality material is likely to cost more than standard, resulting in an adverse material price variance.

16 Further variance analysis

(a)   B

	$
Revenue from 2,550 units should have been (× $27)	68,850
but was	67,320
Sales price variance	1,530 (A)

Actual sales	2,550 units
Budgeted sales	2,400 units
Variance in units	150 units (F)
x standard profit per unit ($(27 – 12))	× $6
Sales volume variance in $	$900 (F)

If you selected option A, C or D, you calculated the monetary values of the variances correctly, but misinterpreted their direction.

(b)   C   Statement (i) is not correct. Fixed overhead is not absorbed into production costs in a marginal costing system.

Statement (ii) is correct. Sales volume variances are calculated using the standard contribution per unit (and not the standard profit per unit which is used in standard absorption costing systems).

Statement (iii) is correct. As stated above, fixed overhead is not absorbed into production costs in a marginal costing system.

17 Cost-volume profit analysis

(a)   A   Breakeven point $= \dfrac{\text{Fixed costs}}{\text{Contribution per unit}} = \dfrac{\$96,000}{\$(12-8)} =$ 24,000 units

Budgeted sales	30,000 units
Margin of safety	6,000 units

Expressed % of budget $= \dfrac{6,000}{30,000} \times 100\% = 20\%$

If you selected option B you calculated the correct margin of safety in units, but you then expressed this as a percentage of the breakeven point. If you selected option C you divided the fixed cost by the selling price to determine the breakeven point, but the selling price also has to cover the variable cost. You should have been able to eliminate option D; the margin of safety expressed as a percentage must always be less than 100 per cent.

(b)   C   Contribution at level of activity x = sales value less variable costs, which is indicated by distance C. Distance A indicates the profit at activity x, B indicates the fixed costs and D indicates the margin of safety in terms of sales value.

18 Relevant costing and decision making

(a)   B $5,000 has been spent on market research already and is therefore a sunk cost and irrelevant to the decision. The further $2,000 will only be spent if Sue continues with the project, therefore it is an incremental (relevant) cost of the decision to go ahead.

The cost is not an opportunity cost (option D) because Sue has not forgone an alternative use for the resources.

(b)   B   The relevant cost of the material in inventory is the opportunity cost of $2 per litre, because the material would be sold if the order was rejected. The remainder of the required material must be purchased at $10 per litre.

Relevant cost is therefore $(85 \times \$2) + (15 \times \$10) = \$320$.

If you selected option A you valued all of the 100 litres required at $2 per litre, but this opportunity cost only applies to the 85 litres in inventory. Option C values the inventory items at their original cost of $8 per litre, but this is a sunk cost which is not relevant to decisions about the future use of the material. Option D values all the material at replacement cost, but the items in inventory will not be replaced by ABC.

(c)   V1 = 1st
         V2 = 3rd
         V3 = 2nd

	V1	V2	V3
	$	$	$
Selling price per unit	30	36	34.00
Variable costs per unit	14	22	25.40
Contribution per unit	16	14	8.60
Labour cost per unit	$4	$8	$3.60
Contribution per $ of labour cost	$4	$1.75	$2.39
Rank order of production	1	3	2

(d)   The profit/volume ratio for product V is   50   %

The profit/volume ratio (P/V ratio) is another term used to describe the contribution/sales ratio (C/S ratio)

$$\text{P/V ratio} = \frac{\text{Contribution per unit}}{\text{Selling price per unit}}$$

$$= \frac{\$(40-8-6-4-2)}{\$40} \times 100\% = 50\%$$

(e)   (a)   The contribution per unit of product FF is $5.60.

Workings

Sales are 60,000 units at the normal level of activity. Variable costs at 60,000 units of production/sales are as follows.

	$	$ per unit
Production overhead	30,000	0.50
Sales costs (5% of $600,000)	30,000	0.50
Distribution costs	15,000	0.25
Administration overhead	9,000	0.15
	84,000	1.40
Direct costs	180,000	3.00
Total variable costs	264,000	4.40
Sales revenue	600,000	10.00
Contribution	336,000	5.60

(b)   The fixed cost per period is $252,000.

Fixed costs	$
Production overhead	126,000
Sales costs	50,000
Distribution costs	45,000
Administration overhead	31,000
	252,000

(c)   The breakeven volume of sales per period is 45,000 units.

Workings

$$\text{Breakeven point} = \frac{\text{fixed costs}}{\text{contribution per unit}}$$

$$= \frac{\$252,000}{\$5.60}$$

$$= 45,000 \text{ units}$$

19 Linear programming

(a)   D   This inequality states that X must be at most 2Y, as required.

The inequality in **option A** states that X must be at least 2Y, whereas 2Y is meant to be the very maximum value of X.

The inequality in **option B** states that Y must be at most 2X, whereas X is meant to be at most 2Y.

The inequality in **option C** states that Y must be at least 2X, whereas X is meant to be at most 2Y.

(b)   D   The region to the left of X = 41 satisfies X ≤ 41 while that above Y = 19 satisfies Y ≥ 19.

Option A is incorrect because the region you have described is bounded by X ≤ 41, but Y ≤ 19 instead of Y ≥ 19.

Option B is incorrect because the region you have described is bounded by X ≥ 41 and Y ≤ 19 instead of by X ≤ 41 and Y ≥ 19.

Option C is incorrect because the region you have described is bounded by Y ≥ 19 but by X ≥ 41 instead of X ≤ 41.

Pilot paper questions and answers

Pilot paper

Paper F2

Management accounting

Time allowed	2 hours

ALL questions are compulsory and MUST be attempted

Do NOT open this paper until instructed by the supervisor.

This question paper must not be removed from the examination hall.

Warning

The pilot paper cannot cover all of the syllabus nor can it include examples of every type of question that will be included in the actual exam. You may see questions in the exam that you think are more difficult than any you see in the pilot paper

---

You can see from this paper that the examiner is able to test right across the syllabus, so you must expect every topic to be examined.

If you take the paper-based exam the questions will be all 1 or 2-mark MCQs. The computer-based exam will have a variety of types of objective test questions. You will get plenty of practice doing these in the Practice and Revision Kit.

ALL 50 questions are compulsory and MUST be attempted

1 The following break-even chart has been drawn showing lines for total cost (TC), total variable cost (TVC), total fixed cost (TFC) and total sales revenue (TSR):

What is the margin of safety at the 1,700 units level of activity?

A   200 units
B   300 units
C   500 units
D   1,025 units   **(2 marks)**

2 The following assertions relate to financial accounting and to cost accounting:

(i)   The main users of financial accounting information are external to an organisation.

(ii)   Cost accounting is that part of financial accounting which records the cash received and payments made by an organisation.

Which of the following statements are true?

A   Assertions (i) and (ii) are both correct.
B   Only assertion (i) is correct.
C   Only assertion (ii) is correct.   **(1 mark)**

3 Regression analysis is being used to find the line of best fit (y = a + bx) from eleven pairs of data. The calculations have produced the following information:

$\Sigma x = 440$, $\Sigma y = 330$, $\Sigma x^2 = 17,986$, $\Sigma y^2 = 10,366$, $\Sigma xy = 13,467$ and $b = 0.69171$

What is the value of 'a' in the equation for the line of best fit (to 2 decimal places)?

A   0.63
B   0.69
C   2.33
D   5.33   **(2 marks)**

4   The purchase price of a stock item is $25 per unit. In each three month period the usage of the item is 20,000 units. The annual holding costs associated with one unit equate to 6% of its purchase price. The cost of placing an order for the item is $20.

What is the Economic Order Quantity (EOQ) for the stock item to the nearest whole unit?

A   730
B   894
C   1,461
D   1,633   **(2 marks)**

5   A company uses an overhead absorption rate of $3.50 per machine hour, based on 32,000 budgeted machine hours for the period. During the same period the actual total overhead expenditure amounted to $108,875 and 30,000 machine hours were recorded on actual production.

By how much was the total overhead under or over absorbed for the period?

A   Under absorbed by $3,875
B   Under absorbed by $7,000
C   Over absorbed by $3,875
D   Over absorbed by $7,000

                                                                                                              (2 marks)

6   **For which of the following is a profit centre manager responsible?**

A   Costs only
B   Revenues only
C   Costs and revenues.   **(1 mark)**

7   An organisation has the following total costs at two activity levels:

Activity level (units)   16,000   22,000
Total costs ($)   135,000   170,000

Variable cost per unit is constant within this range of activity but there is a step up of $5,000 in the total fixed costs when the activity exceeds 17,500 units.

What is the total cost at an activity of 20,000 units?

A $155,000
B $158,000
C $160,000
D $163,000   **(2 marks)**

8   A company manufactures and sells a single product. In two consecutive months the following levels of production and sales (in units) occurred:

	Month 1	Month 2
Sales	3,800	4,400
Production	3,900	4,200

The opening inventory for Month 1 was 400 units. Profits or losses have been calculated for each month using both absorption and marginal costing principles.

Which of the following combination of profits and losses for the two months is consistent with the above data?

	Absorption costing profit/(loss)		Marginal costing profit/(loss)	
	Month 1	Month 2	Month 1	Month 2
	$	$	$	$
A	200	4,400	(400)	3,200
B	(400)	4,400	200	3,200
C	200	3,200	(400)	4,400
D	(400)	3,200	200	4,400

(2 marks)

9   **Which of the following best describes a flexible budget?**

A   A budget which shows variable production costs only.

B   A monthly budget which is changed to reflect the number of days in the month.

C   A budget which shows sales revenue and costs at different levels of activity.

D   A budget that is updated halfway through the year to incorporate the actual results for the first half of the year.   **(2 marks)**

10   Information relating to two processes (F and G) was as follows:

Process	Normal loss as %of input	Input litres	Output litres
F	8	65,000	58,900
G	5	37500	35,700

For each process, was there an abnormal loss or an abnormal gain?

	Process F	Process G
A	Abnormal gain	Abnormal gain
B	Abnormal gain	Abnormal loss
C	Abnormal loss	Abnormal gain
D	Abnormal loss	Abnormal loss

(2 marks)

11   An organisation manufactures a single product which is sold for $80 per unit. The organisation's total monthly fixed costs are $99,000 and it has a contribution to sales ratio of 45%. This month it plans to manufacture and sell 4,000 units.

What is the organisation's margin of safety this month (in units)?

A   1,250
B   1,750
C   2,250
D   2,750   **(2 marks)**

12   **Which one of the following should be classified as indirect labour?**

A   Assembly workers on a car production line
B   Bricklayers in a house building company
C   Machinists in a factory producing clothes
D   Forklift truck drivers in the stores of an engineering company.   **(2 marks)**

13   A company is evaluating a project that requires 400kg of raw material X. The company has 150kg of X in stock that were purchased six months ago for $55 per kg. The company no longer has any use for X. The inventory of X could be sold for $40 per kg. The current purchase price for X is $53 per kg.

What is the total relevant cost of raw material X for the project?

A $17,950
B $19,250
C $21,200
D $21,500   **(2 marks)**

14   **Which of the following is NOT a feasible value for the correlation coefficient?**

A   +1.4
B   +0.7
C   0
D   −0.7   **(2 marks)**

15   The following statements relate to aspects of budget administration:

Statement (1): An important task of a budget committee is to ensure that budgets are properly coordinated.

Statement (2): A budget manual is the document produced at the end of the budget setting process.

Which of the following is true?

A   Only statement (1) is correct.
B   Only statement (2) is correct.
C   Both statements are correct.   **(1 mark)**

16   Up to a given level of activity in each period the purchase price per unit of a raw material is constant. After that point a lower price per unit applies both to further units purchased and also retrospectively to all units already purchased.

Which of the following graphs depicts the total cost of the raw materials for a period?

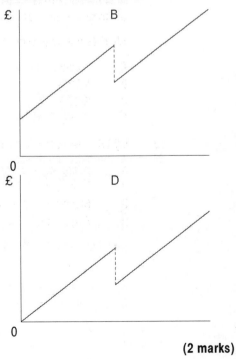

                                                                                                (2 marks)

17   A manufacturing organisation incurs costs relating to the following:

    (1)   Commission payable to salespersons.

    (2)   Inspecting all products.

    (3)   Packing the products at the end of the manufacturing process prior to moving them to the warehouse.

Which of these costs are classified as production costs?

    A   (1) and (2) only
    B   (1) and (3) only
    C   (2) and (3) only
    D   (1), (2) and (3)   **(2 marks)**

18   **Which of the following is correct with regard to expected values?**

    A   Expected values provide a weighted average of anticipated outcomes.
    B   The expected value will always equal one of the possible outcomes.
    C   Expected values will show the decision maker's attitude to risk.
    D   The expected value will never equal one of the possible outcomes.   **(2 marks)**

19   There is a 60% chance that a company will make a profit of $300,000 next year and a 40% chance of making a loss of $400,000.

What is the expected profit or loss for next year?

    A $120,000 Loss
    B $20,000 Loss
    C $20,000 Profit
    D $120,000 Profit   **(2 marks)**

20   A company's budgeted sales for last month were 10,000 units with a standard selling price of $20 per unit and a standard contribution of $8 per unit. Last month actual sales of 10,500 units at an average selling price of $19.50 per unit were achieved.

What were the sales price and sales volume contribution variances for last month?

	Sales price variance ($)	Sales volume contribution variance ($)
A	5,250 Adverse	4,000 Favourable
B	5,250 Adverse	4,000 Adverse
C	5,000 Adverse	4,000 Favourable
D	5,000 Adverse	4,000 Adverse

    (2 marks)

21   A company manufactures and sells one product which requires 8 kg of raw material in its manufacture. The budgeted data relating to the next period are as follows:

	Units
Sales	19,000
Opening inventory of finished goods	4,000
Closing inventory of finished goods	3,000

	Kg
Opening inventory of raw materials	50,000
Closing inventory of raw materials	53,000

What is the budgeted raw material purchases for next period (in kg)?

A   141,000
B   147,000
C   157,000
D   163,000   **(2 marks)**

22   The following statements refer to spreadsheets:

(i)   A spreadsheet is the most suitable software for the storage of large volumes of data.

(ii)   A spreadsheet could be used to produce a flexible budget.

(iii)   Most spreadsheets contain a facility to display the data in them within them in a graphical form.

Which of these statements are correct?

A   (i) and (ii) only
B   (i) and (iii) only
C   (ii) and (iii) only
D   (i), (ii) and (iii)   **(2 marks)**

23   A company always determines its order quantity for a raw material by using the Economic Order Quantity (EOQ) model.

What would be the effects on the EOQ and the total annual holding cost of a decrease in the cost of ordering a batch of raw material?

	EOQ	*Annual holding cost*
A	Higher	Lower
B	Higher	Higher
C	Lower	Higher
D	Lower	Lower

(2 marks)

24   **Which one of the following is most likely to operate a system of service costing?**

A   A printing company
B   A hospital
C   A firm of solicitors.   **(1 mark)**

25   The following budgeted information relates to a manufacturing company for next period:

	Units		$
Production	14,000	Fixed production costs	63,000
Sales	12,000	Fixed selling costs	12,000

The normal level of activity is 14,000 units per period.

Using absorption costing the profit for next period has been calculated as $36,000.

What would the profit for next period be using marginal costing?

A $25,000
B $27,000
C $45,000
D $47,000   **(2 marks)**

26   A company manufactures a single product which it sells for $20 per unit. The product has a contribution to sales ratio of 40%. The company's weekly break-even point is sales revenue of $18,000.

What would be the profit in a week when 1,200 units are sold?

A $1,200
B $2,400
C $3,600
D $6,000   **(2 marks)**

27   The following graph relates to a linear programming problem:

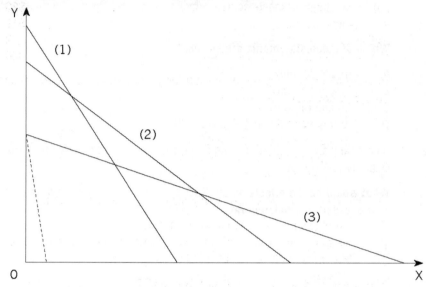

The objective is to maximise contribution and the dotted line on the graph depicts this function. There are three constraints which are all of the "less than or equal to" type which are depicted on the graph by the three solid lines labelled (1), (2) and (3).

At which of the following intersections is contribution maximised?

A   Constraints (1) and (2)
B   Constraints (2) and (3)
C   Constraints (1) and (3)
D   Constraint (1) and the x-axis   **(2 marks)**

28   In an organisation manufacturing a number of different products in one large factory, the rent of that factory is an example of a direct expense when costing a product.

Is this statement true or false?

A   True
B   False   **(1 mark)**

29   A company operates a process in which no losses are incurred. The process account for last month, when there was no opening work-in-progress, was as follows:

Process account

	$		$
Costs arising	624,000	Finished output (10,000 units)	480,000
		Closing work-in progress (4,000 units)	144,000
	624,000		624,000

The closing work-in-progress was complete to the same degree for all elements of cost.

What was the percentage degree of completion of the closing work-in-progress?

A   12%
B   30%
C   40%
D   75%   **(2 marks)**

30   A company manufactures and sells two products (X and Y) both of which utilise the same skilled labour. For the coming period, the supply of skilled labour is limited to 2,000 hours. Data relating to each product are as follows:

Product	X	Y
Selling price per unit	$20	$40
Variable cost per unit	$12	$30
Skilled labour hours per unit	2	4
Maximum demand (units) per period	800	400

In order to maximise profit in the coming period, how many units of each product should the company manufacture and sell?

A   200 units of X and 400 units of Y
B   400 units of X and 300 units of Y
C   600 units of X and 200 units of Y
D   800 units of X and 100 units of Y   **(2 marks)**

31   The following statements refer to organisations using job costing:

(i)   Work is done to customer specification.
(ii)   Work is usually completed within a relatively short period of time.
(iii)   Products manufactured tend to be all identical.

Which two of these statements are CORRECT?

A   (i) and (ii)
B   (i) and (iii)
C   (ii) and (iii)   **(1 mark)**

The following information relates to questions 32 and 33:

A company uses standard costing and the standard variable overhead cost for a product is: 6 direct labour hours @ $10 per hour

Last month when 3,900 units of the product were manufactured, the actual expenditure on variable overheads was $235,000 and 24,000 hours were actually worked.

32   **What was the variable overhead expenditure variance for last month?**

A $5,000 Adverse
B $5,000 Favourable
C $6,000 Adverse
D $6,000 Favourable   **(2 marks)**

33   **What was the variable overhead efficiency variance for last month?**

A $5,000 Adverse
B $5,000 Favourable
C $6,000 Adverse
D $6,000 Favourable   **(2 marks)**

34   When a manufacturing company operates a standard marginal costing system there are no fixed production overhead variances.

Is this statement true or false?

A   True

B   False   **(1 mark)**

35   A company operates a standard costing system. The variance analysis for last month shows a favourable materials price variance and an adverse labour efficiency variance.

The following four statements, which make comparisons with the standards, have been made:

(1)   Inferior quality materials were purchased and used.
(2)   Superior quality materials were purchased and used.
(3)   Lower graded workers were used on production.
(4)   Higher graded workers were used on production.

Which statements are consistent with the variance analysis?

A   (1) and (3)
B   (1) and (4)
C   (2) and (3)
D   (2) and (4)   **(2 marks)**

36   Which of the following best describes a principal budget factor?

A   A factor that affects all budget centres.
B   A factor that is controllable by a budget centre manager.
C   A factor which limits the activities of an organisation.
D   A factor that the management accountant builds into all budgets.   **(2 marks)**

37   Four vertical lines have been labelled G, H, J and K at different levels of activity on the following profit-volume chart:

Which line represents the total contribution at that level of activity?

A   Line G
B   Line H
C   Line J
D   Line K

                                                                                                              (2 marks)

38   Data is information that has been processed in such a way as to be meaningful to its recipients.

Is this statement true or false?

A   True

B   False   **(1 mark)**

39 Two products G and H are created from a joint process. G can be sold immediately after split-off. H requires further processing into product HH before it is in a saleable condition. There are no opening inventories and no work in progress of products G, H or HH. The following data are available for last period:

	$
Total joint production costs	350,000
Further processing costs of product H	66,000

Product	Production	Closing inventory
G	420,000	20,000
HH	330,000	30,000

Using the physical unit method for apportioning joint production costs, what was the cost value of the closing inventory of product HH for last period?

A $16,640
B $18,625
C $20,000
D $21,600 (2 marks)

40 A company purchased a machine several years ago for $50,000. Its written down value is now $10,000. The machine is no longer used on normal production work and it could be sold now for $8,000.

A project is being considered which would make use of this machine for six months. After this time the machine would be sold for $5,000.

What is the relevant cost of the machine to the project?

A $2,000
B $3,000
C $5,000
D $10,000 (2 marks)

41 A company operates a standard absorption costing system. The standard fixed production overhead rate is $15 per hour. The following data relate to last month: Actual hours worked 5,500 Budgeted hours 5,000 Standard hours for actual production 4,800

What was the fixed production overhead capacity variance?

A $7,500 Adverse
B $7,500 Favourable
C $10,500 Adverse
D $10,500 Favourable (2 marks)

42 The following statements relate to relevant cost concepts in decision-making:

(i) Materials can never have an opportunity cost whereas labour can.

(ii) The annual depreciation charge is not a relevant cost.

(iii) Fixed costs would have a relevant cost element if a decision causes a change in their total expenditure

Which statements are correct?

A (i) and (ii) only
B (i) and (iii) only
C (ii) and (iii) only
D (i), (ii) and (iii) (2 marks)

43 A contract is under consideration which requires 600 labour hours to complete. There are 350 hours of spare labour capacity for which the workers are still being paid the normal rate of pay. The remaining hours for the contract can be found either by weekend overtime working paid at double the normal rate of pay or by diverting labour from other production. This other production makes a contribution, net of labour cost, of $5 per hour. The normal rate of pay is $9 per hour.

What is the total relevant cost of labour for the contract?

A $1,250
B $3,500
C $4,500
D $4,900   (2 marks)

44 An organisation operates a piecework system of remuneration, but also guarantees its employees 80% of a time-based rate of pay which is based on $20 per hour for an eight hour working day. Three minutes is the standard time allowed per unit of output. Piecework is paid at the rate of $18 per standard hour.

If an employee produces 200 units in eight hours on a particular day, what is the employee's gross pay for that day?

A $128
B $144
C $160
D $180   (2 marks)

45 A semi-variable cost is one that, in the short term, remains the same over a given range of activity but beyond that increases and then remains constant at the higher level of activity.

Is this statement true or false?

A True
B False   (1 mark)

46 A factory consists of two production cost centres (P and Q) and two service cost centres (X and Y). The total allocated and apportioned overhead for each is as follows:

P	Q	X	Y
$95,000	$82,000	$46,000	$30,000

It has been estimated that each service cost centre does work for other cost centres in the following proportions:

	P	Q	X	Y
Percentage of service cost centre X to	50	50	–	–
Percentage of service cost centre Y to	30	60	10	

The reapportionment of service cost centre costs to other cost centres fully reflects the above proportions.

After the reapportionment of service cost centre costs has been carried out, what is the total overhead for production cost centre P?

A $124,500
B $126,100
C $127,000
D $128,500   (2 marks)

The following information relates to questions 47 and 48:

A company manufactures and sells two products (X and Y) which have contributions per unit of $8 and $20 respectively. The company aims to maximise profit. Two materials (G and H) are used in the manufacture of each product. Each material is in short supply – 1,000 kg of G and 1,800 kg of H are available next period. The company holds no inventories and it can sell all the units produced.

The management accountant has drawn the following graph accurately showing the constraints for materials G and H.

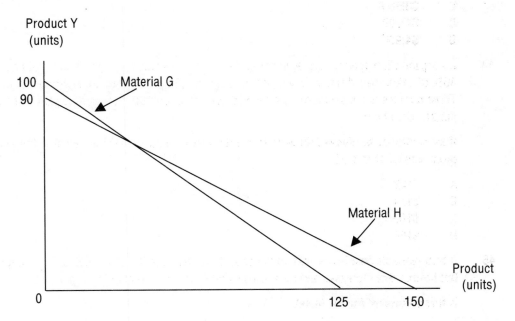

47   **What is the amount (in kg) of material G and material H used in each unit of product Y?**

	Material G	Material H
A	10	20
B	10	10
C	20	20
D	20	10

(2 marks)

48   **What is the optimal mix of production (in units) for the next period?**

	Product X	Product Y
A	0	90
B	50	60
C	60	50
D	125	0

(2 marks)

49   The following statement refers to a quality of good information: The cost of producing information should be greater than the value of the benefits of that information to management.

Is this statement true or false?

A   True
B   False

(1 mark)

50 A company which operates a process costing system had work-in-progress at the start of last month of 300 units (valued at $1,710) which were 60% complete in respect of all costs. Last month a total of 2,000 units were completed and transferred to the finished goods warehouse. The cost per equivalent unit for costs arising last month was $10. The company uses the FIFO method of cost allocation.

What was the total value of the 2,000 units transferred to the finished goods warehouse last month?

A $19,910
B $20,000
C $20,510
D $21,710   **(2 marks)**

FORMULAE SHEET

Regression analysis

$$a = \frac{\Sigma Y}{n} - \frac{b\Sigma x}{n}$$

$$b = \frac{n\Sigma xy - \Sigma x\Sigma y}{n\Sigma x^2 - (\Sigma x)^2}$$

$$r = \frac{x\Sigma xy - \Sigma x\Sigma y}{\sqrt{(n\Sigma x^2 - (\Sigma x^2)(n\Sigma y^2 - (\Sigma y)^2)}}$$

Economic order quantity

$$= \sqrt{\frac{2C_0 D}{C_h}}$$

Economic batch quantity

$$= \sqrt{\frac{2C_0 D}{C_h(1 - \frac{D}{R})}}$$

Pilot Paper F2
Management Accounting

Summarised

1	C		26	B
2	B		27	D
3	C		28	False
4	C		29	D
5	A		30	D
6	C		31	A
7	C		32	B
8	C		33	C
9	C		34	False
10	C		35	A
11	A		36	C
12	D		37	C
13	B		38	False
14	A		39	C
15	A		40	B
16	D		41	B
17	C		42	C
18	A		43	B
19	C		44	D
20	A		45	False
21	B		46	D
22	C		47	A
23	D		48	A
24	B		49	Less
25	B		50	A

In detail

1 C

2 B

3 C $a = (\Sigma y \div n) - [(b\Sigma x) \div n] = (330 \div 11) - [(0.69171 \times 440) \div 11]$
$= (30 - 27.6684)$
$= 2.3316$ (2.33 to 2 decimal places)

4 C $\{[\ 2 \times 20 \times (4 \times 20,000)\ ] \div [0.06 \times 25]\}^{0.5} = 1,461$ units

5 A

Actual cost	$108,875
Absorbed cost (30,000 × 3.50)	$105,000
Under absorption	$ 3,875

6 C

7 C Variable cost per unit: $[(170,000 - 5,000) - 135,000] \div (22,000 - 16,000) = \$5$
Total fixed cost (below 17,500 units): $[135,000 - (16,000 \times 5)] = \$55,000$
Total cost for 20,000 units: $55,000 + 5,000 + (20,000 \times 5) = \$160,000$

8 C Month 1: Production > Sales   Absorption costing profit > Marginal costing profit
Month 2: Sales > Production   Marginal costing profit > absorption costing profit
A and C satisfy Month 1, C and D satisfy Month 2. Therefore C satisfies both.

9 C

10 C

	Normal loss litres	Actual loss litres	Abnormal loss litres	Abnormal gain litres
Process F	5,200	6,100	900	–
Process G	1,875	1,800	–	75

11 A   Contribution per unit (CPU): $(80 \times 0.45) = \$36$
Break even point (units): $(99,000 \div 36) = 2,750$
Margin of safety: $(4,000 - 2,750) = 1,250$ units

12 D

13 B $(150 \times 40) + (250 \times 53) = \$19,250$

14 A

15 A

16 D

17 C

18 A

19 C $(300,000 \times 0.60) - (400,000 \times 0.40) = +\$20,000$ (profit)

20 A   Price variance: $(0.50 \times 10,500) = \$5,250$ Adverse
Volume variance: $(500 \times 8) = \$4,000$ Favourable

21 B   Budgeted production: $(19,000 + 3,000 - 4,000) = 18,000$ units
Raw materials required for budgeted production: $(18,000 \times 8) = 144,000$ kg
Budgeted raw material purchases: $(144,000 + 53,000 - 50,000) = 147,000$ kg

22 C

23 D

24 B

25 B   Production > Sales   Absorption costing profit > Marginal costing profit
Marginal costing profit: $\{36,000 - [2,000 \times (63,000 \div 14,000)]\} = \$27,000$

26 B   CPU: $(20 \times 0.4) = \$8$
Break even point: $(18,000 \div 20) = 900$ units
Profit when 1,200 units produced and sold: $(300 \times 8) = \$2,400$

27 D

28 False

29 D   Cost per equivalent unit: $(480,000 \div 10,000) = \$48$
Closing work in progress valuation: $(4,000 \times$ Degree of completion $\times 48) = 144,000$
Degree of completion $= (144,000 \div 4,000 \div 48) = 0.75 = 75\%$

30 D

	X	Y
CPU	$8	$10
Contribution per hour	$4	$2.50
Ranking	1st	2nd

Therefore produce and sell the maximum 800 units of X using 1,600 hours and with the remaining 400 hours produce ar
100 units of Y.

31 A

32 B

	$
Actual expenditure	235,000
Actual hours × standard rate	
(24,000 × 10)	240,000
Expenditure variance	5,000 Favourable

33 C

	$
Actual hours × standard rate	240,000
Standard cost of actual production	
(3,900 × 6 × 10)	234,000
Efficiency variance	6,000 Adverse

34 False

35 A

36 C

37 C

38 False

39 C   Joint costs apportioned to H: [330,000 ÷ (420,000 + 330,000)] × 350,000 = $154,000
Closing inventory valuation (HH): (30,000 ÷ 330,000) × (154,000 + 66,000) = $20,000

40 B   Relevant cost: (8,000 − 5,000) = $3,000

41 B

Budgeted hours	5,000	
Actual hours worked	5,500	
Capacity variance	500	hours × 15 = $7,500 Favourable

42 C

43 B   Overtime cost for 250 hours: (250 × 9 × 2) = $4,500
Cost of diverting labour: 250 × (9 + 5) = $3,500
Relevant cost (lowest alternative) = $3,500

44 D   200 units × (3 ÷ 60) × 18 = $180

45 False, this is a stepped fixed cost

46 D

	$
Total overhead to cost centre P:	
Direct	95,000
Proportion of cost centre X [46,000 + (0.10 × 30,000)] × 0.50	24,500
Proportion of cost centre Y [30,000 × 0.3]	9,000
	128,500

47 A
100 units of Y with all of material G (1,000 kg) = 10 kg per unit
90 units of Y with all of material H (1,800 kg) = 20 kg per unit

48 A
Total contributions:
A   [(0 × 8) + (90 × 20)] = $1,800
B   [(50 × 8) + (60 × 20)] = $1,600
C   [(60 × 8) + (50 × 20)] = $1,480
D   [(125 × 8) + (0 × 20)] = $1,000

49 Less

50 A

	$
Value of 2,000 units transferred:	
1,700 units × 10	17,000
300 units × 0.40 × 10	1,200
Opening work in progress value	1,710
	19,910

Index

Note: **Key Terms** and their page references are given in **bold.**

Review Form & Free Prize Draw – Paper F2 Management Accounting (4/07)

All original review forms from the entire BPP range, completed with genuine comments, will be entered into one of two draws on 31 January 2008 and 31 July 2008. The names on the first four forms picked out on each occasion will be sent a cheque for £50.

Name: _____   Address: _____

_____

_____

How have you used this Text?
(Tick one box only)

☐ Home study (book only)

☐ On a course: college _____

☐ With 'correspondence' package

☐ Other _____

Why did you decide to purchase this Text? *(Tick one box only)*

☐ Have used BPP Texts in the past

☐ Recommendation by friend/colleague

☐ Recommendation by a lecturer at college

☐ Saw advertising

☐ Saw information on BPP website

☐ Other _____

During the past six months do you recall seeing/receiving any of the following?
(Tick as many boxes as are relevant)

☐ Our advertisement in *ACCA Student Accountant*

☐ Our advertisement in *Pass*

☐ Our advertisement in *PQ*

☐ Our brochure with a letter through the post

☐ Our website www.bpp.com

Which (if any) aspects of our advertising do you find useful?
(Tick as many boxes as are relevant)

☐ Prices and publication dates of new editions

☐ Information on Text content

☐ Facility to order books off-the-page

☐ None of the above

Which BPP products have you used?

Text	☑	Success CD	☐	Learn Online	☐
Kit	☐	i-Learn	☐	Home Study Package	☐
Passcard	☐	i-Pass	☐	Home Study PLUS	☐

Your ratings, comments and suggestions would be appreciated on the following areas.

	Very useful	Useful	Not useful
Introductory section (Key study steps, personal study)	☐	☐	☐
Chapter introductions	☐	☐	☐
Key terms	☐	☐	☐
Quality of explanations	☐	☐	☐
Case studies and other examples	☐	☐	☐
Exam focus points	☐	☐	☐
Questions and answers in each chapter	☐	☐	☐
Fast forwards and chapter roundups	☐	☐	☐
Quick quizzes	☐	☐	☐
Question Bank	☐	☐	☐
Answer Bank	☐	☐	☐
Index	☐	☐	☐

Overall opinion of this Study Text	Excellent ☐	Good ☐	Adequate ☐	Poor ☐

Do you intend to continue using BPP products?   Yes ☐   No ☐

On the reverse of this page are noted particular areas of the text about which we would welcome your feedback.
The BPP author of this edition can be e-mailed at: marymaclean@bpp.com

Please return this form to: Nick Weller, ACCA Publishing Manager, BPP Learning Media Ltd, FREEPOST, London, W12 8BR

Review Form & Free Prize Draw (continued)

TELL US WHAT YOU THINK

Please note any further comments and suggestions/errors below

Free Prize Draw Rules

1   Closing date for 31 January 2008 draw is 31 December 2007. Closing date for 31 July 2008 draw is 30 June 2008.

2   Restricted to entries with UK and Eire addresses only. BPP employees, their families and business associates are excluded.

3   No purchase necessary. Entry forms are available upon request from BPP Learning Media. No more than one entry per title, per person. Draw restricted to persons aged 16 and over.

4   Winners will be notified by post and receive their cheques not later than 6 weeks after the relevant draw date.

5   The decision of the promoter in all matters is final and binding. No correspondence will be entered into.

ACCA

S T U D Y   T E X T

PAPE

MANAGE

In this new sylla

- We **discuss** the
- We **highlight** th
- We **signpost** ho
- We **provide** lots
- We **emphasise**
- We **test your** kn
- We **examine** your u
- We reference all the important topics in our **full index**

BPP's **i-Learn** and **i-Pass** products also support this paper.

FOR EXAMS IN DECEMBER 2007 AND JUNE 2008

LEARNING MEDIA

First edition April 2007

ISBN 9780 7517 3287 0

British Library Cataloguing-in-Publication Data
A catalogue record for this book
is available from the British Library

Published by

BPP Learning Media Ltd
BPP House, Aldine Place
London W12 8AA

www.bpp.com/learningmedia

Printed in Great Britain by
WM Print
45-47 Frederick Street
Walsall
West Midlands
WS2 9NE

Your learning materials, published by BPP Learning
Media Ltd, are printed on paper sourced from
sustainable, managed forests.

We are grateful to the Association of Chartered Certified
Accountants for permission to reproduce past
examination questions. The suggested solutions in the
exam answer bank have been prepared by BPP Learning
Media Ltd, unless otherwise stated.